THE MacARTHUR NEW TESTAMENT COMMENTARY

1 & 2 THESSALONIANS

John MacArthur

MOODY PUBLISHERS/CHICAGO

All Scripture quotations, unless otherwise indicated, are taken from the *New American Standard Bible®*, Copyright © The Lockman Foundation 1960, 1962, 1963, 1968, 1971, 1972, 1973, 1975, 1977, 1995. Used by permission.

Scripture quotations marked NKJV are taken from the *New King James Version.* Copyright © 1982 by Thomas Nelson, Inc. Used by permission. All rights reserved.

Scripture quotations marked NIV are taken from the *Holy Bible, New International Version®*. NIV.® Copyright © 1973, 1978, 1984 by International Bible Society. Used by permission of Zondervan Publishing House. All rights reserved.

Scripture quotations marked KJV are taken from the King James Version.

Library of Congress Cataloging-in-Publication Data

MacArthur, John
   1 & 2 Thessalonians / by John MacArthur
     p. cm. – (MacArthur New Testament commentary)
   Includes bibliographical references and indexes.
   ISBN 978-0-8024-0882-2
    1. Bible. N.T. Thessalonians–Commentaries. I. Title. II. Title: First and Second Thessalonians. III. Series: MacArthur, John, 1939- . MacArthur New Testament commentary.

BS2725.53 .M33 2002
227'.81077–dc21

2002009836

We hope you enjoy this book from Moody Publishers. Our goal is to provide high-quality, thought-provoking books and products that connect truth to your real needs and challenges. For more information on other books and products written and produced from a biblical perspective, go to www.moodypublishers.com or write to:

Moody Publishers
820 N. LaSalle Boulevard
Chicago, IL 60610

15 17 19 20 18 16 14

Printed in the United States of America

*To Doug Virgint who, for a number of years,
has translated and published my writings into the French language
so that the Word of God can shed its glorious light
to a people who have limited biblical resources.
It is a special joy to see the light of truth
shining into another part of the darkness.
Thank you, Doug, for being a friend, a facilitator,
and a true missionary.*

Contents

Preface

It continues to be a rewarding, divine communion for me to preach expositionally through the New Testament. My goal is always to have deep fellowship with the Lord in the understanding of His Word and out of that experience to explain to His people what a passage means. In the words of Nehemiah 8:8, I strive "to give the sense" of it so they may truly hear God speak and, in so doing, may respond to Him.

Obviously, God's people need to understand Him, which demands knowing His Word of truth (2 Tim. 2:15) and allowing that Word to dwell in them richly (Col. 3:16). The dominant thrust of my ministry, therefore, is to help make God's living Word alive to His people. It is a refreshing adventure.

This New Testament commentary series reflects this objective of explaining and applying Scripture. Some commentaries are primarily linguistic, others are mostly theological, and some are mainly homiletical. This one is basically explanatory, or expository. It is not linguistically technical but deals with linguistics when that seems helpful to proper interpretation. It is not theologically expansive but focuses on the major doctrines in each text and how they relate to the whole of Scripture. It is not primarily homiletical, although each unit of thought is generally treated as one chapter, with a clear outline and logical flow of thought.

Most truths are illustrated and applied with other Scripture. After establishing the context of a passage, I have tried to follow closely the writer's development and reasoning.

My prayer is that each reader will fully understand what the Holy Spirit is saying through this part of His Word, so that His revelation may lodge in the mind of believers and bring greater obedience and faithfulness—to the glory of our great God.

Introduction to 1 Thessalonians

In this day of intense interest in prophecy and the end times, there is a tendency to view the Thessalonian epistles merely as treatises on eschatology. But to do so is to overlook the fullness of the riches they contain. They *do* include important teaching on the end times (e.g., 1 Thess. 1:10; 2:19; 3:11–13; 4:13–5:11; 5:23; 2 Thess. 1:7–10; 2:1–12), but only in the context of Paul's passionate pastoral concern for his beloved Thessalonian flock that they not lose the joy and hope of a sound eschatology (e.g., 1 Thess. 1:2–5; 2:7–8, 11–12, 17–20; 3:1–12; 4:1–12; 2 Thess. 1:3–4, 11–12; 2:13–14, 16–17; 3:5, 16, 18). Therefore, they could more accurately be categorized as church epistles.

Though he had ministered for only a brief time in Thessalonica, the apostle Paul was thrilled with what was happening in the church there. His letters reflect joy over the spiritual progress the Thessalonians had made in the short time they had been believers:

> We give thanks to God always for all of you, making mention of you in our prayers. (1 Thess. 1:2)

> For this reason we also constantly thank God that when you received the word of God which you heard from us, you accepted it not as the word of men, but for what it really is, the word of God, which also performs its

work in you who believe. For you, brethren, became imitators of the churches of God in Christ Jesus that are in Judea, for you also endured the same sufferings at the hands of your own countrymen, even as they did from the Jews. (1 Thess. 2:13–14)

For who is our hope or joy or crown of exultation? Is it not even you, in the presence of our Lord Jesus at His coming? For you are our glory and joy. (1 Thess. 2:19–20)

For what thanks can we render to God for you in return for all the joy with which we rejoice before our God on your account? (1 Thess. 3:9)

Now as to the love of the brethren, you have no need for anyone to write to you, for you yourselves are taught by God to love one another; for indeed you do practice it toward all the brethren who are in all Macedonia. But we urge you, brethren, to excel still more. (1 Thess. 4:9–10)

Therefore encourage one another and build up one another, just as you also are doing. (1 Thess. 5:11)

We ought always to give thanks to God for you, brethren, as is only fitting, because your faith is greatly enlarged, and the love of each one of you toward one another grows ever greater; therefore, we ourselves speak proudly of you among the churches of God for your perseverance and faith in the midst of all your persecutions and afflictions which you endure. (2 Thess. 1:3–4)

But we should always give thanks to God for you, brethren beloved by the Lord, because God has chosen you from the beginning for salvation through sanctification by the Spirit and faith in the truth. (2 Thess. 2:13)

The Thessalonian epistles catalog the marks of a healthy, growing church. They give the responsibilities of the leaders to the congregation (1 Thess. 5:12, 14–15); the congregation to the leaders (1 Thess. 5:13, 25–28; 2 Thess. 3:1–2); of believers to grow spiritually (1 Thess. 5:16–22), stand firm in the midst of persecution (1 Thess. 2:14–16), and live orderly lives (2 Thess. 3:6–13); and the church's responsibility to discipline sinning members (2 Thess. 3:6, 14–15). They also emphasize the church's responsibility to reach the lost world with the saving truth of the gospel (1 Thess. 1:8–10).

THE CITY OF THESSALONICA

Thessalonica, modern Thessaloniki (formerly Salonika), was the largest and most important city in the Roman province of Macedonia (the northern part of modern Greece). Located at the head of the Thermaic Gulf (the Gulf of Salonica), a branch of the Aegean Sea, Thessalonica was a thriving seaport. Spreading up the slopes of the hills overlooking the harbor, it had a cosmopolitan population of about a quarter of a million people, including native Greeks, Romans, sailors, travelers, tradesmen, and businessmen. Unlike Philippi, which did not have a large enough Jewish population to support a synagogue (cf. Acts 16:13), the Jewish presence in Thessalonica was significant and influential (cf. Acts 17:1, 5–9).

Perhaps Thessalonica's greatest asset was its location astride the Egnatian Way, the major east-west highway of the Roman Empire, which ran from what is now Albania to Byzantium (Constantinople; Istanbul). Thessalonica's main street was part of that great highway linking Rome with the eastern regions of the empire. Noting the importance of Thessalonica's strategic location on the Egnatian Way to the spread of the gospel, William Barclay writes,

> It is impossible to overstress the importance of the arrival of Christianity in Thessalonica. If Christianity was settled there, it was bound to spread East along the Egnatian Road until all Asia [Minor] was conquered and West until it stormed even the city of Rome. The coming of Christianity to Thessalonica was crucial in the making of it into a world religion. (*The Letters to the Philippians, Colossians, and Thessalonians.* Rev. ed. [Louisville, Ky.: Westminster, 1975], 181)

Thessalonica was founded about 315 B.C. by Cassander, one of Alexander the Great's generals, who became king of Macedonia after the latter's death. He named the new settlement, built on the site of an older town named Therme (presumably because of nearby hot springs), after his wife, the half-sister of Alexander the Great. When the Romans conquered Macedonia (168 B.C.) and divided it into four republics, they made Thessalonica the capital of one of them. And when all of Macedonia became a Roman province (148 B.C.), Thessalonica became its capital. The city was wise (or fortunate) enough to back Antony and Octavian in their successful campaign against Brutus and Cassius. As a reward, it was made a free city in 42 B.C. As such, although it was the seat of the Roman governor, the city was not occupied by Roman troops. It remained largely a Greek city, unlike Philippi, which was heavily influenced by Roman laws and customs. As a free city, Thessalonica also enjoyed freedom from certain taxes. But most important, the city was granted a large measure of self-government; its people chose their own magistrates, known as politarchs ("city authorities"; Acts 17:6). Though skeptics once questioned Luke's use of that term, numerous inscriptions have verified its accuracy.

Thessalonica is one of the few cities visited by Paul that has existed continuously from his day to modern times. According to tradition, Paul's traveling companion Gaius was the first bishop of Thessalonica. He is one of several Thessalonians mentioned in Scripture (Acts 19:29; the Gaius mentioned in Acts 20:4 is apparently a different individual). Other Thessalonians who ministered with Paul include Aristarchus (Acts 19:29; 20:4; 27:2), Secundus (Acts 20:4), and possibly Demas (2 Tim. 4:10).

Thessalonica was the second most important city in the Byzantine Empire, after Constantinople. A famous incident in the city's history took place in A.D. 390 when Emperor Theodosius ordered the massacre of several thousand of its inhabitants following a riot. For that barbarous act the church father Ambrose denied him communion until he publicly repented. The city survived repeated attacks over the centuries from the Avars, Slavs, Arabs, Bulgarians, Saracens, Normans, and Ottoman Turks. The Nazis captured it in 1941, then deported and executed most of its 60,000 Jews. Today Thessalonica (Thessaloniki) remains one of Greece's most important cities, with a population of nearly 400,000.

THE FOUNDING OF THE CHURCH AT THESSALONICA

Paul first came to Thessalonica on his second missionary journey. After traveling west across Asia Minor to the region known as Mysia, the apostle and his entourage reached an impasse. They had been forbidden by the Holy Spirit to preach in the province of Asia (to the south of Mysia), and their attempt to turn north into Bithynia was similarly blocked. With no other way to proceed, they went to Troas, a city on the Aegean Sea. There Paul saw a vision of a Macedonian imploring him to come to that province and preach the gospel (Acts 16:6–10). Crossing the Aegean Sea, they came to Philippi, where Paul's fearless preaching of the gospel sparked a riot. As a result, he and Silas were seized, beaten, and placed in stocks in the city's jail. God miraculously released them by means of an earthquake, as a result of which the jailer came to faith in Christ. Horrified at the realization that they had beaten Roman citizens without benefit of a trial (an act that could have had serious repercussions both for them and their city), the magistrates begged Paul and Silas to leave Philippi.

In what must have been an excruciatingly painful journey, the battered preachers made the one-hundred-mile journey along the Egnatian Way toward Thessalonica. They apparently spent the night at Amphipolis and again at Apollonia, not preaching in those cities because there were no Jewish synagogues. As he customarily did, Paul began his ministry in Thessalonica by preaching the gospel in the synagogue there. He spent three Sabbaths arguing from the Old Testament Scriptures that the Messiah had to die and rise from the dead. Such revolutionary teaching contradicted the prevailing Jewish view of the Messiah as a political and military deliverer who would rescue Israel from her oppressors. Paul further proclaimed Jesus of Nazareth as the promised Messiah. As a result of the apostle's powerful preaching, some Jews, a larger number of Gentile proselytes, and even some of the upper-class Greek women believed the gospel.

Paul most likely stayed longer in Thessalonica than the three Sabbaths Luke mentioned (Acts 17:2). In 1 Thessalonians 2:9 and 2 Thessalonians 3:8, Paul reminded his readers that he had worked to support himself while in their city so as not to be a burden. He would not have needed to do that if he were only there for two or three weeks, nor would he have become a burden to them in such a short time. While some of the Gentile converts were Jewish proselytes who attended the synagogue, many others were converted directly from their pagan idol worship (1 Thess. 1:9). That implies that Paul had a ministry in Thessalonica outside of the synagogue, as he did in Corinth (Acts 18:4–7). The depth of the pastoral care Paul gave the Thessalonian converts (cf. 1 Thess. 2:11–12) and the deep affection that developed between them (cf. 1 Thess. 2:8; 3:6–10) also suggest a longer stay. The size and vitality of the church when Paul left implies that it had not just separated from the synagogue. Finally, and most significant, the Philippians twice sent Paul a gift during his stay in Thessalonica (Phil. 4:16). They would not likely have sent a second gift if he had only stayed a couple of weeks.

As they jealously watched Paul's success at winning Gentile proselytes to Christ, the Jews' smoldering resentment burst into flame. Gathering a gang of thugs from the marketplace, they assaulted Jason's house, looking for the Christian preachers. When they could not find them, the frustrated Jews seized Jason and some of the other Christians and hauled them before the politarchs. The false charge of treason ("they all act contrary to the decrees of Caesar, saying that there is another king, Jesus"; Acts 17:7) was an exceedingly dangerous one, calculated to "[stir] up the crowd and the city authorities who heard these things" (Acts 17:8). The people and the politarchs knew all too well that

> the very suggestion of treason against the Emperors often proved fatal to the accused; and it compelled the politarchs to take steps, for, if they failed to do so, they became exposed to a charge of treason, as having

taken too little care for the honour of the Emperor. Many a man was ruined by such a charge under the earlier Emperors. (Sir William M. Ramsay, *St. Paul the Traveller and the Roman Citizen.* [Reprint; Grand Rapids: Baker, 1975], 229–30)

The threat to Thessalonica's status as a free city was significant; if they failed to maintain order, the Romans would intervene.

Showing a commendable concern for justice, however, the politarchs merely took a pledge, or bond, from Jason and the others and released them. Sir William Ramsay notes that "the step taken by the politarchs was the mildest that was prudent in the circumstances: they bound the accused over in security that peace should be kept" (*St. Paul the Traveller and the Roman Citizen,* 230). Since Jason and the other believers would forfeit that bond if the Jews stirred up any more trouble, Paul and Silas had to leave Thessalonica.

THE OCCASION OF 1 THESSALONIANS

After being forced to leave Thessalonica, the missionary team traveled to Berea, about fifty miles away. There they had a successful ministry until Jews from Thessalonica arrived, stirred up trouble, and Paul was again forced to leave. This time, however, Silas and Timothy were able to stay behind. From Berea, Paul went to Athens, where they later rejoined him (cf. Acts 17:15).

Though forcibly separated from the Thessalonians, Paul was deeply concerned about them. The apostle expressed the anguish he felt in 1 Thessalonians 2:17–18: "But we, brethren, having been taken away from you for a short while—in person, not in spirit—were all the more eager with great desire to see your face. For we wanted to come to you— I, Paul, more than once—and yet Satan hindered us." So great was his concern that he sent Timothy back to Thessalonica—even though that left him to face the formidable task of evangelizing Athens by himself (he also sent Silas from Athens to Macedonia, possibly to Philippi; cf. Acts 18:5):

> Therefore when we could endure it no longer, we thought it best to be left behind at Athens alone, and we sent Timothy, our brother and God's fellow worker in the gospel of Christ, to strengthen and encourage you as to your faith. . . . For this reason, when I could endure it no longer, I also sent to find out about your faith, for fear that the tempter might have tempted you, and our labor would be in vain. (1 Thess. 3:1–2, 5)

To Paul's immense relief and joy, Timothy brought an encouraging report about the situation in Thessalonica when he met Paul at Corinth (Acts 18:5), where the apostle went after he left Athens (Acts 18:1):

> But now that Timothy has come to us from you, and has brought us good news of your faith and love, and that you always think kindly of us, longing to see us just as we also long to see you, for this reason, brethren, in all our distress and affliction we were comforted about you through your faith; for now we really live, if you stand firm in the Lord. For what thanks can we render to God for you in return for all the joy with which we rejoice before our God on your account? (1 Thess. 3:6–9)

But though Timothy's report was on the whole encouraging, there were some issues at Thessalonica that concerned Paul. Because the persecution that drove the missionaries out of Thessalonica had not abated, the church needed encouragement to stand firm (1:2–10; 2:13–16). Further, enemies of the truth were spreading lies and slander about Paul and his companions. They claimed the Christian preachers were only in it to make money and build their reputations. Further, they insinuated that after stirring up trouble the missionaries fled the scene, leaving their duped converts to face the consequences alone. They may even have argued that the missionaries' failure to appear before the politarchs was a tacit admission of guilt. Paul's failure to return to Thessalonica may have been advanced as proof that he really did not care about the Thessalonian believers. To counter their insidious lies and slander, Paul vigorously defended his, Silas's, and Timothy's integrity (2:1–12). He was also concerned that the new converts not slip back into the pagan immorality so prevalent in their culture (4:1–8). The apostle also was concerned about the Thessalonians' reputation with those outside the church; therefore, he encouraged them to continue to love each other fervently and to work diligently (4:9–12). The letter also corrects a wrong understanding about the end times (4:13–5:11), and instructs the Thessalonian congregation in the basics of Christian living (5:12–22).

THE AUTHOR OF 1 THESSALONIANS

The letter twice claims to have been written by Paul (1:1; 2:18), harmonizes with the Acts account of his travels (2:1–2; 3:1–2; Acts 16–18), and contains many intimate details about him. The letter shows clear evidence of having been written early in church history, during Paul's lifetime. There is no reference to church organization or a specialized ministry; only the general reference in 5:12 to "those who diligently labor among you, and have charge over you in the Lord and give you instruction." Nor would a forger, writing long after Paul's death, have allowed for the possibility that Christ could return during the apostle's lifetime (4:15, 17). The vocabulary is consistent with Paul's other inspired letters (cf. William Hendriksen, *New Testament Commentary: Exposition of Thessalonians, Timothy and Titus* [Grand Rapids: Baker, 1981], 20–21).

The testimony of the early church also strongly supports the Pauline authorship of 1 Thessalonians. The Muratorian Canon (c. A.D. 170) and the church fathers Irenaeus, Tertullian, and Clement of Alexandria all affirmed Paul's authorship. Even the heretic Marcion, who denied that Paul wrote several of his other letters, acknowledged the genuineness of 1 Thessalonians. The church historian Eusebius, writing early in the fourth century, also included 1 Thessalonians among Paul's epistles.

THE DATE AND PLACE OF THE WRITING OF 1 THESSALONIANS

Paul wrote this epistle from Corinth where he went, as noted above, after he left Athens. Timothy, having been sent back to check on the situation at Thessalonica, met Paul in Corinth and delivered his report (Acts 18:5; 1 Thess. 3:6). Paul's inclusion of Silas in the greeting of the letter indicates it was written on his second missionary journey, since Silas did not accompany him on his third journey (Silas is not mentioned in Acts after 18:5).

Paul's stay in Corinth can be correlated with Gallio's term as proconsul (Acts 18:12). An inscription found at Delphi, not far from Corinth, refers to Gallio as proconsul at Corinth in early A.D. 52. Since proconsuls took office during the summer, Gallio would have commenced his term in the summer of A.D. 51. Paul's trial before Gallio (Acts 18:12–17) probably took place shortly after he assumed office. Since Paul had apparently been in Corinth for some time before Gallio arrived, and wrote 1 Thessalonians shortly after his arrival in Corinth, the epistle was probably written late in A.D. 50 or early in A.D. 51.

OUTLINE

I. Paul's Salutation (1:1)
II. Paul's Pastoral Care (1:2–3:13)
  A. Describing his thankfulness (1:2–10)
  B. Defending his integrity (2:1–16)
  C. Defining his concerns (2:17–3:13)

III. Paul's Practical Instruction (4:1–5:22)
    A. Moral purity (4:1–8)
    B. Disciplined living (4:9–12)
    C. The Rapture (4:13–18)
    D. The Day of the Lord (5:1–11)
    E. Church relationships (5:12–15)
    F. Basic Christian living (5:16–22)
IV. Paul's Benediction and Closing Admonition (5:23–28)

Identifying the Elect
(1 Thessalonians 1:1–10)

Paul and Silvanus and Timothy, To the church of the Thessalonians in God the Father and the Lord Jesus Christ: Grace to you and peace. We give thanks to God always for all of you, making mention of you in our prayers; constantly bearing in mind your work of faith and labor of love and steadfastness of hope in our Lord Jesus Christ in the presence of our God and Father, knowing, brethren beloved by God, His choice of you; for our gospel did not come to you in word only, but also in power and in the Holy Spirit and with full conviction; just as you know what kind of men we proved to be among you for your sake. You also became imitators of us and of the Lord, having received the word in much tribulation with the joy of the Holy Spirit, so that you became an example to all the believers in Macedonia and in Achaia. For the word of the Lord has sounded forth from you, not only in Macedonia and in Achaia, but also in every place your faith toward God has gone forth, so that we have no need to say anything. For they themselves report about us what kind of a reception we had with you, and how you turned to God from idols to serve a living and true God, and to wait for His Son from heaven, whom He

raised from the dead, that is Jesus, who rescues us from the wrath to come. (1:1–10)

The Thessalonians, like all believers, were the elect of God. That reality caused the apostle Paul to begin his first letter to them by simply pouring out his thanks for the divine gift of their saving faith. The only way believers can discern that someone is elect is after God has regenerated and sanctified that soul. Paul did not know the eternal, elective decree of God, but he could see whose lives gave evidence of genuine salvation (cf. 2:13).

Paul suffered constantly and extremely for the cause of Christ, and he carried on his shoulders an overwhelming burden of responsibility and care for all the churches. He described his burden to the Corinthian church this way:

> Five times I received from the Jews thirty-nine lashes. Three times I was beaten with rods, once I was stoned, three times I was shipwrecked, a night and a day I have spent in the deep. I have been on frequent journeys, in dangers from rivers, dangers from robbers, dangers from my countrymen, dangers from the Gentiles, dangers in the city, dangers in the wilderness, dangers on the sea, dangers among false brethren; I have been in labor and hardship, through many sleepless nights, in hunger and thirst, often without food, in cold and exposure. Apart from such external things, there is the daily pressure on me of concern for all the churches. (2 Cor. 11:24–28)

In view of such severe suffering amid heavy responsibilities, it must have been refreshing and exhilarating for Paul to minister to the Thessalonian elect, whom in this letter he deemed worthy of nothing but commendation and encouragement. In the situation he experienced at Thessalonica, the believers displayed many characteristics that reliably identify the elect. He began his first letter to them with a recognition of those virtues. He arranged them under two categories: the Thessalonians' present condition (a faith that works, a love that labors, a steadfastness of hope) and their past conversion (a reception of the gospel in power and the Holy Spirit, a genuine imitation of the Lord, a joyful endurance in tribulation, a behavior that exemplifies all believers, a proclamation of the Word everywhere, a total transformation from idolatry, and an expectant looking for the return of Christ). Between those two lists Paul paused in verse 4 to affirm his understanding that the church in Thessalonica was elect. Before that, as usual, he opened the letter with identifying words of greeting for his beloved friends.

PAUL'S GREETING

Paul and Silvanus and Timothy, To the church of the Thessalonians in God the Father and the Lord Jesus Christ: Grace to you and peace. We give thanks to God always for all of you, making mention of you in our prayers; (1:1–2)

Though Paul was the most influential apostle of the early church, in his greeting to the Thessalonians, he did not identify himself as an apostle. Apparently in the Macedonian churches, his apostleship was never in question, because in neither of his letters to the church at Thessalonica, nor in his letter to Philippi, did he begin by identifying himself as an apostle. Those churches had not questioned his apostolic status, although he would later defend his integrity and sincerity (1 Thess. 2:1–6). Here he simply and humbly identified himself as **Paul.** And in the same attitude of humility he linked his co-laborers **Silvanus** (Silas) **and Timothy** to himself as if they were all equals.

Silas, probably a Hellenistic Jew, was a prominent member of the Jerusalem church who first accompanied Paul on the apostle's second missionary journey (Acts 15:40) and later was a scribe for Peter (cf. 1 Peter 5:12). **Timothy** was a native of Lystra (Acts 16:1–3), a city in Asia Minor. He was Paul's son in the faith (1 Cor. 4:17; Phil. 2:22; 1 Tim. 1:2; 2 Tim. 1:2; 2:1) and protégé. He toured with Paul on the second and third missionary journeys and remained near the apostle during Paul's first incarceration in Rome (cf. Phil. 1:1; Col. 1:1; Philem. 1). Later Timothy served the church at Ephesus (1 Tim. 1:3) and was himself imprisoned (Heb. 13:23). At the end of Paul's life, when Timothy was in Ephesus, he wrote the two inspired letters to him.

All three men knew the Thessalonian believers well. They founded the church in Thessalonica (Acts 17:4), and Timothy later checked on its well-being and brought back a positive report to Paul (1 Thess. 3:6). Because the Thessalonians were precious to all three of them, Paul included his coworkers' names in the greeting.

Paul's use of the Greek word translated **church** (*ekklēsia*) emphasizes the reality of the Thessalonians' election. *Ekklēsia* is related to the phrase *ek kaleō*, "to call out," and means "the called out ones," or it can mean "the elect ones," especially when connected with the phrase "His choice of you" (v. 4), which is specific. Paul was certain that the Thessalonians were among God's elect because he had seen the evidence of their transformation.

The apostle elaborated on the nature of the church with the somewhat unusual but wonderful expression **in God the Father and the Lord Jesus Christ,** which demonstrates the Thessalonians' vital and inextricable union with God and Christ (cf. 2:14; 2 Thess. 1:1). They participated in the very life of God and the life of Christ. There is an indivisible spiritual union between Christ and His own. In his New Testament letters, Paul taught that believers do not simply believe facts *about* Jesus Christ, but that they are *in* Him. He told the Galatians, "I have been crucified with Christ; and it is no longer I who live, but Christ lives in me" (Gal. 2:20). "For you have died," he reminded the Colossians, "and your life is hidden with Christ in God" (Col. 3:3). That is the inexplicable and incomprehensible mystery of what it is to be a Christian—that God, Christ, and the Holy Spirit (Rom. 8:9, 11; 1 Cor. 3:16; 2 Tim. 1:14) live within the believer and the believer lives in them in a sharing of divine and eternal life.

Significantly, in this profound statement in verse 1, Paul used the preposition **in** just once. Modifying the phrase **God the Father and the Lord Jesus Christ** with a single preposition emphasizes the equality of essence between Father and Son. It is also worth noting here that Paul used the Savior's full title, **the Lord Jesus Christ.** That combines in one phrase all the major aspects of His redemptive work. **Lord** describes Him as creator and sovereign ruler, the One who made us, bought us, rules over us, and to whom we owe full allegiance. **Jesus** ("Jehovah saves") refers to His humanity; it was the name given Him at His birth (Matt. 1:21, 25). **Christ** ("the anointed one") is the Greek term for the Messiah, the one promised by God to fulfill His plan of redemption.

Paul continued the salutation with his common greeting **Grace to you and peace** (cf., for example, 1 Cor. 1:3; 2 Cor. 1:2; Gal. 1:3; Eph. 1:2; Phil. 1:2). **Grace** is God's undeserved favor to the sinner in the form of complete forgiveness of sin and the granting of eternal life, and **peace** is the result of that amazing gift of love. Paul desired that the Thessalonians would continually experience the fullness of God's **grace.** They would then possess not only an unending **peace** with God, but an experience of **peace** in their hearts that always surpassed their human understanding (Phil. 4:7). **Grace** and **peace** are Christians' daily portion—every day they receive divine **grace** to cover their sins and divine **peace** to assuage their guilt.

Because of his sincere wish that the Thessalonians constantly know God's grace and peace, it was understandable for the apostle Paul and his companions to **give thanks to God always for all of** them, **making mention of** them **in** their **prayers** (v. 2). Paul, Silas, and Timothy thanked God continually **for all of** them because all the Thessalonian believers were the elect of God.

The Thessalonians, because they were elect, were living for the honor of Christ. The apostle underscored his thankfulness for that reality by listing the first three qualities that proved God's sovereign choice of them, which were manifest in their sanctification.

THEIR PRESENT CONDITION

constantly bearing in mind your work of faith and labor of love and steadfastness of hope in our Lord Jesus Christ in the presence of our God and Father, (1:3)

Here begins Paul's litany of praise to God for the evidence of salvation the Thessalonians presently displayed. He thanked God for their faith that worked, labor that loved, and hope that endured. This trio of Christian virtues was a favorite of Paul's (cf. 1 Cor. 13:13; Col. 1:4–5; 1 Thess. 5:8).

A FAITH THAT WORKED

constantly bearing in mind your work of faith (1:3*a*)

Paul was **constantly bearing in mind,** or remembering, in thankful prayer these foundational spiritual qualities, the first of which was the Thessalonians' **work of faith.** A true saving belief in Jesus Christ will always result in the mighty **work** of God that produces change in one's nature or disposition. A **work of faith** is action representative of the transforming power of regeneration (2 Cor. 5:17). Simply stated, the elect engage in holy, righteous deeds to the honor of God. **Work** is the Greek word *ergon,* which refers to the deed, achievement, or function itself. Paul was confident of the Thessalonians' election because their **faith**—the authentic saving and sanctifying gift from God—was producing righteous deeds in their lives.

Paul's words here, however, do not in any way contradict his clear teaching elsewhere that salvation is by faith alone, apart from any human works. For example, in Romans 3:20–21 he declares, "By the works of the Law no flesh will be justified in His sight; for through the Law comes the knowledge of sin. But now apart from the Law the righteousness of God has been manifested." Paul goes on to assert that sinners are "justified as a gift by His [God's] grace through the redemption which is in Christ Jesus; whom God displayed publicly as a propitiation in His blood through faith" (vv. 24–25; cf. 4:4; 5:1; Eph. 2:8–9).

However, the New Testament also stresses the active side of faith —salvation will necessarily produce holy conduct. Such teaching is not opposed to justification by faith alone through grace alone and, when properly understood, actually complements that doctrine. Paul is unequivocal early in the book of Romans that works flow from saving faith: "[God] will render to each person according to his deeds: to those who by perseverance in doing good seek for glory and honor and immortality, eternal life" (2:6–7). This does not mean people can *earn* salvation because of their good works, but rather that those works *verify* the reality of their faith.

Paul instructed the Ephesians, "For by grace you have been saved through faith; and that not of yourselves, it is the gift of God; not as a result of works, so that no one may boast. For we are his workmanship, created in Christ Jesus for good works, which God prepared beforehand so that we would walk in them" (Eph. 2:8–10). And the reason believers perform good deeds is because God is at work in them (Phil. 2:13).

Paul described the believer's transformation as going from one kind of slavery to another:

> Do you not know that when you present yourselves to someone as slaves for obedience, you are slaves of the one whom you obey, either of sin resulting in death, or of obedience resulting in righteousness? But thanks be to God that though you were slaves of sin, you became obedient from the heart to that form of teaching to which you were committed, and having been freed from sin, you became slaves of righteousness. . . . Therefore what benefit were you then deriving from the things of which you are now ashamed? For the outcome of those things is death. But now having been freed from sin and enslaved to God, you derive your benefit, resulting in sanctification, and the outcome, eternal life. (Rom. 6:16–18, 21–22)

The apostle James also taught that good works must be present in the lives of those who profess faith in Christ; otherwise that profession is not genuine.

> But someone may well say, "You have faith and I have works; show me your faith without the works, and I will show you my faith by my works." You believe that God is one. You do well; the demons also believe, and shudder. But are you willing to recognize, you foolish fellow, that faith without works is useless? Was not Abraham our father justified by works when he offered up Isaac his son on the altar? You see that faith was working with his works, and as a result of the works, faith was perfected. . . . For just as the body without the spirit is dead, so also faith without works is dead. (James 2:18–22, 26)

Believers will sometimes disobey God's commands and fail to do His will, but they will always long to obey (Rom. 7:18–20) and will manifest some true spiritual fruit of obedience (cf. John 15:5). Genuine saving faith is by definition powerfully inclined toward obedience to God, which leads inevitably to the **work of faith** Paul commended the Thessalonians for.

A LOVE THAT LABORED

and labor of love (1:3*b*)

The second identifying mark of the elect is their **labor of love.** True Christians minister motivated by their love for others. Loving even one's enemies is an expression of the power of salvation (cf. Matt. 5:44; Gal. 6:10). Loving other believers is also evidence of salvation, as 4:9 explicitly states,"Now as to the love of the brethren, you have no need for anyone to write to you, for you yourselves are taught by God to love one another." Peter affirmed this reality:"Since you have in obedience to the truth purified your souls for a sincere love of the brethren, fervently love one another from the heart" (1 Peter 1:22). The apostle John expressed this truth also when he wrote,"The one who loves his brother abides in the Light and there is no cause for stumbling in him" (1 John 2:10). He went on to state that such love is definitive evidence of salvation: "We know that we have passed out of death into life, because we love the brethren. He who does not love abides in death" (3:14; cf. John 13:35; 1 John 2:9, 11; 3:10; 4:20). This **love** is part of the fruit of the Spirit produced in those led by the Spirit (Gal. 5:22). **Labor** is the Greek word *kopos,* which denotes an arduous, wearying kind of toil, done to the point of exhaustion. Unlike *ergon* (**work**), which focuses on the deed itself, *kopos* looks at the effort expended in accomplishing a particular deed. It is an effort that strains all of one's energies to the maximum level. The noblest, most altruistic and selfless form of **love** (*agapē*) motivates this kind of spiritual effort. The apostle Paul referred to the spiritual effort believers make as they work to advance divine truth and the kingdom of the Lord because they sincerely love people.

Furthermore, beyond loving unbelievers and believers, Romans 8:28 identifies the elect—people included in God's eternal, saving purpose —as "those who love God." That is a basic characteristic of anyone who savingly worships the true and living God and the Lord Jesus Christ, and it is the real reason they love others:

> Also the foreigners who join themselves to the Lord, to minister to Him, and to love the name of the Lord, to be His servants, every one who keeps from profaning the sabbath and holds fast My covenant. (Isa. 56:6)

> But just as it is written,"Things which eye has not seen and ear has not heard, and which have not entered the heart of man, all that God has prepared for those who love Him." (1 Cor. 2:9)

> But if anyone loves God, he is known by Him. (1 Cor. 8:3)

Grace be with all those who love our Lord Jesus Christ with incorruptible love. (Eph. 6:24)

Blessed is a man who perseveres under trial; for once he has been approved, he will receive the crown of life which the Lord has promised to those who love Him. (James 1:12)

For a detailed discussion of this love for God, see *Romans 1–8,* The MacArthur New Testament Commentary (Chicago: Moody, 1991), 483–85.

Authentic Christianity has always been defined by loving Christ. In 2 Corinthians 5:14 Paul says, "The love of Christ controls us" (cf. Gal. 5:6). Those who are indifferent to that concern are on their way to hell, unless they repent: "If anyone does not love the Lord, he is to be accursed" (1 Cor. 16:22). The Thessalonian believers' **labor of love** was therefore another mark of their election (cf. 2 Thess. 1:11).

A HOPE THAT ENDURED

and steadfastness of hope in our Lord Jesus Christ in the presence of our God and Father, (1:3c)

The third evidence of election is **steadfastness of hope.** All Christians have a **hope in** the **Lord Jesus Christ**—a persevering anticipation of seeing His future glory and receiving their eternal inheritance.

The redeemed look for the glorious future appearance of the **Lord Jesus Christ** (see the discussion of 1:10 later in this chapter). Paul stated that salvation instructs believers in that **hope:** "For the grace of God has appeared, bringing salvation to all men, instructing us to deny ungodliness and worldly desires and to live sensibly, righteously and godly in the present age, looking for the blessed hope and the appearing of the glory of our great God and Savior, Christ Jesus" (Titus 2:11–13).

The apostle could encourage and teach others regarding this great **hope** (Rom. 5:1–2; Eph. 1:11; Col. 1:27) because he was so confident of it in his own life: "In the future there is laid up for me the crown of righteousness, which the Lord, the righteous Judge, will award to me on that day; and not only to me, but also to all who have loved His appearing" (2 Tim. 4:8).

Peter opened his first epistle with announcement of the blessing of God that transcends all blessings—"a living hope, . . . an inheritance . . . in heaven for you, . . . protected by the power of God, . . . at the revelation of Jesus Christ" (1 Peter 1:3–7). This hope is the same hope Paul referred to when he wrote, "For in hope we have been saved" (Rom. 8:24).

Steadfastness is from the Greek word *hupomonē*, which conveys the idea of endurance or perseverance; literally, it denotes the condition of staying under pressure. It is closely related to the theological concept the Reformers called "the perseverance of the saints" (cf. Rom. 2:7; 2 Thess. 1:4; Rev. 14:12)—that is, Christians will hold fast to their hope until the end. There is nothing that should cause a true Christian to lose his trust in God's promises: "For whatever is born of God overcomes the world; and this is the victory that has overcome the world—our faith. Who is the one who overcomes the world, but he who believes that Jesus is the Son of God?" (1 John 5:4–5). For believers, true hope is a strong longing and groaning to "be at home with the Lord" (see 2 Cor. 5:2–8).

The Thessalonians' **hope** (*elpis*) was firm because it was anchored **in** the unchangeable **Lord Jesus Christ.** The writer of Hebrews richly expressed the security of this **hope** when he wrote:

> so that by two unchangeable things in which it is impossible for God to lie, we who have taken refuge would have strong encouragement to take hold of the hope set before us. This hope we have as an anchor of the soul, a hope both sure and steadfast and one which enters within the veil, where Jesus has entered as a forerunner for us, having become a high priest forever according to the order of Melchizedek. (Heb. 6:18–20)

The context indicates that the "two unchangeable things" are God's promise and His oath (v. 17), which make the believer's hope in the gospel impossible to change. Further, his hope is secured by the intercession of Christ, the eternal High Priest, and kept safe within the impregnable heavenly sanctuary where He stands guard over His own (7:25; cf. 4:15–16). **Hope** transcends mere human, wishful anticipation and rests confidently in the consummation of redemption that Scripture says will certainly occur when Christ returns. Such **hope** will inevitably cause believers to triumph over the struggles of life because it derives from the type of true faith the Thessalonians received from God.

The **steadfastness of** those who have been given that **hope** fulfills Jesus' promise in Matthew 24:13, "The one who endures to the end, he will be saved." That was not a novel concept, but one solidly based on Old Testament teachings, such as Proverbs 4:18, "The path of the righteous is like the light of dawn, that shines brighter and brighter until the full day" (cf. Jer. 32:40). The spiritual path of the righteous does not go from light to darkness; it goes from dim light to full light. It becomes ever brighter as the person's work of faith increases, his labor of love intensifies, and his hope perseveres more and more. Like the Thessalonian believers, those whose faith is genuine are those whose **hope** the Savior secures in heaven and, by the Holy Spirit, empowers to persevere to the end (cf. Job 17:9; John 8:31; Phil. 1:6; Col. 1:21–23; Heb. 3:6, 14). Hebrews 6:10–11 compares with what Paul wrote here: "For God is not unjust so as to forget your work and the love which you have shown toward His name, in having ministered and in still ministering to the saints. And we desire that each one of you show the same diligence so as to realize the full assurance of hope until the end."

An Understanding of Election

knowing, brethren beloved by God, His choice of you; (1:4)

Verse 4 signals the transition from the preceding statement (v. 3), which describes Paul's confidence in the Thessalonians' present spiritual condition, to the following section, which focuses on their past conversion (vv. 5–10).

Knowing, from a form of the Greek verb *oida*, could also be translated "seeing," or "perceiving." Here Paul used it to express his perception that the assembly in Thessalonica was genuine.

The phrase **brethren beloved by God** contains some familiar New Testament terminology. **Brethren** (*adelphoi*) is a common word for the children of God in Christ. **Beloved by God** translates a perfect passive participial phrase in the Greek (*ēgapēmenoi hupo [tou] theou*), explaining the reality that Christians are recipients of the sovereign love of God (cf. Deut. 7:7–8).

When Paul told the Thessalonians he was certain of God's **choice of** them, his words were in perfect harmony with New Testament usage (cf. Matt. 24:22, 24, 31; Luke 18:7; Rom. 8:33; Col. 3:12; 2 Tim. 2:10). Christians are the elect, chosen of God solely by His sovereign, loving purpose, apart from any human merit or wisdom. God in eternity past sovereignly chose all believers to salvation, drawing them to Himself in time, by the work of the Holy Spirit (John 6:37, 44; Rom. 9:15–16; 1 Cor. 1:9; Eph. 1:4–6, 11; 2 Thess. 2:13; 2 Tim. 1:9; cf. Acts 13:46–48; Rev. 13:8; 17:8). Jesus instructed the disciples, "You did not choose Me but I chose you, and appointed you that you would go and bear fruit" (John 15:16). The Father, Son, and Holy Spirit elected not only the apostles but also all who have believed throughout history. In His High Priestly Prayer, Jesus prayed, "I ask on their behalf; I do not ask on behalf of the world, but of those whom You have given Me; for they are Yours" (John 17:9).

As 1 Thessalonians 1:6 and 9 suggest, man's will participates in conversion in response to God's promptings. Thus true evangelism is a call to repent and believe (e.g., Acts 20:21).

THEIR PAST CONVERSION

for our gospel did not come to you in word only, but also in power and in the Holy Spirit and with full conviction; just as you know what kind of men we proved to be among you for your sake. You also became imitators of us and of the Lord, having received the word in much tribulation with the joy of the Holy Spirit, so that you became an example to all the believers in Macedonia and in Achaia. For the word of the Lord has sounded forth from you, not only in Macedonia and Achaia, but also in every place your faith toward God has gone forth, so that we have no need to say anything. For they themselves report about us what kind of a reception we had with you, and how you turned to God from idols to serve a living and true God, and to wait for His Son from heaven, whom He raised from the dead, that is Jesus, who rescues us from the wrath to come. (1:5–10)

Paul's certainty regarding the Thessalonians' election encompassed his memories of their past conversion. The apostle confidently set forth those memories in verses 5–10 as reasons affirming their salvation.

A RECEPTION OF THE GOSPEL IN POWER AND THE HOLY SPIRIT

for our gospel did not come to you in word only, but also in power and in the Holy Spirit and with full conviction; just as you know what kind of men we proved to be among you for your sake. (1:5)

The first past indicator (and the fourth one overall) from the Thessalonians' conversion that attested to the genuineness of their election was the divine power revealed in the preaching of the gospel to them. When Paul said the **gospel** came **in power and in the Holy Spirit and with full conviction,** he was not just describing the Thessalonians' experience but his, Silas's, and Timothy's, when they first declared the saving news in Thessalonica. Paul and the others were so deeply identified with the message of salvation and its power that he called it **our gospel** (cf. 2 Thess. 2:14), though it was from God (Rom. 1:1; 1 Thess. 2:2,9) and concerned the atoning work of Jesus Christ (1 Cor. 15:1–4).

First, Paul asserted that **power** was revealed because the message **did not come to** the Thessalonians **in word only**—it was not merely talk. It was not simply the words themselves that mattered, although any message—including the gospel—by definition has to consist of words setting forth the message (cf. Rom. 10:8, 14; 1 Peter 1:22–25). Faith does come by hearing those words of truth, but the transformation process involves far more than that. Regardless of the erudition, the compelling logic, the soaring rhetoric, or the clever and interesting communication style, if the truth spoken is not accompanied by the power of God, it accomplishes nothing. But when empowered by God as it enters the prepared soul, the gospel truth saves (cf. 1 Peter 1:23–25).

Jesus indicated the inability of all sinners to believe the truth when He said, "This is the judgment, that the Light has come into the world, and men loved the darkness rather than the Light, for their deeds were evil. For everyone who does evil hates the Light, and does not come to the Light for fear that his deeds will be exposed" (John 3:19–20). Along those lines, Paul taught the Corinthians, "And even if our gospel is veiled, it is veiled to those who are perishing, in whose case the god of this world has blinded the minds of the unbelieving so that they might not see the light of the gospel of the glory of Christ" (2 Cor. 4:3–4; cf. Eph. 2:1). He had already told them that the "natural man" cannot understand the gospel (1 Cor. 2:14). Barren words of truth alone, no matter how well presented, cannot penetrate such spiritual blindness and deadness. "For the kingdom of God does not consist in words but in power" (1 Cor. 4:20). God has to powerfully awaken the dead soul and open the blind eyes so the truth can regenerate (Eph. 2:4–5).

Such obvious **power** to quicken the spiritually dead comes from **the Holy Spirit.** Genuine soul-transforming power accompanying gospel preaching is the work of the Spirit energizing both the preacher and the hearer. Jesus alluded to this truth when He promised the apostles just prior to His ascension, "You will receive power when the Holy Spirit has come upon you; and you shall be My witnesses both in Jerusalem, and in all Judea and Samaria, and even to the remotest part of the earth" (Acts 1:8).

Paul knew the preaching at Thessalonica bore divine power because of the **full conviction** ("much assurance," NKJV) he had as he delivered it. Commentator Leon Morris gives a helpful perspective on what Paul meant here:

> The third point is that the gospel came "in much assurance." There is no repetition of the "in" in the Greek. The effect is to link these words very closely with the foregoing. Assurance *[plērophoria]* is not some human device whereby men persuade themselves. Rather it is the result of the activity of the Holy Spirit working within believers. Some have felt that the assurance meant here is that which came to the converts as they put their trust in Christ, and this may not be out of the Apostle's mind. But his primary meaning is the assurance that the Spirit gave to the preachers, for Paul is dealing with the way he and his companions

came to know the election of the Thessalonians. They had the assurance in their own hearts that, as they were preaching, the power of God was at work. The Spirit was working a work of grace. (*The First and Second Epistles to the Thessalonians,* The New International Commentary on the New Testament [Grand Rapids: Eerdmans, 1989], 57–58)

Paul and his fellow preachers were Spirit-empowered, confident, assured, and bold men who depended on God's **power** working through them and in their hearers to effect salvation.

To emphasize his point about the power of the missionaries' preaching, Paul closed verse 5 with these words: **just as you know what kind of men we proved to be among you for your sake.** He told the Thessalonian believers that the spiritual power manifest in his life and the lives of his fellow ministers affirmed the accuracy of their preaching. The apostle (and no doubt Silas and Timothy, as well) was truthful, humble, selfless, gentle, caring, passionate, and compassionate toward the Thessalonians. He worked among them with his own hands so that he would not have to accept any money from them (2 Thess. 3:7–8). The Thessalonians had not only heard the gospel preached, they had seen it lived out in Paul, whose life was a rich example of the power of the gospel he preached (see 2 Cor. 1:12).

A GENUINE IMITATION OF THE LORD

You also became imitators of us and of the Lord, (1:6*a*)

The fifth identifying mark proving the Thessalonians' election was that they **became imitators of** Paul **and of the Lord. Imitators** (*mimētai*) is the word from which the English term *mimics* derives. This transforming work occurred at the moment of salvation when the Thessalonian believers became new creations (cf. 2 Cor. 5:17). Patterns of holy living immediately began replacing the old sinful ones (cf. Eph. 4:22, 24). The Thessalonians, in the middle of a pagan environment, without any veteran church leadership, had in the power of the Holy Spirit become **imitators** of the apostle, his co-laborers, and—most important—Christ. Salvation starts the work of sanctification (cf. 1 Peter 1:1–2). As Paul reminded the Romans, "Do you not know that all of us who have been baptized into Christ Jesus have been baptized into His death? Therefore we have been buried with Him through baptism into death, so that as Christ was raised from the dead through the glory of the Father, so we too might walk in newness of life" (Rom. 6:3–4; cf. 2 Cor. 5:17; Gal. 6:15).

The Thessalonian believers' lifestyles started becoming far different from the sordid, idolatrous paganism of their past and from the legalistic self-righteousness of the Jews in their city. They had become **imitators** of Jesus Christ. Paul commanded believers to pursue that reality as a way of life: "Be imitators of me, just as I also am of Christ" (1 Cor. 11:1). He told the Corinthians that it was a progressive experience of sanctification by the Holy Spirit that moved them upward to increasing levels of glory, more and more into the image of Christ (2 Cor. 3:18).

A JOYFUL ENDURANCE IN TRIBULATION

having received the word in much tribulation with the joy of the Holy Spirit, (1:6b)

A sixth identifying mark that confirmed the Thessalonians were truly elect was their **joy** in the midst of suffering and hardship. No matter how difficult circumstances become, true Christians do not lose their ultimate **joy** because the Holy Spirit dispenses it to the elect. The kingdom of God *is* **joy** (Rom. 14:17).

Paul again noted that the Thessalonians had **received the word,** which was simply a reiteration that they had believed the gospel and been converted. But they did so **in much tribulation,** that is, in severe suffering that began when Paul first preached. As recorded in Acts 17:1–4, and noted earlier, Paul and his fellow missionaries launched an effective evangelistic ministry spanning three Sabbaths in the Thessalonian synagogue, after which they continued their work in another location for several months—long enough to receive two collections from Philippi (cf. Phil. 4:16), be employed (1 Thess. 2:9; 2 Thess. 3:8), and care for the church in depth (1 Thess. 2:7–11). As a result of the transforming impact of that gospel ministry, the Jews hurled tremendous persecution and opposition against the apostle:

> But the Jews, becoming jealous and taking along some wicked men from the market place, formed a mob and set the city in an uproar; and attacking the house of Jason, they were seeking to bring them out to the people. When they did not find them, they began dragging Jason and some brethren before the city authorities, shouting, "These men who have upset the world have come here also; and Jason has welcomed them, and they all act contrary to the decrees of Caesar, saying that there is another king, Jesus." They stirred up the crowd and the city authorities who heard these things. And when they had received a pledge from Jason and the others, they released them. The brethren immediately sent Paul and Silas away by night to Berea. (Acts 17:5–10)

After Paul and his company had left Thessalonica, it is likely the unbelieving Jews and pagan Gentiles intensified the persecution. Paul later reflected on that assault: "For you, brethren, became imitators of the churches of God in Christ Jesus that are in Judea, for you also endured the same sufferings at the hands of your own countrymen, even as they did from the Jews, who both killed the Lord Jesus and the prophets, and drove us out" (1 Thess. 2:14–15).

The Greek word rendered **tribulation** is *thlipsis,* which means "intense pressure," as opposed to something mild. So the new believers in Thessalonica experienced severe persecution, but the genuineness of their salvation transcended that affliction so that they never lost their **joy** (cf. 1 Thess 3:4; 2 Thess. 1:4; in contrast, see Ps. 51:12).

The Thessalonians' responding to persecution and suffering **with the joy of the Holy Spirit** was reminiscent of the apostles' reaction early in the book of Acts. After the Sanhedrin flogged them, ordered them not to preach the gospel again, and released them, "they went on their way from the presence of the Council, rejoicing that they had been considered worthy to suffer shame for His name" (Acts 5:41).

But one should not consider those Spirit-filled responses of joy strange or incomprehensible—joy is a divine benefit of the Christian's standing in Christ, one of the "spiritual blessing(s) in the heavenly places in Christ" (Eph. 1:3). Romans 5:1–4 declares:

> Therefore, having been justified by faith, we have peace with God through our Lord Jesus Christ, through whom also we have obtained our introduction by faith into this grace in which we stand; and we exult in hope of the glory of God. And not only this, but we also exult in our tribulations, knowing that tribulation brings about perseverance; and perseverance, proven character; and proven character, hope. (Cf. Acts 16:22–25; Gal. 5:22; Phil. 4:4.)

Mere human joy will die under persecution; **the joy of the Holy Spirit** will transcend it and grow. Yet again, though such joy is a fruit of the Spirit (Gal. 5:22), all believers are called on to pursue greater and greater joy (Phil. 4:4).

A BEHAVIOR THAT IS EXEMPLARY

so that you became an example to all the believers in Macedonia and in Achaia. (1:7)

A seventh indicator of the Thessalonians' election, and an extension of the others, was their exemplary conduct. They went from commendable imitators of Paul and Christ to those whose own Christian lives became worthy of imitation. The church had become **an example to all the believers,** a model for even older, more mature Christians to follow. **Example** is the Greek word *tupos* ("exact reproduction"), from which the English *type* derives. The Thessalonians became like blueprints for others throughout the region to build their lives on (cf. 1 John 2:6). **Macedonia** was the province in northern Greece that contained Thessalonica, as well as Philippi and Berea. **Achaia** was the southern province of Greece that included such prominent cities as Athens and Corinth.

To illustrate this specifically, the Thessalonians were among those believers Paul cited to the Corinthians as models for giving and financial stewardship. The Thessalonians were in deep poverty, likely because of the persecution they underwent. Yet they gave liberally and sacrificially to help the needy believers in Jerusalem (2 Cor. 8:1–5), thus demonstrating a pattern of godliness, and again in a sacrificial way proving the reality of their election.

A PROCLAMATION OF THE WORD EVERYWHERE

For the word of the Lord has sounded forth from you, not only in Macedonia and Achaia, but also in every place your faith toward God has gone forth, so that we have no need to say anything. For they themselves report about us what kind of a reception we had with you, (1:8–9a)

Another characteristic that verified salvation's power in the Thessalonian saints was their faithfulness in the proclamation of the gospel. **The word of the Lord,** the divine saving truth of the gospel, **sounded forth** from the church in Thessalonica. **Sounded forth** (*exēchētai*) is used only here in the New Testament and means "to blast forth" or "to sound forth very intensely." Outside the New Testament, the term was used to refer to a blaring trumpet, or rolling thunder. The perfect tense form of *exēchētai* indicates the church's bold, continual trumpeting of the gospel message.

From the time the church was founded, its proclamation of the gospel trumpeted out, **not only in Macedonia and Achaia, but also in every place.** Because Thessalonica was a hub of travel and trade, people coming through **Macedonia** from east and west along the Egnatian Highway heard **the word of the Lord** from true believers, as did those who visited the city by ship and used its port facilities. Apparently the Thessalonians who ventured out from the city also carried the gospel with them to **Achaia** and to **every place.** Paul pictured their proclamation as a constant sound, increasing and echoing into a wider and wider circle as the church made the most of a strategic location from which to proclaim the truth.

Their influence was so clear and extensive that Paul said he had **no need to say anything.** In fact, news of the Thessalonians' salvation and subsequent powerful witness was so convincing that Paul said the people who heard the testimony of the church could **themselves report about us what kind of a reception we had with you.** Rather than Paul telling people he met in his travels about what God had done in that city, people were telling him what was becoming commonly known. Every church could wish for such an impact and reputation.

A TOTAL TRANSFORMATION FROM IDOLATRY

and how you turned to God from idols to serve a living and true God, (1:9*b*)

A sure evidence of the Thessalonians' election was that they submitted to a new Master. Salvation meant a decisive break with pagan religion and a redirecting of one's whole life. The Thessalonians abandoned all polytheism and embraced only God and the Lord Jesus Christ. Paul expressed this change as their having **turned to God from idols. Turned** is from the verb *epistrephō*, which is used in the New Testament to indicate the fact that in the sinner's conversion there is a turning in the absolute opposite direction (Acts 9:35; 11:21; 26:18, 20; 2 Cor. 3:16; cf. Luke 1:16; James 5:20). Such conversion entails repentance, a turning **from idols** and in faith submitting to the Savior alone (Acts 20:21). Such turning is far more than merely changing one's belief about who Christ is—it is a complete reversal of allegiance, **from idols** to **serve a living and true God.** The word Paul chose for **serve** (*douleuein*) means to serve as a bond-slave, which was the most demanding form of servitude. Paul knew that the Thessalonians had turned from slavish devotion to false, dead, demonic **idols** to a new and welcome slavery to the one **living and true God** (cf. Rom. 6:16–18).

AN EXPECTANT LOOKING FOR THE RETURN OF CHRIST

and to wait for His Son from heaven, whom He raised from the dead, that is Jesus, who rescues us from the wrath to come. (1:10)

A tenth and final mark that indicated the church in Thessalonica was truly God's elect was that its members waited **for His Son from heaven . . . that is Jesus.**

Those who love Christ long for and anticipate His return. The apostles displayed such a desire when they saw Jesus' ascension:

> He was lifted up while they were looking on, and a cloud received Him out of their sight. And as they were gazing intently into the sky while He was going, behold, two men in white clothing stood beside them. They also said, "Men of Galilee, why do you stand looking into the sky? This Jesus, who has been taken up from you into heaven, will come in just the same way as you have watched Him go into heaven." (Acts 1:9–11)

Paul unquestionably affirmed that the One who once ascended to heaven is also the One believers **wait** for, the One **whom He** [God] **raised from the dead, that is Jesus.** The reference to the Resurrection establishes the ground for the return of Jesus Christ. God **raised** Him **from the dead** because He was pleased with His sacrifice for sin and because He wanted to exalt Him to the heavenly throne from which He will return to exercise His sovereign right to rule as King of Kings (Acts 2:24, 32; 3:15; 4:10–12; 5:30–32; 13:33–35; 17:31; cf. Rom. 1:3–4; 2 Cor. 13:4; Eph. 1:19–23). The word for **wait** is used only here in the New Testament and refers to expectant waiting—sustained, patient, trusting waiting.

To have an expectant looking for Jesus' return from heaven is just one more important aspect in this first chapter that defines a Christian. Waiting is a recurring theme in the Thessalonian letters (1 Thess. 2:17, 19; 3:13; 4:15–17; 5:8, 23; 2 Thess. 3:6–12). In two of his other letters, Paul described this attitude of waiting as follows:

> In the future there is laid up for me the crown of righteousness, which the Lord, the righteous Judge, will award to me on that day; and not only to me, but also to all who have loved His appearing. (2 Tim. 4:8)

> For the grace of God has appeared, bringing salvation to all men, instructing us to deny ungodliness and worldly desires and to live sensibly, righteously and godly in the present age, looking for the blessed hope and the appearing of the glory of our great God and Savior, Christ Jesus. (Titus 2:11–13)

The true believer eagerly looks forward to Christ's return because he knows it brings to fulfillment and satisfaction God's eternal purpose, which is, as Paul stated it, to rescue **us from the wrath to come.**

Rescues denotes the deliverance the Lord provides. He is the Rescuer, Deliverer, and Savior of those otherwise headed for divine judgment and eternal punishment. In the ancient world, the idea of divine wrath was accepted, but there was no genuine hope of rescue from it. By contrast, in the postmodern world the idea of divine wrath is rejected, so the Rescuer is not needed or heeded. *Orgē* (**wrath**) describes God's settled opposition to and displeasure with sin. In this context the **wrath** is God's eternal judgment against sin. Some believe **the wrath to come** refers to the Great Tribulation, and see this rescue as the promise of the pretribulation Rapture, expounded upon later in this epistle (see chapter 11 of this volume). But the immediate context of Paul's discussion of election and salvation rather than eschatology rules out temporal wrath and points to eternal **wrath,** as does the wrath mentioned in 5:9—"For God has not destined us for wrath, but for obtaining salvation through our Lord Jesus Christ."

These ten marks of the elect are true of every genuine follower of Christ. But from time to time it is possible for even true believers to lose touch with those realities in their lives and to live sinfully inconsistent with their position in the body of Christ. Peter urged his readers, "Therefore, brethren, be all the more diligent to make certain about His calling and choosing you" (2 Peter 1:10). It is not that they need to convince God —He already knows who constitutes the elect. But there is nothing more assuring for those who profess faith in Christ than to know their true spiritual condition by means of these ten spiritual benchmarks.

Fail-Proof Spiritual Leadership (1 Thessalonians 2:1–6)

2

For you yourselves know, brethren, that our coming to you was not in vain, but after we had already suffered and been mistreated in Philippi, as you know, we had the boldness in our God to speak to you the gospel of God amid much opposition. For our exhortation does not come from error or impurity or by way of deceit; but just as we have been approved by God to be entrusted with the gospel, so we speak, not as pleasing men, but God who examines our hearts. For we never came with flattering speech, as you know, nor with a pretext for greed—God is witness—nor did we seek glory from men, either from you or from others, even though as apostles of Christ we might have asserted our authority. (2:1–6)

For nearly half a century, beginning in the 1950s, the world has asked the question, "Where have all the leaders gone?" During that time, society has placed more and more of a premium on leadership, but has found few noble leaders with skill and integrity.

Leadership is not easy. When a sports team does not win, the owner fires the head coach. When a corporation loses its competitive edge or fails in a major way to live up to expectations, the board of directors often fires the president. When a church does not grow according to people's expectations, the pastor is often forced out.

And because spiritual and eternal matters are involved, the leadership crisis in the world is insignificant compared to the leadership crisis in the church, God's agency to fulfill His mission on earth (Matt. 28:19-20; cf. 1 Tim. 3:15) until Christ returns.

Those called to be elders in the church, who preach, teach, and lead God's flock, are entrusted with the unequalled duty of proclaiming the gospel to unbelieving sinners, and bringing those who believe and are baptized into the fellowship of the local church. There the Holy Spirit will sanctify them as they worship God in spirit and truth, submitting to the exposition and application of Scripture. Pastors also must intercede for their people through public and private prayer, oversee the administration of the Lord's Table so their people will regularly confess their sins and renew their covenant of obedience, equip other teachers and workers within the church, superintend and enforce church discipline, and provide biblical counseling to the congregation. All of this spiritual work is to build up the saints to maturity—"to the measure of the stature which belongs to the fullness of Christ" (Eph. 4:13).

The elder must be a spiritual physician who can capably apply biblical cures to those vices and heresies that might afflict members of his church. He also must be a tender shepherd who, while feeding the flock, also heals their wounds, calms their fears, protects them from spiritual dangers, and comforts them in their distresses. In short, he is to be a champion for biblical truth (2 Tim. 4:2), a provider of spiritual resources (1 Peter 5:1-2), a guardian and protector (Acts 20:28-31), and always a model of spiritual virtue (1 Tim. 4:12), for all of which he is directly accountable to his Lord Jesus Christ (Heb. 13:17; James 3:1).

Even the uniquely gifted apostle Paul asked the question, "And who is adequate for these things?" (2 Cor. 2:16). He realized that no man could effectively discharge the immense obligation of spiritual leadership by human wisdom, effort, and strength alone. He knew that only God could provide the power to be an effective leader, although he struggled with his flesh and found himself not doing the things he wanted to do and doing the things he did not want to do (Rom. 7:14-25). God graciously gave him suffering and pain to continually humble him and make him dependent on divine power (2 Cor. 12:7-10).

False teachers assailed Paul, as they often do other faithful shepherds, by impugning his character and challenging his authority. Thus the opening statement of chapter 2 is a polemic in defense of Paul's ministry to the Thessalonians. Opponents of his ministry were lying to the church in Thessalonica concerning his integrity and sincerity. They hoped to ruin the new church by destroying its confidence in the person

God had used to found it. That group probably included both unbelieving Jews and pagan Gentiles, both of whom were extremely hostile to the gospel. (This was a similar situation to the one later addressed by Paul in 2 Corinthians.) In a negative response to the coming of Messiah and His redemptive work, as well as to the spread of the gospel message, the attacks on the truth of salvation by grace escalated—and Paul was the main target.

Since the first-century world was full of false spiritual leaders and charlatans, it was easy for the apostle's foes to lump him in with those charlatans who traveled around and ministered merely to gain personal power, wealth, and prestige. W. Neil writes about those times:

> There has probably never been such a variety of religious cults and philosophic systems as in Paul's day. East and West had united and intermingled to produce an amalgam of real piety, high moral principles, crude superstition and gross license. Oriental mysteries, Greek philosophy, and local godlings competed for favour under the tolerant aegis of Roman indifference. "Holy Men" of all creeds and countries, popular philosophers, magicians, astrologers, crack-pots, and cranks; the sincere and the spurious, the righteous and the rogue, swindlers and saints, jostled and clamoured for the attention of the credulous and the sceptical. (Cited in Leon Morris, *The First and Second Epistles to the Thessalonians.* The New International Commentary on the New Testament [Grand Rapids: Eerdmans, 1989], 68, n.3)

In spite of the purity of Paul's life and the transforming power of his message (sufficient and convincing proof of his legitimacy as an apostle of Jesus Christ), the enemies of the gospel were having some success in convincing the Thessalonians that Paul and his companions were men of wicked intentions, nothing more than self-seeking frauds like so many other "spiritual teachers" of that time. Therefore, as distasteful as it was for Paul to have to defend himself, he answered his detractors directly and concisely for the sake of the truth.

PAUL'S OPENING REMINDER

For you yourselves know, brethren, that our coming to you was not in vain, (2:1)

Paul opened the defense of his spiritual leadership with a general statement about the effectiveness of his ministry: **For you yourselves know, brethren, that our coming to you was not in vain.** The apostle immediately urged his audience to remember their own experience with him and his companions—what had occurred was obvious and self-evident. Awareness of how Paul ministered among the Thessalonians did not come from a secondhand report (cf. 1 Thess. 1:9) but from their own firsthand involvement.

The phrase **our coming to you** refers to the missionaries' arrival in Thessalonica with the message of the gospel. **Vain** translates *kenos,* which means "empty." The term also could denote something that was without purpose, effect, or importance and was thus inconsequential. But the ministry of Paul, Silas, and Timothy in Thessalonica **was not** so insipid. On the contrary, it had a powerful impact because it produced deep and far-reaching effects in the lives of the Thessalonians—the marks of genuine faith recollected in 1:1–10. The strength of the Thessalonian church, even after Paul's leaving, was evidence that he had not labored **in vain.** As he continued the defense of his ministry in this section of the letter, Paul expressed five ingredients that opened his ministry to divine power: his confidence in God's power, his commitment to God's truth, his commissioning by God's will, his motivation by God's knowledge, and his dedication to God's glory.

PAUL'S CONFIDENCE IN GOD'S POWER

but after we had already suffered and been mistreated in Philippi, as you know, we had the boldness in our God to speak to you the gospel of God amid much opposition. (2:2)

Paul's confidence in the power of God, both to energize his ministry and protect him from harm, gave him boldness, courage, tenacity, and fearlessness in the face of his enemies.

Paul was thinking of those enemies when he reminded the Thessalonians that he and his companions **had already suffered and been mistreated in Philippi.** Luke recorded that episode in Acts 16:16–24:

> It happened that as we were going to the place of prayer, a slave-girl having a spirit of divination met us, who was bringing her masters much profit by fortune-telling. Following after Paul and us, she kept crying out, saying, "These men are bond-servants of the Most High God, who are proclaiming to you the way of salvation." She continued doing this for many days. But Paul was greatly annoyed, and turned and said to the spirit, "I command you in the name of Jesus Christ to come out of her!" And it came out at that very moment. But when her masters saw that their hope of profit was gone, they seized Paul and Silas and dragged them into the market place before the authorities, and when they had brought them to the chief magistrates, they said, "These men

are throwing our city into confusion, being Jews, and are proclaiming customs which it is not lawful for us to accept or to observe, being Romans." The crowd rose up together against them, and the chief magistrates tore their robes off them and proceeded to order them to be beaten with rods. When they had struck them with many blows, they threw them into prison, commanding the jailer to guard them securely; and he, having received such a command, threw them into the inner prison and fastened their feet in the stocks.

Paul and Silas were actually harmed in two ways at Philippi, as indicated by the two words **suffered** and **mistreated.** They were treated brutally, being beaten and imprisoned in stocks, falsely accused, and illegally punished. **Suffered** refers primarily to the physical abuse, whereas **mistreated** refers to public disgrace, or even legal abuse—they were unjustly judged and made prisoners when they had committed no crime. In the first century, *hubrizō* (**mistreated**) meant to treat shamefully, insultingly, or outrageously in public—all with intent to humiliate.

Paul declared that even **after** they had experienced such bad treatment **in Philippi** they continued to preach the gospel in Thessalonica, where they were falsely accused of treason (Acts 17:7) and unfairly assaulted by a mob (17:5–6). The word rendered **but after** (*alla*) by the *New American Standard Bible* is a strong adversative that in this context might better be translated "but on the other hand" or "although." Even though the missionaries encountered such a terrible reaction in Philippi when they proclaimed the gospel, they came to Thessalonica committed to the same privileged duty of preaching **the gospel of God.** In fact, Paul reasoned that the pagan Philippians' hostile reaction was a sure indicator he and his friends were preaching the truth. Paul's statement here makes it clear that confident, bold, biblical preaching does not lead to popularity. Rather, it leads to conflict that requires courage and renewed boldness.

Paul's confidence was not in himself. On the contrary, his confidence or **boldness** was solely **in God.** Paul wholeheartedly trusted that God would sustain him. As he would later write to the Ephesians, he was "strong in the Lord and in the strength of His might" (Eph. 6:10). His human weakness was the best tool for God's power (2 Cor. 12:9–10).

The term **gospel of God** appears two more times in chapter 2 (vv. 8, 9) as well as in Mark 1:14; Romans 1:1; 15:16; 2 Corinthians 11:7; and 1 Peter 4:17. It describes the gospel from the perspective of God as the source. It is the good news designed by and revealed from God about what He has done to redeem sinners through His grace and by His Son Jesus Christ.

As in Philippi and so many other places, the apostle ministered the gospel in Thessalonica **amid much opposition.** The Greek word translated **opposition** is *agōn* ("struggle," "conflict," "fight"), from which the English word *agonize* derives. It referred to an agonizing life and death struggle. In the ministry, there is always pressure to mitigate the message, to be inoffensive to sinners, to make the gospel acceptable to them. But such a compromise had no place in Paul's strategy. Instead, he had full confidence in God's power to overcome all opposition and achieve His redemptive purpose. The servant of God preaches the true, unmitigated message God has laid out in His Word, not some other message. He does so for the sake of truth, not for personal popularity. And when opposition comes, he trusts in the power of God and stays obedient to his calling. All that was true of Paul and his companions. As with all dedicated preachers of the gospel, they counted the cost of faithfully confronting sinners with the truth and rested boldly in the sovereign, supreme power of God.

PAUL'S COMMITMENT TO GOD'S TRUTH

For our exhortation does not come from error or impurity or by way of deceit; (2:3)

The apostle Paul knew he could be confident in God's power because he was committed to God's truth, not only in his preaching but also in his living. Enemies of the truth often try to destroy ministers of the gospel by persecution. But when that does not work, as it did not with Paul, they try to undermine people's trust in the spiritual leader's message or his personal integrity.

That often happened to Paul and his associates. He believed it necessary to defend his integrity by affirming his unwavering commitment to God's truth, in both speech and conduct. First he declared, **our exhortation does not come from error.** The word **exhortation** (*paraklēsis*) means an urgent cry, appeal, or call, with an emphasis on judgment. Such usage stressed for Paul's readers the urgency and directness of his preaching. He did not stray from the truth or operate apart from the standard of divine revelation. Paul assured them there was no false teaching or living—in other words, **error**—in his ministry.

Paul's critics must have accused him not only of **error** but of outright heresy. Perhaps the antagonistic Jews accused him of ignorance regarding the Old Testament. But such charges were completely false (cf. 2 Cor. 2:17). From the time of his conversion, Paul was a guardian of God's truth and he would later admonish Timothy about the importance of being such a guardian:

> If anyone advocates a different doctrine and does not agree with sound words, those of our Lord Jesus Christ, and with the doctrine conforming to godliness, he is conceited and understands nothing.... O Timothy, guard what has been entrusted to you, avoiding worldly and empty chatter and the opposing arguments of what is falsely called "knowledge"—which some have professed and thus gone astray from the faith. (1 Tim. 6:3–4, 20)

> Retain the standard of sound words which you have heard from me, in the faith and love which are in Christ Jesus. Guard, through the Holy Spirit who dwells in us, the treasure which has been entrusted to you. (2 Tim. 1:13–14)

> Be diligent to present yourself approved to God as a workman who does not need to be ashamed, accurately handling the word of truth. (2 Tim. 2:15)

As noted, Paul was committed not only to speaking and guarding the truth but also to living the truth. Thus he affirmed that his message did not originate from **impurity** (*akatharsias*), a compound word composed of *katharos*, which means "pure" or "clean," and the prefix *a*, which gives the expression a negative meaning, literally "without purity." (*Katharos* is the source of the English word *catharsis*, meaning purifying or cleansing.) Although the word could refer to physical uncleanness and social uncleanness (stigma), it primarily referred to sexual uncleanness.

In Paul's day many of the mystery religions and Greek cults practiced and even exalted sexual perversion. Those religions were very popular because in most of them the primary religious experience centered on the cult adherents having sex with a ritual temple prostitute or the cult leader. Temple orgies were not uncommon. Sexual intercourse had such a central role in those pagan religions because the members believed that when one had sex with a male leader or female prostitute—those supposedly closest to the gods—the individual connected with the deities. Therefore, through fornication they supposedly achieved some sort of mystical or metaphysical union with the gods. Thus wicked, unscrupulous leaders would seek converts for the purpose of having a sexual encounter with them.

So it was typical for religious charlatans to enter a locale and seek women for personal sexual satisfaction under the pretext of offering them a deeper, more complete, more intimate religious experience. Those unscrupulous teachers even enlisted women to pass those "religious experiences" on to other men. Other New Testament references to those practices imply how commonly such perverse teaching was promoted in Paul's day. The apostle Peter wrote, "Many will follow their [false prophets'] sensuality, and because of them the way of the truth will be maligned; and in their greed they will exploit you with false words" (2 Peter 2:2–3; cf. vv. 12–15). Later, the apostle John, in conveying the Lord's warning to the church in Thyatira, said, "But I have this against you, that you tolerate the woman Jezebel, who calls herself a prophetess, and she teaches and leads My bond-servants astray so that they commit acts of immorality and eat things sacrificed to idols" (Rev. 2:20).

Incredibly, Paul's enemies were accusing him of the same kind of **impurity** as the false teachers—seeking converts for sexual favors. But that is unimaginable, as seen by his categorical denial of such accusations. In fact, in denying his foes' wicked allegations, Paul specifically chose the word *akatharsias* because the wider connotation for that word likely indicated a lecherous love for the sake of fornication. The apostle and his companions had no impure ulterior motives, nor were they sexually immoral spiritual leaders. They spoke the truth out of pure lives.

Finally, Paul affirmed his commitment to God's truth by declaring that he had not come **by way of deceit.** With those words he elevated the argument to the realm of motives and asserted the honesty and straightforwardness of his intentions. **Deceit** translates *dolos*, literally, a fishhook, trap, or trick (forms of deception). False teachers often used sorcery, magic, and theatrics to appear as if they had supernatural power and thereby gain converts, both for sexual favors and for money (cf. Acts 8:9–11; 2 Peter 2:15–18; Jude 11). But Paul's motives were righteous, and he lived and ministered with the utmost integrity (1 Cor. 4:1–5; 2 Cor. 3:1–3; 4:1–6). Paul—and by extension, his colleagues—wanted nothing more than to discharge his responsibility of speaking and living the truth, without deception of any kind.

Paul was the opposite of a false teacher: his message was the truth; his life was pure; and his ministry was honest, without hypocrisy or deception.

PAUL'S COMMISSIONING BY GOD'S WILL

but just as we have been approved by God to be entrusted with the gospel, (2:4*a*)

A third and essential element in Paul's powerful impact was that his ministry was **approved by God.** With this point, the discussion moved from the apostle's commitment to the truth to his commission from God, from which he derived that commitment to truth.

The perfect tense of the verb *dedokimasmetha* (**have been ap-**

proved) means Paul was tested and found valid, he was given a lasting approval. God had validated and continued to approve Paul's ministry.

Clearly God had called Paul to be an apostle; he was not self-appointed (Acts 9:1–18). He was not ministering on his own authority, but he had been **entrusted with the gospel.** Shortly after Paul's conversion, the Lord said to Ananias about him: "Go, for he is a chosen instrument of Mine, to bear My name before the Gentiles and kings and the sons of Israel" (Acts 9:15). Paul reiterated the truth of that concept a number of times in his other epistles:

> But by the grace of God I am what I am, and His grace toward me did not prove vain; but I labored even more than all of them, yet not I, but the grace of God with me. (1 Cor. 15:10)

> To me, the very least of all saints, this grace was given, to preach to the Gentiles the unfathomable riches of Christ. (Eph. 3:8)

> According to the glorious gospel of the blessed God, with which I have been entrusted. I thank Christ Jesus our Lord, who has strengthened me, because He considered me faithful, putting me into service. (1 Tim. 1:11–12)

> But at the proper time manifested, even His word, in the proclamation with which I was entrusted according to the commandment of God our Savior. (Titus 1:3)

Thus the apostle Paul was a man under God's call, command, and authority, to whom God had given massive responsibility for preaching **the gospel,** establishing the church, and writing Scripture. For such noble services, Paul was **approved by God,** and he labored under that calling as one who had divinely delegated authority and was promised supernatural blessing.

PAUL'S MOTIVATION BY GOD'S KNOWLEDGE

so we speak, not as pleasing men, but God who examines our hearts. For we never came with flattering speech, as you know, nor with a pretext for greed—God is witness— (2:4b–5)

While he rejoiced in the privilege of his high calling, a strong sense of accountability to God balanced Paul's authority to preach the Word. That accountability came from the constant realization that the omniscient Lord knew and examined everything in his heart and life.

Paul was keenly aware that he was not merely accountable to men. He assured the Thessalonians that when he spoke God's Word, he did so **not as pleasing men.** Nowhere did he make that more clear than when he responded to the allegation from false teachers in Galatia that he was nothing but a men pleaser. After attacking them with a powerful denunciation and curse, pronouncing *anathema* on those false teachers and all who corrupt the gospel (Gal. 1:6–9), he then said, "For am I now seeking the favor of men, or of God? Or am I striving to please men? If I were still trying to please men, I would not be a bond-servant of Christ" (v. 10; cf. Heb. 13:17; James 3:1).

The apostle Paul was consumed with pleasing God because he knew that only God truly **examines** the **hearts** of those who serve Him. Here **hearts** refers to the inner self, the real person, where thought, feeling, will, and motive converge. God scrutinizes all those factors and knows with certainty whether His servants are seeking to please Him or people. Paul's recognition of that omniscience was what motivated his service.

Paul addressed the matter of motivation and accountability at greater length in a critically instructive section of his first epistle to the church at Corinth:

> Let a man regard us in this manner, as servants of Christ and stewards of the mysteries of God. In this case, moreover, it is required of stewards that one be found trustworthy. But to me it is a very small thing that I may be examined by you, or by any human court; in fact, I do not even examine myself. For I am conscious of nothing against myself, yet I am not by this acquitted; but the one who examines me is the Lord. Therefore do not go on passing judgment before the time, but wait until the Lord comes who will both bring to light the things hidden in the darkness and disclose the motives of men's hearts; and then each man's praise will come to him from God. (1 Cor. 4:1–5)

Paul, though leaving the final assessment of his faithfulness to his omniscient Lord, nevertheless kept his own heart clean. His personal testimony in 2 Corinthians 1:12 is remarkable: "For our proud confidence is this: the testimony of our conscience, that in holiness and godly sincerity, not in fleshly wisdom but in the grace of God, we have conducted ourselves in the world, and especially toward you."

Since the Lord is the true Judge, the apostle called upon **God** as his **witness** in the care of this church and asked Him to confirm that he and his friends had not come to exploit the Thessalonians **with flattering speech.** The person using **flattering speech** compliments someone else merely as a ploy to win favor with that person or to gain power over him. Paul did not stoop to the sin of flattery, no doubt remembering the Old Testament words: "May the Lord cut off all flattering lips, the tongue that speaks great things" (Ps. 12:3; cf. 5:9; Job 32:21–22; Prov. 20:19; 28:23; Rom. 16:18).

False teachers not only seek to gain power and influence through their flattering words, but also their underlying motivation is usually greed. This was common for false religionists in Paul's day, and it is now. Therefore, Paul also asserted that he had not come **with a pretext for greed. Pretext** is from *prophasis*, which means "cloak." Paul and his companions did not come to Thessalonica with a cloak hiding greedy intentions. They were not at all like the spiritual deceivers who come cloaking their real desires for sexual favors and money, using flattery to win over their audience, and then exploiting them for all sorts of personal satisfaction and gain.

In contrast, Paul's ministry was consistent with his later words to the Ephesian elders: "I have coveted no one's silver or gold or clothes. You yourselves know that these hands ministered to my own needs and to the men who were with me" (Acts 20:33–34). Unlike most false teachers, he worked with his hands, demonstrating that he did not preach the gospel for crass monetary reward. God knew his heart and his motives, and He was the One to whom Paul was accountable.

PAUL'S DEDICATION TO GOD'S GLORY

nor did we seek glory from men, either from you or from others, even though as apostles of Christ we might have asserted our authority. (2:6)

Also unlike typical spiritual deceivers, Paul did not **seek glory**—esteem, honor, or praise—**from men.** The present tense of the Greek participle *zētountes* indicates that Paul did not habitually **seek** accolades, applause, awards, recognition, and prestige **either from** the Thessalonians **or from others.** The only **glory** Paul ever sought was eternal. To the Ephesians he wrote: "Now to Him who is able to do far more abundantly beyond all that we ask or think, according to the power that works within us, to Him be the glory in the church and in Christ Jesus to all generations forever and ever. Amen" (Eph. 3:20–21). Paul was not in the ministry because of his own ambition. God had gifted, prepared, and placed him there, and therefore he did not deserve any human commendation (cf. 1 Cor. 9:16–18; 10:31; 2 Cor. 4:5).

Even though as apostles of Christ Paul and his associates **might have asserted** their divinely delegated **authority** and thereby gained some prestige, they were preoccupied with giving all the glory to

God. **Apostles** refers to specially called messengers. In the strictest sense, the plural **apostles** was likely intended to link Paul (as one who had seen the risen Christ and been personally commissioned by Him) to the Twelve so as to identify his unique authority. In a less specific sense, it could designate Silas and Timothy as apostles of the churches, chosen not directly by Christ but by the churches (cf. Rom. 16:7; Phil. 2:25).

Paul never abused his **authority** as an apostle but always balanced it with accountability and humility. And he knew that God's omniscience discerned every thought and intention of the heart, so he was careful not to desire praise from men but always to seek to give all the glory to God. "For from Him and through Him and to Him are all things. To Him be the glory forever. Amen" (Rom. 11:36) expresses the divine doxology of the apostle.

This passage sets forth five key qualities of fail-proof spiritual leadership: tenacity, because the leader trusts totally in the power of God; integrity, because the leader is fully committed to the truth of God; authority, because the leader is commissioned by the will of God; accountability, because the leader knows the omniscient God examines his heart; and humility, because the leader is consumed with the glory of God. If he has these qualities, he will be well on his way to exercising fail-proof spiritual leadership.

Parental Pictures of Spiritual Leadership (1 Thessalonians 2:7–12)

3

But we proved to be gentle among you, as a nursing mother tenderly cares for her own children. Having so fond an affection for you, we were well-pleased to impart to you not only the gospel of God but also our own lives, because you had become very dear to us. For you recall, brethren, our labor and hardship, how working night and day so as not to be a burden to any of you, we proclaimed to you the gospel of God. You are witnesses, and so is God, how devoutly and uprightly and blamelessly we behaved toward you believers; just as you know how we were exhorting and encouraging and imploring each one of you as a father would his own children, so that you would walk in a manner worthy of the God who calls you into His own kingdom and glory. (2:7–12)

Scripture offers much guidance, by example and direct instruction, on the subject of spiritual leadership. From the very beginning of creation, God established leadership in human relationships. In the marriage relationship between Adam and Eve, God designed Adam to be the leader (Gen. 2:18). Ever since then, He has commanded the husband and father to be the leader of the family (1 Cor. 11:3, 8–9; Eph. 5:22; Col. 3:18; 1 Tim. 2:12–14).

On the national level, God used the patriarchs, priests, judges, kings, prophets, and military leaders through Old Testament times to lead His people. The Holy Spirit forthrightly discloses from Genesis to Malachi the blessings and cursings of good and bad leadership.

In the gospels the greatest leader of all, Jesus Christ, appears (cf. Heb. 2:10). Early in His ministry, He chose the twelve apostles (cf. Luke 6:12–13), an eternally preordained choice of ordinary men who would receive the Son of God's unique leadership training. That preparation, along with their receiving the Holy Spirit (Acts 1:6–11; 2:1–4), enabled them to reproduce additional spiritual leaders, who in turn conveyed what they knew to other men in a discipling process that has continued throughout church history (cf. 2 Tim. 2:2). The church has always had the responsibility to identify and appoint biblically qualified men who lead and, at the same time, are capable of selecting and training the next generation of spiritual leaders (see 1 Tim. 3:1ff.; Titus 1:4ff.).

Effective spiritual leadership is a combination of character and activity. First Thessalonians 2:1–6 presented the exemplary leadership virtues of Paul's inner life (and the lives of Silas and Timothy): tenacity, integrity, authority, accountability, and humility. In this subsequent passage, however, the apostle views the outward functions of the divinely approved spiritual leader. He could have presented these functions by discussing preaching, discipling, protecting, and overseeing. But as the New Testament writers often did for the sake of vividness and richness, the apostle used a metaphor. He could have chosen any one of several metaphors: a steward or household manager (1 Cor. 4:1–2); a bond-slave or servant (Col. 4:12); a herald or proclaimer of the message (1 Tim. 2:7 NIV); a teacher, soldier, athlete, farmer (2 Tim. 2:2–6); or the common image of a shepherd (1 Peter 5:1–4; cf. Ps. 23). All those metaphors are replete with significance and paint helpful pictures. However, Paul chose to use the most intimate, compelling metaphors of a mother and father, which illustrate the primary kinds of spiritual care a leader must provide his people.

Such metaphors are not limited to this epistle. In Galatians 4:19 he wrote, as if a mother calling believers, "My children, with whom I am again in labor until Christ is formed in you." He pictured himself as a mother who first labored to give birth and then, as it were, labored longer to bring her children to spiritual maturity. In 1 Corinthians 4:15 he pictured himself as a spiritual father: "For if you were to have countless tutors in Christ, yet you would not have many fathers, for in Christ Jesus I became your father through the gospel." He was the human source of their spiritual life as well as their teacher and protector. Paul's use of these familial metaphors emphasizes the care and affection of shared life that he had with those he brought the gospel to.

THE SPIRITUAL LEADER AS MOTHER

But we proved to be gentle among you, as a nursing mother tenderly cares for her own children. Having so fond an affection for you, we were well-pleased to impart to you not only the gospel of God but also our own lives, because you had become very dear to us. For you recall, brethren, our labor and hardship, how working night and day so as not to be a burden to any of you, we proclaimed to you the gospel of God. (2:7–9)

As mothers are absolutely and indisputably essential to the well-being of children, so spiritual leaders who minister with a mother's gentleness, intimate affection, sacrificial love, and unselfish labor are essential for the health of the church.

GENTLENESS

But we proved to be gentle among you, as a nursing mother tenderly cares for her own children. (2:7)

Paul begins with the important adversative **but,** which again contrasts the conduct of his colleagues and him with the sinful behavior of the false teachers (vv. 2, 4). Paul reminded the Thessalonians that instead of operating by the deceitful abusiveness of Satan's agents, they **proved to be gentle among you.**

The term **gentle** is at the heart of this verse. It means to be kind to someone and encompasses a host of other virtues: acceptance, respect, compassion, tolerance of imperfections, patience, tenderheartedness, and loyalty. Unlike many itinerant teachers, Paul and his preacher friends did not come to Thessalonica to exploit the people for their own prosperity but to live and serve **among** them with kindness. Paul explained his degree of gentleness toward the Thessalonians by comparing it to **a nursing mother** who **tenderly cares for her own children,** the imagery Moses had used for his relationship to Israel (Num. 11:12). As the phrase **her own children** indicates, Paul was no paid surrogate mother or modern-style, hired day care worker. The apostle exhibited the same feelings as **a nursing mother** when he cared for the Thessalonians' spiritual needs. This picture is usually foreign to all leaders outside the true church of Jesus Christ. In fact, for most, it would appear to be sentimental, weak, and unproductive. The standard for worldly leadership is to accomplish the leader's desires *through* people. In the church, pastors have the privilege of seeing things God desires done in people.

That changes the dynamic. As good parents are concerned about their children's hearts, so are good pastors. The preceding metaphors make that clear.

The verb rendered **tenderly cares** literally means to warm with body heat. The loving mother would take the little one in her arms and warm the child with her own body heat. Such a vivid metaphor perfectly illustrates the kind of personal care the Thessalonians received. Paul, unlike the enemies of the truth, was not harsh or indifferent, but tenderly nurturing.

INTIMATE AFFECTION

Having so fond an affection for you, (2:8*a*)

In extending the metaphor of a nursing mother, it was logical for Paul to mention the motive for such nurturing gentleness—love. He possessed **fond affection** for the Thessalonians. A mother who carries an infant son or daughter on her breast has a naturally **fond affection** that is unequalled in other human contexts. The Greek word translated **fond affection** (*homeiromai;* used only here in the New Testament) means to long for someone passionately and earnestly, and, being linked to a mother's love, is intended here to express an affection so deep and compelling as to be unsurpassed. Ancient inscriptions on the tombs of dead babies sometimes contained this term when parents wanted to describe their sad longing for a too-soon-departed child.

Paul acknowledged that God naturally designed such intimate **affection** into the hearts of mothers. The hearts of all righteous spiritual leaders have been supernaturally given the same type of **affection** for their people, even as he and his companions had for those who were Christ's.

SACRIFICIAL LOVE

we were well-pleased to impart to you not only the gospel of God but also our own lives, because you had become very dear to us. (2:8*b*)

Such personal and intimate supernatural affection was not out of a sense of obligation; they were not merely carrying out an assignment as God's messengers. It was, rather, the highest joy of their hearts to so love. Paul said they **were well-pleased** to so minister. That desire defined an eagerness and zealousness generated from love-filled hearts (cf. 3:12).

They came first of all **to impart . . . the gospel of God.** The verb translated **impart** means to share, or give someone something of which one retains a part. That is exactly what happens when Christians **impart** to other people divine truth. They give someone else the good news of salvation, yet without losing possession of it themselves.

Paul and his fellow workers taught the transforming truths of the **gospel of God** (see comments on 2:2) and yet retained those truths, even strengthening them by the giving (as all good teachers know), thus forming a loving, enriching fellowship with those who accepted the message. Implicit in the expression **gospel of God** is a doctrinal fullness that encompasses justification, sanctification, and glorification (cf. Titus 1:1–2). (And because God is the source of the good news, even election is included.) The missionaries understood and obeyed the Great Commission's injunction that said Christians were to "make disciples of all the nations . . . teaching them to observe all that I commanded you" (Matt. 28:19–20). They exhorted the Thessalonians to repent and embrace Christ's death and resurrection (justification). They also instructed them on how to live holy lives in obedience to Scripture and in the power of the Holy Spirit (sanctification) and to wait for their eternal glory at the glorious coming of the Lord for His beloved church (glorification). (In reality, all New Testament teaching relates to the complete gospel in some way.)

Besides imparting the complete gospel, Paul, Silas, and Timothy shared **also** their **own lives.** Literally, they gave up their souls—their real inner beings—for the sake of the Thessalonians. There was nothing superficial or partial about their sacrificial service. A woman who fulfills the biblical role for motherhood does the same thing when she, at great cost to herself, unselfishly and generously sets aside her life for the benefit of her beloved children. That is especially true of the nursing mother as she provides nourishing milk for her little one and cares for her newborn baby's every need.

Paul ministered to his people with that same attitude of all-out commitment **because,** as babies to a mother, they **had become very dear** to him. **Very dear** adds to the images and descriptions intended by Paul to unmistakably demonstrate the heart of a godly pastor.

UNSELFISH LABOR

For you recall, brethren, our labor and hardship, how working

night and day so as not to be a burden to any of you, we proclaimed to you the gospel of God. (2:9)

For proof of his affection for them, Paul again urged the Thessalonians to **recall** the character of the ministry he had with them. **Labor and hardship** appropriately summarize the ministry at Thessalonica. **Labor** emphasizes the difficulty of a particular deed itself, and **hardship** underscores the strenuous toil and struggle in performing it. Those two words combine to reflect not only the loving attitude of motherly concern, but also the sincere application of that concern. Every mother knows there is no price her children can pay her for what she does for them. She does not expect them to compensate her for nursing them, for displaying a deep affection for them, or for embracing their every need sacrificially in heartfelt love. Likewise, Paul told the church that he and his colleagues eagerly ministered to them, with no desire for the compensation they had a right to expect (cf. 1 Cor. 9:7–11; 1 Tim. 5:17–18).

Paul gives a further explanation of this sacrifice in 2 Thessalonians 3:7–9:

> For you yourselves know how you ought to follow our example, because we did not act in an undisciplined manner among you, nor did we eat anyone's bread without paying for it, but with labor and hardship we kept working night and day so that we would not be a burden to any of you; not because we do not have the right to this, but in order to offer ourselves as a model for you, so that you would follow our example.

He and his companions lived on what he received from the Philippians (Phil. 4:16) and what he earned in his trade as a tent maker. Since he clearly stayed in Thessalonica beyond the three Sabbaths which he first taught at the synagogue, he had time to set up a tent making business—which he did, **working night and day** with his hands to support himself and those with him.

Paul did not want **to be a burden to any** of the Thessalonians because he knew they lacked material resources (cf. 2 Cor. 8:1–2). Though they gave generously and sacrificially for the impoverished believers in Jerusalem (cf. vv. 3–4), it was out of the "deep poverty" that was typical of believers (cf. 1 Cor. 1:26–28), especially in the war-ravaged, oft-plundered Roman province of Macedonia.

So Paul pictured Silas, Timothy, and himself as spiritual mothers who made the maximum effort to provide gentleness, intimate affection, sacrificial love, and hard-working provision as they **proclaimed** to them **the gospel of God.** That maternal metaphor, however, only partially describes the effective spiritual leader. Describing the spiritual leader as a father completes Paul's picture of leadership.

The Spiritual Leader as Father

You are witnesses, and so is God, how devoutly and uprightly and blamelessly we behaved toward you believers; just as you know how we were exhorting and encouraging and imploring each one of you as a father would his own children, so that you would walk in a manner worthy of the God who calls you into His own kingdom and glory. (2:10–12)

First Corinthians 16:13 contains the distinctive New Testament definition of manliness, which is a helpful corollary to understanding the paternal aspect of spiritual leadership. After instructing the Corinthian believers on how to stand firm and be alert in the face of sinful factionalism and compromising weakness, Paul exhorted them to "act like men, be strong." The Greek verb translated "act like men" means "to conduct oneself in a courageous way." That injunction further clarifies the command to "be strong," summing up the matter of manliness and being the equivalent of the old English term *fortitude*. (*Merriam-Webster's Collegiate Dictionary* defines fortitude as "strength of mind that enables a person to encounter danger or bear pain or adversity with [resolute] courage.")

Effective spiritual leaders, then, will be men who have strength of conviction and the courage to stand on it. God has called them to noble spiritual standards (cf. Eph. 4:11–12; 1 Tim. 3:1–13; 2 Tim. 2:2; 1 Peter 5:1–4) and granted them by truth and the Holy Spirit the fortitude to uphold those standards and remain firm, unmoved, and uncompromising in the face of any opposition.

That Corinthian text is the only place in the New Testament where the phrase "act like men, be strong" appears. But the Septuagint translators used it a number of times, and some of those key passages provide additional insight and richness to the phrase's implications for leadership.

Then Moses called to Joshua and said to him in the sight of all Israel, "Be strong and courageous, for you shall go with this people into the land which the Lord has sworn to their fathers to give them, and you shall give it to them as an inheritance. The Lord is the one who goes ahead of you; He will be with you. He will not fail you or forsake you. Do not fear or be dismayed."... Then He commissioned Joshua the son of Nun, and said, "Be strong and courageous, for you shall bring the sons of Israel into the land which I swore to them, and I will be with you." (Deut. 31:7–8, 23)

No man will be able to stand before you all the days of your life. Just as I have been with Moses, I will be with you; I will not fail you or forsake you. Be strong and courageous, for you shall give this people possession of the land which I swore to their fathers to give them. Only be strong and very courageous; be careful to do according to all the law which Moses My servant commanded you; do not turn from it to the right or to the left, so that you may have success wherever you go. This book of the law shall not depart from your mouth, but you shall meditate on it day and night, so that you may be careful to do according to all that is written in it; for then you will make your way prosperous, and then you will have success. Have I not commanded you? Be strong and courageous! Do not tremble or be dismayed, for the Lord your God is with you wherever you go. (Josh. 1:5–9)

"Be strong, and let us show ourselves courageous for the sake of our people and for the cities of our God; and may the Lord do what is good in His sight." So Joab and the people who were with him drew near to the battle against the Arameans, and they fled before him. (2 Sam. 10:12–13)

As unfolded in the Joshua passage, the first source of courage for Joshua in his task as spiritual leader was the continuing presence of God ("I will be with you"); the second was the promise of God ("I swore to their fathers"); and the third was the power of God ("Do not tremble or be dismayed, for the Lord your God is with you wherever you go"). Based on those divine resources, God called Joshua to obey His law, knowing that such obedience would make him a successful leader. Those truths, so simply given, apply to all who lead in God's kingdom.

Perhaps the apostle Paul drew from the above-cited passages as he elucidated the paternal metaphor of spiritual leadership and reminded the Thessalonians how he and his missionary companions exemplified it.

THE FATHER AS MODEL

You are witnesses, and so is God, how devoutly and uprightly and blamelessly we behaved toward you believers; (2:10)

As with all leaders, a father's duty is to lead by example, setting the standard of virtuous integrity in his family (Deut. 4:9; Prov. 13:24; Eph. 6:4; Col. 3:21; Heb. 12:9); and that is also the spiritual leader's responsibility to his people. With that in mind, Paul called upon the Thessalonians again to remember what he had said and how he had ministered among them (2:1, 2, 5, and 9). The phrase **You are witnesses** repeats the reminder of verse 1, "for you yourselves know," and the phrase **and so is God** looks back to verses 4 and 5 in which Paul described God's omniscient examination of his motive and his own testimony of his personal integrity.

Thus Paul pointed both to the Thessalonians' firsthand knowledge and God's perfect insight into **how devoutly and uprightly and blamelessly** he and his friends **behaved toward** them. **Devoutly** means "in a holy manner" and emphasizes how Paul, Silas, and Timothy lived before God. The adverb **uprightly** ("righteously") refers to how well the men dealt righteously under divine law toward both God and man. And finally, the word **blamelessly** pertains to their reputation before people. In every respect, they were exemplary spiritual fathers, setting the standard for all who have followed.

THE FATHER AS TEACHER AND MOTIVATOR

just as you know how we were exhorting and encouraging and imploring each one of you as a father would his own children, (2:11)

As a father would his own children expresses the natural, normal function of **a father** concerned about the well-being of **his own children.** Fathers are not only examples, but also instructors. So the spiritual father is not to be merely a model but also a personal teacher and motivator. This fatherly instruction is conveyed in three verbs describing what fathers do and what Paul had done continually.

Exhorting is from *parakaleō*, literally "to call alongside," and is related to the noun *paraklētos*, "one who comes alongside," which is one of the titles for the Holy Spirit (John 14:16–17, 26; 15:26; cf. Gen. 1:2; Isa. 11:2; John 3:6; Rom. 8:9, 15–16; Eph. 1:13; 1 Peter 4:14). The apostle referred to coming alongside **children** for the purpose of aiding, directing, and instructing wisely as a source of character conduct.

Encouraging (*paramutheomai*), meaning to encourage in the sense of comfort and consolation, is so critical in assisting toward spiritual growth because of the many obstacles and failures Christians can experience. Used in John 11:19 and 31 for the consolation given to the grieving family of Lazarus, the word was reserved for the tender, restorative, compassionate uplifting needed by a struggling, burdened, heartbroken child. This beautiful expression of natural fatherly kindness also fits the spiritual father.

Finally, Paul reminded the believers that he had been **imploring each one** (singling them out personally). **Imploring** is the Greek participle *marturomenoi,* which is usually translated "testifying," or "witnessing," is related to the word *martyr* because so many faithful witnesses died for their boldness. Paul warned the Thessalonians that any deviation from the divinely prescribed course of conduct had serious consequences. The warning was an admonishment that if they did not follow the course laid out for them, they, as disobedient children would receive from a father, could expect to receive spiritual discipline from the apostle.

THE FATHER AS PRODUCER

so that you would walk in a manner worthy of the God who calls you into His own kingdom and glory. (2:12)

Like a father whose goal is the mature wisdom of his children, the apostle Paul concluded his exhortation by affirming that a spiritual father will endeavor to continue his efforts until he produces sons and daughters who **walk in a manner worthy**—live mature lives. **Walk** refers to daily conduct, as it often does in the New Testament epistles (e.g., Rom. 6:4; 2 Cor. 5:7; Gal. 5:16, 25; Eph. 2:10; 4:1; 5:8; Col. 1:10; 2:6; 1 John 2:6). In referring to the **God who calls,** Paul was again directly referring to the truth of the Thessalonians' election, which he stated in 1:4 (see the discussion in chapter 1 of this volume) and again mentions in 5:24.

Here the divine call, as always in the epistles, refers to the effectual saving call. By it God, through the faith graciously and sovereignly granted to sinners, regenerates, justifies, and sanctifies them. And Paul stated the singular end of that call—entrance **into His own kingdom and glory.** Though they, as all believers, had not yet seen either the millennial kingdom or the eternal kingdom, they were already citizens of the redeemed **kingdom** over which God now rules (Luke 17:21; Col. 1:13; cf. Rom. 14:17). Thus they had a present share in the **glory** of God as well as a promise of the future glory in the **kingdom** yet to come. All believers look forward to sharing in the full **glory** of the heavenly kingdom when God raises them to be like Christ and with Him for eternity (Ps. 73:24; Prov. 3:35; Rom. 9:23; 1 Cor. 15:43; Phil. 3:20–21; Col. 3:4; 2 Thess. 2:14; 1 Peter 5:10; cf. Matt. 5:12; John 14:2; Rom. 8:18; 2 Cor. 4:17; Heb. 4:9; 11:16; 1 Peter 1:3–4; Rev. 7:16–17).

The parental pictures of spiritual leadership in 1 Thessalonians 2:7–12 clearly demonstrate that leadership in the church must be balanced. It is not enough for leaders just to be compassionate, tender, and caring as spiritual mothers. They also need to live uncompromising, pure, and exemplary lives as spiritual fathers—lives that, in their motives and actions, set the standard for all to follow (cf. 1 Cor. 11:1). Furthermore, they need to teach the truth faithfully, building up the saints in spiritual wisdom (cf. Eph. 4:11–16) and displaying the courage of conviction to come alongside and exhort and call their spiritual children to obedience, through both strong discipline and tender consolation. These efforts lead their congregation to live in a way that honors God, who has called them to His eternal kingdom and glory.

A People to Be Glad for and a People to Be Sad For
(1 Thessalonians 2:13–16)

For this reason we also constantly thank God that when you received the word of God which you heard from us, you accepted it not as the word of men, but for what it really is, the word of God, which also performs its work in you who believe. For you, brethren, became imitators of the churches of God in Christ Jesus that are in Judea, for you also endured the same sufferings at the hands of your own countrymen, even as they did from the Jews, who both killed the Lord Jesus and the prophets, and drove us out. They are not pleasing to God, but hostile to all men, hindering us from speaking to the Gentiles so that they may be saved; with the result that they always fill up the measure of their sins. But wrath has come upon them to the utmost. (2:13–16)

Since God first revealed it to mankind, the plan of redemption has been a bittersweet reality (cf. Rev. 10:8–10). One finds sweetness in contemplating the bliss and glory of eternal life that awaits those who embrace the gospel. By contrast, one finds only bitterness in the endless shame and punishment of eternal damnation that awaits those who reject the gospel. That contrast is never more strikingly seen than when one compares people who have made the most of limited spiritual opportunity to people who have squandered great spiritual opportunity and privilege. Throughout redemptive history, the Jews have exemplified the latter reality, which illustrates the ultimate tragedy of apostasy (cf. Rom. 2:4–11; 3:1–4; 9:30–33). On the other hand, the Thessalonians epitomized the former reality and believed God's truth after only a brief initial exposure to it (Acts 17:1–4).

This striking contrast is the object of the apostle Paul's focus in 1 Thessalonians 2:13–16. He distinguishes sharply between a people to be glad for, the believing Thessalonians, and a people to be sad for, the unbelieving Jews. In just a few weeks, the Thessalonians readily chose the blessing of obedience to the gospel of God, whereas after centuries of revelation from God, the Jews stubbornly chose the cursing resulting from disobedience to the gospel. Such opposite responses to God's truth and grace prompted Paul to sort out the reasons he rejoiced for the Thessalonians and sorrowed for the Jews.

A PEOPLE TO BE GLAD FOR

For this reason we also constantly thank God that when you received the word of God which you heard from us, you accepted it not as the word of men, but for what it really is, the word of God, which also performs its work in you who believe. For you, brethren, became imitators of the churches of God in Christ Jesus that are in Judea, for you also endured the same sufferings at the hands of your own countrymen, even as they did from the Jews, (2:13–14)

Paul, Silas, and Timothy had ministered only a short while in Thessalonica when they saw miraculous results from their preaching (Acts 17:2–3). Because of the immorality and strong pagan religious environment in the city, and the realities that the truth of salvation was so new to the people, and the apostle had been with them only a few months, Paul was concerned that the Thessalonians' faith might have faltered. Consequently, after leaving Thessalonica, Paul sent Timothy back there to check on the church's progress: "When I could endure it no longer, I also sent to find out about your faith, for fear that the tempter might have tempted you, and our labor would be in vain" (1 Thess. 3:5). However, the apostle's fears proved unfounded: "But now that Timothy has come to us from you, and has brought us good news of your faith and love, and that you always think kindly of us, longing to see us just as we also long to see you" (v. 6). That positive report prompted this expression of gratitude for the Thessalonians.

Paul was always thankful for the privilege of ministry, and he ceaselessly acknowledged God as the One who empowered the truth through him. He had already expressed this to the Thessalonians when he opened his letter: "We give thanks to God always for all of you" (1:2; cf. Rom. 1:8). Here he rehearses the **reason** he had to **constantly thank God** for the Thessalonians. The expression **for this reason,** though singular, encompasses a threefold cause for Paul's gratitude: the Thessalonians' reception of God's Word, their honoring of the saints, and their perseverance in suffering.

THE THESSALONIANS' RECEPTION OF GOD'S WORD

that when you received the word of God which you heard from us, you accepted it not as the word of men, but for what it really is, the word of God, which also performs its work in you who believe. (2:13)

Paul was first of all thankful the people willingly **received the word of God.** They were open and receptive in listening to the preaching from Paul, Silas, and Timothy (Acts 17:4; cf. 28:24). *Paralabontes* (**received**) refers to an objective reception of a particular message, in this case the gospel.

The phrase **the word of God which you heard from us** literally reads, "A word heard from us out from God." The missionaries spoke the words, but those words came from God. That is why Paul several times in this letter refers to his message as "the gospel of God" (2:2, 8, 9; cf. Acts 8:14; 13:44). As **the word of God,** it was infinitely superior to the words of human opinion the Thessalonians were accustomed to hearing. Because of Thessalonica's strategic location (see Introduction 1 Thessalonians and chapter 1 of this volume), the city attracted many false philosophers and religious teachers. Its residents therefore had heard a wide range of human wisdom and rhetoric. But, in contrast to all others, when they heard the preaching of Paul and his companions, they **accepted** it as the true message of salvation from God.

The Thessalonians' reception of God's Word was subjective as well as objective. *Edexasthe* (**accepted**) connotes an inward welcome of the message, a transference from the mind to the heart. Such an eager embracing of what the Thessalonians had heard indicated that God had granted them faith and regeneration. Luke's record says: "Some of them were persuaded and joined Paul and Silas, along with a large number of the God-fearing Greeks and a number of the leading women" (Acts 17:4; cf. Rom. 10:10, 17).

Paul underscored what the Thessalonians affirmed—that the message they had accepted was **not . . . the word of men.** The recipients of Paul's letters knew that what he taught was from God. To the Corinthians he wrote:

> Now I make known to you, brethren, the gospel which I preached to you, which also you received, in which you also stand. . . . For I delivered to you as of first importance what I also received, that Christ died for our sins according to the Scriptures, and that He was buried, and that He was raised on the third day according to the Scriptures. (1 Cor. 15:1, 3–4)

He assured the Galatians, "For I would have you know, brethren, that the gospel which was preached by me is not according to man. For I neither received it from man, nor was I taught it, but I received it through a revelation of Jesus Christ" (Gal. 1:11–12). Likewise, what the Thessalonians heard **really** was **the word of God** (cf. 1 Thess. 4:15).

Unlike the **word of men,** the Word of God is not empty, inert, or powerless. The verb rendered **performs its work** means to work effectively, efficiently, and productively on a supernatural (divine) level (cf. 1 Cor. 12:6; Phil. 2:13). God's Word always **performs** His purposes **in** the lives of all **who believe** (cf. Isa. 55:11). Scripture works on behalf of believers in a multitude of ways: it saves them (James 1:18; 1 Peter 1:23); it sanctifies them (John 17:17); it matures them (1 Peter 2:2); it frees them (John 8:31–32); it perfects them (2 Tim. 3:16–17); it counsels them (Ps. 119:24); it builds them up (Acts 20:32); it ensures their spiritual success (Josh. 1:8–9; Ps. 1:2–3); and it gives them hope (Ps. 119:147; Acts 20:32).

In spite of its claims to the contrary, human wisdom cannot produce any of those results. That is the clear message of 1 Corinthians 1:18–25, which records Paul's Spirit-inspired testimony on the emptiness and folly of human wisdom:

> For the word of the cross is foolishness to those who are perishing, but to us who are being saved it is the power of God. For it is written, "I will destroy the wisdom of the wise, and the cleverness of the clever I will set aside." Where is the wise man? Where is the scribe? Where is the debater of this age? Has not God made foolish the wisdom of the world? For since in the wisdom of God the world through its wisdom did not come to know God, God was well-pleased through the foolishness of the message preached to save those who believe. For indeed Jews ask for signs and Greeks search for wisdom; but we preach Christ crucified, to Jews a stumbling block and to Gentiles foolishness, but to those who are the called, both Jews and Greeks, Christ the power of God and the wisdom of God. Because the foolishness of God is wiser than men, and the weakness of God is stronger than men.

The Thessalonians progressed spiritually because they savingly believed the message of the Cross and that belief powerfully affected their daily lives. Paul was thankful for that reality, just as he was later for the Colossians' reception of the Word: "It is constantly bearing fruit and increasing, even as it has been doing in you also since the day you heard of it and understood the grace of God in truth" (Col. 1:6).

THE THESSALONIANS' HONORING OF THE SAINTS

For you, brethren, became imitators of the churches of God in Christ Jesus that are in Judea, (2:14a)

The proof of their complete acceptance of the gospel and the Lord of that gospel is that the church in Thessalonica had become **imitators** of the apostle and his coworkers, Silas and Timothy (see discussion of 1:6 in chapter 1 of this volume). Here Paul expands his commendation and says the Thessalonians also imitated the believers **in Judea,** giving him further reason to be thankful to God for His work in saving the Thessalonians.

Though the Thessalonians probably had never been to **the churches in Judea** to see a pattern they could follow, the Holy Spirit's sanctifying work was making the Thessalonian church a duplicate of His work in Judea, in that both churches experienced suffering (v. 14b).

In the first century, **Judea** was a Roman province in Palestine. It was the home of the first local Christian assembly, the Jerusalem church, which began on the day of Pentecost (Acts 2). During the first few years following the birth of that church, believers founded other local churches (cf. Acts 8:4) that, by the time of the Thessalonians' conversion, were all mature assemblies, having benefited from the refining of persecution.

Paul refers to the Judean congregations as **the churches of God,** which emphasizes their divine source (cf. Acts 20:28; Gal. 1:22). The plural **churches** indicates that by this time there were a number of local **churches** scattered around **Judea,** individual assemblies of people who were **in Christ Jesus,** which is true of all genuine churches (cf. 1 Cor. 1:2; Eph. 1:1; Phil. 1:1; Col. 1:2; 1 Thess. 1:1). True churches are both **of God** and **in Christ** because all individual believers are in Christ (Rom. 6:11; 8:1; 12:5; 2 Cor. 5:17; Gal. 3:28; Eph. 2:10; Phil. 4:21; Col. 1:28; 2 Tim. 2:10; 1 Peter 5:14).

THE THESSALONIANS' PERSEVERANCE IN SUFFERING

for you also endured the same sufferings at the hands of your own countrymen, even as they did from the Jews, (2:14*b*)

After the stoning of Stephen, the Judean Christians suffered a period of persecution that was mainly led by Saul of Tarsus (Acts 7:54–8:4). When the risen Christ saved Saul on the Damascus road (9:1–19), the persecution waned somewhat. But it was not long before the persecution—which this time included the first murder of an apostle, James, by the sword—flared up again under Herod. At that time also, the Jewish leaders imprisoned Peter (Acts 12:1–4). Thus the Judean churches had a history of dealing with severe harassment, and had persevered in suffering—an experience the Thessalonian church was imitating.

Even as the believers in Judea suffered persecution **from** their own people, **the Jews,** the Thessalonians, immediately after receiving the gospel (Acts 17:1–4), **endured** persecution **at the hands of** their **own countrymen.** Acts 17:5–8 identifies those persecutors as both unbelieving Jews and their Gentile accomplices:

> But the Jews, becoming jealous and taking along some wicked men from the market place, formed a mob and set the city in an uproar; and attacking the house of Jason, they were seeking to bring them out to the people. When they did not find them, they began dragging Jason and some brethren before the city authorities, shouting, "These men who have upset the world have come here also; and Jason has welcomed them, and they all act contrary to the decrees of Caesar, saying that there is another king, Jesus." They stirred up the crowd and the city authorities who heard these things.

In that instance, the mob sought Paul and his friends at Jason's house on the assumption that they were protected there. (Jason was a name adopted by many dispersed Jews, so he was possibly an Israelite.) The episode illustrates the kind of persecution the Thessalonian church was suffering.

Paul and his companions left Thessalonica immediately after the mob uproar (Acts 17:10), but it is likely that the persecution resumed and intensified during the subsequent weeks before Paul sent this epistle from Corinth. The Thessalonians nevertheless triumphed in their sufferings, being joyful in affliction (1 Thess. 1:6), which to Paul was an evidence of their true conversion and thus the culmination of his thanks to God for them.

A PEOPLE TO BE SAD FOR

who both killed the Lord Jesus and the prophets, and drove us out. They are not pleasing to God, but hostile to all men, hindering us from speaking to the Gentiles so that they may be saved; with the result that they always fill up the measure of their sins. But wrath has come upon them to the utmost. (2:15–16)

The apostle Paul made an unusually abrupt transition as he began his criticism of the Jews. It is almost as if the mention of the word **Jews** at the end of verse 14 instantly catapulted him into the harsh words of verses 15 and 16. The unbelieving Jews were the tragic antithesis of the believers in Thessalonica.

Such a harsh, condemning outburst as this against the Jews was not unusual for Paul, in light of their long-standing, persistent resentment of the apostle, which began shortly after his conversion. The book of Acts chronicles numerous examples of the Jews' hostility. "Now for several days he was with the disciples who were at Damascus, and immediately he began to proclaim Jesus in the synagogues, saying, 'He is the Son of God.' . . . [And] Saul kept increasing in strength and confounding the [disbelieving] Jews who lived at Damascus by proving that this Jesus is the Christ" (Acts 9:20, 22; cf. 14:1–7, 19–20; 18:12–17; 19:8–10; 2 Cor. 11:24). In Acts 13, when the Jews observed Paul and his companions effectively proclaiming the gospel among the Gentiles, they reacted with prejudicial hatred. They were filled with envy and rage over the efforts of Paul, a Jew, to reach unclean Gentiles. Acts 13:40–50 describes that sort of prejudice:

"Therefore take heed, so that the thing spoken of in the Prophets may not come upon you: 'Behold, you scoffers, and marvel, and perish; for I am accomplishing a work in your days, a work which you will never believe, though someone should describe it to you.'" As Paul and Barnabas were going out, the people kept begging that these things might be spoken to them the next Sabbath. Now when the meeting of the synagogue had broken up, many of the Jews and of the God-fearing proselytes followed Paul and Barnabas, who, speaking to them, were urging them to continue in the grace of God. The next Sabbath nearly the whole city assembled to hear the word of the Lord. But when the Jews saw the crowds, they were filled with jealousy and began contradicting the things spoken by Paul, and were blaspheming. Paul and Barnabas spoke out boldly and said, "It was necessary that the word of God be spoken to you first; since you repudiate it and judge yourselves unworthy of eternal life, behold, we are turning to the Gentiles. For so the Lord has commanded us, 'I have placed you as a light for the Gentiles, that you may bring salvation to the end of the earth.'" When the Gentiles heard this, they began rejoicing and glorifying the word of the Lord; and as many as had been appointed to eternal life believed. And the word of the Lord was being spread through the whole region. But the Jews incited the devout women of prominence and the leading men of the city, and instigated a persecution against Paul and Barnabas, and drove them out of their district.

The Jewish people had already turned their backs on the spiritual privilege that Paul alluded to in the book of Romans:

Who are Israelites, to whom belongs the adoption as sons, and the glory and the covenants and the giving of the Law and the temple service and the promises, whose are the fathers, and from whom is the Christ according to the flesh, who is over all, God blessed forever. Amen. (9:4–5; cf. Gen. 17:2; Ex. 4:22; Deut. 4:13; 29:14–15; 1 Sam. 4:21; Pss. 26:8; 147:19; Heb. 9:1, 6)

The apostle subsequently summarized their apostate position: "For I testify about them that they have a zeal for God, but not in accordance with knowledge. For not knowing about God's righteousness and seeking to establish their own, they did not subject themselves to the righteousness of God" (Rom. 10:2–3; cf. Matt. 23:13–30).

Knowing that the Jews' hateful attitude had not changed but rather had intensified since their original hostility in the early days at Thessalonica, Paul made a strong statement about their spiritual condition. His statement consists of three reasons they are a people to be sad for: they rejected God's Word, they hindered the saints, and they faced punishment in suffering. These three are in direct contrast to the reasons Paul was joyful over the Thessalonians.

THE JEWS' REJECTION OF GOD'S WORD

who both killed the Lord Jesus and the prophets, and drove us out. (2:15a)

Amazingly, in clear contrast to the Thessalonian believers' immediate love of the truth, throughout their long history the Jews rejected the message and messengers God sent them. Most notably, the **Lord Jesus,** their Messiah, declared the truth of God, and they **killed** Him (Acts 2:22–23, 36). The Old Testament **prophets** delivered God's words to His people, and they **killed** those men also (Jer. 26:23; Heb. 11:32–37; cf. 1 Kings 19:10; 2 Chron. 24:20–21). Matthew 23:31–35 sums up the Jews' attitude toward God's messengers:

> So you testify against yourselves, that you are sons of those who murdered the prophets. Fill up, then, the measure of the guilt of your fathers. You serpents, you brood of vipers, how will you escape the sentence of hell? Therefore, behold, I am sending you prophets and wise men and scribes; some of them you will kill and crucify, and some of them you will scourge in your synagogues, and persecute from city to city, so that upon you may fall the guilt of all the righteous blood shed on earth, from the blood of righteous Abel to the blood of Zechariah, the son of Berechiah, whom you murdered between the temple and the altar.

Jesus' parable in Matthew 21:33–46 vividly reveals their murderous acts toward the prophets and the Lord:

> "Listen to another parable. There was a landowner who planted a vineyard and put a wall around it and dug a wine press in it, and built a tower, and rented it out to vine-growers and went on a journey. When the harvest time approached, he sent his slaves to the vine-growers to receive his produce. The vine-growers took his slaves and beat one, and killed another, and stoned a third. Again he sent another group of slaves larger than the first; and they did the same thing to them. But afterward he sent his son to them, saying, 'They will respect my son.' But when the vine-growers saw the son, they said among themselves, 'This is the heir; come, let us kill him and seize his inheritance.' They took him, and threw him out of the vineyard and killed him. Therefore when the owner of the vineyard comes, what will he do to those vine-growers?" They said to Him, "He will bring those wretches to a wretched end, and will rent out the vineyard to other vine-growers who will pay him the proceeds at the proper seasons." Jesus said to them, "Did you never read in the Scriptures, 'The stone which the builders rejected, this became the chief corner stone; this came about from the Lord, and it is marvelous in our eyes'? Therefore I say to you, the kingdom of God will be taken away from you and given to a people, producing the fruit of it. And he who falls on this stone will be broken to pieces; but on whomever it falls, it will scatter him like dust." When the chief priests and the Pharisees heard His parables, they understood that He was speaking about them. When they sought to seize Him, they feared the people, because they considered Him to be a prophet.

The gospels support Paul's statement that the Jews **killed the Lord Jesus** (Matt. 27:20–25; Mark 14:61–65; 15:11–14; Luke 23:20–25). The Romans executed Him, but only at the instigation of the Jews (John 19:12–16). Obviously it is not all Jews of all time who were responsible for killing Christ. However, the apostate Jewish mob that insisted Pontius Pilate should carry out the crucifixion of Jesus was guilty of murdering Him. Those Jews represented the historic apex of their people's unbelief and opposition to God's will (Acts 2:22–23, 36; 4:10; 5:30; 10:39). Thus Paul's strong words in verse 15 are without doubt in harmony with God's centuries-old disapproval of the Jews who apostatized (cf. 2 Kings 17:13; 2 Chron. 15:1–2; 36:16; Jer. 25:4–5; Lam. 2:9; Ezek. 3:19; Matt. 23:35–38).

The Jewish people's culpability for the murder of Jesus also correlates with their deadly hostility toward **the prophets.** Other than Zechariah's (2 Chron. 24:20–22), the Old Testament spokesmen's murders are not detailed in Scripture. However, the writer of the letter to the Hebrews provides a general indication of what occurred: "They were stoned, they were sawn in two, they were tempted, they were put to death with the sword; they went about in sheepskins, in goatskins, being destitute, afflicted, ill-treated" (Heb. 11:37).

The Jews' long-established rejection of anyone who brought God's Word to them (2 Chron. 24:19) extended to Paul and the other New Testament apostles. Hence Paul wrote that the Jews **drove** his associates and him **out** of Thessalonica (Acts 17:10). The verb rendered **drove us out** refers to the hunting down of an animal with the intention of killing it. Such stubborn and overt Jewish rejection of God's Word profoundly saddened the apostle's heart (cf. Rom. 9:1–5; 10:1).

THE JEWS' HINDRANCE OF THE SAINTS

They are not pleasing to God, but hostile to all men, hindering us from speaking to the Gentiles so that they may be saved; (2:15*b*–16*a*)

Whereas the Thessalonians honored the messengers of God, the Jews hindered the gospel preachers by trying to prevent them from preaching their message. By **hindering** the spread of the gospel **to the Gentiles,** the Jews, in similar fashion to the unconverted Saul of Tarsus, thought they were rendering God a service. However, Paul said they were **not pleasing to God** and used the present tense, denoting that the Jews' antagonistic attitude was habitual.

The Jews were not only displeasing to God, but they were also **hostile to all men.** That hostility was not so much a racial prejudice as it was a religious prejudice. They resented, even hated, any religion but their own—and especially the gospel of Jesus Christ, whom they rejected as a satanic, counterfeit messiah (cf. Matt. 12:24). That animosity was expressed in **hindering** the apostles **from speaking** the gospel **to the Gentiles.** The Jews refused to believe the gospel, and they resented it being preached so that others might **be saved.** Such sinful religious prejudice had appeared before, in the earliest days of the Jerusalem church, when the Sanhedrin attempted to silence the apostles:

> But someone came and reported to them, "The men whom you put in prison are standing in the temple and teaching the people!" Then the captain went along with the officers and proceeded to bring them back without violence (for they were afraid of the people, that they might be stoned). When they had brought them, they stood them before the Council. The high priest questioned them, saying, "We gave you strict orders not to continue teaching in this name, and yet, you have filled Jerusalem with your teaching and intend to bring this man's blood upon us." But Peter and the apostles answered, "We must obey God rather than men. The God of our fathers raised up Jesus, whom you had put to death by hanging Him on a cross. He is the one whom God exalted to His right hand as a Prince and a Savior, to grant repentance to Israel, and forgiveness of sins. And we are witnesses of these things; and so is the Holy Spirit, whom God has given to those who obey Him." But when they heard this, they were cut to the quick and intended to kill them. (Acts 5:25–33; cf. 4:1–22; 5:17–18, 40–41)

That indicates how strongly the Jews rejected the gospel of Jesus Christ, and how determined some of them were to stop its proclamation—even by killing the proclaimers!

THE JEWS' PUNISHMENT IN SUFFERING

with the result that they always fill up the measure of their sins. But wrath has come upon them to the utmost. (2:16*b*)

The Thessalonians had demonstrated perseverance in suffering and emerged triumphant in the hope of eternal glory. However, the Jews faced an entirely different situation. They would not be able to endure their fearful, deadly, final punishment.

The result of the Jews' hostility to God's Word and His saints is that they **always fill up the measure of their sins.** Literally, that phrase says, "They always heap up their sins to the limit." There is a well-defined point at which people reach the limit of their sins (cf. Gen. 6:3, 5–6; Matt. 23:32). Paul's language stems from the kind of expression first seen in Scripture in Genesis 15:16, "The iniquity of the Amorite is not yet complete." It means God brings judgment only when sin has reached a certain limit (Dan. 8:23; Acts 17:30–31; Rom. 2:5–6; cf. Matt. 23:32; Heb. 10:28–30).

God's judgmental **wrath has come upon** the Jews **to the utmost.** The verb translated **has come** is in the aorist tense, which affirms that

Paul was so certain that divine **wrath** would come that he expressed the notion as if it had already occurred. And historically, it had occurred—in the Babylonian exile (Ezek. 8–11). His expression likely includes the destruction of Jerusalem in A.D. 70, although then nearly twenty years off; and it denotes the eschatological **wrath** to come when Jesus returns to earth in judgment (Rev. 19). But primarily the expression points to the damnation of people who reject God (cf. John 3:36). That, too, was so certain that Paul could write of it as if it had already occurred. Those Jews had met all the prerequisites for future damnation. They had completed **the measure of their sins** in rejecting the only truth of salvation and murdering their Messiah and His messengers; therefore, God's **wrath** would **come upon them to the utmost.** The expression **to the utmost** means God will extend His wrath to the unbelieving Jews to its extreme limit, or fullest expression (cf. 2 Kings 22:17; 2 Chron. 24:18; 36:16; Neh. 13:18; Ps. 78:59; Jer. 4:4; Matt. 3:7; Rom. 9:22). Their future punishment in hell was by that time irreversible. (However, that does not mean God is through with Israel. As Paul writes in Romans 11:26–27, someday God will save all Israel, in accord with His promises to that nation: "All Israel will be saved; just as it is written, 'The Deliverer will come from Zion, He will remove ungodliness from Jacob. This is My covenant with them, when I take away their sins'" [cf. Jer. 33:19–26; Zech. 12:10].)

Today, as in Paul's day, the choice between God's blessing and His cursing (cf. Deut. 28:1, 15) remains. Those who believe and obey the Word and honor other believers by imitating their lives will persevere to eternal glory, which is good reason to be glad for them. But those who reject the Word and hinder those who preach it will ultimately suffer eternal condemnation, which is good reason to be sad for them.

Out of Sight, but Not Out of Mind (1 Thessalonians 2:17–20)

5

But we, brethren, having been taken away from you for a short while—in person, not in spirit—were all the more eager with great desire to see your face. For we wanted to come to you—I, Paul, more than once—and yet Satan hindered us. For who is our hope or joy or crown of exultation? Is it not even you, in the presence of our Lord Jesus at His coming? For you are our glory and joy. (2:17–20)

Conflict between people persists in spite of all human effort to mitigate it. Some reports estimate that ninety percent of the people who fail in their life's vocation do so because they cannot get along properly with other people. Ultimately, job failure usually has little connection with ability or even performance. Instead, such failure often stems from an inability to be unselfish and to understand and care about the concerns of others. People may be well trained and highly skilled in a technical or professional field, but they are a liability in the workplace if they are self-centered. Likewise, the most academically well-prepared pastor can be a liability in the church if he does not seek to sacrificially love and serve his people.

The apostle Paul set the standard for pastors in all his ministry and here confirmed the genuineness of his love and concern for the Thessalonians as he answered another accusation from his critics. In addition to their earlier criticisms that he lacked integrity, was greedy, was a deceitful flatterer, and was power hungry, Paul's foes apparently told the Thessalonians that he really had no affection for them and had willfully and callously deserted them. Thus he concludes 1 Thessalonians 2 by telling his people why he had not been back and how he truly cared for them.

Paul left Thessalonica only because he was forced out (Acts 17:1–10). The unbelieving mob came to the house of a believing resident of Thessalonica, Jason, with the mistaken notion they would find Paul there. The angry crowd relented only when Jason and some others pledged themselves as sureties or guarantors for Paul and his companions. Jason and his friends put up something of their possessions as bonds that promised that Paul would not cause further trouble in the city. Therefore, the apostle did not leave the Thessalonians willingly. His words in 3:1–3,5 (see chapter 6 of this volume) assert Paul's true attitude toward them:

> Therefore when we could endure it no longer, we thought it best to be left behind at Athens alone, and we sent Timothy, our brother and God's fellow worker in the gospel of Christ, to strengthen and encourage you as to your faith, so that no one would be disturbed by these afflictions; for you yourselves know that we have been destined for this. ... For this reason, when I could endure it no longer, I also sent to find out about your faith, for fear that the tempter might have tempted you, and our labor would be in vain.

Even though he had known the Thessalonians for only a few months and had been away from them just a short while, he struggled to endure the separation from them. In this paragraph, the apostle focuses on how deeply he cared for the Thessalonians by explaining three elements of his relationship to them: his desire to be with them, his understanding of his spiritual enemy, and his anticipation of eternal reward.

PAUL'S LOVE FOR THE THESSALONIANS

But we, brethren, having been taken away from you for a short while—in person, not in spirit—were all the more eager with great desire to see your face. For we wanted to come to you—I, Paul, more than once— (2:17–18a)

The apostle Paul repeatedly wrote of his strong love for fellow believers (Rom. 1:7–12; Eph. 6:21–24; Phil. 1:3–8; 4:1; Col. 1:3–12; 2 Thess. 1:3–5; 2:13–14; 2 Tim. 1:3–5; Titus 1:4; Philem. 1–7). Even though he had to write some especially stern words of rebuke to the church in Corinth, Paul still loved the Corinthians: "For out of much affliction and anguish of heart I wrote to you with many tears; not so that you would be made sorrowful, but that you might know the love which I have especially for you" (2 Cor. 2:4). Even to the Galatians, whom he severely rebuked, he wrote:

> So have I become your enemy by telling you the truth? They eagerly seek you, not commendably, but they wish to shut you out so that you will seek them. But it is good always to be eagerly sought in a commendable manner, and not only when I am present with you. My children, with whom I am again in labor until Christ is formed in you—but I could wish to be present with you now and to change my tone, for I am perplexed about you. (Gal. 4:16–20)

Paul also had an unflagging love for the Philippians: "For it is only right for me to feel this way about you all, because I have you in my heart, since both in my imprisonment and in the defense and confirmation of the gospel, you all are partakers of grace with me. For God is my witness, how I long for you all with the affection of Christ Jesus" (Phil. 1:7–8). At the conclusion of his letter to the Romans, Paul listed name after name of fellow Christians he loved and worked alongside for the sake of the gospel (16:1–15). He truly loved the Ephesian elders and in return they deeply loved him. The account of Paul's departure from them clearly illustrates that mutual affection: "When he had said these things, he knelt down and prayed with them all. And they began to weep aloud and embraced Paul, and repeatedly kissed him, grieving especially over the word which he had spoken, that they would not see his face again. And they were accompanying him to the ship" (Acts 20:36–38).

Likewise, Paul loved the Thessalonians. The words **but we** contrast again that love he, Silas, and Timothy had with the strong hostility the Jews had for the Thessalonians. Contrary to the Jews, who did not want the Thessalonians to know Christ and did not care about their spiritual health, Paul and his colleagues sincerely did care. The apostle called the Thessalonians **brethren,** a familiar term of endearment that expressed his filial, heartfelt affection for them. It was a sound repudiation of the criticism that he was indifferently refusing to return to Thessalonica.

Even though it was clear from the incident that forced him out that Paul had not wanted to leave Thessalonica, he nevertheless emphasized that he had **been taken away from** them. The participle translated **having been taken away** can mean "to be torn away from" in the harsh sense that a parent is bereft of a deceased child or a child is orphaned from its deceased parents. That illustrates how Paul felt about his premature separation from the Thessalonians.

Paul's lengthier stays with his other churches illustrate that he likely would have stayed much longer at Thessalonica had his unbelieving opponents allowed him to. He lived and ministered in Ephesus for three years, and it is doubtful that the church there equaled the quality of the one at Thessalonica (cf. 1 Tim. 1:3–7; Rev. 2:1–7). He stayed in Corinth eighteen to twenty months and, on a human level, certainly would not have loved the problem-plagued Corinthian church more than the spiritually growing one in Thessalonica. Because he was forced to leave Thessalonica after a relatively short stay, he felt like a parent whose children had been torn away from him (see the parental perspective in 2:7, 11, chapter 3 of this volume), as evidenced by what he wrote to them: "But now that Timothy has come to us from you, and has brought us good news of your faith and love, and that you always think kindly of us, longing to see us just as we also long to see you, for this reason, brethren, in all our distress and affliction we were comforted about you through your faith" (3:6–7; cf. vv. 10–13).

Although the apostle's separation **from** them had been only **for a short while,** he nevertheless had a great longing in his heart to be with the Thessalonians—a longing that did not derive simply from the sentiment of friendship and socialization but from his sense of responsibility for their spiritual welfare. Paul exhibited the same trait for which he commended Epaphras, "For I testify for him that he has a deep concern for you and for those who are in Laodicea and Hierapolis" (Col. 4:13).

Paul's enemies had **taken** him **away from** the Thessalonians **in person,** but they could **not** remove him **in spirit;** they were still in Paul's thoughts and prayers (1 Thess. 1:2–4; 2:13; 3:9–13; 5:23–24; 2 Thess. 1:3, 11–12; 2:13–16; 3:16). Their spiritual needs burdened his heart, and that kind of burden prompted Paul later to tell the Corinthians, "There is the daily pressure on me of concern for all the churches. Who is weak without my being weak? Who is led into sin without my intense concern?" (2 Cor. 11:28–29).

That continual concern for the various churches he knew and the individual believers he loved is why Paul assured the Thessalonians that he was **all the more eager with great desire to see** their **face.** That phrase is loaded with intensity and emotion; it was as though the apostle were short of breath with eagerness and anticipation as he expressed his **desire** to see the Thessalonians. Furthermore, that aspiration was no ordinary wish. **Great desire** translates *pollē epithumia,* a general expression for any kind of dominant passion or compelling, controlling **desire,** and which was most often used in secular Greek to denote sexual passion. Such usage here indicates how dominant and compelling Paul's **desire** was **to see** the collective **face** of the Thessalonians again soon. In its truest biblical context, "seeing one's face" means to come into intimate communication with him or her (cf. Gen. 33:10; 48:11; Ex. 10:29; 1 Thess. 3:10; 2 John 12). That is why God did not allow Moses to see His face (Ex. 33:17–23). Seeing God's face would be the same as seeing the full expression of His glory and holiness, which for Moses or any other mortal would mean death. In Paul's understanding, seeing one's face was not at all insignificant.

Thus, contrary to the critics' charges that they were glad to leave Thessalonica and had no desire to ever return, Paul and his companions **wanted to come** back, see the faces of their newly beloved Thessalonian brethren, and renew their fellowship with them at the earliest opportunity.

As if to underscore his strong feelings, Paul abruptly shifts from the plural **we** to the emphatic singular **I, Paul.** Leon Morris comments, "Throughout these two [Thessalonian] Epistles . . . the plural is used more than in most of Paul's letters. This makes the singular the more significant when it does occur. Here the intense personal feeling breaks through, and we have the emphatic singular reinforced by the personal name" (*The First and Second Epistles to the Thessalonians,* The New International Commentary on the New Testament [Grand Rapids: Eerdmans, 1989], 94–95). The apostle asserts that he personally **more than once** ("repeatedly") desired to be with the Thessalonians again. But there had been a formidable obstacle preventing his return, and he clearly identified that barrier in the next phrase.

PAUL'S UNDERSTANDING OF HIS ENEMY

and yet Satan hindered us. (2:18*b*)

A second reality that Paul understood well in his ministry and relationship with the Thessalonians was that he faced satanic opposition. He had the spiritual discernment and understanding to realize that God has allowed **Satan** to oppose the kingdom of God in a variety of ways. Scripture mentions many of them: the devil tempted Christ (Matt. 4:3–10); he opposes the gospel (Matt. 13:19; 2 Cor. 4:4); he performs counterfeit miracles (Ex. 7:11; Acts 8:9–24; 13:8; cf. 2 Thess. 2:9; Rev. 16:14); he seeks to deceive believers (2 Cor. 11:3, 14; Eph. 6:11); he perpetrates lies and murders (1 Kings 22:22; John 8:44); he attacks individual churches (Acts 5:1–11; Rev. 2:9, 13, 24; 3:9); and he especially attacks spiritual leaders (Job 1:6–2:8; Luke 22:31–32; 2 Cor. 12:7–9; 1 Tim. 3:7). The New Testament reports that he was present at the churches of Jerusalem

(Acts 5:1–10), Corinth (2 Cor. 2:1–11), Ephesus (1 Tim. 3:6–7), Smyrna (Rev. 2:9–10), Pergamum (2:13), Thyatira (2:24), and Philadelphia (3:9).

Satan wants to thwart the progress of God's kingdom much as an army seeks to disrupt the advance of an opposing army. The word translated **hindered** is a military term referring to digging a trench or breaking up a road. One of the countermeasures an ancient army would take against the opposition was to dig a massive trench that would prevent enemy troops from reaching its men. Another way to frustrate the enemy's progress would be to tear up a brick or stone road so that he could not traverse it. Thus Paul depicted the powerful devil as supernaturally obstructing the apostle's strong desire to revisit Thessalonica. Paul did not state specifically how Satan thwarted his desire, but the hindrance could refer to the trouble at Jason's house and the pledge that Jason made (Acts 17:9).

Other New Testament writers portray **Satan** as a roaring lion who seeks victims to devour (1 Peter 5:8), and as one whom Christians must resist so he will flee from them (James 4:7; 1 Peter 5:9). However, the devil is not omnipresent, and against believers he can do nothing that is outside God's overruling providence (cf. Job 1:12; 2:6). In this regard, commentator R. C. H. Lenski wrote:

> This by no means excludes divine providence which rules in the midst of our enemies. Satan entered the heart of Judas so that he made plans to betray Jesus, and God permitted the betrayal for his own divine and blessed ends. So Satan succeeded in frustrating Paul's two plans to return to Thessalonica, but only because this accorded with God's own plans regarding the work Paul was to do. Satan has brought many a martyr to his death, and God permitted it. The death of these martyrs was more blessed for them and for the cause of the gospel than their life would have been. It is ever so with Satan's successes. No thanks to Satan! His guilt is the greater. It was due to Satan that the Thessalonians suffered just as the original churches in Judea had to suffer (v. 14) although God permitted this suffering. (*The Interpretation of St. Paul's Epistles to the Colossians, to the Thessalonians, to Timothy, to Titus and to Philemon* [Minneapolis: Augsburg, 1961], 275–76)

PAUL'S ANTICIPATION OF CHRIST'S RETURN

For who is our hope or joy or crown of exultation? Is it not even you, in the presence of our Lord Jesus at His coming? For you are our glory and joy. (2:19–20)

The apostle Paul always lived and taught others to live in the light of Jesus Christ's return (Rom. 13:12; Phil. 3:20; 2 Tim. 2:12; 4:8, 18; cf. 1 Cor. 1:7–8; Phil. 4:5; Titus 2:13), and he plainly stated to the Thessalonians that the glory to come to believers when Christ returned was powerful motivation for ministering. That anticipation of the future perfection of believers is the third reality in Paul's relationship with the Thessalonians. To emphasize this point, he asked a threefold question and answered it. First he asked them **who** was the object of his **hope** in the promised future reward and eternal blessing (cf. Rom. 5:2; Col. 1:5, 27; 1 Thess. 1:3; Titus 1:2; 2:13; 3:7; Heb. 3:6; 6:11; 1 Peter 1:13). Then he asked who was the source of his **joy,** or eternal happiness and satisfaction (cf. Matt. 25:21, 23; Phil. 4:1; Jude 24). Finally he inquired concerning the identity of his **crown of exultation.** The **crown** (cf. Prov. 1:9; 1 Cor. 9:25; 2 Tim. 4:8; James 1:12; 1 Peter 5:4; Rev. 2:10; 3:11; 6:2) is the festive wreath or victor's crown, awarded for athletic triumph, and **exultation** denotes the exuberant expression of joyful feelings, and sometimes is translated "boasting," in the righteous sense. From the Greek, one can literally render this phrase, "the crown which is rejoicing." Similarly, "the crown of life" (James 1:12) is "the crown which is life," and "the crown of righteousness" (2 Tim. 4:8) is "the crown which is righteousness." The "incorruptible" crown (1 Cor. 9:25 KJV) is the reality of salvation's triumph over believers' corruption. The **crown** or wreath denotes the overwhelming victory God gives His own over sin, suffering, death, and judgment (cf. 1 Peter 5:4).

Paul immediately answered the question of what brought him **joy** with a rhetorical question that is somewhat surprising. One might think the answer should be the Lord Jesus Christ. But the apostle said, **Is it not even you, in the presence of our Lord Jesus at His coming?** Paul's anticipation for the future was the assurance that he would be **in the presence of** his Savior (cf. 1:10; 1 Cor. 1:7; Rom. 8:19–20; Phil. 3:20; Titus 2:13), but a crucial element of the joy of that experience is that **at His coming** he would see all the believers to whom he had ministered, including the Thessalonians (cf. 2 Cor. 1:14; Phil. 2:16).

Paul understood that when believers reach heaven, they do not receive literal crowns to place on their glorified heads. Instead, the Lord will crown all believers with life, righteousness, glory, perfection, and joy. A great part of heaven's bliss for the redeemed will be the joyful **presence** of those whom they have been used to reach. The believer's hope of such reward is in part what Jesus in His parable of the unjust steward alluded to: "Make friends for yourselves by means of the wealth of unrighteousness, so that when it fails, they will receive you into the eternal dwellings" (Luke 16:9). Even as the unbelieving steward or manager used his master's resources to purchase earthly friends, Christ said believers should use the resources their Master provides to bring people to salvation. Whether or not believers know those people now as friends, they will know them in glory as friends forever and as sources of eternal **joy.**

The time to receive in full the promised joys is still in the future, at Christ's return. He has promised, "Behold, I am coming quickly, and My reward is with Me, to render to every man according to what he has done" (Rev. 22:12). The Lord will officially render that reward individually to every believer at the judgment seat (*bēma*) of Christ (Rom. 14:10; 1 Cor. 3:12–15; 2 Cor. 5:10; cf. Matt. 12:36; 2 Cor. 9:6; Gal. 6:7, 9; Eph. 6:8; Col. 3:24–25). God will seal it at the marriage supper of the Lamb (Rev. 19:6–9; cf. Matt. 25:1–13; Rom. 8:16–17; Gal. 3:29; Col. 1:12; 1 Peter 1:4).

Coming is the important New Testament word *parousia,* "presence," which in the majority of its occurrences has an eschatological meaning (1 Cor. 15:23; 1 Thess. 3:13; 4:15; 5:23; 2 Thess. 2:1, 8–9; James 5:7–8; 2 Peter 3:4, 12; 1 John 2:28). Sometimes it refers to the time after the Tribulation when Christ returns to establish His millennial kingdom (Matt. 24:3, 27, 37, 39). However, in 1 Thessalonians *parousia* refers more specifically to the Rapture because Paul was writing to believers whom he knew were already waiting for Jesus to return from heaven (1 Thess. 1:10). In addition to the present verse, this epistle uses *parousia* three other times to denote the Rapture (3:13; 4:15; 5:23).

So Paul encouraged the Thessalonians with the truth that he did love them, evidenced by his desire to see them, the supernatural opposition it took to keep him away, and his view of heaven in which they would be central to his eternal **joy.** They also were his **glory,** which is the true honor bestowed on him by God, who used him to reach them. The pronoun **you** is in the emphatic position so as to remove any doubt that Paul was identifying his Thessalonian brethren as the source of both his eternal honor and happiness.

The Pastor's Heart
(1 Thessalonians 3:1–10)

6

Therefore when we could endure it no longer, we thought it best to be left behind at Athens alone, and we sent Timothy, our brother and God's fellow worker in the gospel of Christ, to strengthen and encourage you as to your faith, so that no one would be disturbed by these afflictions; for you yourselves know that we have been destined for this. For indeed when we were with you, we kept telling you in advance that we were going to suffer affliction; and so it came to pass, as you know. For this reason, when I could endure it no longer, I also sent to find out about your faith, for fear that the tempter might have tempted you, and our labor would be in vain. But now that Timothy has come to us from you, and has brought us good news of your faith and love, and that you always think kindly of us, longing to see us just as we also long to see you, for this reason, brethren, in all our distress and affliction we were comforted about you through your faith; for now we really live, if you stand firm in the Lord. For what thanks can we render to God for you in return for all the joy with which we rejoice before our God on your account, as we night and day keep praying most earnestly that we may see your face, and may complete what is lacking in your faith? (3:1–10)

Anyone who serves the church as a pastor or elder realizes that the scriptural requirements for his service are high. He also knows he must understand the important issues of what a pastor does, says, is, and feels. In chapters 1–2 of this epistle, Paul's words reveal the true concerns of a pastor (1:2–3, 5; 2:2–4, 5–7, 9–11, 13). As earlier noted, coming through his inspired pen are some of the pastoral attitudes Paul had for the church: he was thankful for them (1:2; 2:13); he appreciated their testimony (1:3); he was encouraged by what he heard about them (1:9); he loved them (2:8); and he longed to be with them (2:17–20). Here as he recorded matters related to Timothy and himself, in connection with the church, he opened his heart even more as he expressed concerns for them in a much more focused and specific way. His forced separation from the Thessalonians seemed to intensify his pastoral concern for them. Paul's narrative implies seven elements of his exemplary pastor's heart: affection for his people, sacrifice for them, compassion for them, protectiveness toward them, delight in seeing them, gratitude for them, and intercession for them.

THE PASTOR'S AFFECTION FOR HIS PEOPLE

Therefore when we could endure it no longer, (3:1*a*)

Because of a rather arbitrary chapter break, this passage opens with **therefore,** which specifically links it to the closing section of the previous chapter. Because of Paul's attitude toward the Thessalonian believers —"For you are our glory and joy" (2:20)—he **could endure it no longer.** He could **no longer** tolerate his distance from his spiritual children and the consequent lack of knowledge of their condition. Paul's strong affection for them resulted in intense emotional pain during this forced separation.

Even though he faced his own trials (3:7), Paul was more concerned about his people's spiritual well-being in the midst of their difficulties. In fact, his affection for them was so strong that in 3:5 he also declared, "I could endure it no longer."

That love was far more than a mere sentimental desire for social fellowship with the church. It was Paul's desire to help the Thessalonians fulfill God's calling to be loyal to the truth and to experience spiritual maturity in their lives. As discussed in the previous chapter of this volume, the enemies of the gospel forced Paul and his companions to leave Thessalonica, creating a potentially dangerous situation (cf. Acts 20:29–32) that increased his concern for the Thessalonians.

A man with a true and faithful pastoral heart is not concerned about his own success or his own reputation; nor is he preoccupied with his own trials. Rather, he is deeply concerned with the spiritual condition of his people, for whom he will suffer and rejoice with an unflagging affection. Paul exhibited that kind of spiritual care no matter what the response was. He wrote to the Corinthians, "I will most gladly spend and be expended for your souls. If I love you more, am I to be loved less?" (2 Cor. 12:15; cf. 2:12–13; 11:28–29).

THE PASTOR'S SACRIFICE FOR HIS PEOPLE

we thought it best to be left behind at Athens alone, and we sent Timothy, our brother and God's fellow worker in the gospel of Christ, (3:1b–2a)

Strong affection always leads to sacrifice. Love gives itself away for its object. Selfless commitment to meet others' needs is the measure of true care for others. Paul exemplified that reality when he **thought it best to be left behind at Athens alone, and . . . sent Timothy** back to Thessalonica. The apostle used the plural pronoun **we,** but the context makes it clear that Paul referred to himself. At times in his letters, he appears to have an aversion to the pronoun "I," as if its use was a breach of his humility.

Paul initially came to Athens without **Timothy** and Silas (Acts 17:14), but they eventually joined him there (v. 15). After an indeterminate period, Paul **sent Timothy** again to Thessalonica (Acts 18:5) to determine their condition (1 Thess. 3:5), and he apparently dispatched Silas somewhere else in Macedonia, perhaps Philippi (18:5; cf. 2 Cor. 11:9; Phil. 4:15). Thus for a second time, Paul was **left behind at Athens alone.** The verb translated **left behind** means "abandoned" or "forsaken" and was used in secular contexts of leaving a loved one behind at death. It expresses how serious Paul's separation from his friends was. Even though he could have benefited greatly by their assistance and fellowship in Athens, Paul **thought it best** to send his colleagues to Thessalonica and Macedonia for the well-being of the believers in those places.

The kind of sacrifice Paul made indicates again the strength of his pastoral concern for the Thessalonians. For their sakes he gladly **sent** to them his most precious friend and fellow missionary, **Timothy.** Paul dispatched to several of the churches his beloved son in the faith as his representative (cf. 1 Cor. 4:17; 16:10; Phil. 2:19–24; 1 Tim. 1:3).

Paul's warm and positive appellations for Timothy demonstrate the close, trusting relationship the apostle had with his younger colleague. First, Paul called him his **brother,** which Timothy was as a fellow believer by the grace of God (1 Tim. 1:2; 2 Tim. 1:2; 2:1; cf. Phil. 1:1). Because of experience through the rigors they had endured in ministering together (cf. Acts 16:1–3; 17:1–15; 18:5–7; 19:22; 20:4–5), they were more than just spiritual brothers.

Second, Paul referred to **Timothy** not only in relation to himself but as **God's fellow worker** (*sunergon tou theou;* some manuscripts prefer "minister," *diakonos,* rather than **fellow worker**). That is a startling truth—that a man could be a fellow worker with the Holy One. He worked with God because he, as Paul, faithfully proclaimed **the gospel of Christ** (cf. 1 Tim. 1:18; 6:12; 2 Tim. 1:6–7; 4:2, 5). The salvation message is called "the gospel of God" three times in 1 Thessalonians 2 (vv. 2, 8, and 9), and **the gospel of Christ,** because God provided it in and through Christ.

Paul gave his descriptions of noble and beloved Timothy to emphasize how precious he was to him. They also revealed to the Thessalonians Paul's love in the sacrifice of sending him to them.

THE PASTOR'S COMPASSION FOR HIS PEOPLE

to strengthen and encourage you as to your faith, so that no one would be disturbed by these afflictions; for you yourselves know that we have been destined for this. For indeed when we were with you, we kept telling you in advance that we were going to suffer affliction; and so it came to pass, as you know. (3:2b–4)

Compassion born of love motivated Paul to send Timothy back to the Thessalonians, **to strengthen and encourage** them concerning their **faith,** which Paul mentions five times in this section (vv. 2, 5, 6, 7, 10). This is not *the* faith (cf. Jude 3) that is the body of gospel truths, but the Thessalonians' *belief* in it. As the discussion of 1:1–10 in chapter 1 of this volume indicates, the Thessalonian believers constituted a model church with many noble virtues. But they were still young in a faith being tested by affliction and needed further guidance toward spiritual maturity (cf. 1 Thess. 3:13; 4:1, 10).

Timothy's assignment was first of all **to strengthen** the Thessalonians' **faith. Strengthen** means to support or buttress something with the intent of establishing it. Strong faith is a result of knowing all that God has revealed, and has a firm foundation in sound doctrine. No faith can be strong without knowledge and understanding of the truth. Second, he was to **encourage** them, which denotes coming alongside and motivating them to live that sound doctrine. Timothy's task was to make the foundation of the Thessalonians' **faith** solid and unwavering so they could have confidence to apply the truth.

Timothy conducted the sort of follow-up, strengthening and encouraging ministry that Paul had done. For example, Paul, Barnabas, and their entourage often returned to cities where they had previously taught: "After they had preached the gospel to that city and had made many disciples, they returned to Lystra and to Iconium and to Antioch, strengthening the souls of the disciples, encouraging them to continue in the faith, and saying, 'Through many tribulations we must enter the kingdom of God'" (Acts 14:21–22; cf. 15:32, 41; 18:23; Rom. 1:11). Spiritual maturity is what Paul desired for the churches: "I pray that the eyes of your heart may be enlightened, so that you will know what is the hope of His calling, what are the riches of the glory of His inheritance in the saints, and what is the surpassing greatness of His power toward us who believe" (Eph. 1:18–19; cf. 2 Thess. 2:16–17; 3:3). More specifically, he told the Galatians that the goal of his labor for believers was that Christ be formed in them (Gal. 4:19).

Paul knew they faced and could **be disturbed by** certain **afflictions** (pressure, tests of faith in suffering). The verb rendered **would be disturbed** (*sainesthai*) originally designated the wagging of a dog's tail, but through the years it came to mean, "to allure, fascinate, flatter, or beguile." When a dog wags its tail, it often does so to draw attention to itself and gain something it wants. Hence *sainō*, the root verb of *sainesthai,* later referred to a person who tried to flatter or beguile other people. Paul did not want anyone to lure the Thessalonians away from the truth in that manner, because they had been made vulnerable by persecution and suffering.

The apostle reminded them that all believers should expect tribulations and persecutions because all **have been destined** for such temporal difficulties. Actually it is not clear from verse 3 whether **we** refers primarily to Paul or the Thessalonians. Some assert that **we** denotes Paul, and the **afflictions** the sufferings to which he had **been destined** (cf. Acts 9:16). That interpretation sees Paul reminding the Thessalonians of his God-ordained difficulties so that they would not equate them with God's disapproval of him or with nullification of His plans for him or even as evidence that he was not an apostle. Others see Paul's statement as a reminder to the Thessalonians and all Christians that they should expect **afflictions.** Paul later exhorted Timothy, "Indeed, all who desire to live godly in Christ Jesus will be persecuted" (2 Tim. 3:12; cf. John 16:33; James 1:2–4; 1 Peter 5:10). Jesus told the disciples, "Blessed are you when people insult you and persecute you, and falsely say all kinds of evil against you because of Me. Rejoice and be glad, for your reward in heaven is great; for in the same way they persecuted the prophets who were before you" (Matt. 5:11–12; cf. 10:24–25).

The widest interpretation, which includes Paul and believers within the statement, may be best, since it truly applies to both.

To make sure the Thessalonians got his point, Paul reminded them that **indeed when** he was **with** them, he told them **in advance that** they **were going to suffer** earthly **affliction.** As William Hendriksen observed, "Afflictions that have been *predicted,* and that take place in accordance with this prediction, serve to strengthen faith" (*New Testament Commentary: Exposition of Thessalonians, Timothy, and Titus* [Grand Rapids: Baker, 1981], 85; emphasis in original).

THE PASTOR'S PROTECTIVENESS TOWARD HIS PEOPLE

For this reason, when I could endure it no longer, I also sent to find out about your faith, for fear that the tempter might have tempted you, and our labor would be in vain. (3:5)

By essentially repeating what he wrote just a few lines earlier (3:1–2), the apostle Paul reveals another attitude of his pastoral heart— his protectiveness toward his people. **For** that **reason, when** Paul **could endure it no longer,** he **sent** Timothy **to find out about** their **faith.**

When he **sent** Timothy, the apostle did not know how the Thessalonians' **faith** had weathered the storm of trials, tribulations, and persecutions. Paul's constant concern for the churches under his care (cf. 2 Cor. 11:28) is expressed in his warning words to the Ephesian elders, "I know that after my departure savage wolves will come in among you, not sparing the flock; and from among your own selves men will arise, speaking perverse things, to draw away the disciples after them" (Acts 20:29–30; cf. 1 Tim. 4:1).

The apostle's fear was that **the tempter,** Satan, **might have tempted** them successfully to reject the gospel truth. To do that, the devil uses three basic approaches. His first assault is to prevent people from believing: "The god of this world has blinded the minds of the unbelieving so that they might not see the light of the gospel of the glory of Christ" (2 Cor. 4:4). If he cannot do that, his second assault is to destroy someone's initial interest in the gospel: "The one on whom seed was sown on the rocky places, this is the man who hears the word and immediately receives it with joy; yet he has no firm root in himself, but is only temporary, and when affliction or persecution arises because of the word, immediately he falls away" (Matt. 13:20–21). Finally, if he cannot stop them from embracing the gospel, Satan strives to weaken the faith of those who do believe: "But I am afraid that, as the serpent deceived Eve by his craftiness, your minds will be led astray from the simplicity and purity of devotion to Christ" (2 Cor. 11:3; cf. 1 Cor. 7:5; 2 Cor. 2:11; 3:14–15; James 1:12–18; 1 Peter 5:8).

If Satan had succeeded in his assault on the Thessalonians, Paul knew that his **labor** among them would have been **in vain** (*eis kenon*), "empty, void, pointless, for nothing." This was not the only time Paul expressed such feelings. He wrote to the Galatians, "Then after an interval of fourteen years I went up again to Jerusalem with Barnabas, taking Titus along also. It was because of a revelation that I went up; and I submitted to them the gospel which I preach among the Gentiles, but I did so in private to those who were of reputation, for fear that I might be running, or had run, in vain" (Gal. 2:1–2; cf. 4:11). He urged the Philippians to "prove yourselves to be blameless and innocent, children of God above reproach in the midst of a crooked and perverse generation, among whom you appear as lights in the world, holding fast the word of life, so that in the day of Christ I will have reason to glory because I did not run in vain nor toil in vain" (2:15–16). Likewise Paul was concerned about the Thessalonians' faith. He wanted to know that it was real rather than superficial.

THE PASTOR'S DELIGHT IN HIS PEOPLE

But now that Timothy has come to us from you, and has brought us good news of your faith and love, and that you always think kindly of us, longing to see us just as we also long to see you, for this reason, brethren, in all our distress and affliction we were comforted about you through your faith; for now we really live, if you stand firm in the Lord. (3:6–8)

When Timothy arrived back from Thessalonica and presented his report to Paul, the apostle was by that time in Corinth. Timothy's report was so encouraging to Paul that to describe it the apostle called it **good news,** using the word *euangelisamenou* (from which the English words *evangel* and *evangelism* derive), from a root word (*euangelion*) whose every other occurrence in the New Testament refers to the gospel message of salvation by grace through faith.

Timothy conveyed a four-part report on the Thessalonians' spiritual status to Paul. First, he delivered the **good news** that their **faith** in God and Jesus Christ was genuine. Their hearts had been like the good soil that received the seed of the gospel and bore much fruit (Matt. 13:23). Second, he told Paul the **good news** about their authentic **love** for the Lord, which was the clearest evidence that they were Christians (cf. Ps. 5:11; Matt. 22:37–40; John 8:42; 13:34–35; Rom. 13:8–10; Gal. 5:6, 22; 1 Peter 1:8; 1 John 2:5, 10; 3:14; 4:20; 5:1–3). Third, Timothy announced that the

Thessalonians **always** thought **kindly of** Paul. It was **good news** for the apostle that they had cherished memories of him and were still confidently loyal to him as Christ's true apostle. In view of his many enemies (Acts 21:27; 2 Tim. 1:15) and the concern that Satan or false teachers would draw the Thessalonians away from the truth, as they endeavored to do in so many places (cf. 2 Cor. 12:19–21; Gal. 3:1), Paul was thrilled to know that the church trusted him. Finally, Timothy declared that the Thessalonians' affection was so strong they were **longing to see** Paul. Pained by the separation from his spiritual children (1 Thess. 2:7–12), Paul rejoiced in the **good news** that they were eager to renew fellowship with him (cf. Acts 2:42; Rom. 15:32; Heb. 10:25; 1 John 1:3).

Timothy's report was the source of the apostle's shift from anxiety to delight. In the midst of all his **distress and affliction**—all the persecutions, pressures, and trials he was experiencing (cf. 2 Cor. 4:7–12; 11:23–28, 32–33; 2 Tim. 3:11; cf. Acts 9:23–25; 14:1–20; 16:16–34; 17:1–10; 19:13–41; 21:27–36; 27:14–26)—Paul was **comforted about** the true, saving **faith** of his children. It should be noted that when churches were unfaithful and succumbed to sin and false teachers, the apostle was devastated. That was the case in the Corinthian church, over which he actually became "depressed" (2 Cor. 7:6) and lost interest in preaching the gospel in a city where God had opened a door for the message (cf. 2 Cor. 2:12–13). It was as though he began to **really live** again once he received a positive report about the Thessalonians. The knowledge that they stood **firm in the Lord** further stimulated Paul to renewed zeal in ministry. Whenever he saw any believers **stand firm** (*stēkete,* a military term meaning not to retreat in the face of an attack), strong in their **faith,** he was delighted, yet he exhorted them to continued resolve. For example, in his second letter to the Thessalonians he declared:

> But we should always give thanks to God for you, brethren beloved by the Lord, because God has chosen you from the beginning for salvation through sanctification by the Spirit and faith in the truth. It was for this He called you through our gospel, that you may gain the glory of our Lord Jesus Christ. So then, brethren, stand firm and hold to the traditions which you were taught, whether by word of mouth or by letter from us. (2:13–15; cf. 1 Cor. 16:13; Gal. 5:1; Phil. 1:27; 4:1)

THE PASTOR'S GRATITUDE FOR HIS PEOPLE

For what thanks can we render to God for you in return for all the joy with which we rejoice before our God on your account, (3:9)

The devoted pastor recognizes that all thanks for spiritual progress goes to God. That the apostle Paul acknowledged that his gratitude for the Thessalonians must primarily go to God, but found no adequate words to express the fullness of his heart, is clear because he asked rhetorically, **For what thanks can we render to God for you?**

Paul was so profoundly in debt to God **in return for all the joy** Timothy's report had brought him, and he realized he had no means to express an adequate thanks. **Render . . . in return** translates one word (*antapodounai*), and expresses the impossibility of repaying the Lord for all the divine work that caused him to **rejoice before . . . God.** The out-workings of God's grace in their lives had made Paul grateful beyond expression.

THE PASTOR'S INTERCESSION FOR HIS PEOPLE

as we night and day keep praying most earnestly that we may see your face, and may complete what is lacking in your faith? (3:10)

Even though the true pastor will have joy and gratitude because of his people, he will still realize the need for prayerful intercession on their behalf. He will understand that their lives are not yet perfect and that his ministry among them is incomplete. For those reasons he, like the apostle, will engage in sincere intercession to God that he may have opportunity to minister again among them (cf. Rom. 1:8–12; 15:5–7, 13; 2 Cor. 1:3–5; Eph. 1:15–21; 3:14–21; Phil. 1:3–11; Col. 1:9–12; 2 Thess. 1:11–12; Philem. 4–7).

Paul's **praying** was constant and fervent. He interceded for them **night and day,** and did so **most earnestly.** The ultimate goal of his praying was to **complete** whatever was still **lacking** in their lives before God. The immediate goal was **that** he **may see** their **face,** to supply the instruction they needed right away. Chapters 4 and 5 of this letter provide some of the truth they were lacking.

If Paul is the ideal human model of one with a pastor's heart, that is only because he carefully patterned his pastoral ministry after that of Jesus Christ, who perfectly modeled the pastor's heart during His earthly ministry. He was the ultimate example of affection for His sheep (John 10:11–16, 27–28), unselfishness for His disciples (John 13:3–17), compassion for His people (John 11:33–44; cf. Matt. 23:37–39), protectiveness toward His lambs (John 10:2–5), delight for His church (Matt. 16:18–19), gratitude for His followers (Matt. 11:25–30), and intercession for His beloved children (John 17:6–26). That model of the shepherd's heart is the divine standard for all pastors today.

A Pastoral Prayer
(1 Thessalonians 3:11–13)

7

Now may our God and Father Himself and Jesus our Lord direct our way to you; and may the Lord cause you to increase and abound in love for one another, and for all people, just as we also do for you; so that He may establish your hearts without blame in holiness before our God and Father at the coming of our Lord Jesus with all His saints. (3:11–13)

The New Testament contains many rich and instructive examples of prayers that are pleasing to God (e.g., Matt. 26:36–42; John 11:41–42; 17:9–24; Acts 4:24–30; 7:60; Heb. 13:20–21; Jude 24–25). Arthur W. Pink (1886–1952), the English-born Christian writer, theologian, and Bible teacher, noted in the late 1940s how valuable those prayers are for current believers:

> How blessed it is to hear some aged saint, who has long walked with God and enjoyed intimate communion with Him, pouring out his heart before Him in adoration and supplication. But how much more blessed should we esteem it could we have listened to the utterances of those who companied with Christ in person during the days when He tabernacled in this scene. And if one of the apostles were still here upon earth what a high privilege we should deem it to hear him

engage in prayer! Such a high privilege that most of us would be willing to go to considerable inconvenience and to travel a long distance in order to be thus favored. And if our desire were granted, how closely we would listen to his words, how diligently we would seek to treasure them up in our memories. Well, no such inconvenience, no such journey, is required: it has pleased the Holy Spirit to record quite a number of the apostolic prayers for our instruction and satisfaction. (*Gleanings from Paul: Studies in the Prayers of the Apostle* [reprint; Chicago: Moody, 1967; 1981 paperback edition], 9)

The majority of prayers recorded in the New Testament are from the apostle Paul. It devotes more pages to his words and ministry than to those of any other individual except Jesus. Paul is the main character in Acts 14–28 (although Acts records no prayers of individual apostles, it does portray them as men of prayer in 1:24–25; 4:24–30; 6:4; 9:40; 10:9; 20:36; 21:5; 28:8) and the author of thirteen letters that record many of his prayers (e.g., Rom. 15:5–7, 13; 1 Cor. 1:4–7; 2 Cor. 1:3–5; Eph. 1:15–23; 3:14–21; Phil. 1:8–11; Col. 1:9–12; 2 Thess. 1:11–12; Philem. 4–6). Consistent with this picture of the apostle is Luke's description of the newly converted Paul:"he [was] praying"(Acts 9:11).

Certainly the apostle Paul modeled prayer to the Thessalonians. He also exemplified the pastoral prayer life once described by Charles Spurgeon:"I take it that as a minister *he is always praying.* . . . He is not always in the act of prayer, but he lives in the spirit of it. . . . If you are a genuine minister of God you will stand as a priest before the Lord, spiritually wearing the ephod and the breast-plate whereon you bear the names of [your] children . . . pleading for them within the veil" (*Lectures to My Students* [reprint; Grand Rapids: Zondervan/Ministry Resources Library, 1985], 42, 47; emphasis in the original). It is obvious that Paul was in the spirit of prayer from 1:1 to 3:10, even though he did not offer a formal prayer until 3:11. Breaking into a prayer at a crucial juncture in one of his letters was typical of Paul (e.g., Rom. 1:8–12; Eph. 1:15–23; Col. 1:9–12; 2 Thess. 1:11–12). And certainly he could not conclude the expression of his pastor's heart here without praying for the accomplishment of God's will in his people's lives.

THE FORM OF PAUL'S PRAYER

Now may our God and Father Himself and Jesus our Lord (3:11a)

Paul's prayer took a distinctive form. Rather than addressing **God** by the usual second person pronoun, Paul, including the Thessalonians in his petition, addressed Him by name in the first person—**our God**

and Father. Paul's petition utilized the Greek optative mood, indicated in English by **may,** which expresses a wish. That form of prayer was not Paul's normal approach, but he did use it at other times (5:23; 2 Thess. 3:5, 16). Use of the optative here allowed him to reiterate to the Thessalonians the sincere heart wishes he had concerning them. Paul also directed this prayer to **God** the **Father** and **Jesus** the **Lord,** expressing the desire that both the Father and Son might act to answer his longings. Such linkings of the Father and the Son are frequent in the epistles and emphasize equality in divine nature between God the Father and Jesus the Son (cf. Rom. 1:7; 1 Cor. 1:3; 2 Cor. 1:2; Gal. 1:3; Eph. 1:2; Phil. 1:2; Col. 1:3; 1 Thess. 1:1, 3; 2 Thess. 1:1–2; 1 Tim. 1:2; 2 Tim. 1:2; Titus 1:4; Philem. 3; James 1:1; 1 Peter 1:3; 2 Peter 1:1; 1 John 1:3; 2 John 3; Jude 1).

By calling God **our . . . Father,** an address emphasizing personal relationship, and Jesus **our Lord,** an address emphasizing personal rulership, Paul switched the usual popular ideas about God being the ruler and Christ being the one with whom believers have a relationship. The use of **our** before both **God** and **Jesus** underscores the relationship Paul and the Thessalonians enjoyed with both Persons of the Trinity. God came down to be intimate with them as their gracious, loving, and forgiving Father, and Jesus ascended to heaven's throne to be their sovereign Lord.

That **Himself** (*autos*) is singular and in the emphatic position in the Greek word order provides further insight into the nature of the Godhead. Literally, verse 11 reads, "Now may Himself, our God and Father and Jesus Christ our Lord, direct our way to you." The use of the singular pronoun (**Himself**) and the singular verb (**direct**) with the plural subject (**our God and Father . . . and Jesus our Lord**) emphasizes again the unmistakable unity of the Father and the Son in the Godhead.

That grammatical consideration helps explain why Paul's prayer could assume the deity of Jesus and address Him equally with the divine Father. The Father and Son are equally sovereign and perfectly agree in all matters. Assured of those truths, Christians, like Paul, can direct all their prayers to either or to both (cf. Job 8:5; Pss. 5:2; 143:1; John 16:23–24; Acts 7:59; 1 John 5:14). Romans 8:27 indicates that the Holy Spirit is also in perfect agreement: "He who searches the hearts knows what the mind of the Spirit is, because He intercedes for the saints according to the will of God."

THE PURPOSE OF PAUL'S PRAYER

direct our way to you; and may the Lord cause you to increase and abound in love for one another, and for all people, just as we

also do for you; so that He may establish your hearts without blame in holiness before our God and Father at the coming of our Lord Jesus with all His saints. (3:11*b*–13)

Paul's prayer here is a definitive model of conscientious pastoral intercession. He had a threefold purpose in offering it: that God would grant the Thessalonians a perfecting faith, a prospering love, and a purifying hope. That is the familiar triad of Christian virtues (1 Cor. 13:13). Paul was genuinely concerned that his people grow in each of those spiritual realities, as is evident at the beginning of this letter: "constantly bearing in mind your work of faith and labor of love and steadfastness of hope" (1:3), and at the end: "let us ... put on the breastplate of faith and love, and as a helmet, the hope of salvation" (5:8).

A PERFECTING FAITH

direct our way to you; (3:11*b*)

The foremost motive for Paul's prayer for the Thessalonians was that their faith would grow. The apostle did not explicitly say that within his prayer but identified it as the goal of his prayer: "as we night and day keep praying most earnestly that we may see your face, and may complete what is lacking in your faith" (v. 10). "Complete" could also be translated "perfect"—Paul wanted to return to help perfect any weakness or defect in their faith (see the comments on 3:10, page 83), in the sense of Ephesians 4:11–12, "He gave some as apostles, and some as prophets, and some as evangelists, and some as pastors and teachers, for the equipping of the saints for the work of service, to the building up of the body of Christ."

For that spiritual work of edification, he asked God and Jesus to **direct** his **way** to them. **Direct** conveys the idea of laying out a straight, smooth path with all the obstacles removed. Up to this time, satanically instigated circumstances had prevented Paul from coming to the Thessalonians (cf. the discussion of 2:18 in chapter 5 of this volume). The apostle knew that only the power of the Lord could overcome Satan (cf. Gen. 3:15; Matt. 10:1; Luke 11:21–22; Rom. 16:20; Col. 2:15; 1 John 3:8; 4:4; Jude 6; Rev. 12:10; 20:10) and allow him to return. It was his desire to return, but only by the will of his Lord and God (cf. Ps. 37:1–5; Prov. 3:5–6).

Paul's intention was not to return and lead the Thessalonians into some emotional experience that would merely attempt to get them believing more fervently in the things they already knew. Rather, he wanted to expand their knowledge of God through His revealed truth, which in turn would enlarge their trust in Him and enable them to walk in greater obedience to His will. Paul was ministering under a divine mandate to teach the truth (Acts 9:15–18; 13:1–4; 1 Cor. 9:16; Eph. 3:1–8), which meant feeding them Scripture so they could mature by it. That is the principle found in 1 Peter 2:2:"Like newborn babies, long for the pure milk of the word, so that by it you may grow in respect to salvation" (cf. Acts 20:32).

The precepts, principles, and promises of Scripture are the windows through which believers look to see God and understand His glory and will for their lives (cf. Pss. 19:7–8, 11; 119:9, 93, 99, 105, 130; Prov. 6:23; Luke 11:28; John 17:17; 20:31; Rom. 15:4; 2 Tim. 3:15–17; James 1:21–22, 25). Their response to the truths of God's Word also allows them to know if their faith is growing. That growth is evident when (1) their knowledge of God's Word is increasing (cf. Col. 3:16); (2) their confidence in God is greater than before (cf. Eph. 3:12); (3) their trust in His sovereignty is stronger than before (cf. Job 42:2); (4) their obedience to Him is consistent (cf. Deut. 17:19–20); and (5) they are finding joy in their trials (cf. James 1:2–3).

So Paul's pastoral prayer began with a request that the Father and Son would use him to mature and strengthen the Thessalonians' faith, which was the foundation they needed for obedient and powerful Christian living (cf. Acts 14:22; 2 Cor. 1:24; 5:7; Col. 1:23; 1 Tim. 1:4; Heb. 11:6; Jude 20). Even though he did not return to Thessalonica, Paul saw his desire realized, as evidenced by what he wrote to them a few months later in his second letter, "We ought always to give thanks to God for you, brethren, as is only fitting, because your faith is greatly enlarged" (2 Thess. 1:3).

A PROSPERING LOVE

and may the Lord cause you to increase and abound in love for one another, and for all people, just as we also do for you; (3:12)

The apostle Paul knew that genuine believers would always exhibit love (cf. John 13:34–35), therefore he prayed that the Thessalonians' growing faith would be accompanied by a prospering love. That Paul asked **the Lord** to **cause** the Thessalonians' **love** to grow indicates he depended on God for the development of spiritual virtues. Whether it was the beginning of the Christian life (justification—Rom. 3:30; 8:30, 33; cf. Isa. 50:8; Jonah 2:9; John 1:12–13) or the process of spiritual growth (sanctification—John 17:17; 1 Thess. 5:23; Jude 1; cf. Ezek. 37:28; Eph. 5:26), God revealed that He ultimately deserves the credit for believers' maturity (1 Cor. 3:6–7; cf. 2 Cor. 3:5; 9:8; Gal. 2:20).

Paul's statements in 1:3,"constantly bearing in mind your work of faith and labor of love," and 3:6,"good news of your faith and love," are clear evidence of the Thessalonians' love. Here he prayed they would **increase and abound in love** (*agapē*),**in** that **love** which is the purest and noblest (Rom. 13:8–10; 1 Cor. 13:4,13; 16:14; Gal. 5:13–14,22; Eph. 1:15; 4:2; 5:2,25,28,33; Phil. 1:9; Col. 3:19; 1 John 3:16–17). Paul asked first that their love would **increase and abound . . . for one another,** that is, within the church (cf. Eph. 1:15; 4:16; Phil. 2:2; Col. 2:2; 3:14; 1 Thess. 4:9; 2 Thess. 1:3; 1 Peter 1:22; 4:8). There are more than thirty positive and negative "one anothers" in the New Testament, and **love** appears by far the most often (1 Thess. 4:9; Rom. 12:10; 13:8; 2 Thess. 1:3; 1 Peter 1:22; 1 John 3:11,23; 4:7, 11; 2 John 5). Second, the apostle prayed that their love **for all people** would increase. He wanted them to have a greater love for the lost and for those who persecuted them, as Jesus commanded His disciples, "Love your enemies and pray for those who persecute you" (Matt. 5:44; cf. Deut. 10:19; Rom. 12:14,20; 1 Tim. 2:1–4). Other New Testament injunctions concerning **all people** include pursuing peace (Rom. 12:18), doing good (Gal. 6:10), being patient (Eph. 4:2), praying (1 Tim. 2:1),showing consideration (Titus 3:2),and honoring (1 Peter 2:17).

To provide them a practical example to understand that **love,** Paul told the Thessalonians they should love **just as** he **also** loved them. He loved them when they were strangers in the greatest spiritual need by sacrificially bringing the gospel to them (1 Thess. 1:9; 2:1–2).Then, after they received justification,he loved them by the living sacrifice of his life for their sanctification (2:10–12).

A PURIFYING HOPE

so that He may establish your hearts without blame in holiness before our God and Father at the coming of our Lord Jesus with all His saints. (3:13)

The final objective of Paul's prayer for the Thessalonians was **that** they might look to their glorification, which produces a purifying hope. All the good qualities of a strong faith and a vibrant love are incomplete unless they point one toward genuine hope. Paul reminded the Romans, "Therefore, having been justified by faith, we have peace with God through our Lord Jesus Christ, through whom also we have obtained our introduction by faith into this grace in which we stand; and we exult in hope of the glory of God" (Rom. 5:1–2; cf. 15:13; Titus 2:13; Heb. 6:11).The nature of that hope is best stated in 1 John 3:2,"Beloved, now we are children of God,and it has not appeared as yet what we will be. We know that when He appears, we will be like Him, because we will see Him just as He is" (cf. Phil. 3:20–21).

The only way the Thessalonians would actually live in such hope was for God to **establish** their **hearts without blame in holiness before** (literally, "in the presence of") Him. Paul expresses a similar sentiment in 5:23, "Now may the God of peace Himself sanctify you entirely; and may your spirit and soul and body be preserved complete, without blame at the coming of our Lord Jesus Christ." He knew the one person who cared most about the Thessalonians' purifying hope was God, and only He truly knows what is in people's hearts (2 Chron. 6:30; Ps. 44:21; Prov. 24:12; cf. 1 Sam. 16:7; Prov. 21:2). Paul wanted them to be pure at heart, so as to desire **the coming** (*parousia*, "presence") **of** the **Lord Jesus,** who is the Judge (cf. 2 Tim. 4:1). The apostle knew that the promise of Christ's return to Rapture and reward the church is the essence of believers' purifying hope. He explains the event in 4:13–18 as the hope that produces comfort (cf. Jude 24; the discussion in chapter 11 of this volume). Believers' knowing that when Christ comes to reward His people, they will have their works evaluated before the judgment seat (2 Cor. 5:10), is motivation to holy living. (See also the discussion of 2:19–20 in chapter 5 of this volume.)

Paul focused on the heart because it is the seat of human emotion, thought, and purpose (cf. Prov. 4:23; 1 Chron. 28:9; Matt. 12:35; 15:16–20). If their **hearts** were pure, clean, and righteous, and they were able to stand against temptation (cf. Matt. 4:4–11; 26:41; 1 Cor. 10:13; Eph. 6:16; James 1:12; 1 Peter 5:8–9), that would free them from shame and embarrassment before the Lord and cause them to eagerly look for His coming. The believer's appearance before God is truly the consummation of his sanctification (Rom. 8:17, 30).

In contrast to obedient believers who look forward to Christ's appearing, sinning believers are not eager to have their sin interrupted and exposed to the presence of the Lord. Such disobedient Christians are like disobedient children who do not want their parents to catch them doing wrong, or like lawbreakers who least of all wish for the arrival of the police. What makes obedient believers long for the Lord's return is holiness that seeks pure fellowship with the Holy One. And such purity that initially inspires hope also produces greater hope, as John wrote: "And everyone who has this hope fixed on Him purifies himself, just as He is pure" (1 John 3:3).

Whereas Paul prayed that God would purify the Thessalonians' hope, Peter pled directly with his readers that they would live pure in hope:

> Therefore, prepare your minds for action, keep sober in spirit, fix your hope completely on the grace to be brought to you at the revelation of Jesus Christ. As obedient children, do not be conformed to the former

lusts which were yours in your ignorance, but like the Holy One who called you, be holy yourselves also in all your behavior; because it is written, "You shall be holy, for I am holy." If you address as Father the One who impartially judges according to each one's work, conduct yourselves in fear during the time of your stay on earth; knowing that you were not redeemed with perishable things like silver or gold from your futile way of life inherited from your forefathers, but with precious blood, as of a lamb unblemished and spotless, the blood of Christ. (1 Peter 1:13–19)

Again, the supernatural reality of sanctification is all the work of God and, at the same time, dependent on the obedience of the believer.

The apostle Paul's prayer that the Thessalonians would have a purifying hope actually extends beyond that congregation. His request was that God would **establish** their **hearts without blame in holiness . . . with all His saints.** Paul wanted all the other elect to be pure and set apart from worldliness. Some commentators identify **all His saints** more specifically as the angels and believers who accompany Christ at His return to establish His millennial kingdom (cf. Matt. 16:27). Since that expression is *not* used in the New Testament to denote angels but *is* commonly used to denote believers, it is best to equate this **coming of** the **Lord Jesus** with the Rapture of the church (see 4:13–18) and her arrival in the place prepared for her (cf. John 14:1–6). Then comes the reward (Rev. 22:12) at the judgment seat of Christ where believers will be rewarded for their faithfulness and obedience. First Corinthians 3:11–14 describes this reward event as a judgment of works. Yet, in 1 Corinthians 4:5 it is clear that rewards will come on the basis of what motivated those works. The glory of this reward is the theme of Romans 8:17–18; Colossians 3:4; Philippians 3:20–21; 2 Timothy 4:8; James 1:12; and 1 Peter 1:4; 5:4 (cf. 1 Cor. 9:25).

This focus on hope concludes the apostle Paul's brief pastoral prayer for his beloved Thessalonians. His requests that God perfect their faith, prosper their love, and purify their hope model how all pastors and elders ought to pray for their people. His entreaty also establishes a general devotion to prayer that must accompany any sincere ministry of the Word (cf. Acts 6:4).

Excelling Still More
(1 Thessalonians 4:1-2)

8

Finally then, brethren, we request and exhort you in the Lord Jesus, that as you received from us instruction as to how you ought to walk and please God (just as you actually do walk), that you excel still more. For you know what commandments we gave you by the authority of the Lord Jesus. (4:1-2)

Historians generally consider Jonathan Edwards (1703–1758) to be among the handful of superior intellectuals and writers in American history, whether in secular or ecclesiastical annals. Edwards was also the leading evangelical theologian of his day and the most prominent pastor in the First Great Awakening (1735–1737; 1740–1744) in New England. He was the faithful shepherd of the same church in Northampton, Massachusetts, for twenty-three years and had an unparalleled influence through preaching, writing, and evangelism that continues to this day. The underlying drive and motive to Edwards' powerful and lasting impact was not mere personal devotion to his profession but was his insatiable thirst for God and the things that concern God—purity, holiness, virtue, and truth—what he called "religious affections." God saved him at age seventeen and the change was thorough. He reflected on the profound, divine transformation in his thoughts and actions subsequent to his conversion:

My mind was greatly fixed on divine things; almost perpetually in the contemplation of them. I spent most of my time in thinking of divine things, year after year; often walking alone in the woods, and solitary places, for meditation, soliloquy, and prayer, and converse with God; and it was always my manner, at such times, to sing forth my contemplations. I was almost constantly in ejaculatory prayer, wherever I was. Prayer seemed to be natural to me, as the breath by which the inward burnings of my heart had vent. The delights which I now felt in those things of religion, were of an exceedingly different kind from those before mentioned, that I had when a boy; and what then I had no more notion of, than one born blind has of pleasant and beautiful colours. They were of a more inward, pure, soul-animating and refreshing nature. Those former delights never reached the heart; and did not arise from any sight of the divine excellency of the things of God; or any taste of the soul-satisfying and life-giving good there is in them. (*Memoirs of Jonathan Edwards,* lv. In vol. 1 of *The Works of Jonathan Edwards,* edited by Edward Hickman [London: Henry G. Bohn, 1865], 10th ed.)

Edwards' sentiments highlight an important element of the apostle Paul's exhortation in these two verses. He could urge them and all believers to excel in Christian living more and more, but only when believers nurture that new nature with its resolute longing for God do they attain the kind of spiritual progress Paul had in mind.

There is always a danger of Christians thinking they have no further need to progress in sanctification; but this side of eternity, no believer has even come close to what God desires for him spiritually (cf. Phil. 3:12–16). Because it knew so much truth, even a church as strong as the one in Thessalonica might have been tempted to settle for the spiritual status quo. Thanks to Paul's solid instruction when he was with them, the saints were living exemplary lives and he had commended them for that (1 Thess. 1:2–4, 7; 2:13–14). As a result, they might have thought their condition was ideal and in no need of improvement. But Paul knew they could do better and encouraged them accordingly. He was not satisfied even with his own progress:

Not that I have already obtained it or have already become perfect, but I press on so that I may lay hold of that for which also I was laid hold of by Christ Jesus. Brethren, I do not regard myself as having laid hold of it yet; but one thing I do: forgetting what lies behind and reaching forward to what lies ahead, I press on toward the goal for the prize of the upward call of God in Christ Jesus. (Phil. 3:12–14)

As a faithful teacher and overseer, Paul was diligent not only to impart truth to his flock but also to apply that truth himself and to motivate his people to apply it in an ever-increasing way (1 Cor. 15:58; 2 Cor. 8:7; Phil. 1:9; 1 Thess. 4:10; cf. 1 Thess. 3:10). From 4:1 to the end of the body of the letter (5:22), Paul's primary purpose was to exhort the church to strive for spiritual excellence. In 4:1–2 he introduced three foundational elements concerning that pursuit of excellence: the priority of excelling, the power and principles for excelling, and the progress and pressure of excelling.

THE PRIORITY OF EXCELLING

Finally then, brethren, we request and exhort you . . . that you excel still more. (4:1a, d)

That 4:1–2 turns to a discussion of the goal of spiritual excellence for the Thessalonians is clear from Paul's opening words, **finally then.** The main teaching section of the epistle concludes at 3:13, and on the basis of that content comes the apostle's exhortation to excellence.

Request denotes a gentle, humble suggestion offered among equals. It does not contain the military overtones of a commander ordering a soldier, or the slavery overtones of a master dictating to a servant, or the sovereignty overtones of a monarch commanding a subject. Unlike one of those leaders, Paul was not browbeating the Thessalonians but lovingly, gently, and kindly requesting that they as his **brethren** persevere in sanctification. Similarly, **exhort** (*parakaloumen*) means "to come alongside and encourage." The word could be used in an authoritative sense (2 Thess. 3:12; 2 Tim. 4:2; Titus 2:15), but here Paul used it to express his desire to help their spiritual growth.

Paul exhibited much humility and pastoral warmth toward these faithful believers. There was no reason to be overbearing toward them because they were already living in a way that pleased God. Therefore, his attitude was gracious and considerate, with just enough urgency that they accept his exhortation not to be content with their spiritual growth but to **excel still more.**

The word translated **excel** (*perisseuēte*) means "to abound, to be abundantly supplied, to overflow, to exist in full quantity, to be over and above and around, to be advanced." A closely related form of the word can mean "extraordinary," or "surpassing." Paul used *perisseuēte* here in a comparative way (cf. 1 Cor. 8:8) to tell the Thessalonians he was intent that they become spiritually extraordinary, that they **excel** to a higher degree (cf. 1 Cor. 14:12; Phil. 1:9; 1 Thess. 3:12; 4:10).

Paul's priority for believers was spiritual progress motivated by a desire to know God—the kind of strong desire the psalmist described:

"As the deer pants for the water brooks, so my soul pants for You, O God" (Ps. 42:1; cf. 34:8; 63:1–2). For all believers, the pursuit of knowing God is the basic component of spiritual growth (Jer. 9:23–24; 2 Cor. 8:7; Eph. 4:13; Phil. 3:7–10; Col. 1:9–10; 2:2; 3:10; 2 Peter 1:2–9; cf. Pss. 25:10; 71:15–16; 138:2; Jer. 31:34; 2 Cor. 7:1; Heb. 6:12, 15; 10:36). The objective of knowing God should supersede even the desire to know His Word; that desire is simply the means to knowing the God of the Word. If gaining more information about the Bible and participating in additional spiritual activities—praying, witnessing, and serving—are not linked to the desire to know God better, they will not bring spiritual growth to those who profess faith in Christ (cf. Hos. 6:6; Matt. 6:1–18; John 15:4–5; 1 Cor. 13:1–3; Phil. 2:13; Col. 3:17).

This is the sense of 1 John 2:12–14:

> I am writing to you, little children, because your sins have been forgiven you for His name's sake. I am writing to you, fathers, because you know Him who has been from the beginning. I am writing to you, young men, because you have overcome the evil one. I have written to you, children, because you know the Father. I have written to you, fathers, because you know Him who has been from the beginning. I have written to you, young men, because you are strong, and the word of God abides in you, and you have overcome the evil one.

In that text, John identifies three steps in a believer's growth: (1) "little children" who know their sins are forgiven, (2) "young men" who know doctrine and are strong against Satan's lies (unlike children, cf. Eph. 4:14), and (3) "fathers" who know not just doctrine but the eternal God. That is the final goal of every believer.

THE POWER AND PRINCIPLES FOR EXCELLING

in the Lord Jesus, that as you received from us instruction as to how you ought to walk and please God (4:1b)

In the Lord Jesus can modify **you** and refer to those who are regenerate and share the divine life of God by being in Christ. Certainly only the regenerate possess the spiritual power and insight to accomplish the objectives of spiritual growth (cf. 1 Cor. 2:14). This reality clearly burdened the apostle's heart, as demonstrated by his prayer for the Thessalonians: "May the Lord cause you to increase and abound in love for one another" (1 Thess. 3:12). The only way love or any other Christian virtue can increase is when the Lord causes it to happen. The power to excel comes from the power of the indwelling Christ (John 17:23; Gal. 2:20; Eph. 3:17; 4:15–16; Col. 2:7; 1 John 5:20). Paul called the Thessalonians to spiritual excellence, which they could attain because they were **in the Lord Jesus.**

That phrase could also refer to the verbs *request* and *exhort* and therefore mean **in** behalf of **the Lord Jesus,** that is, with His authority (v. 2). Paul often added force to his appeals by reminding the church leaders of the authority he had as Christ's apostle (cf. vv. 2, 15; 5:27; 2 Thess. 3:6, 12).

The power for excelling, however, does not operate in a vacuum. It works according to scripturally delineated, time-tested, God-approved principles. Paul refers to the divine principles, spiritual truths, and gospel doctrine that the Thessalonians had **received from** him and his companions when they first arrived in Thessalonica (cf. Acts 17:2–4; 1 Thess. 1:5–6; 2:7–8, 14). Although the term **instruction** is not in the original text, it is implied in the doctrines Paul taught concerning **how** they **ought to walk,** or conduct their daily lives (cf. Rom. 12:9–21; Gal. 5:16–26; 6:6–10; Eph. 4:25–5:21; 6:10–18; Col. 3:12–4:6).

So the saints already knew the fundamentals of Christian living. They knew what they needed to do to **please God** (literally, "to strive to please" Him) and glorify Him in everything: they needed to confess their sins regularly (cf. Ps. 32:5; Isa. 1:18–19; Matt. 6:12; 1 John 1:9); to pray continually and trust Him (cf. Ps. 27:8; Phil. 4:6; 1 Thess. 5:17; 1 Tim. 2:8; Heb. 4:16; 10:22; James 1:6); to pursue humility (cf. Matt. 20:26–28; Eph. 4:1–2; Phil. 2:3–4; Col. 3:12; James 4:6); to be content with God's will (cf. Ps. 37:16; 1 Tim. 6:6, 8; Heb. 13:5), as it is revealed in His Word (cf. Ps. 119:105; Prov. 6:23; 2 Tim. 3:16–17; 2 Peter 1:19); to be willing to suffer for His name (cf. Matt. 5:10–12; John 15:20; Acts 5:41; 2 Tim. 3:12); to evangelize the lost (cf. Matt. 4:19; 28:19–20; Mark 16:15; 2 Cor. 5:20; 2 Tim. 4:5); to celebrate the Lord's Table (cf. Luke 22:19; 1 Cor. 11:23–28); to care for one another (cf. Acts 2:44–46; Gal. 6:2; Phil. 2:3–4; 1 Thess. 5:11, 14; Heb. 13:1–3; James 1:27; 2:15–17); to honor God in their marriages and families (cf. Eph. 5:22–6:4; Col. 3:18–21; 1 Tim. 5:3–16; Titus 2:1–8; Heb. 13:4); and to be diligent and fruitful in all avenues of service (cf. Matt. 3:8; Eph. 2:10; Col. 1:10; 2 Tim. 3:16–17; Titus 3:8, 14; Heb. 10:24; 13:21). Paul, Silas, and Timothy had taught the Thessalonians how they ought to live as Christians, and they were already obeying what they had heard.

THE PROGRESS AND PRESSURE OF EXCELLING

(just as you actually do walk), . . . For you know what commandments we gave you by the authority of the Lord Jesus. (4:1c, 2)

Spiritual growth is not an instantaneous process; it does not culminate overnight. Instead, the pursuit of spiritual excellence is a lifelong commitment. As they **walk** in daily obedience, believers gradually but surely become more and more like Christ. Paul's exhortation to the Thessalonians was a confirmation of that fact and a reminder to them to keep progressing, **just as** they already **actually** did **walk.** They were on the pathway of progressive sanctification, and Paul wanted them to stay on it and have the patient, determined mind-set of the long-distance runner or the boxer, as he later described it to the Corinthians:

> Do you not know that those who run in a race all run, but only one receives the prize? Run in such a way that you may win. Everyone who competes in the games exercises self-control in all things. They then do it to receive a perishable wreath, but we an imperishable. Therefore I run in such a way, as not without aim; I box in such a way, as not beating the air; but I discipline my body and make it my slave, so that, after I have preached to others, I myself will not be disqualified. (1 Cor. 9:24–27; cf. Phil. 3:12–14; Heb. 12:1–2)

The pressure for the Thessalonians to stay on the path of righteousness and excel more and more in their walk with Christ derived from the fact that they knew **what commandments** Paul **gave** them **by the authority of the Lord Jesus.** Christ Himself authorized Paul's exhortation to the church in Thessalonica. **Commandments** (*parangelias*) refers to strong, authoritative directives delivered by a commanding officer to his subordinates. That meant the church could not take the apostle's admonition lightly. He not only reminded them of the various **commandments** he **gave** them, as he implicitly did concerning his earlier instruction to them, but he also reminded them of the divine authority by which he ministered (cf. 1 Cor. 2:1–5; 2 Cor. 10:1–5; 1 Thess. 2:13). Paul's directives did not originate from some arbitrary human sanction or some remote ecclesiastical authority (cf. Gal. 1:1, 15–16; 2 Peter 1:20–21). Instead, they came from **the authority of the Lord Jesus,** and obedience to them was mandatory (cf. Matt. 7:21; John 15:14–17; 1 John 2:3–5).

Christians who seek to know God better, to love Him more, and to obey Him more thoroughly, must live according to the commands of Scripture. Such believers will then experience growth toward spiritual excellence, through the power of the indwelling Christ and by their obedience to the truth of the Word. Paul spoke of this progress as "beholding . . . the glory of the Lord" and "being transformed into the same image from glory to glory" by the Holy Spirit (2 Cor. 3:18). "The glory of the Lord" is in the Scripture that, when comprehended by the sanctified mind, progressively changes and elevates believers to increasing Christlikeness.

This occurs when with "unveiled face"—undistracted, unhindered—the child of God looks into the magnificent mirror of Scripture, which reflects the Lord's glory.

Abstaining from Sexual Sin (1 Thessalonians 4:3–8)

9

For this is the will of God, your sanctification; that is, that you abstain from sexual immorality; that each of you know how to possess his own vessel in sanctification and honor, not in lustful passion, like the Gentiles who do not know God; and that no man transgress and defraud his brother in the matter because the Lord is the avenger in all these things, just as we also told you before and solemnly warned you. For God has not called us for the purpose of impurity, but in sanctification. So, he who rejects this is not rejecting man but the God who gives His Holy Spirit to you. (4:3–8)

Since the 1960s, when the modern sexual revolution really accelerated, Western society has had fewer and fewer rules governing sexual attitudes and behaviors. Freedom of sexual expression has in many ways become the cultural god that rules over all the other idolatrous gods of postmodern culture. People want the right, for themselves and others, to express their sexual desires at any cost, even if that means aborting the unwanted child resulting from a sexual union or risking a sexually transmitted disease.

Several obvious tenets constitute the world's immoral, unscriptural outlook regarding sex. First, people are basically good and all but the most heinous activities should be tolerated. Therefore, virtually any kind of consensual sexual activity is good (except for child molestation), especially if one views sex as merely a way to personal gratification. Second, since sexual activity is only a biological function (cf. 1 Cor. 6:13), it is normal and necessary to engage in it without placing on it any moral restrictions. Third, since "casual" sex is just another form of fun and pleasure, it is permissible to enjoy sexual activity recreationally, any time with any consenting partner. Fourth, fulfilling one's sexual desire is a major goal in life, more important than developing meaningful personal relationships. Fifth, instant gratification is more important than delayed satisfaction. Therefore, having premarital sex is legitimate and preferable to waiting until marriage to have sex. Sixth, enjoyable sexual intercourse is the most important factor in establishing a good marital relationship. Therefore, the early stage of every romantic relationship should include sex. The couple should live together to determine sexual compatibility and fulfillment before they marry.

Christians understand that those are the dogmas of society's permissive sexual outlook. The apostle Paul could have recognized the same tendencies in his day because, if anything, the utterly pagan Greco-Roman culture he ministered in was more sexually perverse and debauched than contemporary Western culture, which for centuries has had the beneficial influence of Christianity on its institutions. Thessalonica was part of that debased Greco-Roman culture. The city was rife with such sinful practices as fornication, adultery, homosexuality (including pedophilia), transvestism (men dressing like women), and a wide variety of pornographic and erotic perversions, all done with a seared conscience and society's acceptance, hence with little or no accompanying shame or guilt. Unlike people in Western nations today, the Thessalonians grew up with no Christian tradition to support laws and standards that forbid the grosser manifestations of immorality. Pagan Greek society apparently did not have civil laws to prohibit immoral behavior.

Further contributing to the sexually permissive environment in Thessalonica was the influence of the mystery religions that advocated ritual prostitution. They taught that if a follower engaged with a temple prostitute, he would be communing transcendentally with the deity the prostitute represented. For example, the Temple of Aphrodite on the Corinthian acropolis employed one thousand priestesses who were essentially religious prostitutes. Thus people did not consider fornication and adultery illegal or immoral; the idolatrous religions actually condoned them.

For the Thessalonians, then, sexual sin was more customary and more tolerated than it is even by today's standards. That reality provides a clearer perspective of Paul's ministry at Thessalonica. When he, Silas, and Timothy planted the church there, they rescued people out of that pornographic society. Many of those new converts, who had lived in immorality, no doubt had mistresses, and many of the women likely engaged in harlotry. Their rather sudden entrance into the kingdom of God required the Thessalonians to break with their pagan background. That requirement presented them with strong challenges—old habits and the pressures from a wicked culture would seek to draw them away from their new life and back to the old. Paul, as their pastor, was concerned enough to begin the exhortation portion of this epistle with commands regarding immoral conduct.

Though the surrounding culture continually lowered its moral standards, the Thessalonians could not lower theirs. Paul's requirement that the Thessalonian believers abstain from sexual sin did not involve a relative morality; it encompassed an absolute standard. Such an unambiguous command, however, did not single out—the way Paul would with the Corinthians—specific groups or individuals within the church who were committing certain sins (cf. 1 Cor. 5:1–13). But that lack of specificity in no way mitigated Paul's concern for the Thessalonians' purity. That this general, preventive exhortation to sexual morality began his list of practical instructions in the final two chapters of 1 Thessalonians highlights Paul's major concern for sexual fidelity in Thessalonica. With this background in mind, one can examine this passage by asking three questions: What kind of sexual conduct does God require? How can a believer be sexually moral? Why should a believer be sexually moral?

What Kind of Sexual Conduct Does God Require?

For this is the will of God, your sanctification; that is, that you abstain from sexual immorality; (4:3)

The will of God for Christians concerning proper sexual behavior is quite clear, namely, **that** they **abstain from sexual immorality.** The conjunction **for** links this command to Paul's previous exhortation that the Thessalonians strive to excel more (4:1–2). Paul already knew his readers desired to do God's will (cf. 1:3–10), but he also realized they needed to know more specifically what that will encompasses.

But before mentioning specifics, Paul defined **the will of God** under the broad governing principle of **sanctification** (*hagiosmos*), which is the process of being separated from sin and set apart to God's holiness (Ps. 4:3; Jer. 1:5; John 17:17, 19; Acts 20:32; 26:18; Rom. 6:22;

15:16; 1 Cor. 6:11; Eph. 5:26–27; 2 Tim. 2:21; Heb. 2:11; 10:10; 13:12; cf. 2 Cor. 6:17; Eph. 5:7–9; Phil. 2:12–13). God wants believers to separate from all that is evil, fleshly, and impure. The **sanctification** process is the direct result of salvation, as Paul instructed the Corinthians: "Such [sexually immoral] were some of you; but you were washed, but you were sanctified, but you were justified in the name of the Lord Jesus Christ and in the Spirit of our God" (1 Cor. 6:11; cf. 1:2, 30; Acts 20:32; 26:18; 2 Thess. 2:13; Heb. 2:11; 10:14; 1 Peter 1:2). The apostle's reference to sanctification points back to one of the requests he had just prayed for the Thessalonians: "that He may establish your hearts without blame in holiness before our God and Father" (1 Thess. 3:13).

In view of the permissive culture in Thessalonica, Paul considered abstention **from sexual immorality** to be the first priority in the Thessalonians' devotion to sanctification. As already discussed, every imaginable sexual vice was rampant in and around Thessalonica; therefore, Paul was especially concerned that the Thessalonians could easily fall back into their former habits. So he gave them the direct, uncomplicated command to **abstain from sexual immorality. Abstain** means complete abstinence, in this case, staying completely away from any thought or behavior that violates the principles of God's Word and results in any act of sexual sin. **Sexual immorality** (*porneias*) is a term used to describe any form of illicit sexual behavior (John 8:41; Acts 15:20, 29; 21:25; 1 Cor. 5:1; 6:13, 18; 2 Cor. 12:21; Gal. 5:19; Eph. 5:3; Col. 3:5; Rev. 2:21; 9:21). Any sexual activity that deviates from the monogamous relationship between a husband and a wife is immoral by God's standard. The Lord does bless the sexual relationship in matrimony: "Marriage is to be held in honor among all, and the marriage bed is to be undefiled" (Heb. 13:4*a*). But He is not pleased with sexual activity of any kind other than that: "for fornicators and adulterers God will judge" (Heb. 13:4*b*; cf. Rom. 1:24–32; 2:2).

Paul's Spirit-inspired teaching on the subject of sexual morality is so strict and demanding that it extends beyond just the physical acts of immorality, as his later teachings to the Ephesians and the Colossians illustrate:

But immorality or any impurity or greed must not even be named among you, as is proper among saints. (Eph. 5:3)

For you have died and your life is hidden with Christ in God. . . . Therefore consider the members of your earthly body as dead to immorality, impurity, passion, evil desire, and greed, which amounts to idolatry. (Col. 3:3, 5)

In both passages, *impurity* is from the same Greek word, whose meaning extends beyond acts of sexual sin to include unclean thoughts and intentions. That use of *impurity*, along with the general tenor of Paul's warnings against sexual immorality, places him in complete agreement with Jesus' teaching on sexual sin: "You have heard that it was said, 'You shall not commit adultery'; but I say to you that everyone who looks at a woman with lust for her has already committed adultery with her in his heart" (Matt. 5:27–28; cf. 15:19; Mark 7:21–22). Total abstinence from sexual sin is a duty of the utmost importance for all believers (Ex. 20:14; Acts 15:20; Rom. 13:13; 1 Cor. 6:15–18; Gal. 5:19–21; Eph. 5:5–6; Col. 3:5; cf. Gen. 39:7–10; 1 Cor. 5:11; 1 Peter 4:3).

Scripture makes it clear that people who habitually engage in sexual immorality thereby demonstrate that they are not Christians: "Or do you not know that the unrighteous will not inherit the kingdom of God? Do not be deceived; neither fornicators, nor idolaters, nor adulterers, nor effeminate, nor homosexuals, nor thieves, nor the covetous, nor drunkards, nor revilers, nor swindlers, will inherit the kingdom of God" (1 Cor. 6:9–10; cf. Gal. 5:19–21; Rev. 21:8; 22:15). But that same chapter of 1 Corinthians also indicates that believers can sometimes commit sexual sins:

> Do you not know that your bodies are members of Christ? Shall I then take away the members of Christ and make them members of a prostitute? May it never be! Or do you not know that the one who joins himself to a prostitute is one body with her? For He says, "The two shall become one flesh." But the one who joins himself to the Lord is one spirit with Him. Flee immorality. Every other sin that a man commits is outside the body, but the immoral man sins against his own body. Or do you not know that your body is a temple of the Holy Spirit who is in you, whom you have from God, and that you are not your own? For you have been bought with a price: therefore glorify God in your body. (6:15–20)

Paul may have had such sins in mind when he later told the Corinthians, "You cannot drink the cup of the Lord and the cup of demons; you cannot partake of the table of the Lord and the table of demons" (1 Cor. 10:21). The demonic cup and table refer to the worship in pagan temples in Corinth, and part of that idolatrous ritual entailed the worshipers having sexual intercourse with temple prostitutes. The apostle was concerned that the new Corinthian believers had not completely abandoned such activities. The situation at Corinth, where Paul was when he wrote the Thessalonian epistles, surely highlighted the danger of sexual sin and motivated Paul's warning to the Thessalonians. The command, then, is for total abstinence from any sexual activity outside marriage.

HOW CAN A BELIEVER BE SEXUALLY MORAL?

that each of you know how to possess his own vessel in sanctification and honor, not in lustful passion, like the Gentiles who do not know God; and that no man transgress and defraud his brother in the matter (4:4–6a)

Because Christians today are incessantly exposed to all kinds of sights, sounds, and philosophies that tempt their fallen flesh to immoral thoughts and actions, they must know how to resist such temptations. Because the need was equally great for the Thessalonians, Paul gave them three timeless principles for maintaining sexual morality: the body should not control the believer; the believer should not act like the unbeliever; and the believer should not take advantage of others.

THE BODY SHOULD NOT CONTROL THE BELIEVER

that each of you know how to possess his own vessel in sanctification and honor, (4:4)

Believers must maintain self-control over the desires of their flesh. Hence Paul exhorted the Thessalonians **that each of** them had to **know how to** control their body's appetites. **Each** believer had the same personal responsibility to control his body. **Know** is from *oida*, which carries the idea of having the knowledge or skill necessary to accomplish a desired goal. Every Christian needs to know himself well, so as to understand his weaknesses and evil propensities and, thereby, **know how to possess** ("gain mastery over") **his own vessel.**

Over the years many commentators have asserted that **vessel** (*skeuos*) means "wife," but that definition does not fit the context or the usual meaning of the word. Leon Morris notes:

> A few early commentators like Theodore of Mopsuestia and Augustine held that the word means "wife," and a good number of modern writers follow them. The strongest argument for this view appears to be that there are a few passages (Grimm-Thayer cite two in the Septuagint and one in Xenophon) where the combination of this noun and verb means "to marry." This is said to be supported by the reference to the wife as "the weaker vessel" in I Pet. 3:7. This latter point must, however, be discounted, for the wife is not spoken of as the husband's "vessel" at all. Both are "vessels" of the Holy Ghost, the wife being the weaker. Thus the passage does not really bear on our problem. Among the Rabbis

the Hebrew equivalent of the Greek word here is used of the wife, and this may have influenced Paul.

It is not easy to decide the point, but it does seem to me that it would not be very natural for a Greek writer to speak of a wife as a "vessel." And in this case it would be the less likely since Paul is inculcating a high view of marriage, and it is a very low view that thinks of the wife as no more than a vessel for gratifying the husband's sexual desires. This . . . inclines me to the view that "body" is meant. Paul then is exhorting his Thessalonian friends to keep their bodies pure. (*The First and Second Epistles to the Thessalonians.* The New International Commentary on the New Testament [Grand Rapids: Eerdmans, 1989], 123–24)

The New Testament uses *skeuos* metaphorically for utensils, implements, or tools (Rom. 9:21; 2 Cor. 4:7; 2 Tim. 2:21); it also uses the term in reference to people (Acts 9:15; Rom. 9:22–23). But the present verse uses it for "body," which matches some rabbinical uses of the word. Paul was admonishing the Thessalonians to control their bodies, the unredeemed human flesh that is the beachhead for sin and immorality (cf. Rom. 7:18; 8:5–8, 23). For that reason, Paul urged believers to kill the flesh (cf. Rom. 13:14; 2 Cor. 7:1), live by the Spirit (Rom. 8:13), and dedicate their bodies to God and allow His Spirit to renew their minds so that the body would not control them (Rom 12:1–2).

As in today's culture, the culture of Paul's day operated largely according to physical appetites and impulsive, superficial emotions. (The words of the slogan "If it feels right, do it" are of contemporary origin, but the philosophy they express is not.) That is why Paul gave such strong instruction to the Corinthians,

Food is for the stomach and the stomach is for food, but God will do away with both of them. Yet the body is not for immorality, but for the Lord, and the Lord is for the body. . . . Do you not know that your bodies are members of Christ? Shall I then take away the members of Christ and make them members of a prostitute? May it never be! (1 Cor. 6:13, 15)

The statement regarding "food" and "the stomach" was likely a proverbial saying that called all physical gratification natural and normal, and viewed sex, like eating, as purely biological. Apparently some of the Corinthians used that analogy to justify their sexual immorality. But sexual sin is not a servant; it is a powerful master. Therefore, the apostle warned the Corinthians, as he had the Thessalonians, that believers must not allow that sin to control them. Instead, all Christians must know the importance of disciplining their bodies so they will honor God (cf. 1 Cor. 9:27).

In several of his other letters, the apostle Paul made it crystal clear that in order to control their bodies believers must rely on the Holy Spirit. "Walk by the Spirit, and you will not carry out the desire of the flesh" (Gal. 5:16). The key to walking in the Spirit is being filled with the Spirit (Eph. 5:17–18), and the key to being filled with the Spirit is for believers to let God's Word dwell within them (Col. 3:16; cf. Pss. 19:7–11; 119:11, 105). They must sincerely read, study, and apply Scripture so that it saturates their lives and allows them to yield complete control to the Holy Spirit (Deut. 6:7; Pss. 1:2; 119:97; John 5:39; Acts 17:11; 20:32; Rom. 15:4; 1 Peter 2:2; 2 Peter 1:19; cf. Isa. 30:20–21; Ezek. 36:27; John 14:26; 1 Cor. 2:12–13; 2 Tim. 3:15).

Along those lines, Paul urged the Thessalonians to control their bodies for the purpose of **sanctification and honor.** As noted in the discussion of 4:3, **sanctification** means to be set apart from sin to God, for the purpose of living a pure and holy life. **Honor** is the result of separation from sin. They would show respect for their bodies as temples of the Spirit and instruments of service to Christ (cf. 1 Cor. 3:17; 6:19; 2 Cor. 6:16). The goal is positive—pursue separation and virtue with all one's heart. No Christian should ever ask how far his or her moral behavior can depart from God's standard and still avoid sin. Rather, believers should strive to be utterly separate from immorality so that they can honor their bodies, which belong to God, and use them to glorify Jesus Christ, the Head of the church (Eph. 1:21–23; 2:20–21; 4:15–16; 5:23; Col. 1:18, 24; cf. John 10:1–16, 27–28; Heb. 13:20; 1 Peter 2:25; 5:4).

THE BELIEVER SHOULD NOT ACT LIKE THE UNBELIEVER

not in lustful passion, like the Gentiles who do not know God; (4:5)

The second principle Paul gave the Thessalonians concerning how to maintain sexual purity and abstain from immorality was that they were not to behave like their pagan neighbors or relatives, **who** did **not know God**—that is, were not transformed by the divine work of salvation. Scripture often designates those outside salvation in this way (cf. Judg. 2:10; Ps. 79:6; Isa. 45:4–5; Jer. 9:3; 10:25; Acts 17:23; Rom. 1:28; 1 Cor. 1:21; 15:34; Gal. 4:8; 2 Thess. 1:8). The uncontrolled desire for sexual gratification, which is typical of unregenerate people (Rom. 1:24–27; 1 Cor. 5:9–11; Gal. 5:19–21; Eph. 5:3–5; Col. 3:5–7; 1 Peter 4:1–4; cf. 2 Tim. 3:1–7; 2 Peter 2:12–14; Jude 17–19), was not to be true of the Thessalonians or any other true believer (cf. 1 Thess. 3:13).

Passion (*pathos*) means "uncontrollable desires, compelling feelings, overpowering urges" and has a negative connotation here (cf. Rom. 1:26; Col. 3:5). **Lustful** (*epithumias*) refers to an out-of-control craving, usually for that which is unrighteous or illegitimate (cf. Rom. 6:12; 2 Tim. 2:22; Titus 3:3; 1 Peter 4:3), although it can refer to legitimate desires and longings (cf. Phil. 1:23; 1 Thess. 2:17). The words used together forcefully characterize the immorality of those **who do not know God.**

Christians, however, cannot any longer live in the same unwholesome patterns of sin that the godless people (in this context **the Gentiles**) do. The apostle instructed the Galatians: "Now those who belong to Christ Jesus have crucified the flesh with its passions and desires" (Gal. 5:24; cf. Col. 3:5–10). Unregenerate people practice, as a way of life, all sorts of sexual immorality (cf. Rom. 1:24–28); but God has delivered the regenerate from such habitual sinning (cf. 1 John 3:9–10). But believers can cultivate immoral thoughts and commit immoral acts—so they need this instruction.

Christians must not lower themselves to a level of pagan sexual behavior determined merely by unthinking passions and uncontrolled fleshly urges. Because of their intimate relationship with a holy God, believers must not subject themselves to an ungodly society's vast array of sexually immoral temptations (cf. 2 Tim. 2:22; 1 John 2:15–16). Overexposure to such temptations will only lower one's resistance and diminish one's outrage, thus weakening spiritual resolve and virtue. Scripture warns God's children to stay far away from, even to flee, all immorality (1 Cor. 6:18). Lustful thoughts and feelings can lead believers to actions that are completely incongruous with their position in the body of Christ (see 1 Cor. 6:15–20).

THE BELIEVER SHOULD NOT TAKE ADVANTAGE OF OTHERS

and that no man transgress and defraud his brother in the matter (4:6a)

A third practical, unambiguous principle emerges from the apostle Paul's admonition to the Thessalonians on sexual morality: They should never sexually take advantage of other believers. The word rendered **transgress** means "to sin against," which includes the concept of stepping over the line and exceeding the lawful limits. In some modern Scripture translations, such as the *New King James Version* and the *New International Version*, the translators provide further insight by rendering **transgress,** "take advantage of."

Paul warns that a believer should not take such advantage described so as to **defraud his brother in the matter. Defraud** means to selfishly, greedily take something for personal gain and pleasure at someone else's expense. As is true with **transgress,** the definition of **defraud** includes the notion of taking advantage of someone, and in this context it concerns **the matter** of sexual sin. Whenever believers seek to satisfy their physical desires and gain sexual pleasure at the expense of another believer, they have violated this command.

God considers this subject of sinfully taking advantage of another believer so serious that Jesus warned,

> Whoever causes one of these little ones who believe in Me to stumble, it would be better for him to have a heavy millstone hung around his neck, and to be drowned in the depth of the sea. Woe to the world because of its stumbling blocks! For it is inevitable that stumbling blocks come; but woe to that man through whom the stumbling block comes! (Matt. 18:6–7)

Those Christians who cause other Christians ("little ones") to stumble (sin) would be better off drowned. One expects the world to offend believers and sometimes cause them to sin, but believers should never be stumbling blocks for fellow believers (cf. Matt. 5:23–24; Rom. 14:13; 1 Cor. 10:32–33; Col. 2:18). The seriousness of Christ's admonition to believers in Matthew 18:6 has no equal in all His teaching. He said that a believer who defrauds another believer deserves to be killed! So Christians must take heed to their own holiness, avoid all ungodly influences, and never use other people, especially fellow believers, to achieve sinful gratification.

WHY SHOULD A BELIEVER BE SEXUALLY MORAL?

because the Lord is the avenger in all these things, just as we also told you before and solemnly warned you. For God has not called us for the purpose of impurity, but in sanctification. So, he who rejects this is not rejecting man but the God who gives His Holy Spirit to you. (4:6b–8)

The apostle Paul, through the inspiration of the Holy Spirit, anticipated his readers' asking why they should keep his command concerning sexual morality. He offered three reasons that the Thessalonians and all believers should abstain from sexual immorality: because of God's vengeance, because of God's purpose, and because of God's Holy Spirit.

BECAUSE OF GOD'S VENGEANCE

because the Lord is the avenger in all these things, just as we also told you before and solemnly warned you. (4:6*b*)

The first compelling motive Paul gave the Thessalonians for obeying his command to abstain from sexual immorality is **because the Lord is the avenger in all these things.** Only God has the right to exact vengeance for the sins people commit: "Never take your own revenge, beloved, but leave room for the wrath of God, for it is written, 'Vengeance is Mine, I will repay,' says the Lord" (Rom. 12:19; cf. Deut. 32:35). He is the one who metes out judgment, and sexual sin is one of the specific reasons He does so: "The marriage bed is to be undefiled; for fornicators and adulterers God will judge" (Heb. 13:4).

If a believer engages in sexual immorality, God **the avenger** may judge **all these things** by allowing one or more of several consequences to affect that believer's life. For example, the outcome could be a severely damaged marriage, accompanied by loss of family love and respect; the sin could lead to a divorce (Matt. 5:32; 19:9); God may chasten the person by allowing him or her to be afflicted with venereal disease or some other physical affliction; or the sin could result in the absence of blessing, the presence of a greater than average number of trials and troubles, or even an untimely death (cf. 1 Cor. 10:8). Sexual sin by a believer will certainly result to some degree in the loss of eternal reward (cf. Prov. 11:18; 1 Cor. 3:12–15; 2 Cor. 5:10; 2 John 8).

The concept of God's judgment against sexual immorality was not new to the Thessalonians. Paul reminded them that he **also told** them about it **before and solemnly warned** them. That he **solemnly warned** them about these matters shows that the apostle taught them "the whole purpose of God" (Acts 20:27). He had done a thorough job of evangelizing the Thessalonians, imparting to them not only a complete understanding of the gospel, but also what it means to observe all the commands of Christ (cf. Matt. 28:18–20).

BECAUSE OF GOD'S PURPOSE

For God has not called us for the purpose of impurity, but in sanctification. (4:7)

That Christians should strive to be sexually moral is in complete accord with God's general plan for their lives. Therefore, a second reason Paul gave for abstaining from sexual immorality was because that command fit God's **purpose** for the Thessalonians. For the third time in this passage, Paul used a form of the word **sanctification,** which emphasized to them that when **God** effectually **called** them to salvation, He also **called** them to holiness. A life **of impurity** was inconsistent with believers' high calling (Eph. 4:1).

The phrase **in sanctification** indicates that the believer's position of holiness is the direct result of God's effectual call. God's **purpose** in salvation was to produce a holy people who would walk worthy of the divine call into His kingdom and glory (cf. Eph. 4:1; 1 Thess. 2:12). The call to salvation is inseparable from the call to holy and pure living. Ephesians 2:8–10 says:

> For by grace you have been saved through faith; and that not of yourselves, it is the gift of God; not as a result of works, so that no one may boast. For we are His workmanship, created in Christ Jesus for good works, which God prepared beforehand so that we would walk in them.

Paul was intent on presenting the church at Thessalonica and the church everywhere as a bride "having no spot or wrinkle or any such thing" (Eph. 5:27), but as one set apart and pure before God. Therefore sexual sin is utterly inconsistent with God's present and ultimate purpose for believers.

BECAUSE OF GOD'S HOLY SPIRIT

So, he who rejects this is not rejecting man but the God who gives His Holy Spirit to you. (4:8)

The final reason for the Thessalonians to obey Paul's admonition was that their disobeying it would mean they were **rejecting** God's **Holy Spirit.** Any believer who **rejects** ("nullifies, makes void, cancels, disregards, despises") the command to abstain from sexual immorality **is not rejecting man but the God who gives His Holy Spirit.** Thus if the Thessalonians disobeyed Paul's words, they would not merely be rejecting him, the church elders, or some faction in the church, but the **Spirit** of **God.** The standard of sexual morality is God's, and He gave believers the **Holy Spirit** to enable them to keep that norm (cf. Ezek. 36:27; John 14:16–17; Rom. 8:9; Gal. 5:16; 1 John 3:24; 4:13).

The Greek verb **gives** denotes timelessness. Paul told the Thessalonians that **God gives** believers the timeless gift of **His Holy Spirit** (cf. Isa. 59:21; 2 Cor. 1:22; Eph. 1:13–14; 2 Tim. 1:14) so that they might live pure and holy lives (cf. 1 Cor. 6:19–20; Rom. 8:16; 2 Cor. 5:5; 1 John 2:27). If they understood that precise identification of God's **Spirit,** it should have been unthinkable for the Thessalonians to enter into sexual sin and thereby reject the Lord who gave them the Spirit.

The practice of sexual sin violates the work of the Father, the Son, and the Holy Spirit. It spurns the Lord's will, disregards His purposes, defies His commands, rejects His love, and flouts and abuses His grace. Perhaps most frightening and sobering of all, those who engage in sexual immorality discount the reality of God's righteous judgment against sin. Thus the apostle's exhortation to the Thessalonians ought to prompt all believers to faithfully heed these words and diligently use the means God has given them to abstain from all forms of sexual sin (Rom. 13:13–14; 1 Peter 2:11).

Shoe-Leather Faith
(1 Thessalonians 4:9–12)

10

Now as to the love of the brethren, you have no need for anyone to write to you, for you yourselves are taught by God to love one another; for indeed you do practice it toward all the brethren who are in all Macedonia. But we urge you, brethren, to excel still more, and to make it your ambition to lead a quiet life and attend to your own business and work with your hands, just as we commanded you, so that you will behave properly toward outsiders and not be in any need. (4:9–12)

Christianity is a shoe-leather faith—a living, practical faith that hits the streets in normal, everyday life, affecting everything from believers' simplest attitudes and most mundane actions to their profoundest thoughts and noblest deeds. Although any religion should affect the way its adherents live, no false religion—no matter how high its ethical standards—can genuinely transform the lives of its followers in a way that restrains the fallen flesh. Only by belief in the gospel of Jesus Christ does the power of God transform lives so that what believers profess they are able to live. The apostle Paul's continued insistence that the Thessalonians live that way was the motive for the practical expressions in this passage.

An unsettling situation within the church at Thessalonica intensified his concern for the Thessalonians' spiritual growth. From the beginning, their church was genuine, and Paul recognized that—"Constantly bearing in mind your work of faith and labor of love and steadfastness of hope in our Lord Jesus Christ in the presence of our God and Father, knowing, brethren beloved by God, His choice of you" (1 Thess. 1:3–4; cf. 2:13). They were soon a model church in their region; they "became an example to all the believers in Macedonia and in Achaia. For the word of the Lord . . . sounded forth from [them], not only in Macedonia and Achaia, but also in every place [their] faith toward God [went] forth, so that we [had] no need to say anything" (1:7–8; cf. 2 Cor. 8:1–5; 2 Thess. 1:3–4). However, at the conclusion of Paul's commendations, there is the hint of a problem.

The apostle had taught the Thessalonians about the return of Christ, and they eagerly anticipated that glorious coming (1:10). However, they were apparently overly anxious about the Lord's return and wanted to make sure they did not miss it. Their zealous preoccupation with Jesus' coming led to the mistaken notion that temporal responsibilities no longer mattered in light of His return. Thus Paul had to give them substantial instruction to correct their misunderstandings and unhealthy responses to the promise of the imminent return of the Savior (4:13–5:11; 2 Thess. 2:1–12).

A zealous but balanced anticipation of the return of Christ is a good thing. The apostle John had such an earnest expectation for the Parousia in his conclusion to the book of Revelation:"He who testifies to these things says, 'Yes, I am coming quickly.' Amen. Come, Lord Jesus" (Rev. 22:20). The apostle James told his readers, "Therefore be patient, brethren, until the coming of the Lord. The farmer waits for the precious produce of the soil, being patient about it, until it gets the early and late rains. You too be patient; strengthen your hearts, for the coming of the Lord is near" (James 5:7–8). The apostle Peter wrote, "But according to His promise we are looking for new heavens and a new earth, in which righteousness dwells. Therefore, beloved, since you look for these things, be diligent to be found by Him in peace, spotless and blameless" (2 Peter 3:13–14). Paul desired that the Corinthians would be "awaiting eagerly the revelation of our Lord Jesus Christ" (1 Cor. 1:7).

But the Thessalonians were allowing their excitement and enthusiasm for the second coming of Christ to overshadow the ordinary responsibilities of life. They seemed to lose their balance and composure (2 Thess. 2:2; 3:10) and became so zealous and agitated concerning eschatological events that they neglected their everyday duties. Such an unbalanced perspective on Jesus' return, however, contradicted the Lord's teaching, for example, in the parable of the ten minas, in which He sought to correct the disciples' mistaken idea that "the kingdom of God was going to appear immediately" (Luke 19:11; cf. 24:21; Acts 1:6). As He introduced the parable, Christ indicated how believers ought to live in view of His coming earthly kingdom: "A nobleman went to a distant country to receive a kingdom for himself, and then return. And he called ten of his slaves, and gave them ten minas and said to them, 'Do business with this until I come back'" (Luke 19:12–13). Christians are to carry on with their everyday lives and responsibilities until Christ returns.

Because of the Thessalonians' skewed and unsettled outlook concerning the return of Christ, Paul needed to bring them down to earth and give them four practical exhortations for life until Jesus comes: love each other more, lead a quiet life, mind your own business, and work with your hands. Obedience to these commands would be a more appropriate testimony to unbelievers than the Thessalonians' extreme preoccupation with the Lord's return, which preoccupation came at the expense of caring for life's responsibilities.

LOVE EACH OTHER MORE

Now as to the love of the brethren, you have no need for anyone to write to you, for you yourselves are taught by God to love one another; for indeed you do practice it toward all the brethren who are in all Macedonia. But we urge you, brethren, to excel still more, (4:9–10)

The apostle Paul's exhortation to love contrasts with what he admonished them concerning immorality and lust (4:3–8; cf. Eph. 5:1–3). The phrase **now as to** introduces a change in subject (cf. 5:1), from a discussion about lust and sexual sin to a consideration of **the love of the brethren.** Believers must not only abstain from illicit forms of affection but also exchange all that for the kind of brotherly love characterized by only the purest motives and conduct. This would be the truest expression of the change regeneration had made in the Thessalonians.

Love of the brethren (*philadelphia*) originally referred to affection for blood relatives but is always used in the New Testament in reference to Christian affection (Rom. 12:10; Heb. 13:1; 1 Peter 1:22; 2 Peter 1:7). True biblical love, a recurring New Testament theme, always expresses itself in acts of service—meeting needs and doing things sacrificially to benefit others (Matt. 25:35–40; John 13:34–35; Rom. 12:15; 1 Cor. 12:26; 16:14; 2 Cor. 8:7; Gal. 5:13; 6:2; Eph. 5:2; Phil. 1:9; Col. 3:14; Heb. 6:10; 10:24; James 1:27; cf. Matt. 22:37–39; 1 Cor. 13:13; Gal. 5:22; 1 John 3:18).

Even as Paul mentioned it in his letter, it was only to affirm that there was **no need for anyone to write to** the Thessalonians (cf. 5:1) about **love of the brethren** because they were already **taught by God to love one another.** Paul's use of the emphatic expression **you yourselves** indicates that, apart from him or any other teacher, the believers were **taught by God** (*theodidaktos,* literally "God taught," and used only here in the New Testament) **to love one another.** That type of love was characteristic of the divine nature they now possessed.

Romans 5:5 supports that reality: "The love of God has been poured out within our hearts through the Holy Spirit who was given to us." At conversion Christians receive the Holy Spirit (Acts 2:38–39; 15:8; 1 Cor. 12:13) who indwells them (John 14:16–17; Rom. 8:11; Eph. 1:13–14; 5:18; 2 Tim. 1:14; 1 John 2:27; cf. Ezek. 36:27) and teaches them to love (John 14:26; 16:13; Rom. 5:3–5; 1 Cor. 2:10). Thus it is impossible for believers not to love (John 13:34–35; 1 John 3:17; 4:20–21; 5:1). In his first letter, the apostle John emphasized several times, positively and negatively, that truth. "The one who says he is in the Light and yet hates his brother is in the darkness until now. The one who loves his brother abides in the Light and there is no cause for stumbling in him" (1 John 2:9–10). "We know that we have passed out of death into life, because we love the brethren. He who does not love abides in death" (3:14; cf. 4:7–8, 12).

Love is from the familiar verb *agapaō,* related to the noun *agapē.* It expresses the purest, noblest form of love, which is volitionally driven, not motivated by superficial appearance, emotional attraction, or sentimental relationship. Paul was convinced that they **indeed** (in reality, without question) were exhibiting this love **toward all the brethren.** The Thessalonians demonstrated *agapē* love not only in their congregation but also for the other **brethren** (Christians) **who** were **in all Macedonia.** Paul planted churches in the other Macedonian towns of Philippi and Berea (Acts 16:12–40; 17:10–14; cf. 16:6–10), and his companions in Thessalonica, Silas and Timothy, also ministered in those towns (Acts 16:19, 25, 29; 17:14). Just as they had proclaimed their faith to the entire region (1 Thess. 1:8), thus demonstrating the reality of their conversion, so had the Thessalonians demonstrated their sanctification by manifesting spiritual love toward all. Believers all across their region (**Macedonia**) had received their generous hospitality, their kind acts of mercy, and their sacrificial deeds of service.

However, as exemplary as the Thessalonians' **love** was, it was not perfect. Even as Paul wanted to see them strengthen their faith (1 Thess. 3:10), he also sought to have them strengthen their love. Hence he again urged them **to excel still more** ("super abound") in this virtue (cf. 4:1). Specific opportunity remained for the Thessalonians' love to abound toward their pastors (5:12–13) and fellow believers (5:14–15, 26). Along similar lines, Peter encouraged his readers, "Since you have in obedience to the truth purified your souls for a sincere love of the brethren, fervently love one another from the heart" (1 Peter 1:22; cf. 2:17; 4:8; 2 Peter 1:7). "Fervently love one another" could literally be rendered "stretch out to the limits of love for one another."

Thus, in view of the truth that Jesus is returning, Paul urged the Thessalonians to love others more, not less. As they had in the past, they were to live in the hope of the Lord's return, yet never lose sight of the priority of love (cf. James 1:27; 2:15–16; 1 John 3:17–18).

LEAD A QUIET LIFE

and to make it your ambition to lead a quiet life (4:11*a*)

Though there is a great urgency in the imminent coming of the Lord, which prompts earnestness about proclaiming the gospel while there is yet time, the apostle Paul did not command the Thessalonians to live lives of noisy, frenetic evangelistic agitation. Instead, and as a result of their excelling still more in brotherly love, they were **to make it** their **ambition to lead a quiet life.**

In that phrase Paul used the two verb forms in almost a contradictory fashion. **Make it your ambition** (from *philotimeomai*) means to be zealous and strive eagerly, even to consider it an honor (as in Rom. 15:20; 2 Cor. 5:9), whereas **lead a quiet life** (from *hēsuchazō*) means to be silent (as in Luke 14:4; Acts 21:14), not speaking out inappropriately (see 1 Tim. 2:11–12), remaining at rest and tranquil (as in Luke 23:56). In anticipation of the Lord's return, believers are to lead peaceful lives, free of conflict and hostility toward others, which is a witness to the transforming power of the gospel.

The goal of Paul's directive, as it was when he instructed Timothy and the church at Ephesus to pray for those in authority, was that believers "may lead a tranquil and quiet life in all godliness and dignity" (1 Tim. 2:2; cf. Isa. 30:15; 32:17; 2 Thess. 3:12).

MIND YOUR OWN BUSINESS

and attend to your own business (4:11*b*)

The admonition to **attend to your own business** was a common one in secular Greek writings but used only here in the New Testament. It is not clear, however, whether Paul was speaking to a particular group within the Thessalonian church or addressing a specific issue. The apostle may have used the expression as a general exhortation for the

Thessalonians to concentrate on their own lives, take care of their own jobs, and not meddle in the affairs of others.

Paul issued them a follow-up exhortation in 2 Thessalonians 3:11-12: "For we hear that some among you are leading an undisciplined life, doing no work at all, but acting like busybodies. Now such persons we command and exhort in the Lord Jesus Christ to work in quiet fashion and eat their own bread." Those who did not **attend to** their **own business** were "acting like busybodies" (*periergazomai,* "wasting their labor"), running around meddling in everyone's problems.

Paul's antidote for such unwise, undisciplined behavior was that the Thessalonians work diligently and faithfully at their jobs (cf. Prov. 27:23-27; Gal. 6:5; Eph. 4:28; 6:5-7; Col. 3:22-24; 1 Tim. 6:1-2), stay out of other people's business, and lead quiet, unobtrusive lives that serve fellow believers and glorify the Lord before unbelievers.

WORK WITH YOUR HANDS

and work with your hands, just as we commanded you, so that you will behave properly toward outsiders and not be in any need. (4:11c-12)

The Greeks believed free men should never stoop to do manual labor. **Work** done **with** the **hands** was degrading to them; therefore, they made their slaves do all of it. However, with most of the early Christians coming from the working classes, the church dignified manual labor as an honorable endeavor. Therefore, Paul **commanded** the Thessalonians to persevere at their jobs.

Apparently many of the working class and slave laborers from among the Thessalonian converts had taken the attitude that, since they had become free in Christ, perhaps they were no longer subject to their masters and the obligations of their jobs. The new believers' preoccupation with Jesus' return may have intensified that attitude. Instead of supporting themselves through honest labor, some of the Thessalonians were likely depending on others' resources to sustain themselves for what they thought would be a brief interlude. Hence Paul exhorted them here to **work with** their own **hands** and warned them in 2 Thessalonians 3:10 that "if anyone is not willing to work, then he is not to eat, either."

The purpose underlying Paul's exhortation on work and motivating all his other injunctions—to love, to live quietly, and to mind their own business—was evangelistic, so that the Thessalonians would **behave properly toward outsiders.** For him, the key to evangelism was the integrity Christians manifest to a sinful, confused, and agitated world (cf.

Job 2:3; Ps. 26:1; Matt. 5:16; Phil. 2:15–16; 1 Peter 2:12). When believers display diligent work attitudes and habits and live in a loving and tranquil manner that respects others' privacy and does not intrude or gossip, it constitutes a powerful testimony to unbelievers and makes the gospel credible.

Furthermore, the Thessalonians' proper behavior (acceptable daily conduct) would ensure that they would **not be in any need.** If they obeyed Paul's exhortations, they would not always have to depend on more industrious Christians to supply their livelihood.

Such practical, straightforward living, as embodied in the apostle Paul's exhortations to the Thessalonians, is the foundation of all evangelism. Believers who sacrificially love other people, exhibit tranquil lives, conscientiously focus on keeping their own lives in order, and faithfully carry out their daily responsibilities in the workplace (thus avoiding any welfare dependence)—all the while proclaiming the gospel in light of the return of Christ—are the most effective witnesses to their unsaved neighbors and loved ones.

What Happens to Christians Who Die? (1 Thessalonians 4:13–18)

11

But we do not want you to be uninformed, brethren, about those who are asleep, so that you will not grieve as do the rest who have no hope. For if we believe that Jesus died and rose again, even so God will bring with Him those who have fallen asleep in Jesus. For this we say to you by the word of the Lord, that we who are alive and remain until the coming of the Lord, will not precede those who have fallen asleep. For the Lord Himself will descend from heaven with a shout, with the voice of the archangel and with the trumpet of God, and the dead in Christ will rise first. Then we who are alive and remain will be caught up together with them in the clouds to meet the Lord in the air, and so we shall always be with the Lord. Therefore comfort one another with these words. (4:13–18)

The study of the end times is the consuming passion of many in the church today. Sensational best-selling authors argue that current events fulfill their often dubious interpretations of biblical prophecy. Some claim to have figured out the secret that even Jesus in His Incarnation did not know—the time of the Second Coming (cf. Matt. 24:36). Tragically, some people get so caught up in the study of eschatology that they neglect the basic principles of spiritual growth and evangelism that the Second Coming is designed to motivate.

Of all the end-time events, the Rapture of the church seems to generate the most interest and discussion. The young church at Thessalonica also had questions about that event, so Paul addressed their concerns in this passage. But unlike most modern-day treatises on the subject, Paul's concern was not just doctrinal, but pastoral. His intent was not to give a detailed description of the Rapture, but to comfort the Thessalonians. The intent of the other two passages in the New Testament that discuss the Rapture (John 14:1–3; 1 Cor. 15:51–58) is also to provide comfort and encouragement for believers, not to fuel their prophetic speculations.

When Paul penned this epistle, the Thessalonians had been in Christ only for a few months. The apostle had taught them about end-time events, such as Christ's return to gather believers to Himself (e.g., 1:9–10; 2:19; 3:13). They also knew about the Day of the Lord (5:1–3), a time of coming judgment on the ungodly. But some issues about the details of their gathering to Christ troubled them. First, they seem to have been afraid that they had missed the Rapture, since the persecution they were suffering (3:3–4) caused some to fear they were in the Day of the Lord, which they obviously had not expected to experience (2 Thess. 2:1–2). Furthering that misconception were some false teachers, about whom Paul warned in 2 Thessalonians 2:2, "[Do] not be quickly shaken from your composure or be disturbed either by a spirit or a message or a letter as if from us, to the effect that the day of the Lord has come." But the persecution they were experiencing was not that associated with the Tribulation or the Day of the Lord. It was merely the persecution that all believers can expect (2 Tim. 3:12) and that Paul had warned the Thessalonians about (3:3–4).

The Thessalonians' fears that they were in the Day of the Lord and thus had missed the Rapture imply that the Rapture precedes the Tribulation. If the Thessalonians knew that the Rapture came at the end of the Tribulation, persecution would not have caused them to fear they had missed it. Instead, that persecution would have been a cause for joy, not concern. If the Day of the Lord had arrived, and the Rapture was after the Tribulation, then that blessed event would have been drawing near.

But of gravest concern to the Thessalonians were those of their number who had died. Would they receive their resurrection bodies at the Rapture, or would they have to wait until after the Tribulation? Would they miss the Rapture altogether? Would they therefore be second-class citizens in heaven? Were their deaths chastisement for their sins (cf. 1 Cor. 11:30)? They loved each other so deeply (cf. 4:9–10) that those thoughts greatly disturbed them. Their concern for those who had died shows that the Thessalonians believed the return of Christ was imminent and could happen in their lifetime. Otherwise, there would have been no reason for their concern. The Thessalonians' fear that their fellow believers who had died might miss the Rapture also implies that they believed in a pretribulational Rapture. If the Rapture precedes the Tribulation, they might have wondered when believers who died would receive their resurrection bodies. But there would have been no such confusion if the Rapture follows the Tribulation; all believers would then receive their resurrection bodies at the same time. Further, if they had been taught that they would go through the Tribulation, they would not have grieved for those who died, but rather would have been glad to see them spared from that horrible time.

Paul wrote this section of his epistle to alleviate the Thessalonians' grief and confusion. He was concerned that they **not . . . be uninformed . . . about those who are asleep** and thus **grieve as do the rest who have no hope.** Since their grief was based on ignorance, Paul comforted them by giving them knowledge.

The phrase **we do not want you to be uninformed** or its equivalent frequently introduces a new topic in Paul's epistles (cf. Rom. 1:13; 1 Cor. 10:1; 11:3; 12:1; 2 Cor. 1:8; Phil. 1:12; Col. 2:1). The conjunction **but** and the affectionate term **brethren** (cf. vv. 1, 10; 1:4; 2:1, 9, 14, 17; 3:7; 5:1, 4, 12, 14, 25) emphasize the change in subject and call attention to the new topic's importance. In this case, Paul introduced not only a new subject but also new revelation he had received "by the word of the Lord" (v. 15).

Since it was their primary concern, Paul first addressed the question of **those who are asleep.** While *koimaō* (**asleep**) can be used of normal sleep (Matt. 28:13; Luke 22:45; Acts 12:6), it more often refers to believers who have died (vv. 13–15; Matt. 27:52; John 11:11; Acts 7:60; 13:36; 1 Cor. 11:30; 15:6, 18, 20, 51; 2 Peter 3:4). In verse 14 **those who are asleep** are identified as "the dead in Christ." The present tense participle *koimōmenōn* (v. 13) refers to those who are continually falling **asleep** as a regular course of life in the church. They had grown increasingly concerned as their fellow believers continued to die.

It is important to remember that in the New Testament "sleep" applies only to the body, never to the soul. "Soul sleep," the false teaching that the souls of the dead are in a state of unconscious existence in the afterlife, is foreign to Scripture. In 2 Corinthians 5:8 Paul wrote that he "prefer[red] rather to be absent from the body and to be at home with the Lord," while in Philippians 1:23 he expressed his "desire to depart and be with Christ, for that is very much better." Those statements teach that believers go consciously into the Lord's presence at death, for how could unconsciousness be "very much better" than conscious communion with Jesus Christ in this life? Jesus promised the repentant thief on the cross,"Truly I say to you,today you shall be with Me in Paradise [heaven; cf. 2 Cor. 12:4; Rev. 2:7]" (Luke 23:43). Moses' and Elijah's souls were not asleep,since they appeared with Jesus at the Transfiguration (Matt. 17:3), nor are those of the Tribulation martyrs in Revelation 6:9–11,who will be awake and able to speak to God. After death the redeemed go consciously into the presence of the Lord, while the unsaved go into conscious punishment (Luke 16:19–31).

Paul related this information to the Thessalonians so that they would **not grieve.** There is a normal sorrow that accompanies the death of a loved one, caused by the pain of separation and loneliness. Jesus grieved over the death of Lazarus (John 11:33,35),and Paul exhorted the Romans to "weep with those who weep" (Rom. 12:15). However,the apostle did not have that kind of grief in mind here, but grief like **the rest who have no hope.** In Ephesians 2:12 Paul described unbelievers as "having no hope and without God in the world."There is an awful,terrifying, hopeless finality for unbelievers when a loved one dies, a sorrow unmitigated by any hope of reunion. Commenting on the hopeless despair of unbelievers in the ancient world,William Barclay writes,

> In the face of death the pagan world stood in despair. They met it with grim resignation and bleak hopelessness. Aeschylus wrote, "Once a man dies there is no resurrection."Theocritus wrote,"There is hope for those who are alive, but those who have died are without hope." Catullus wrote,"When once our brief light sets, there is one perpetual night through which we must sleep."On their tombstones grim epitaphs were carved. "I was not; I became; I am not; I care not." (*The Letters to the Philippians, Colossians, and Thessalonians*, rev. ed. [Louisville: Westminster, 1975], 203)

Even those pagans who believed in life after death did not have that hope confirmed by the Holy Spirit; they merely clung to it without affirmation from God. But Christians do not experience the hopeless grief of nonbelievers, for whom death marks the permanent severing of relationships. Unlike them, Christians never say a final farewell to each other; there will be a "gathering together [of all believers] to Him" (2 Thess. 2:1). Partings in this life are only temporary.

The Thessalonians' ignorance about the Rapture caused them to grieve. It was to give them hope and to comfort them that Paul discussed that momentous event, giving a fourfold description of it: its pillars, participants,plan,and profit.

THE PILLARS OF THE RAPTURE

For if we believe that Jesus died and rose again, even so God will bring with Him those who have fallen asleep in Jesus. For this we say to you by the word of the Lord, (4:14–15*a*)

The blessed hope of the Rapture is not based on the shifting sands of philosophical speculation. Nor is it religious mythology, a fable concocted by well-meaning people to comfort those who grieve. The marvelous truth that the Lord Jesus Christ will return to gather believers to Himself is based on three unshakeable pillars: the death of Christ, the resurrection of Christ, and the revelation of Christ.

THE DEATH OF CHRIST

For if we believe that Jesus died (4:14*a*)

If does not suggest uncertainty or doubt, but rather logical sequence. Paul says "since," or "based on the fact that" **we believe that Jesus died** certain things logically follow. The apostle's simple statement summarizes all the richness of Christ's atoning work, which provides the necessary foundation for the gathering of the church. His death satisfied the demands of God's righteousness, holiness, and justice by paying in full the penalty for believers' sins. By virtue of Christ's substitutionary death, when God "made Him who knew no sin to be sin on our behalf, so that we might become the righteousness of God in Him" (2 Cor. 5:21), Christians have been made acceptable to God and thus fit to be gathered into His presence.

Significantly, Paul did not use the metaphor of sleep to refer to Jesus, but says that He **died**. Jesus experienced the full fury of death in all its dimensions as He "bore our sins in His body on the cross, so that we might die to sin and live to righteousness" (1 Peter 2:24). His death transformed death into sleep for believers. T. E. Wilson notes, "Death has been changed to sleep by the work of Christ. It is an apt metaphor in which the whole concept of death is transformed. 'Christ made it the name for death in the dialect of the church (Acts 7:60) (Findlay)'" (*What the Bible Teaches: 1 and 2 Thessalonians* [Kilmarnock, Scotland: John Ritchie Ltd., 1983], 45). When believers die, their spirit goes immediately into conscious fellowship with the Lord, while their bodies temporarily sleep in the grave, awaiting the Rapture.

THE RESURRECTION OF CHRIST

and rose again, even so God will bring with Him those who have fallen asleep in Jesus. (4:14*b*)

The resurrection of Christ indicates that the Father accepted His sacrifice, enabling Him to "be just and the justifier of the one who has faith in Jesus" (Rom. 3:26). Paul taught that truth to the Romans when he wrote that "[Christ] was raised because of our justification" (Rom. 4:25). Christ's resurrection proves that He conquered sin and death, and became the source of resurrection life for every Christian. I. Howard Marshall writes, "The death of believers does not take place apart from Jesus, and hence Paul can conclude that God will raise them up and bring them into the presence of Jesus at the *parousia*. God will treat those who died trusting in Jesus in the same way He treated Jesus Himself, namely by resurrecting them" (*1 and 2 Thessalonians*, The New Century Bible Commentary [Grand Rapids: Eerdmans, 1983], 124).

The phrase **even so** links believers' resurrections inextricably to the resurrection of Christ. In John 14:19 Jesus said, "Because I live, you will live also." In the most detailed passage on the resurrection in Scripture, Paul wrote that "Christ [is] the first fruits, after that those who are Christ's at His coming" (1 Cor. 15:23). Earlier in that same epistle, he stated plainly, "Now God has not only raised the Lord, but will also raise us up through His power" (1 Cor. 6:14). In his second inspired letter to the Corinthians, Paul wrote, "He who raised the Lord Jesus will raise us also with Jesus" (2 Cor. 4:14).

To further assuage their fears, Paul reassured believers that **God will bring with Him** [Jesus] **those who have fallen asleep in Jesus.** Their fellow believers who died will not miss out on the Rapture but will return with Christ in glory. Some interpret the phrase **God will bring** to mean that the spirits of dead believers will come from heaven with Christ to meet their resurrected bodies. Others see in it the truth that at the Rapture, God will bring all believers, living and dead, back to heaven with Christ. While the first view is certainly true, the second one seems to be the emphasis of this passage.

What the passage does not teach is that the spirits of dead believers immediately return to earth with Christ for the establishing of the millennial kingdom. That view places the Rapture at the end of the Tribulation and essentially equates it with the Second Coming. It trivializes the Rapture into a meaningless sideshow that serves no purpose. Commenting on the pointlessness of a posttribulational Rapture, Thomas R. Edgar asks,

What can be the purpose for keeping a remnant alive through the tribulation so that some of the church survive and then take them out of their situation and make them the same as those who did not survive? Why keep them for this? [The] explanation that they provide an escort for Jesus does not hold up. Raptured living saints will be exactly the same as resurrected dead saints. Why cannot the dead believers fulfill this purpose? Why keep a remnant alive [through the Tribulation], then Rapture them and accomplish no more than by letting them die? There is no purpose or accomplishment in [such] a Rapture....

With all the saints of all the ages past and the armies [of angels] in heaven available as escorts and the fact that [raptured] saints provide no different escort than if they had been killed, why permit the church to suffer immensely, most believers [to] be killed, and spare a few for a Rapture which has no apparent purpose, immediately before the [Tribulation] period ends?... Is this the promise? You will suffer, be killed, but I will keep a few alive, and take them out just before the good times come. Such reasoning, of course, calls for some explanation of the apparent lack of purpose for a posttribulational Rapture of any sort.

We can note the following:

(1) An unusual, portentous, one-time event such as the Rapture must have a specific purpose. God has purposes for his actions. This purpose must be one that can be accomplished only by such an unusual event as a Rapture of living saints.

(2) This purpose must agree with God's general principles of operation.

(3) There is little or no apparent reason to Rapture believers when the Lord returns and just prior to setting up the long-awaited kingdom with all of its joyful prospects.

(4) There is good reason to deliver all who are already believers from the tribulation, where they would be special targets of persecution.

(5) To deliver from a period of universal trial and physical destruction such as the tribulation requires a removal from the earth by death or Rapture. Death is not appropriate as a promise in Rev. 3:10.

(6) Deliverance from the tribulation before it starts agrees with God's previous dealings with Noah and Lot and is directly stated as a principle of God's action toward believers in 2 Pet. 2:9. ("Robert H. Gundry and Revelation 3:10," *Grace Theological Journal* 3 [Spring 1982], 43–44)

The view that the raptured saints immediately return to earth with Christ also contradicts John 14:1–3:

> Do not let your heart be troubled; believe in God, believe also in Me. In My Father's house are many dwelling places; if it were not so, I would have told you; for I go to prepare a place for you. If I go and prepare a place for you, I will come again and receive you to Myself, that where I am, there you may be also.

The phrases "My Father's house" and "where I am" clearly refer to heaven (cf. John 7:34). Jesus promised to take believers back to heaven with Him when He returns to gather His people. There has to be a time interval, then, between Christ's return to gather His people (the Rapture) and His return to earth to establish the millennial kingdom (the Second Coming). During that interval between the Rapture and the Second Coming, the believers' judgment takes place (1 Cor. 3:11–15; 2 Cor. 5:10); a post-tribulational Rapture would leave no time for that event.

The phrase **in Jesus** is best understood as describing the circumstances in which the departed saints fell **asleep**. They died in the condition of being related to Jesus Christ. Paul used essentially the same phrase in 1 Corinthians 15:18 when he wrote of those "who have fallen asleep in Christ."

By demonstrating God's acceptance of His atoning sacrifice, the resurrection of Christ buttresses the first pillar on which the Rapture is based, the death of Christ.

THE REVELATION OF CHRIST

For this we say to you by the word of the Lord, (4:15*a*)

Paul's teaching on the Rapture was not his own speculation but direct revelation from God. The phrase **this we say to you by the word of the Lord** has the authoritative tone of an inspired writer revealing what God has disclosed to him. Some argue that **the word of the Lord** was something Jesus said while He was here on earth. But there are no close parallels to the present passage in any of the Gospels. Nor is there any specific teaching in the Gospels to which Paul could be alluding. Although the Lord talked in the Gospels about a trumpet and the gathering of the elect, the differences between those passages and the present one outweigh the similarities, as Robert L. Thomas notes:

Similarities between this passage in 1 Thessalonians and the gospel accounts include a trumpet (Matt. 24:31), a resurrection (John 11:25, 26), and a gathering of the elect (Matt. 24:31). . . . Yet dissimilarities between it and the canonical sayings of Christ far outweigh the resemblances. . . . Some of the differences between Matthew 24:30, 31 and 1 Thessalonians 4:15–17 are as follows: (1) In Matthew the Son of Man is coming on the clouds, . . . in 1 Thessalonians ascending believers are in them. (2) In the former the angels gather, in the latter the Son does so personally. (3) In the former nothing is said about resurrection, while in the latter this is the main theme. (4) Matthew records nothing about the order of ascent, which is the principal lesson in Thessalonians. ("1, 2 Thessalonians," in Frank E. Gaebelein, ed. *The Expositor's Bible Commentary,* vol. 11 [Grand Rapids: Zondervan, 1979], 276–77)

Nor is it likely that Paul is referring to a saying of Jesus not recorded in the Gospels (cf. Acts 20:35); he does not state or imply that he is directly quoting Christ's words. Further, in 1 Corinthians 15:51 Paul referred to the Rapture as a mystery; that is, a truth formerly hidden but now revealed. That indicates that Jesus did not disclose the details of the Rapture during His earthly ministry. (He referred to the Rapture in John 14:1–3 in a general, nonspecific sense.) Paul's teaching on the Rapture was new revelation, possibly given by God through a prophet (such as Agabus; Acts 21:11) but more likely directly to Paul himself. The Thessalonians had apparently been informed about the Day of the Lord judgment (5:1–2), but not about the preceding event—the Rapture of the church—until the Holy Spirit through Paul revealed it to them. This was new revelation, unveiled mystery.

The Rapture, then, does not rest on the shaky foundation of whimsical theological speculation, but on the sure foundation of death, resurrection, and revelation of the Lord Jesus Christ.

THE PARTICIPANTS OF THE RAPTURE

we who are alive and remain until the coming of the Lord, will not precede those who have fallen asleep. (4:15b)

Two groups of people will participate in the Rapture: those **who are alive** at **the coming of the Lord** and **those who have fallen asleep.** That Paul used the plural pronoun **we** indicates that he believed the Rapture could happen in his lifetime. He had a proper anticipation of and expectation for the Lord's return, though unlike many throughout church history, the apostle did not predict a specific time for it. He accepted Christ's words in Matthew 24:36, "But of that day and hour no one knows, not even the angels of heaven, nor the Son, but the Father alone," and Acts 1:7, "It is not for you to know times or epochs which the Father has fixed by His own authority." At the same time, Paul understood the parable of the wise and foolish virgins, which illustrates the foolishness of not being constantly prepared for the Lord's return (Matt. 25:1–13). The Lord expressed the point of that parable when He declared, "Be on the alert then, for you do not know the day nor the hour" (Matt. 25:13; cf. 24:45–51). Paul thus avoided both common errors regarding Christ's return; he neither got involved in date setting, nor did he push the return of Christ into the distant, nebulous future.

Several other passages express Paul's fervent hope and expectation that he himself might be among those **who are alive and remain until the coming of the Lord.** In Romans 13:11 he wrote, "Do this, knowing the time, that it is already the hour for you to awaken from sleep; for now salvation is nearer to us than when we believed." The salvation of which he wrote was the redemption of the body (Rom. 8:23) that takes place when Christ returns. In verse 12 Paul added, "The night [of man's sin and Satan's rule] is almost gone, and the day [of Christ's return] is near." He wrote to the Corinthians, "Now these things happened to them as an example, and they were written for our instruction, upon whom the ends of the ages have come" (1 Cor. 10:11). Paul knew he was in the messianic age, the period between Christ's first and second comings, the last days of human history. He likely had no idea that they would last as long as they have. Later in that epistle, Paul, as he does here in 1 Thessalonians, includes himself among those who might still be alive at the Rapture: "Behold, I tell you a mystery; we will not all sleep, but we will all be changed, in a moment, in the twinkling of an eye, at the last trumpet; for the trumpet will sound, and the dead will be raised imperishable, and we will be changed" (1 Cor. 15:51–52). As he concluded that letter Paul wrote, "If anyone does not love the Lord, he is to be accursed. Maranatha" (1 Cor. 16:22). *Maranatha* comes from two Aramaic words that mean "Oh Lord, come!" and expresses Paul's strong hope that the Lord would return soon. Earlier in this epistle, he commended the Thessalonians for waiting "for His Son from heaven" (1:10). He expressed his desire for them that God "may establish [their] hearts without blame in holiness before our God and Father at the coming of our Lord Jesus with all His saints" (3:13). Pronouncing a final benediction as he concluded this letter, Paul wrote, "Now may the God of peace Himself sanctify you entirely; and may your spirit and soul and body be preserved complete, without blame at the coming of our Lord Jesus Christ" (5:23). The apostle wrote to Titus that he was "looking for the blessed hope and the appearing of the glory of our great God and Savior, Christ Jesus" (Titus 2:13).

On the other hand, Paul fully realized that he might die before the Rapture. In 1 Corinthians 6:14 he acknowledged that he might be among those resurrected at the Rapture: "Now God has not only raised the Lord, but will also raise us up through His power." He affirmed to the Philippians his desire that "Christ will even now, as always, be exalted in my body, whether by life or by death" (Phil. 1:20). At the end of his life, sensing his imminent death, he wrote to Timothy, "For I am already being poured out as a drink offering, and the time of my departure has come. I have fought the good fight, I have finished the course, I have kept the faith" (2 Tim. 4:6–7). While acknowledging both possibilities, Paul used **we** because when he wrote, it was still possible for the Lord to return in his lifetime. By so doing, he conveyed to the Thessalonians his own long-ing for Christ's imminent return.

Paul lived in constant expectation of Christ's return. But the apos-tle nevertheless reassured the Thessalonians that those of their number who had died would not miss the Rapture, which will also include **those who have fallen asleep**. Moreover, the living **will not precede** the dead. They will not take precedence over them or gain an advantage over them. Those who die before the Rapture will in no sense be inferior to those who are alive. All Christians will participate in the Rapture.

THE PLAN OF THE RAPTURE

For the Lord Himself will descend from heaven with a shout, with the voice of the archangel and with the trumpet of God, and the dead in Christ will rise first. Then we who are alive and remain will be caught up together with them in the clouds to meet the Lord in the air, and so we shall always be with the Lord. (4:16–17)

Having reassured the Thessalonians that their departed loved ones will not miss out on the Rapture, Paul gave a step-by-step descrip-tion of that event.

First, **the Lord Himself** will return for His church. He will not send angels for it, in contrast to the gathering of the elect that takes place at the Second Coming (Mark 13:26–27).

Second, Jesus **will descend from heaven,** where He has been since His ascension (Acts 1:9–11). Earlier in this epistle, Paul commend-ed the Thessalonians because they were waiting "for His Son from heav-en, whom He raised from the dead, that is Jesus" (1:10). At his trial before the Sanhedrin, Stephen cried out, "Behold, I see the heavens opened up and the Son of Man standing at the right hand of God" (Acts 7:56). The writer of Hebrews said of Christ, "When He had made purification of sins, He sat down at the right hand of the Majesty on high" (Heb. 1:3).

Third, when Jesus comes down from heaven, He will do so **with a shout**. *Keleusma* (command) has a military ring to it, as if the Commander is calling His troops to fall in. The dead saints in their resurrected bodies will join the raptured living believers in the ranks. The Lord's shout of command will be similar to His raising of Lazarus, when "He cried out with a loud voice, 'Lazarus, come forth'" (John 11:43). This is the hour "when the dead will hear the voice of the Son of God, and those who hear will live" (John 5:25). The righteous dead of the church age will be the first to rise—a truth that must have greatly comforted the anxious Thessalonians.

Fourth, **the voice of the archangel** will sound. There is no definite article in the Greek text, which literally reads, "an archangel." In Jude 9, the only other passage in Scripture that mentions an archangel, the archangel is Michael. Scripture does not say whether or not he is the only archangel (there were seven archangels according to Jewish tradition). Thus, it is impossible to say who the **archangel** whose **voice** will be heard at that Rapture is. Whoever he is, he adds his **voice** to the Lord's shout of command.

Fifth, to the Lord's command and the archangel's voice will be added the sounding of **the trumpet of God** (cf. 1 Cor. 15:52). Trumpets were used in Scripture for many reasons. They sounded at Israel's feasts (Num. 10:10), celebrations (2 Sam. 6:15), and convocations (Lev. 23:24), to sound an alarm in time of war (Num. 10:9) or for any other reason it was necessary to gather a crowd (Num. 10:2; Judg. 6:34) or make an announcement (1 Sam. 13:3; 2 Sam. 15:10; 20:1; 1 Kings 1:34, 39, 41). The **trumpet** at the Rapture has no connection to the trumpets of judgment in Revelation 8–11. It seems to have a twofold purpose: to assemble God's people (cf. Ex. 19:16–19) and to signal His deliverance of them (cf. Zech. 1:16; 9:14–16).

Sixth, **the dead in Christ will rise first**. As noted above, the **dead** saints will in no way be inferior to those alive at the Rapture. In fact, they **will rise first**, their glorified bodies joining with their glorified spirits to make them into the image of Christ, as the apostle John wrote: "We know that when He appears, we will be like Him, because we will see Him just as He is" (1 John 3:2). Those who were **in Christ** in life will be so in death; death cannot separate believers from God (Rom. 8:38): "therefore whether we live or die, we are the Lord's" (Rom. 14:8).

Finally, those believers **who are alive and remain will be caught up together** with the dead saints **in the clouds to meet the Lord in the air, and so we shall always be with the Lord.** *Harpazō* (**caught up**) refers to a strong, irresistible, even violent act. In Matthew 11:12 it describes the taking of the kingdom of heaven by force. In John 10:12 it describes a wolf snatching sheep; in John 10:28–29 it speaks of the impossibility of anyone's snatching believers out of the hands of Jesus Christ and God the Father; in Acts 8:39 it speaks of Philip's being snatched away from the Ethiopian eunuch; and in 2 Corinthians 12:2,4 it describes Paul's being caught up into the third heaven. It is when living believers are **caught up** that they are transformed and receive their glorified bodies (Phil. 3:21). "In a moment, in the twinkling of an eye" believers "will be changed" (1 Cor. 15:52), rescued from the grasp of Satan, the fallen flesh, the evil world system, and the coming wrath of God.

The time of the Rapture cannot be discerned from this passage alone. But when it is read with other Rapture texts (John 14:3; Rev. 3:10; cf. 1 Cor. 15:51–52; Phil. 3:20–21), and compared to judgment texts (Matt. 13:34–50; 24:29–44; Rev. 19:11–21), it is clear that there is no mention of judgment at all in the Rapture passages, whereas the others major on judgment. It is therefore necessary to conclude that the Rapture occurs at a time other than the judgment.

It is best, then, to separate the two events. That initiates the case for the Rapture to occur imminently, before the elements of judgment described in Scripture as leading up to the Second Coming in judgment.

Again, no solitary text of Scripture makes the entire case for the pretribulation Rapture. However, when one considers all the New Testament evidence, a very compelling case for the pretribulational position emerges, which answers more questions and solves more problems than any other Rapture position. The following arguments present a strong case in favor of the pretribulation Rapture.

First, the earthly kingdom of Christ promised in Revelation 6–18 does not mention the church as being on earth. Because Revelation 1–3 uses the Greek word for church nineteen times, one would reasonably assume that if the church were on earth rather than in heaven in chapters 6–18, they would use "church" with similar frequency, but such is not the case. Therefore, one can assume that the church is not present on the earth during the period of tribulation described in Revelation 6–18 and that therefore the Lord has removed it from the earth and relocated it to heaven by means of the Rapture.

Second, Revelation 19 does not mention a Rapture even though that is where a posttribulational Rapture (if true) would logically occur. Thus, one can conclude that the Rapture will have already occurred.

Third, a posttribulational Rapture renders the Rapture concept itself inconsequential. If God preserves the church during the Tribulation, as posttribulationists assert, then why have a Rapture at all? It makes no sense to Rapture believers from earth to heaven for no apparent purpose other than to return them immediately with Christ to earth. Further, a posttribulational Rapture makes the unique separation of the sheep (believers) from the goats (unbelievers) at the return of Christ in judgment redundant because a posttribulational Rapture would have already accomplished that.

Fourth, if God raptures and glorifies all believers just prior to the inauguration of the millennial kingdom (as a posttribulational Rapture demands), no one would be left to populate and propagate the earthly kingdom of Christ promised to Israel. It is not within the Lord's plan and purpose to use glorified individuals to propagate the earth during the Millennium. Therefore, the Rapture needs to occur earlier so that after God has raptured all believers, He can save more souls—including Israel's remnant—during the seven-year Tribulation. Those people can then enter the millennial kingdom in earthly form. The most reasonable possibility for this scenario is the pretribulational Rapture.

Fifth, the New Testament does not warn of an impending tribulation, such as is experienced during Daniel's seventieth week, for church-age believers. It does warn of error and false prophets (Acts 20:29–30; 2 Peter 2:1; 1 John 4:1–3), against ungodly living (Eph. 4:25–5:7; 1 Thess. 4:3–8; Heb. 12:1), and of present tribulation (1 Thess. 2:14–16; 2 Thess. 1:4; all of 2 Peter). Thus it is incongruous that the New Testament would be silent concerning such a traumatic change as Daniel's seventieth week if posttribulationism were true.

Sixth, Paul's instructions here to the Thessalonians demand a pretribulational Rapture because, if Paul were teaching them posttribulationism, one would expect them to rejoice that loved ones were home with the Lord and spared the horrors of the Tribulation. But, in actuality, the Thessalonians grieved. In addition, with a posttribulational teaching one would expect them to sorrow over their own impending trial and inquire about their future doom; however, they expressed no such dread or questioning. Further, one might expect Paul to instruct and exhort them concerning such a supreme test as the Tribulation, but Paul wrote only about the hope of the Rapture.

Seventh, the sequence of events at Christ's coming following the Tribulation demands a pretribulational Rapture. A comparing and contrasting of Rapture passages with Second Coming passages yields strong indicators that the Rapture could not be posttribulational. For example: (a) at the Rapture, Christ gathers His own (vv. 16–17 of the present passage), but at the Second Coming, angels gather the elect (Matt. 24:31); (b) at the Rapture, resurrection is prominent (vv. 15–16 of the present passage), but regarding the Second Coming, Scripture does not mention the resurrection; (c) at the Rapture, Christ comes to reward believers (v. 17 of the present passage), but at the Second Coming, Christ comes to judge the earth (Matt. 25:31–46); (d) at the Rapture, the Lord snatches away true believers from the earth (vv. 15–17 of the present passage), but at the Second Coming, He takes away unbelievers (Matt. 24:37–41); (e) at the Rapture, unbelievers remain on the earth, whereas at the Second Coming, believers remain on the earth; (f) concerning the Rapture, Scripture does not mention the establishment of Christ's kingdom, but at His second coming, Christ sets up His kingdom; and (g) at the Rapture, believers will receive glorified bodies, whereas at the Second Coming, no one will receive glorified bodies.

Eighth, certain of Jesus' teachings demand a pretribulational Rapture. For instance, the parable of the wheat and the tares (Matt. 13:24–30) portrays the reapers (angels) removing the tares (unbelievers) from among the wheat (believers) in order to judge the tares, which demonstrates that at the Second Coming, the Lord has unbelievers removed from among believers. However, at the Rapture, He takes believers from among unbelievers. This is also true in the parable of the dragnet (Matt. 13:47–50) and in the discussion of the days of Noah and the description of the nations' judgment, both in the Olivet Discourse (Matt. 24–25).

Ninth, Revelation 3:10 teaches that the Lord will remove the church prior to the Tribulation. In the Greek, the phrase "I also will keep you from" can mean nothing other than "I will prevent you from entering into." Jesus Christ will honor the church by preventing it from entering the hour of testing, namely Daniel's seventieth week, which is about to come upon the entire world. Only a pretribulational Rapture can explain how this will happen.

Thus, the Rapture (being **caught up**) must be pretribulational, before the wrath of God described in the Tribulation (Rev. 6–19). At the Rapture, living believers will be caught up **together with** the believers raised from the dead as the church triumphant joins the church militant to become the church glorified. **Clouds** are often associated in Scripture with divine appearances. When God appeared at Mount Sinai, "The glory of the Lord rested on Mount Sinai, and the cloud covered it for six days" (Ex. 24:16). Clouds marked God's presence in the tabernacle (Ex. 40:34), the temple (1 Kings 8:10), and at Christ's transfiguration (Matt. 17:5). At His ascension Christ "was lifted up while they were looking on, and a cloud received Him out of their sight" (Acts 1:9).

Some argue that the word **meet** suggests meeting a dignitary, king, or famous person and escorting him back to his city. They then argue that after the meeting described in this passage, believers will return to earth with Christ. But such an analogy is arbitrary and assumes a technical meaning for **meet** not required by either the word or the context. As noted earlier in this chapter, that explanation also renders the Rapture pointless; why have believers **meet** Christ **in the air** and immediately return to earth? Why should they not just meet Him when He gets here? Gleason L. Archer comments, "The most that can be said of such a

'Rapture' is that it is a rather secondary sideshow of minimal importance" (Gleason L. Archer, Jr., Paul D. Feinberg, Douglas J. Moo, and Richard Reiter, *The Rapture: Pre-, Mid-, or Post-Tribulational?* [Grand Rapids: Zondervan, 1984], 215). As was also noted earlier in this chapter, a posttribulational Rapture contradicts the teaching of Christ in John 14:1–3 that He will return to take believers to heaven, not immediately back to earth.

The final step in the plan of the Rapture is the blessed, comforting truth that after Christ returns to gather us (believers) to Himself, **we shall always be with the Lord.**

THE PROFIT OF THE RAPTURE

Therefore comfort one another with these words. (4:18)

The benefit of understanding the Rapture is not to fill the gaps in one's eschatological scheme. As noted at the beginning of this chapter, Paul's goal in teaching the Thessalonians about the Rapture was to **comfort** them. The "God of all comfort" (2 Cor. 1:3) grants to all believers the encouraging comfort of knowing that Christ will one day return for them. At that monumental event, the dead in Christ will be raised, join with the living saints in experiencing a complete transformation of body and soul, and be with God forever. Therefore, there was no need for the Thessalonians to grieve or sorrow over their fellow believers who had died. No wonder Paul calls the return of Christ "the blessed hope" (Titus 2:13).

The Day of the Lord (1 Thessalonians 5:1–3)

12

Now as to the times and the epochs, brethren, you have no need of anything to be written to you. For you yourselves know full well that the day of the Lord will come just like a thief in the night. While they are saying, "Peace and safety!" then destruction will come upon them suddenly like labor pains upon a woman with child, and they will not escape. (5:1–3)

After a century that experienced the terror of two world wars, the horror of the Holocaust, the brutality of the Korean conflict, the hopeless futility of the war in Vietnam, as well as innumerable revolutions, riots, assassinations, and acts of terrorism, a crucial question is, Where (if anywhere) is history going? Does it have a purpose, goal, or meaning? Or is it merely an endless succession of events leading nowhere? How are we to live, work, play, and love amidst the chaos, confusion, and meaninglessness of life? In his book *Christ the Meaning of History*, Hendrikus Berkhof writes,

> Our generation is strangled by fear: fear for man, for his future, and for the direction in which we are driven against our will and desire. And out of this comes a cry for illumination concerning the meaning of the existence of mankind, and concerning the goal to which we are directed. It

is a cry for an answer to the old question of the meaning of history. ([Grand Rapids: Baker, 1979], 13)

There are three popular contemporary views of history. The first is the cyclical view, which sees history as an endless circle, spiraling back through the same things over and over again. In the cynical words of the Preacher, "That which has been is that which will be, and that which has been done is that which will be done. So there is nothing new under the sun" (Eccl. 1:9). The cyclical view was popular among the ancient Greeks. Today it characterizes much of Eastern thought—especially Hinduism, with its continual cycle of death and rebirth (*samsara*). Through the influence of the New Age movement, it has also become increasingly popular in the West.

But the cyclical view evacuates any meaning or purpose from history, as John Marsh notes:

> If such a view be true, then historical existence has been deprived of its significance. What I do now I have done in a previous world cycle, and will do again in future world cycles. Responsibility and decision disappear, and with them any real significance to historical life, which in fact becomes a rather grandiose natural cycle. Just as the corn is sown, grows, and ripens each year, so will the events of history recur time after time. Moreover, if all that can happen is the constant repetition of an event-cycle, there is no possibility of meaning in the cycle itself. It achieves nothing in itself, neither can it contribute to anything outside itself. The events of history are devoid of significance. (*The Fulness of Time* [London: Nisbet, 1952], 167)

A second view of history is that of atheistic naturalism. Unlike the cyclical view, this view sees history as linear and non-repetitive. But like the cyclical view, the naturalistic view assigns no meaning to history. History may be proceeding in a straight line instead of going around in circles, but it is not leading anywhere; it has no ultimate goal or purpose. Anthony Hoekema notes that according to this view, "No significant pattern can be found in history, no movement toward a goal; only a meaningless succession of events" (*The Bible and the Future* [Grand Rapids: Eerdmans, 1989], 25). The celebrated British philosopher and vocal critic of Christianity Bertrand Russell admitted, "There is no law of cosmic progress. . . . From evolution, so far as our present knowledge shows, no ultimately optimistic philosophy can be validly inferred" (cited in Henry M. Morris, *That Their Words May Be Used Against Them* [Green Forest, Ark.: Master Books, 1997], 418). The zealous defender of Darwinism Richard Dawkins acknowledges, "Evolution has no long-term goal. There is no long distance target, no final perfection to serve as a criterion for selection, although human vanity cherishes the absurd notion that our species is the final goal of evolution" (cited in Morris, 412). Thus, human history is just one phase of the meaningless flow of evolutionary history. The influential evolutionary paleontologist George Gaylord Simpson put it bluntly: "Man is the result of a purposeless and natural process that did not have him in mind" (cited in Phillip E. Johnson, *Darwin on Trial* [Downers Grove, Ill.: InterVarsity, 1993], 116). Such a hopeless, purposeless, empty view of history reduces man to insignificance, to nothing more than a "chance configuration of atoms in the slip stream of meaningless chance history" (Francis A. Schaeffer, *Death in the City* [Downers Grove, Ill.: InterVarsity, 1972], 18).

The Christian view of history stands in sharp contrast to the hopeless despair of the first two views. The Bible reveals history to be the outworking of the purposeful plan of the sovereign, creator God. Job confessed, "I know that You can do all things, and that no purpose of Yours can be thwarted" (Job 42:2). Through the prophet Isaiah, God declared, "My purpose will be established, and I will accomplish all My good pleasure" (Isa. 46:10), and "I act and who can reverse it?" (Isa. 43:13). Jesus Christ is the central figure in history; the Old Testament points to His coming, and the New Testament describes and expounds His life, death, resurrection, and second coming.

As history continues to unfold the eternally planned purposes of God, one event looms large on the horizon: the Day of the Lord. That event will mark the end of man's day, as God acts in judgment to take back direct control of the earth from the usurpers (both human and demonic) who presently rule it. It will be an unprecedented time of cataclysmic judgment on all unrepentant sinners.

Most preachers strive to be positive, affirming, and comforting, and hence rarely preach on God's wrath, vengeance, and judgment. But to ignore such truth is to "shrink from declaring . . . the whole purpose of God" (Acts 20:27). It is to forsake the preacher's responsibility to "preach the word; be ready in season and out of season; reprove, rebuke, exhort, with great patience and instruction" (2 Tim. 4:2). Scripture repeatedly warns of God's judgment and the eternal punishment of unbelievers. Judgment was a major emphasis of both the Old Testament prophets and the New Testament apostles. But the one who spoke most often about judgment was the Lord Jesus Christ. All true preachers must follow His example, as did Paul (cf. 1:10; 2:16; 4:6; 5:9; 2 Thess. 1:5–9).

Paul had preached the sobering truth about the Day of the Lord to the Thessalonians during his relatively brief stay in their city (2 Thess. 2:5). After he left, questions arose in their minds about both the Rapture and the Day of the Lord. Timothy likely conveyed those concerns to Paul when he returned from his trip to Thessalonica (3:2, 6). Having answered their questions about the Rapture in the previous passage (4:13–18), Paul now dealt with the Thessalonians' concerns about the Day of the Lord. From the blessed event of the catching away of the church, Paul turned to the horrible event that follows it—the destruction of the wicked rejecters of the Lord Jesus Christ. As it was in dealing with the Rapture, Paul's purpose in writing this section on the Day of the Lord was not primarily theological and eschatological but pastoral and practical.

Paul introduced his discussion of the Day of the Lord with the transitional phrase *peri de* (**now as to**). The apostle used that phrase frequently in his writings to signal a change of subject (e.g., 4:9; 1 Cor. 7:1, 25; 8:1; 12:1; 16:1, 12). Paul's use of the affectionate term **brethren** as a call to renewed attention also suggests a new topic (cf. 2:1, 17; 4:1, 13). In his discussion of end-time events, Paul turned from the Rapture (4:13–18) to a new subject, the Day of the Lord.

The phrase **the times** (*chronos*) **and the epochs** (*kairos*) refers in a general sense to the end times (cf. Dan. 2:21; Acts 1:7). Though the two words may be used here in an overlapping sense, there is a subtle difference in meaning between them. *Chronos* refers to chronological time, to clock time or calendar time. *Kairos*, on the other hand, views time in terms of events, eras, or seasons, such as the times of the Gentiles (Luke 21:24). Taken together, the two terms suggest that the Thessalonians were curious about the timing of the end-time events. That both nouns are plural indicates that many different time periods (cf. Dan. 7:25; 9:24–27; 12:7, 11, 12; Rev. 11:2–3; 13:5) and events (e.g., the Rapture, the rise of Antichrist, the salvation of Israel, the seal, trumpet, and bowl judgments, the Second Coming, the battle of Armageddon, the sheep and goat judgment, the binding of Satan, the millennial kingdom, the loosing of Satan and subsequent worldwide rebellion at the end of the Millennium, the Great White Throne judgment, and the new heavens and the new earth) make up the end times.

Specifically, the congregation wanted to know when the Rapture and the Day of the Lord would take place. As noted in the previous chapter of this volume, they were concerned that they had somehow missed the Rapture and were in the Day of the Lord (cf. 2 Thess. 2:1–2). In verse 4 of this chapter, Paul reassured them that they would not experience the Day of the Lord. (See the discussion of 5:4–11 in chapter 13 of this volume.)

But to their question as to when the Day of the Lord would come, Paul replied, **you have no need of anything to be written to you.** The Lord Jesus Christ gave a similar answer to His disciples; when they asked Him, "Lord, is it at this time You are restoring the kingdom to Israel?" (Acts 1:6) He replied, "It is not for you to know times or epochs which the Father has fixed by His own authority" (Acts 1:7; cf. Matt. 24:36, 44, 50; 25:13). The Thessalonians did not need to know when the Day of the Lord would come; they already knew all that God intended them to know. To know when the Day of the Lord will come would foster spiritual indifference if it were still a long way off, or panic if it were coming soon. Being spiritually prepared for the return of Christ does not involve date setting, clock-watching, or sign seeking. God has chosen not to reveal the specific time of end-time events so that all believers will live in constant anticipation of them.

As he replied to the Thessalonians' questions about the Day of the Lord, Paul discussed three aspects of that momentous event: its coming, character, and completeness.

THE COMING OF THE DAY OF THE LORD

For you yourselves know full well that the day of the Lord will come just like a thief in the night. While they are saying, "Peace and safety!" (5:2–3*a*)

What the Thessalonians already knew **full well** was that **the day of the Lord will come just like a thief in the night**—suddenly, unexpectedly, unwelcomed, and harmfully. It will be a terrifying shock to those who do not know the Lord Jesus Christ. *Akribōs* (**full well**) describes careful, accurate, painstaking research (cf. Matt. 2:8; Luke 1:3; Acts 18:25). The Thessalonians knew for certain that the Day of the Lord will arrive unexpectedly. Obviously, then, the time of its arrival will not be revealed; no sane **thief** announces in advance what time of the **night** he plans to rob someone.

In the Olivet Discourse—Jesus' own sermon on His second coming—He used the imagery of **a thief in the night** to refer to the unexpectedness of His return: "But be sure of this, that if the head of the house had known at what time of the night the thief was coming, he would have been on the alert and would not have allowed his house to be broken into" (Matt. 24:43; cf. Rev. 16:15). Like the Day of the Lord, the exact time of the Second Coming will not be revealed, though there will be signs that Christ's return is imminent (Matt. 24:4–33). Jesus put every generation on notice that they must live in expectation of His return and the events of the Day of the Lord that lead up to it.

The metaphor of a **thief** coming is never used to refer to the Rapture of the church. It describes the coming of the Lord in judgment at the end of the seven-year Tribulation period, and the judgment at the end of the thousand-year kingdom of Christ on earth (2 Peter 3:10). A **thief** coming is not a hopeful, joyful event of deliverance, but an unexpected calamity.

The important biblical term **the day of the Lord** describes God's cataclysmic future judgment on the wicked. It is mentioned explicitly nineteen times in the Old Testament (Isa. 2:12; 13:6, 9; Ezek. 13:5; 30:3; Joel 1:15; 2:1, 11, 31; 3:14; Amos 5:18 [2 times], 20; Obad. 15; Zeph. 1:7, 14 [2 times]; Zech. 14:1; Mal. 4:5) and four times in the New Testament (cf. Acts 2:20; 2 Thess. 2:2; 2 Peter 3:10), and is alluded to in other passages (cf. Rev. 6:17; 16:14). It will be the time when God pours out His fury on the wicked; in fact, Scripture three times calls the Day of the Lord the "day of vengeance" (Isa. 34:8; 61:2; 63:4).

The Day of the Lord must be distinguished from the "day of Christ" (Phil. 1:10; 2:16), the "day of Christ Jesus" (Phil. 1:6), the "day of the Lord Jesus" (1 Cor. 5:5), and the "day of our Lord Jesus Christ" (1 Cor. 1:8); all of those terms refer to the time when believers will receive their rewards from the Lord Jesus Christ (Rom. 14:10; 1 Cor. 3:11–14; 4:1–5; 2 Cor. 5:9–10). The Day of the Lord must also be distinguished from the "day of God" (2 Peter 3:12), which refers to the eternal state.

The Old Testament passages dealing with the Day of the Lord often convey a sense of imminence, nearness, and expectation: "Wail, for the day of the Lord is near!" (Isa. 13:6); "For the day is near, even the day of the Lord is near" (Ezek. 30:3); "For the day of the Lord is near" (Joel 1:15); "Let all the inhabitants of the land tremble, for the day of the Lord is coming; surely it is near" (Joel 2:1); "Multitudes, multitudes in the valley of decision! For the day of the Lord is near in the valley of decision" (Joel 3:14); "For the day of the Lord draws near on all the nations" (Obad. 15); "Be silent before the Lord God! For the day of the Lord is near" (Zeph. 1:7); "Near is the great day of the Lord, near and coming very quickly" (Zeph. 1:14).

The Old Testament prophets envisioned historical days of the Lord that would preview the final, eschatological Day of the Lord. God often used providentially controlled circumstances, such as using one nation to destroy another, or natural disasters, as instruments of His judgment. But those historical days of the Lord were merely a prelude to the final eschatological Day of the Lord, which will be far greater in extent and more terrible in its destruction.

The Old Testament Day of the Lord passages often have both a near and a far fulfillment, as does much Old Testament prophecy. In Psalm 69:9 David wrote, "Zeal for Your house has consumed me, and the reproaches of those who reproach You have fallen on me"; yet after Jesus cleansed the temple, "His disciples remembered that it was written, 'zeal for Your house will consume me'" (John 2:17). Psalm 22 has in view both David's suffering and the crucifixion of Christ. Isaiah 7:14 refers both to the historical birth of Isaiah's son and prophetically to the virgin birth of Christ. Similarly, Isaiah 13:6 points to a historical day of the Lord, while verse 9 of that same chapter has the final, eschatological Day of the Lord in view. Joel 1:15; 2:1, 11 describe a historical day of the Lord; Joel 3:1–14 the eschatological Day of the Lord. Obadiah 1–14 depicts the historical day of the Lord in which Edom was judged; verses 15–21 describe the eschatological Day of the Lord. Zephaniah 1:7–14 predicts an imminent, historical day of the Lord judgment on Judah, which was fulfilled shortly afterward in the Babylonian Captivity; 3:8–20 predicts the final Day of the Lord.

Summarizing the interplay of the historical and eschatological Days of the Lord in the writings of the Old Testament prophets, George Eldon Ladd writes,

> The Day of the Lord was near because God was about to act; and the historical event was in a real sense an anticipation of the final eschatological deed. . . . The historical imminence of the Day of the Lord did not include all that the Day of the Lord meant; history and eschatology were held in dynamic tension, for *both were the Day of the Lord.* (The Presence of the Future [Grand Rapids: Eerdmans, 1976], 320. Italics in original.)

Unlike the Rapture, which will not be preceded by any signs, there will be several precursors that will herald the arrival of the eschatological Day of the Lord. They will not, however, reveal the specific time that it will come.

The first sign that the Day of the Lord is drawing near will be the appearance of an Elijah-like forerunner. In Malachi 4:5 the Lord declared, "Behold, I am going to send you Elijah the prophet before the coming of the great and terrible day of the Lord." Like many other Day of the Lord prophecies, this one had a historical fulfillment in John the Baptist (Luke 1:17) and will also have a future fulfillment in the end times. Some have speculated that this forerunner will be one of the two witnesses (Rev. 11:3). Whoever he is, he will herald the imminent return of the Lord Jesus Christ and the arrival of the Day of the Lord that precedes it.

Second, a worldwide rebellion against God and His Word will precede the Day of the Lord. In 2 Thessalonians 2:3 Paul reminded the Thessalonians that the Day of the Lord (v. 2) "will not come unless the apostasy comes first." That apostasy will include a worldwide system of false religion. (See the discussion of 2 Thessalonians 2:3 in chapter 23 of this volume.)

Third, the Day of the Lord will not come until "the man of lawlessness is revealed, the son of destruction, who opposes and exalts himself above every so-called god or object of worship, so that he takes his seat in the temple of God, displaying himself as being God" (2 Thess. 2:3–4).

The rise of Antichrist and his desecration of the temple (Dan. 9:27; 11:31; 12:11; Matt. 24:15) will precede the coming of the Day of the Lord. (See the discussion of 2:3–4 in chapter 23 of this volume.)

Fourth, the nations will begin to assemble in the valley of decision for the battle of Armageddon (Joel 3:2–14).

Fifth, dramatic signs in the heavens will precede the coming of the Day of the Lord; God "will display wonders in the sky and on the earth, blood, fire and columns of smoke. The sun will be turned into darkness and the moon into blood before the great and awesome day of the Lord comes. . . . The sun and moon grow dark and the stars lose their brightness" (Joel 2:30–31; 3:15; cf. Isa. 13:10; Matt. 24:29; Luke 21:25; Rev. 6:12–13; 8:12).

In the Olivet Discourse, Jesus gave another list of precursors to the Day of the Lord—a list paralleled in the first five seal judgments in Revelation. The Lord described these judgments as "birth pangs" (Matt. 24:8)—an apt analogy to the labor pains that come suddenly upon a pregnant woman and intensify until she gives birth. Just as a woman's labor pains warn her that her time to give birth is imminent, so these birth pangs should warn people that the Day of the Lord is near.

The first birth pang is a proliferation of false teachers, false prophets, and false religions. They will succeed in explaining away the signs so that people will not recognize that they point to the Day of the Lord. In Matthew 24:5 Jesus warned, "Many will come in My name, saying, 'I am the Christ,' and will mislead many." But the epitome of all of them will be the ultimate false prophet, the final world ruler, the Antichrist. He is known in Scripture by many names: the little horn (Dan. 7:8), the king who does as he pleases (Dan. 11:36–45), the man of lawlessness (2 Thess. 2:3), the son of destruction (2 Thess. 2:3), and the beast (Rev. 11:7; 13:2–8). This demon-indwelled individual will be a man of charisma, charm, persuasiveness, brilliance, authority, ruthlessness—and consummate wickedness. He will at first appear to be everything a desperate world longs for—a man who will unify the world under his leadership and usher in a short-lived era of global peace and prosperity. He will even make a seven-year pact with Israel (Dan. 9:27), promising to provide the security and protection that nation has always longed for. But halfway through that pact, Antichrist will reveal his true colors. He will put a stop to Israel's religion and desecrate the temple by setting himself up as God and demanding that the world worship him (2 Thess. 2:4).

The first of the seal judgments (Rev. 6:2) depicts Antichrist's rise to power: "I looked, and behold, a white horse, and he who sat on it had a bow; and a crown was given to him, and he went out conquering and to conquer." The bow depicts Antichrist's power, but the absence of arrows and the fact that the crown was freely given to him indicate his victory will not come through war. Antichrist's victory will be a bloodless, political, ideological conquest, as the world turns to him to lead them through the unparalleled crisis of the time of Tribulation.

Antichrist's false peace will not last long, for the second birth pang is war. In Matthew 24:6–7 Jesus warned, "You will be hearing of wars and rumors of wars. See that you are not frightened, for those things must take place, but that is not yet the end. For nation will rise against nation, and kingdom against kingdom." War on an unprecedented scale will characterize the Tribulation (Dan. 11:36–45), culminating in the unimaginable slaughter of the battle of Armageddon (Rev. 19:17–21).

The second seal judgment (Rev. 6:3–4) also depicts the devastating wars that will precede the Day of the Lord: "When He broke the second seal, I heard the second living creature saying, 'Come.' And another, a red horse, went out; and to him who sat on it, it was granted to take peace from the earth, and that men would slay one another; and a great sword was given to him." War personified rides the red horse of battle and slaughter.

Adding to the misery and suffering caused by war will be the natural disasters associated with the third birth pang: "In various places there will be famines and earthquakes" (Matt. 24:7). The third and fourth seal judgments also describe the natural disasters that precede the Day of the Lord:

> When He broke the third seal, I heard the third living creature saying, "Come." I looked, and behold, a black horse; and he who sat on it had a pair of scales in his hand. And I heard something like a voice in the center of the four living creatures saying, "A quart of wheat for a denarius, and three quarts of barley for a denarius; and do not damage the oil and the wine." (Rev. 6:5–6)

That a denarius (one day's wages) would purchase only a quart of wheat (one day's supply for one person) and enough barley (low quality grain usually fed to livestock) to feed a small family for one day graphically depicts the famine conditions that will prevail.

The fourth seal pictures death on a scale unprecedented in human history:

> When the Lamb broke the fourth seal, I heard the voice of the fourth living creature saying, "Come." I looked, and behold, an ashen horse; and he who sat on it had the name Death; and Hades was following with him. Authority was given to them over a fourth of the earth, to kill with sword and with famine and with pestilence and by the wild beasts of the earth. (Rev. 6:7–8)

The devastation caused by war and famine will result in a staggering death toll—one fourth of the earth's population.

The fourth birth pang describes the martyrdom of many of the Tribulation believers. In the midst of the devastation, slaughter, and horror of the Tribulation, many (Rev. 7:9) will be redeemed through the preaching of the two witnesses (Rev. 11:2–6), the 144,000 Jewish evangelists (Rev. 7), and the "angel flying in midheaven, having an eternal gospel to preach to those who live on the earth, and to every nation and tribe and tongue and people" (Rev. 14:6). Jesus warned those believers, "They will deliver you to tribulation, and will kill you, and you will be hated by all nations because of My name" (Matt. 24:9). When the Lord Jesus Christ broke the fifth seal, John

> saw underneath the altar the souls of those who had been slain because of the word of God, and because of the testimony which they had maintained; and they cried out with a loud voice, saying, "How long, O Lord, holy and true, will You refrain from judging and avenging our blood on those who dwell on the earth?" And there was given to each of them a white robe; and they were told that they should rest for a little while longer, until the number of their fellow servants and their brethren who were to be killed even as they had been, would be completed also. (Rev. 6:9–11)

The final birth pang, unlike the first four, is a positive sign. Jesus said in Matthew 24:14, "This gospel of the kingdom shall be preached in the whole world as a testimony to all the nations, and then the end will come." As noted above, there will be vast numbers of people converted during the Tribulation as a result of the preaching of the two witnesses, the 144,000 Jewish evangelists, and the angel flying in midheaven.

Unbelievably, incomprehensibly, despite these obvious, unmistakable signs, most people will still be caught by surprise when the Day of the Lord comes. The terrible outpouring of God's wrath in judgment will happen **while they are saying, "Peace and safety!"** The only explanation for such a ludicrous, absurd response is that people will be deceived by false prophets. Jesus warned, "Many will come in My name, saying, 'I am the Christ,' and will mislead many. . . . Many false prophets will arise and will mislead many. . . . For false Christs and false prophets will arise and will show great signs and wonders, so as to mislead, if possible, even the elect" (Matt. 24:5, 11, 24). Those lying deceivers will dupe the world into believing that peace and prosperity are just around the corner, despite the ominous signs that the Day of the Lord is fast approaching.

The Old Testament prophets also encountered deceiving false prophets who scoffed at their warnings of impending doom. Jeremiah warned his countrymen, "Flee for safety, O sons of Benjamin, from the midst of Jerusalem! Now blow a trumpet in Tekoa and raise a signal over Beth-haccerem; for evil looks down from the north, and a great destruction" (Jer. 6:1). But in spite of Jeremiah's warning, the false prophets were "saying, 'Peace, peace,' but there is no peace" (Jer. 6:14; cf. 8:11). In Jeremiah 14:13 Jeremiah complained, "'Ah, Lord God!' I said, 'Look, the prophets are telling them, "You will not see the sword nor will you have famine, but I will give you lasting peace in this place."'" In verse 14 God replied, "The prophets are prophesying falsehood in My name. I have neither sent them nor commanded them nor spoken to them; they are prophesying to you a false vision, divination, futility and the deception of their own minds." Lamentations 2:14 notes, "Your prophets have seen for you false and foolish visions; and they have not exposed your iniquity so as to restore you from captivity, but they have seen for you false and misleading oracles" (cf. Micah 3:5). God declared of the false prophets who plagued Israel:

> It is definitely because they have misled My people by saying, "Peace!" when there is no peace. And when anyone builds a wall, behold, they plaster it over with whitewash; so tell those who plaster it over with whitewash, that it will fall. A flooding rain will come, and you, O hailstones, will fall; and a violent wind will break out. Behold, when the wall has fallen, will you not be asked, "Where is the plaster with which you plastered it?" Therefore, thus says the Lord God, "I will make a violent wind break out in My wrath. There will also be in My anger a flooding rain and hailstones to consume it in wrath. So I will tear down the wall which you plastered over with whitewash and bring it down to the ground, so that its foundation is laid bare; and when it falls, you will be consumed in its midst. And you will know that I am the Lord. Thus I will spend My wrath on the wall and on those who have plastered it over with whitewash; and I will say to you, 'The wall is gone and its plasterers are gone, along with the prophets of Israel who prophesy to Jerusalem, and who see visions of peace for her when there is no peace,'" declares the Lord God. (Ezek. 13:10–16)

In the end time, the false prophets will use "great signs and wonders" (Matt. 24:24) to mislead the world. As a result of their deception, life will go on with some semblance of normalcy, just as it did before the Flood:

> For the coming of the Son of Man will be just like the days of Noah. For as in those days before the flood they were eating and drinking, marrying and giving in marriage, until the day that Noah entered the ark, and they did not understand until the flood came and took them all away; so will the coming of the Son of Man be. (Matt. 24:37–39)

The false prophet, the associate of the Antichrist, will use signs and wonders to persuade people to worship the Antichrist: "He performs great signs, so that he even makes fire come down out of heaven to the earth in the presence of men" (Rev. 13:13).

Unbelievers' susceptibility to the false prophets' deception is a sign of God's judgment on them. In 2 Thessalonians 2:10–12 Paul wrote that those deceived by the Antichrist will "perish, because they did not receive the love of the truth so as to be saved. For this reason God will send upon them a deluding influence so that they will believe what is false, in order that they all may be judged who did not believe the truth, but took pleasure in wickedness." As a result, the sudden, unexpected coming of the Day of the Lord will sweep them away in judgment.

THE CHARACTER OF THE DAY OF THE LORD

then destruction will come upon them suddenly like labor pains upon a woman with child, (5:3b)

Olethros (**destruction**) does not refer to annihilation, but separation from God (cf. 2 Thess. 1:9). It does not mean the destruction of being, but of well-being (cf. 1 Tim. 6:9); not the end of existence, but the destruction of the purpose for existence. God will accomplish the **destruction** of unbelievers by casting them into the eternal torment of hell (2 Thess. 1:9).

Revelation 6:12–17 graphically depicts the destructiveness of the Day of the Lord:

I looked when He broke the sixth seal, and there was a great earthquake; and the sun became black as sackcloth made of hair, and the whole moon became like blood; and the stars of the sky fell to the earth, as a fig tree casts its unripe figs when shaken by a great wind. The sky was split apart like a scroll when it is rolled up, and every mountain and island were moved out of their places. Then the kings of the earth and the great men and the commanders and the rich and the strong and every slave and free man hid themselves in the caves and among the rocks of the mountains; and they said to the mountains and to the rocks, "Fall on us and hide us from the presence of Him who sits on the throne, and from the wrath of the Lamb; for the great day of their wrath has come, and who is able to stand?"

Acts 2:19–20 describes the Day of the Lord as a time of "wonders in the sky above and signs on the earth below, blood, and fire, and vapor of smoke. The sun will be turned into darkness and the moon into blood, before the great and glorious day of the Lord shall come."

By using the term **them** (a reference to unbelievers), Paul reassured the Thessalonians that they will not face **destruction**. As he states plainly in verse 4, the Thessalonians will not experience the Day of the Lord; they will be raptured before it begins. (See the discussion of v. 4 in chapter 13 of this volume.) As noted earlier in this chapter, the Day of the Lord will come **suddenly** and unexpectedly on unbelievers. They will fail to heed the many precursors that should have warned them of its imminent arrival, just as **labor pains** coming **upon a woman with child** warn her that the birth of her child is imminent. (See the discussion of "birth pangs" above.)

THE COMPLETENESS OF THE DAY OF THE LORD

and they will not escape. (5:3c)

The tragic result of unbelievers' unpreparedness for the Day of the Lord is that **they will not escape** divine judgment. The use of the double negative *ou mē* stresses the comprehensiveness of the Day of the Lord, which will bring destruction on every unbeliever alive when it comes.

Believers should be comforted by the reality that they will be raptured before the coming of the Day of the Lord and not experience its horrors. Yet the knowledge that that event looms large on the prophetic horizon should also motivate them to evangelize the lost. The tragic reality is that those who reject the Lord Jesus Christ will experience God's temporal and eternal wrath. In the sobering, pensive words of the writer of Hebrews, "How will we escape if we neglect so great a salvation?" (Heb. 2:3).

Night People/
Day People
(1 Thessalonians 5:4–11)

13

**But you, brethren, are not in darkness, that the day would over-
take you like a thief; for you are all sons of light and sons of day.
We are not of night nor of darkness; so then let us not sleep as
others do, but let us be alert and sober. For those who sleep do
their sleeping at night, and those who get drunk get drunk at
night. But since we are of the day, let us be sober, having put on
the breastplate of faith and love, and as a helmet, the hope of salvation. For God has not destined us for wrath, but for obtaining
salvation through our Lord Jesus Christ, who died for us, so that
whether we are awake or asleep, we will live together with Him.
Therefore encourage one another and build up one another, just
as you also are doing.** (5:4–11)

Our world is a diverse mixture of ethnic groups, cultures, languages, religions, and political systems. Yet despite all of those distinctions, there are only two kinds of people in the world. There are believers
and unbelievers; the redeemed and the unredeemed; the saved and the
lost; the children of God and the children of the devil; those in the kingdom of God and those in the kingdom of darkness; those who are in
Adam and those who are in Christ; those who love God and those who

hate God; those who go into eternal life and those who go into eternal punishment; those who will be forever with the Lord and those who will be forever apart from the Lord; or, as someone humorously put it, the saints and the ain'ts.

In this passage Paul contrasts night people (unbelievers) with day people (believers). Night people are associated with darkness, sleep, and drunkenness; day people with light, alertness, and soberness.

The truth that unbelievers are in the darkness and believers in the light has its roots in the Old Testament. In Psalm 107:10–12 the psalmist described unbelievers as "those who dwelt in darkness and in the shadow of death, prisoners in misery and chains, because they had rebelled against the words of God and spurned the counsel of the Most High. Therefore He humbled their heart with labor; they stumbled and there was none to help."Then in verses 13–16 the psalmist described the transformation of those night people into day people:

> Then they cried out to the Lord in their trouble; He saved them out of their distresses. He brought them out of darkness and the shadow of death and broke their bands apart. Let them give thanks to the Lord for His lovingkindness, and for His wonders to the sons of men! For He has shattered gates of bronze and cut bars of iron asunder.

Isaiah 9:2 also describes the transformation from spiritual darkness to light:"The people who walk in darkness will see a great light; those who live in a dark land, the light will shine on them."Verses 6 and 7 reveal that the light is the Messiah:

> For a child will be born to us, a son will be given to us; and the government will rest on His shoulders; and His name will be called Wonderful Counselor, Mighty God, Eternal Father, Prince of Peace. There will be no end to the increase of His government or of peace, on the throne of David and over his kingdom, to establish it and to uphold it with justice and righteousness from then on and forevermore. The zeal of the Lord of hosts will accomplish this.

Zacharias, the father of the Messiah's forerunner John the Baptist, prophesied concerning his son,

> And you, child, will be called the prophet of the Most High; for you will go on before the Lord to prepare His ways; to give to His people the knowledge of salvation by the forgiveness of their sins, because of the tender mercy of our God, with which the Sunrise from on high will visit us, to shine upon those who sit in darkness and the shadow of death, to guide our feet into the way of peace. (Luke 1:76–79)

Matthew recorded the fulfillment of the Old Testament prophecy that the Messiah would be a light not only for His people but also for the Gentiles:

> Now when Jesus heard that John had been taken into custody, He withdrew into Galilee; and leaving Nazareth, He came and settled in Capernaum, which is by the sea, in the region of Zebulun and Naphtali. This was to fulfill what was spoken through Isaiah the prophet: "The land of Zebulun and the land of Naphtali, by the way of the sea, beyond the Jordan, Galilee of the Gentiles—the people who were sitting in darkness saw a great light, and those who were sitting in the land and shadow of death, upon them a light dawned." (Matt. 4:12–16)

In John 8:12 Jesus declared, "I am the Light of the world; he who follows Me will not walk in the darkness, but will have the Light of life" (cf. 3:19; 12:35, 46).

How do people turn from darkness to light? Recounting the dramatic story of his conversion, Paul told King Agrippa that Jesus had sent him to the Gentiles "to open their eyes so that they may turn from darkness to light and from the dominion of Satan to God, that they may receive forgiveness of sins and an inheritance among those who have been sanctified by faith in Me" (Acts 26:18). The last phrase is the key; to leave the darkness of sin and unbelief and become a redeemed day person, one must be "sanctified by faith in [Jesus Christ]." Those who put their faith in Him are "rescued . . . from the domain of darkness, and transferred . . . to the kingdom of His beloved Son" (Col. 1:13); those who "were formerly darkness, . . . now . . . are Light in the Lord" (Eph. 5:8); God "has called [them] out of darkness into His marvelous light" (1 Peter 2:9).

The apostle's purpose in contrasting the saved and the lost in this passage was to comfort the Thessalonians (4:18; 5:11). Despite Paul's teaching during his stay in their city (2 Thess. 2:5), they were worried about their future. Exacerbating their fears were false teachers who were attempting to deceive them (2 Thess. 2:1–3). As a result, numerous questions troubled them, questions no doubt relayed to Paul by Timothy, who had recently returned from Thessalonica (3: 2, 6). They feared that their loved ones who had died would miss the Rapture, so Paul assured them in 4:13–18 that they would not. In fact, "the dead in Christ will rise first" (4:16). The apostle addressed the Thessalonians' curiosity about when the Day of the Lord would come by reminding them, "As to the times and the epochs, brethren, you have no need of anything to be written to you" (5:1). Because "the day of the Lord will come just like a thief in the night" (5:2), the time of its coming will not be revealed.

The Thessalonians' fears and concerns find an Old Testament

parallel in the book of Malachi. Malachi preached a sobering, frightening message of judgment (cf. 3:5; 4:5), which caused concern and anxiety among the redeemed. But the Lord reassured His people that they would not experience His judgment:

> Then those who feared the Lord spoke to one another, and the Lord gave attention and heard it, and a book of remembrance was written before Him for those who fear the Lord and who esteem His name. "They will be Mine," says the Lord of hosts, "on the day that I prepare My own possession, and I will spare them as a man spares his own son who serves him." So you will again distinguish between the righteous and the wicked, between one who serves God and one who does not serve Him. (Mal. 3:16–18)

Paul likewise reassured the troubled new believers in Thessalonica that they would not face God's wrath. His use of the pronouns "they" and "them" (5:3) distinguishes the Thessalonians from the unbelievers who will experience God's wrath. He did so by presenting a series of contrasts between night people and day people. Paul gave the Thessalonians a multifaceted description of the distinction between believers and unbelievers, and the implications for each concerning the Day of the Lord. By so doing, the apostle made it plain that the Thessalonians' fears that they were already in the Day of the Lord were groundless. Believers are light people and will not experience the darkness of the Day of the Lord.

Three distinctive characteristics set day people (believers) apart from night people (unbelievers): their nature, behavior, and destiny.

THE DISTINCTIVENESS OF BELIEVERS' NATURE

But you, brethren, are not in darkness, that the day would overtake you like a thief; for you are all sons of light and sons of day. We are not of night nor of darkness; (5:4–5)

The phrase **but you** introduces a contrast with verse 3, where Paul used the pronouns "they" and "them" to refer to unbelievers who will not escape the Day of the Lord. The familial term **brethren** further emphasizes Paul's point. As God's children, the Thessalonians would not experience the Day of the Lord, because unlike unbelievers, believers **are not in darkness;** they possess an entirely different nature. They do not belong to the night; they are not part of Satan's evil kingdom.

The spiritual night that engulfs unbelievers includes both intellectual and moral darkness. It is the intellectual darkness of ignorance on the one hand, and the moral darkness of sin on the other; of not knowing what is true, and of not doing what is right. God invaded the sin-darkened world in the Person of Jesus Christ (John 1:4, 9). Tragically, however, most people choose to remain in darkness; though "the Light shines in the darkness, . . . the darkness did not comprehend it" (John 1:5). As Jesus explained to Nicodemus, "The Light has come into the world, and men loved the darkness rather than the Light, for their deeds were evil. For everyone who does evil hates the Light, and does not come to the Light for fear that his deeds will be exposed" (John 3:19–20). To the Ephesians Paul wrote, "This I say, and affirm together with the Lord, that you walk no longer just as the Gentiles also walk, in the futility of their mind, being darkened in their understanding, excluded from the life of God because of the ignorance that is in them, because of the hardness of their heart" (Eph. 4:17–18). Unbelievers are in the dark not only because they do not know the truth, but also because they love wickedness.

All believers once "were formerly darkness, but now . . . are Light in the Lord" (Eph. 5:8). Earlier in that epistle, Paul graphically described believers' former lives in darkness:

> You were dead in your trespasses and sins, in which you formerly walked according to the course of this world, according to the prince of the power of the air, of the spirit that is now working in the sons of disobedience. Among them we too all formerly lived in the lusts of our flesh, indulging the desires of the flesh and of the mind, and were by nature children of wrath, even as the rest. (Eph. 2:1–3)

In Luke 22:53 Jesus called Satan, described in Ephesians 2:2 as "the prince of the power of the air," "the power of darkness," while in Ephesians 6:12 Paul called Satan's demon hosts "the world forces of this darkness." Fittingly, they all inhabit "the domain of darkness" (Col. 1:13). And the ultimate destiny of Satan, his demon hosts, and all unbelievers is the eternal darkness of hell (Matt. 8:12; 2 Peter 2:4, 17; Jude 6, 13).

But believers are not lost in this darkness of ignorance, sin, and rebellion. "I am the Light of the world," Jesus said; "he who follows Me will not walk in the darkness, but will have the Light of life" (John 8:12). In the Sermon on the Mount, He called believers "the light of the world" (Matt. 5:14). In his first epistle John described believers as those who "walk in the Light as He Himself is in the Light" (1 John 1:7). Believers are not in intellectual darkness, because they know the truth (John 8:32; 1 Tim. 4:3; 2 Peter 1:12; 1 John 2:21; 2 John 1); nor are they in moral darkness, because they practice the truth (John 3:21; 3 John 11).

Because their nature is distinct from unbelievers, believers need not fear that the day **would overtake** them **like a thief.** The Day of the

Lord is a "day of darkness" (Joel 2:2; Zeph. 1:15); "the day of the Lord . . . will be darkness and not light. . . . Will not the day of the Lord be darkness instead of light?" (Amos 5:18, 20). It is for the night people; thus day people need not fear the Day of the Lord; they will not be part of it.

Far from being in the darkness, believers are **all sons of light and sons of day** (cf. Luke 16:8; John 12:36; Eph. 5:8). The phrase **sons of** is often part of an idiomatic Hebrew expression describing the dominant influence in a person's life. The Old Testament uses the phrase "sons of Belial" (Judg. 19:22; 1 Sam. 2:12; 2 Sam. 23:6; 1 Kings 21:10 KJV) to describe worthless men who are by nature children of the devil (cf. 2 Cor. 6:15). Jesus nicknamed James and John "Sons of Thunder" (Mark 3:17) because of their volatile, aggressive personalities. Barnabas's name literally means "Son of Encouragement" (Acts 4:36), denoting his gentle, encouraging nature. Thus, to describe believers as **sons of light** is to say that **light** is the dominant influence in their lives. Adding the parallel phrase **sons of day** reinforces Paul's point; light belongs to day just as darkness belongs to night.

To drive home his point, Paul declared emphatically, **We are not of night nor of darkness.** Believers live in an entirely different sphere than those who will experience God's wrath in the Day of the Lord. As **sons of light** and **sons of day,** believers "walk in newness of life" (Rom. 6:4), are new creatures in Christ (2 Cor. 5:17), are new creations (Gal. 6:15), are "seated . . . in the heavenly places in Christ Jesus" (Eph. 2:6), and have their lives "hidden with Christ in God" (Col. 3:3). Therefore, the Thessalonians did not need to fear missing the Rapture, being caught in the Day of the Lord, or experiencing God's wrath and condemnation. Believers live in a separate sphere of life, where judgment cannot come.

THE DISTINCTIVENESS OF BELIEVERS' BEHAVIOR

so then let us not sleep as others do, but let us be alert and sober. For those who sleep do their sleeping at night, and those who get drunk get drunk at night. But since we are of the day, let us be sober, having put on the breastplate of faith and love, and as a helmet, the hope of salvation. (5:6–8)

The phrase **so then** emphasizes the inseparable link between Christians' nature and their behavior, between their character and their conduct—a truth taught throughout the New Testament (cf. 2:12; 4:1; Eph. 4:1, 17; Phil. 1:27; Col. 1:10). What people are determines how they act; believers are day people and must act accordingly.

On that basis, Paul exhorted the Thessalonians, **let us not sleep**

as others do, but let us be alert and sober. The apostle did not need to exhort them to be day people, because their nature was permanently fixed by the transforming, regenerating power of God in salvation. But because that new nature is incarcerated in fallen, sinful human flesh (cf. Rom. 7:14–25), it is possible for day people to do deeds of the darkness. Therefore, Paul exhorted the Thessalonians to live consistently with their new natures. The present tense verbs indicate that the Thessalonians were to be continuously awake, alert, and sober. Rather than threaten them with chastening, the apostle appealed to their sense of spiritual dignity. As children of the day and the light, it was unthinkable for them to participate in the deeds of darkness (cf. Eph. 4:1; 5:11).

The term **sleep** (*katheudō*; a different word than the one used to refer metaphorically to "death" in 4:13–15) adds yet another dimension to Paul's portrayal of the night people (the **others** to whom he refers). As children of the night and the darkness, it is not surprising to find them asleep in spiritual indifference, living as if there will be no judgment. Like the man in the Lord's parable (Matt. 24:43), who was unaware that he was about to be robbed, they are foolish, unwitting, and unaware of the disaster that threatens to overtake them. That they **sleep** further compounds their dilemma; not only is the night they exist in pitch black, but they also are in a coma. In verse 7 the apostle will complete his description of their sorry plight by noting that they are asleep in the darkness in a drunken stupor. Sadly, though they are asleep to spiritual reality, night people are wide awake to the lusts of the flesh.

As day people, the Thessalonians had been delivered out of the dark night of sin, ignorance, rebellion, and unbelief. Therefore, it was ridiculous for them to walk in the darkness. There is no place for night life among day people—a truth Paul reinforced in another exhortation:

> The night is almost gone, and the day is near. Therefore let us lay aside the deeds of darkness and put on the armor of light. Let us behave properly as in the day, not in carousing and drunkenness, not in sexual promiscuity and sensuality, not in strife and jealousy. But put on the Lord Jesus Christ, and make no provision for the flesh in regard to its lusts. (Rom. 13:12–14)

The apostle reminded Titus that "the grace of God has appeared, bringing salvation to all men, instructing us to deny ungodliness and worldly desires and to live sensibly, righteously and godly in the present age" (Titus 2:11–12). Redeeming grace is also sanctifying grace.

Living consistent with their nature as day people provides believers with comfort, because living a righteous, godly life brings assurance of salvation (cf. 2 Peter 1:5–10). When day people walk in the darkness, however, they forfeit that assurance and become fearful of God's judgment. They become "blind or short-sighted, having forgotten [their] purification from [their] former sins" (2 Peter 1:9). Though it is not possible for day people to be caught in the Day of the Lord, it is possible for sinning ones to lose assurance and fear they might be.

Sleep is the natural condition of night people, but day people are to be **alert**. *Grēgoreō* (**alert**), the source of the name "Gregory," means to be awake or watchful. Unlike the slumbering, witless night people, day people are awake and able to rightly assess what is happening in the spiritual dimension. They heed Peter's injunction, "Prepare your minds for action" (1 Peter 1:13) and, knowing the Day of the Lord is coming (2 Peter 3:10), they are "diligent to be found by Him in peace, spotless and blameless" (2 Peter 3:14).

In contrast to the drunken stupor that envelops night people, day people are also **sober**. To be **sober** means to be free from the influence of intoxicants. A **sober** person exhibits self-control, lives a serious, balanced, calm, steady life, and maintains proper priorities. To be **sober** is to be alert; the two terms are essentially synonyms. Just as sleep and drunkenness define night people's insensitivity to spiritual reality, so alertness and soberness describe day people's sensitivity to it. William Hendriksen notes:

> The *sober* person lives deeply. His pleasures are not primarily those of the senses, like the pleasures of the drunkard for instance, but those of the soul. He is by no means a Stoic. On the contrary, with a full measure of joyful anticipation he looks forward to the return of the Lord (1 Peter 1:13). But he does not run away from his task! Note how both here and also in 1 Peter 5:8 the two verbs *to be watchful* and *to be sober* are used as synonyms.

> The apostle's exhortation, then, amounts to this: "Let us not be lax and unprepared, but let us be prepared, being spiritually alert, firm in the faith, courageous, strong, calmly but with glad anticipation looking forward to the future day. Let us, moreover, do all this because we belong to the day and not to the night." (*New Testament Commentary: Exposition of Thessalonians, Timothy, and Titus* [Grand Rapids: Baker, 1981], 125–26; emphasis in original)

The self-evident observation that **those who sleep do their sleeping at night, and those who get drunk get drunk at night,** further strengthens Paul's point. He also may have been alluding to a parable told by Jesus:

> But if that slave says in his heart, "My master will be a long time in coming," and begins to beat the slaves, both men and women, and to eat and drink and get drunk; the master of that slave will come on a day

when he does not expect him and at an hour he does not know, and will cut him in pieces, and assign him a place with the unbelievers. (Luke 12:45–46)

Both **sleeping** and **getting drunk** are things generally done **at night. Sleeping** refers metaphorically to passive indifference; **getting drunk** to active sin.

Repeating what he said in verse 6 for emphasis, Paul wrote, **But—** in sharp contrast to the sleeping, drunken night people—**since we are of the day, let us be sober.** The apostle's repetition suggests that their fear of being in the Day of the Lord was a major concern for the Thessalonians. In fact, they were so concerned that Paul had to address the issue again in his second inspired letter to them (2 Thess. 2:1ff.). Once again, he stressed that as day people, the Thessalonians would have no part in the Day of the Lord. Both their nature and their behavior set them apart from the night people on whom the Day of the Lord will descend.

The concepts of alertness and sobriety suggested to Paul the image of a soldier on duty. He therefore viewed day people as **having put on** the "armor of light" (Rom. 13:12; cf. Isa. 59:17; Eph. 6:13–17). A soldier's **breastplate** protected his vital organs, the area where he was most vulnerable. It was the ancient equivalent of a bulletproof vest. The obvious function of a soldier's **helmet** (like a modern football or motorcycle helmet) was to protect his head from blows that otherwise might crush his skull. The **breastplate of faith and love** and **the helmet** of **the hope of salvation** equip the Christian soldier to "stand firm against the schemes of the devil. . . . against the spiritual forces of wickedness in the heavenly places" (Eph. 6:11–12).

Faith, love, and **hope** form the supreme triad of Christian virtues (cf. 1:3; 1 Cor. 13:13). They also provide an excellent defense against temptation. **Faith** is trust in God's power, promises, and plan. It is the unwavering belief that God is completely trustworthy in all that He says and does.

First, believers can trust God's Person. He will never deviate from His nature as revealed in Scripture, but will always act consistently with His attributes. The writer of Hebrews declared of God the Son, "Jesus Christ is the same yesterday and today and forever" (Heb. 13:8).

Second, believers can trust God's power. God rhetorically asked Abraham, "Is anything too difficult for the Lord?" (Gen. 18:14; cf. Jer. 32:17, 27).

Third, believers can trust God's promises. "God is not a man, that He should lie, nor a son of man, that He should repent; has He said, and will He not do it? Or has He spoken, and will He not make it good?" (Num. 23:19).

Fourth, believers can trust God's sovereign plan, which can neither be halted nor hindered. Through Isaiah the prophet, God declared, "I act and who can reverse it?" (Isa. 43:13).

Faith provides a defense against temptation, because all sin results from a lack of trust in God. For example, worry is the failure to believe that God will act in love on behalf of His people; lying substitutes man's selfish plans for God's sovereign purposes; adultery denies God's wisdom in instituting the monogamous marriage bond. Thus, **faith** is an impenetrable **breastplate,** providing sure protection against temptation. But to put it on, believers must study and meditate on the rich depths of God's nature as revealed in Scripture, and then translate that knowledge into action in their lives.

If **faith** forms the hard, protective outer surface of a Christian's **breastplate,** then **love** is its soft inner lining. **Love** toward God involves delight in and devotion to God as the supreme object of affection. It, too, provides a powerful deterrent to sin, since all sin involves a failure to love God. The greatest command, the injunction that sums up the whole law of God, is to "love the Lord your God with all your heart, and with all your soul, and with all your mind" (Matt. 22:37). "Love is the fulfillment of the law" (Rom. 13:10), because those who genuinely love God will not do what grieves and offends Him. So **love** and **faith** form an impregnable barrier against temptation; it is only when one or both are lacking that Christians fall victim to sin. Perfect trust in and love for God leads to perfect obedience.

The final piece of armor is the **helmet** of the **hope of salvation.** The **salvation** in view here is not the past aspect of salvation (justification), or its present aspect (sanctification), but rather its future aspect (glorification). Paul described that future aspect of salvation in Romans 13:11 when he wrote, "Now salvation is nearer to us than when we believed." It is then that believers will receive the eagerly anticipated redemption of their bodies (Rom. 8:23), when the Lord Jesus Christ "will transform the body of our humble state into conformity with the body of His glory" (Phil. 3:21). Focusing on the eternal glory that awaits them (2 Tim. 2:10; 1 Peter 5:10) protects believers against temptation. "Beloved, now we are children of God," wrote John, "and it has not appeared as yet what we will be. We know that when He appears, we will be like Him, because we will see Him just as He is. And everyone who has this hope fixed on Him purifies himself, just as He is pure" (1 John 3:2–3).

When **faith** is weak, **love** grows cold. When love grows cold, hope is lost. When **hope** in God's promise of future glory is weak, believers are vulnerable to temptation and sin. Only those who keep the **breastplate of faith and love,** and the **helmet** of **the hope of salvation** firmly in place can resist effectively the onslaught of the forces of darkness.

THE DISTINCTIVENESS OF BELIEVERS' DESTINY

For God has not destined us for wrath, but for obtaining salvation through our Lord Jesus Christ, who died for us, so that whether we are awake or asleep, we will live together with Him. Therefore encourage one another and build up one another, just as you also are doing. (5:9–11)

The most sobering truth in Scripture is that God will judge the wicked and sentence them to eternal hell (Matt. 3:12; 13:40–42, 50; 18:8; 25:41, 46; John 3:36; 5:29; Acts 24:25; Rom. 2:5, 8; 9:22; 2 Thess. 1:9; Heb. 6:2; 10:26–27; 2 Peter 2:9; 3:7; Rev. 14:9–11; 20:11–15; 21:8). On the other hand, the blessed truth for believers is that **God has not destined us for wrath** (cf. 1:10; John 3:18, 36; 5:24; Rom. 5:1, 9; 8:1, 33–34). Like their nature, established in the past at salvation, and their present pattern of obedience, day people's future destiny sets them apart from night people. Believers will not experience the **wrath** God will pour out on unbelievers on the Day of the Lord, and for eternity in hell.

The word **destined** expresses the inexorable outworking of God's sovereign plan for believers' salvation. In Matthew 25:34 Jesus promised that believers will "inherit the kingdom prepared for [them] from the foundation of the world." To the Ephesians Paul wrote, "He chose us in Him before the foundation of the world, that we would be holy and blameless before Him" (Eph. 1:4), while in 2 Timothy 1:9 he added, "[God] has saved us and called us with a holy calling, not according to our works, but according to His own purpose and grace which was granted us in Christ Jesus from all eternity."

Orgē (**wrath**) does not refer to a momentary outburst of rage, but to "an abiding and settled habit of mind" (Richard C. Trench, *Synonyms of the New Testament* [reprint; Grand Rapids: Eerdmans, 1983], 131). It is a general reference to the final judgment, when God's wrath will be poured out on the wicked (Matt. 3:7; John 3:36; Rom. 1:18; 2:5, 8; 3:5; 4:15; 5:9; 9:22; 12:19; Eph. 5:6; Col. 3:6; Rev. 14:9–11). But God's **wrath** here must also include the Day of the Lord, since that was the Thessalonians' primary concern. Paul assured them that they would face neither temporal **wrath** on the Day of the Lord (cf. Rev. 6:17), nor eternal **wrath** in hell.

But—in contrast to the doomed night people—God has destined believers **for obtaining** (lit., "gaining," or "acquiring") **salvation through our Lord Jesus Christ.** Once again, Paul referred to the future dimension of believers' **salvation,** their glorification (see the discussion of verse 8 above). But all three aspects of salvation—justification (Isa. 53:11; Rom. 3:24, 26; 5:8–9; 1 Cor. 6:11; Gal. 2:16), sanctification (1 Cor. 1:30; 6:11; Heb. 7:25), and glorification (cf. Phil. 3:21)—come only **through our Lord**

Jesus Christ. The simple, yet profound phrase **who died for** (*huper,* "on our behalf"; "with reference to us"; "in our place"; "as our substitute") **us** (cf. Rom. 5:8) expresses the sole basis for believers' salvation. God "made Him who knew no sin to be sin on our behalf, so that we might become the righteousness of God in Him" (2 Cor. 5:21); "He Himself bore our sins in His body on the cross, so that we might die to sin and live to righteousness" (1 Peter 2:24; cf. John 10:11; Rom. 8:3; Gal. 1:4; 3:13; Eph. 5:2; 1 Peter 3:18; 1 John 2:2). The glorious message of the gospel is that Christ's substitutionary death paid in full the penalty for believers' sins and therefore believers will not face God's judgment. In John 5:24 Jesus declared, "Truly, truly, I say to you, he who hears My word, and believes Him who sent Me, has eternal life, and does not come into judgment, but has passed out of death into life." Nor will they face His condemnation, because "there is now no condemnation for those who are in Christ Jesus" (Rom. 8:1).

Christ's death on their behalf sets all day people—both those who are **awake** (alive) and those who are **asleep** (dead; cf. 4:13–15)—apart from night people. The marvelous reality is that all believers **will live together with Him,** as Jesus Himself promised:

> Do not let your heart be troubled; believe in God, believe also in Me. In My Father's house are many dwelling places; if it were not so, I would have told you; for I go to prepare a place for you. If I go and prepare a place for you, I will come again and receive you to Myself, that where I am, there you may be also. (John 14:1–3; cf. 1 Thess. 4:17)

As he did with his discussion of the Rapture (cf. 4:18 where he used the same word rendered here "encourage"), Paul concluded his discussion of the Day of the Lord by exhorting the Thessalonians to **encourage one another and build up one another.** Based on the truth he had given them, they were to reassure the anxious and fearful that they would not experience the Day of the Lord. His concluding phrase, **just as you also are doing,** affirms that they were already committed to encouragement. Ever the faithful pastor, passionately concerned for his people, Paul wanted them to "excel still more" (4:1).

One of two possible destinies awaits every member of the human race. Those who stubbornly remain in spiritual darkness will ultimately "be cast out into the outer darkness" of eternal hell (Matt. 8:12; cf. 22:13; 25:30). But those who through faith in Jesus Christ come to the light of salvation (Acts 13:47; cf. John 8:12; 9:5; 11:9; 12:46) will "share in the inheritance of the saints in Light" (Col. 1:12). They will live forever in God's glorious presence, where "there will no longer be any night; and they will not have need of the light of a lamp nor the light of the sun, because the Lord God will illumine them; and they will reign forever and ever" (Rev. 22:5).

Growing a Healthy Flock—Part 1: The Relationship Between Shepherds and Sheep (1 Thessalonians 5:12-13)

14

But we request of you, brethren, that you appreciate those who diligently labor among you, and have charge over you in the Lord and give you instruction, and that you esteem them very highly in love because of their work. Live in peace with one another. (5:12-13)

The church is the most blessed institution on earth, the only one built by the Lord Jesus Christ Himself (Matt. 16:18; cf. Acts 4:11-12; 20:28; 1 Cor. 3:9; Heb. 3:6; 1 Peter 2:5-7), the only institution He promised to eternally bless (cf. Eph. 5:25-27), and the one about which He declared "the gates of Hades will not overpower it" (Matt. 16:18). The apostle Paul was so convinced of the overarching significance of the church that he described it to Timothy as "the pillar and support of the truth" (1 Tim. 3:15). But those powerful descriptions do not mean the church is free from difficulties. Because redeemed sinners within the church are still battling fallen flesh—and some members of local churches are spiritually immature or even unregenerate—the church faces challenges and deals constantly with sin problems. Only as it recognizes and confronts the weaknesses, imperfections, and difficulties caused by sin does Christ's church begin and continue to grow spiritually (Matt. 18:15–18; 1 Cor. 5:1–7; 1 John 1:9; cf. James 5:16).

The true church also faces strong opposition from Satan, his demons, and his human agents (Matt. 13:19; 2 Cor. 2:11; 4:4; Eph. 6:12; 1 Thess. 2:18; 3:5; cf. Acts 8:1–3). Nevertheless it has supernatural resources because it is the body of Christ in the world (Rom. 12:5; Gal. 3:28; Eph. 1:22–23; 3:21; Col. 1:24; Heb. 3:6), the Holy Spirit energizes its life (John 14:26; Acts 1:8; 9:31; 13:2–4; 20:28; 1 Cor. 2:12–13; 3:16–17; 12:13; 1 John 2:27; 3:24; 4:13), the Word of God instructs it (John 17:17; Rom. 15:4; Col. 3:16; 2 Tim. 3:16–17; Heb. 4:12; 1 Peter 2:2), and its people possess divinely granted spiritual gifts to edify one another and reach the lost (Rom. 12:4–13; 1 Cor. 12:4–11, 28; 14:12; Eph. 4:11–12). True believers in the church love and obey the Lord and sincerely strive toward greater holiness (1 Cor. 6:11; Col. 1:21–23; Heb. 2:11; cf. Acts 14:22). The church at Thessalonica was a church successfully striving toward holiness, as Paul's excellent summary of its life reveals: "Finally then, brethren, we request and exhort you in the Lord Jesus, that as you received from us instruction as to how you ought to walk and please God (just as you actually do walk), that you excel still more" (1 Thess. 4:1). Numerous times already in this letter the apostle had commended the Thessalonians (1:2, 3, 6, 8, 9, 10; 2:13, 17, 19, 20; 3:6, 8, 9), indicating that their church was headed in the right spiritual direction. Whatever spiritual deficiencies existed in Thessalonica, they did not threaten the basic spiritual life of the people. Paul did not point out any scandalous sins or false doctrines. But he did encourage the believers that there was still a sanctification process to follow and much room for additional growth—they needed to "excel still more."

First Thessalonians 5:12–13 begins a series of direct exhortations to the Thessalonians to persevere and grow in their Christian walk. Even though they eagerly anticipated the return of Christ for His church and their deliverance from the final Day of the Lord, the Thessalonians' pressing responsibility was to live holy lives in the present and continue to grow in grace.

Verses 12 and 13 present directives concerning the relationship between pastors and people. It is crucial that the relationship between a pastor and his flock be healthy so as to guarantee the spiritual progress of the church (cf. 1 Cor. 14:40; Heb. 13:17; 1 Peter 5:1–5). If the shepherds and the sheep do not fulfill their proper spiritual responsibilities to each other, the church cannot be what God intends it to be. This emphasis permeates the other New Testament epistles (e.g., Rom. 1:9–12; 1 Cor. 16:10–11; 2 Cor. 7:13–16; Eph. 4:15–16; 2 Thess. 3:4; 1 Tim. 3:14–15; 5:17–22; Titus 2:1–10; Heb. 10:24–25). (For a more complete discussion of what constitutes a healthy church, see John MacArthur, *The Master's Plan* for the Church [Chicago: Moody, 1991] and *The Body Dynamic* [Colorado Springs: ChariotVictor/Victor Books, 1996].)

THE SHEPHERDS' RESPONSIBILITY TO THE SHEEP

But we request of you, brethren, . . . who diligently labor among you, and have charge over you in the Lord and give you instruction, (5:12)

  From the beginning, the apostles made leadership a high priority for the churches. In his letters to Timothy and Titus, Paul clearly outlined the qualifications and duties of those leaders (1 Tim. 3:1–7; Titus 1:5–9). Four basic New Testament terms identify and describe church leaders. First is the familiar term *elder* (*presbuteros*), which characterizes leaders as spiritually mature and wise (Acts 15:2ff.; 20:17; 1 Tim. 5:17, 19; Titus 1:5; James 5:14; 1 Peter 5:1, 5; 2 John 1; 3 John 1). Second is the word *overseer* (*episkopos*; Acts 20:28; Phil. 1:1; 1 Tim. 3:1–2; Titus 1:7), which describes the leader's spiritual oversight and authority. (Except in Acts 20:28, the KJV renders this term "bishop" in the preceding references.) Third, the familiar term *pastor* (*poimēn*) emphasizes the leader's responsibility to feed and protect his flock (Eph. 4:11; cf. Matt. 9:36; Mark 6:34). Finally, the term *leader* (*hegemōn*) indicates that the church leader must be able to provide spiritual discernment and guidance for his flock (cf. Heb. 13:7, 17, 24).

  Placing such men into leadership positions within the early church was essential (cf. Acts 14:23), but the task was not easy. In Thessalonica, as in other Greco-Roman cities where Paul planted churches, it was difficult to find qualified elders. First of all, the church was less than a year old and contained primarily new converts. Therefore, few, if any, of the members would have been sufficiently mature and wise enough to articulate the truth and direct the congregation with discernment. But the apostle Paul nevertheless exercised his Spirit-given authority (cf. Acts 13:1–3; 15:22–29; 16:1–5; 2 Cor. 10:8, 14) and discernment, identified certain qualified men, and started training them to become elders. Although 1 Thessalonians makes no mention of elders, overseers, pastors, or leaders, they are in view as those who had **charge over** the Thessalonians.

  Second, finding qualified elders from among the Thessalonians was difficult because those new believers generally were common people. Many of them were slaves who were not accustomed to leadership responsibilities. Thus they would have had to learn how to grow spiritually and develop as leaders at the same time.

  The difficulty in identifying qualified elders in Thessalonica led to a conflict within the church (5:14–15). Apparently some in the flock, wondering why other equally new believers in Christ were given charge over them, were not submissive to the new leaders. That conflict, although not a threat to the life of the church (such as the factionalism and charismatic excesses at Corinth were to that church), was serious enough that Paul wanted it resolved as soon as possible. To a great extent, the resolution of that conflict lay in the proper fulfillment of pastoral and congregational roles. Hence Paul admonished the Thessalonians about the relationship between shepherds and sheep, starting with the shepherd's responsibility to the sheep.

Because that subject was new to the Thessalonians, and inasmuch as they were already growing spiritually and becoming models for other churches (1:7–9), Paul gently introduced the matter to them. **But we request of you, brethren,** was an amiable, gentle approach by the apostle. It is not the forceful expression of apostolic authority Paul was capable of (e.g., Acts 13:9–11; 27:21–26; 1 Cor. 1:10; 5:1–8; 11:17–22; 2 Cor. 2:8–11; Gal. 1:6–9; 3:1–9), but more like a request from a good friend; it is also the same expression he used in 4:1 (see the discussion of that verse in chapter 8 of this volume). The Thessalonians were already doing well; this was just an encouraging appeal for them to do better. Paul therefore told the church of three responsibilities its shepherds had to the sheep: to labor among them, to exercise authority over them, and to provide instruction for them.

THE RESPONSIBILITY TO LABOR

who diligently labor among you, (5:12b)

Diligently labor is from *kopiaō*, which means to exhibit great effort and exertion, to the point of sweat and exhaustion. The faithful pastor works hard among his people and ministers to them as a shepherd cares for his sheep, or a father leads his family. Spiritual shepherds must proclaim the gospel (2 Tim. 4:5), explain and apply the truth (1 Tim. 3:2; 2 Tim. 4:2; Titus 1:9), warn and admonish the sheep (cf. Rom. 15:14; Col. 1:28; 3:16; 1 Thess. 5:14), and counsel them from Scripture (2 Tim. 3:16–4:4; cf. Prov. 17:17; 27:6, 9, 17).

The apostle Paul was the consummate example of such a hardworking, conscientious shepherd and had already stated that: "For you recall, brethren, our labor and hardship, how working night and day so as not to be a burden to any of you, we proclaimed to you the gospel of God" (1 Thess. 2:9; see the discussion of this verse, and the preceding two verses, in chapter 3 of this volume). Then in his second letter to them,

Paul commanded the Thessalonians: "Keep away from every brother who leads an unruly life and not according to the tradition which you received from us. For you yourselves know how you ought to follow our example, because we did not act in an undisciplined manner among you" (3:6–7). Paul worked as a tentmaker (Acts 18:3) to support himself, not because he did not have a right to receive support solely from his ministry efforts, but to be an example to believers of one who worked hard and did not unduly burden anyone (cf. 1 Cor. 9:1–15). Pastors expect their people to minister diligently for the church and to work hard in their jobs (cf. 1 Cor. 3:13). Paul knew if he was going to teach the Thessalonians to do both, he had to be a good example of one who did both.

In Paul's farewell exhortation to the Ephesian elders he reminded them several times of how diligently he had labored among them:

> You yourselves know, from the first day that I set foot in Asia, how I was with you the whole time, serving the Lord with all humility and with tears and with trials which came upon me through the plots of the Jews; how I did not shrink from declaring to you anything that was profitable, and teaching you publicly and from house to house. (Acts 20:18–20; cf. Col. 1:28; 1 Tim. 4:10)

> Therefore be on the alert, remembering that night and day for a period of three years I did not cease to admonish each one with tears. (v. 31; cf. 1 Cor. 15:10)

> I have coveted no one's silver or gold or clothes. You yourselves know that these hands ministered to my own needs and to the men who were with me. In everything I showed you that by working hard in this manner you must help the weak. (vv. 33–35)

Paul was a model of the diligent servant ministry that should characterize every shepherd. Successful leadership in the church comes to those willing to work to exhaustion for the sake of divine mandates and spiritual objectives, embracing the proclamation of the gospel, the establishment of churches, and the edification of believers.

THE RESPONSIBILITY TO EXERCISE AUTHORITY

and have charge over you in the Lord (5:12c)

Have charge over (*proistēmi*) literally means "to stand before" and conveys the notion of authoritatively presiding, leading, or directing.

Paul later used the word four times as he instructed Timothy about the character and duties of church elders (1 Tim. 3:4, 5, 12; 5:17). Pastors stand in the place of the Chief Shepherd as His delegated undershepherds exercising oversight and authority in His name (cf. 1 Peter 5:1–4).

The Thessalonian shepherds' responsibility to give their flock spiritual guidance and direction involved many duties, such as setting a positive spiritual tone, bringing about a functioning unity, relating well on an individual basis to people in the church, helping them to cope with life's difficulties and find biblical solutions for their problems, and working for necessary change within the church—all by diligent effort and reliance on the Holy Spirit.

The phrase **in the Lord** emphasizes that true shepherds are not self-appointed, and their authority does not derive from fallible human beings. Equipped and appointed by God (1 Cor. 4:1; 2 Cor. 3:5–6; Heb. 5:4), it is their duty to lead the sheep for His sake, and never because they want power, prestige, wealth, or an advancement to their own careers (1 Peter 5:2–3; cf. 1 Tim. 6:9–10).

THE RESPONSIBILITY TO PROVIDE INSTRUCTION

and give you instruction, (5:12*d*)

The third responsibility of shepherds to their sheep is to **give** them **instruction.** That expression comes from the verb *noutheteō*, which is often translated "admonish" in the New Testament (Acts 20:31; Rom. 15:14; 1 Cor. 4:14; Col. 1:28; 3:16; 1 Thess. 5:14; 2 Thess. 3:15). It refers not merely to academic data imparted impersonally but to **instruction** for the purpose of correcting and changing people. It is teaching with an element of warning, designed to direct the sheep to holy living (cf. 1 Cor. 4:14).

Shepherds, then, are to be skilled instructors of the Word of God. (In fact, no pastor's authority ever extends beyond the expression of God's will as revealed by His Spirit in Scripture.) In addition to the character qualities Paul stipulated for elders (1 Tim. 3:2–7; Titus 1:7–9), the ability to teach is the only specific skill he said they must possess (cf. 1 Tim. 4:6, 16). The apostle knew, furthermore, that teaching the Word has positive and negative aspects, involving "holding fast the faithful word which is in accordance with the teaching, so that [the pastor] will be able both to exhort in sound doctrine and to refute those who contradict" (Titus 1:9). The shepherd must be able to teach in a manner that exhorts believers to practice the truth (cf. Acts 20:32; Eph. 4:11–12; Titus 2:15) and, as necessary, urges those who deny the truth to give up their error and accept the truth (2 Tim. 2:24–26; cf. 3 John 9–10). The Puritan Richard Baxter wrote concerning the importance of the pastor's being able to teach the truth effectively,

> To preach a sermon, I think, is not the hardest part; and yet what skill is necessary to make the truth plain; to convince the hearers, to let irresistible light in to their consciences, and to keep it there, and drive all home; to screw the truth into their minds, and work Christ into their affections; to meet every objection, and clearly to resolve it; to drive sinners to a stand, and make them see that there is no hope, but that they must unavoidably either be converted or condemned—and to do all this, as regards language and manner, as beseems our work, and yet as is most suitable to the capacities of our hearers. This, and a great deal more that should be done in every sermon, must surely require a great deal of holy skill. So great a God, whose message we deliver, should be honoured by our delivery of it. It is a lamentable case, that in a message from the God of heaven, of everlasting moment to the souls of men, we should behave ourselves so weakly, so unhandsomely, so imprudently, or so slightly, that the whole business should miscarry in our hands, and God should be dishonoured, and his work disgraced, and sinners rather hardened than converted; and all this through our weakness or neglect! How often have carnal hearers gone home jeering at the palpable and dishonourable failings of the preacher! How many sleep under us, because our hearts and tongues are sleepy, and we bring not with us so much skill and zeal as to awake them! (*The Reformed Pastor* [1656; Edinburgh: Banner of Truth, 1974 reprint of 1862 abridgement], 70)

THE SHEEP'S RESPONSIBILITY TO THE SHEPHERDS

that you appreciate those . . . and that you esteem them very highly in love because of their work. Live in peace with one another. (5:12a, 13)

Those who herd sheep for a living know that the animals can be quite difficult to deal with. Sheep are dirty, weak, unorganized creatures that are prone to wander. Yet they can also be demanding and have no regard for those who get in the way of their sharp hooves. Thus sheep can make life quite joyless for the shepherd if they do not obey him. Likewise, when believers do not obey the Lord's commands or submit to the leadership of His appointed leaders, they can make life in the local church miserable and unproductive (cf. Heb. 13:17). That is why it is imperative that Christians realize and fulfill their responsibility to their pastors. Paul gave the Thessalonians a threefold expression of that duty to pastors: appreciate them, esteem them, and submit to them.

THE RESPONSIBILITY TO APPRECIATE

that you appreciate those (5:12a)

Appreciate is a translation of the common New Testament word *oida*, which means to know by experience (e.g., Matt. 7:11; 9:6; Mark 2:10; Luke 20:21; John 4:22; 10:4; Acts 3:16; Rom. 6:16; 8:28; 1 Cor. 2:12; 2 Cor. 9:2; Eph. 1:18; Phil. 4:12; Col. 4:6; 2 Thess. 3:7; 1 Tim. 3:15; 2 Tim. 1:12; Heb. 10:30; James 1:19; 1 John 2:20; 3:2; 3 John 12; Rev. 2:2; 3:8). The connotation here is that believers are to know their shepherds deeply and respectfully and to value their service. Such knowledge is much more than the mere recall of their names or the general awareness of some facts about their personal lives. Instead, it entails a close, personal acquaintance that results in the caring appreciation of the Lord's servant.

It is common for people to be unkind, critical, and indifferent toward their pastors when they do not know them well. But believers will not be as likely to have such negative attitudes toward pastors they truly know. Rather, they are more likely to treat them with heartfelt respect and gratitude.

Appreciation also involves giving pastors financial support. Paul's later instruction concerning elders implies such support even more clearly: "The elders who rule well are to be considered worthy of double honor, especially those who work hard at preaching and teaching" (1 Tim. 5:17). *Timē* ("honor") means "respect," or "high regard," but the context of 1 Timothy 5 (vv. 3–16, the discussion of support for widows) suggests the word can also refer to money (cf. Matt. 27:6, 9; Acts 5:2–3; 7:16; 19:19). Paul told Timothy that diligent, faithful elders were worthy of double respect and generous pay, particularly those who are the most diligent and sacrificial in preaching and teaching. The church must generously support those shepherds who labor hard to expound the Word. First Corinthians 9:14 well summarizes the principle: "So also the Lord directed those who proclaim the gospel to get their living from the gospel" (cf. 9:9; 2 Cor. 8:1–5; 1 Tim. 5:18).

So Paul's request that the Thessalonians appreciate their pastors included knowledgeable acquaintance that leads to loving respect, sincere admiration, and generous financial remuneration that shows gratitude for the shepherds' ministry and trust in their stewardship of the church's resources.

THE RESPONSIBILITY TO ESTEEM

and that you esteem them very highly in love because of their work. (5:13a)

The congregation of believers has the duty to **esteem** ("regard," "think about") its pastors **very highly** ("beyond all measure"). Similar, obviously, to showing appreciation, this second verb, however, indicates something more than simply knowing in a respectful way. This phrase calls for limitless respect for church leaders.

Paul intensified this responsibility even further by telling the Thessalonians they must have high esteem for their shepherds **in love,** not because of their personalities or the favors they rendered, but **because of their work.** So beyond appreciating the man because they know him, the saints are to hold him in even greater regard because of his divinely designed and energized calling. **Love** is the familiar word *agapē* and refers to selfless, sacrificial service for others. The **work** the shepherds do is their ministry of the Word, which feeds the souls of the flock. In his letter to the churches in Galatia, Paul had commended the Galatian believers for the godly way they had esteemed him:

> That which was a trial to you in my bodily condition you did not despise or loathe, but you received me as an angel of God, as Christ Jesus Himself. . . . For I bear you witness that, if possible, you would have plucked out your eyes and given them to me. (Gal. 4:14–15)

In spite of some kind of repulsive physical ailment from which Paul suffered, the Galatians welcomed him as their shepherd. Paul's ailment may have been some type of eye disease, which may explain the Galatians' willingness to pluck out their eyes. (The reference also may be figurative, illustrating their willingness to go to any extreme for him, cf. Matt. 5:29; 18:8–9.) In any case, though from a human standpoint there was nothing attractive about Paul, the Galatians displayed the same kind of respectful attitude toward him as he commanded the Thessalonians to have for their shepherds.

God has called pastors and set them apart for the important work of leading His church (1 Tim. 3:1–7; Titus 1:5–9; cf. Mark 3:13–19; Acts 6:3–6; 13:1–3). Therefore the people under them are to lovingly acknowledge their ministry labors, greatly respect them, overlook their non-sinful human frailties (cf. Prov. 10:12; 1 Peter 4:8), speak well of them, encourage them, and give their best for them.

THE RESPONSIBILITY TO SUBMIT

Live in peace with one another. (5:13*b*)

The concept of believers living in **peace with one another** is a familiar New Testament exhortation (Rom. 14:19; 2 Cor. 13:11; Eph. 4:3; Col. 3:15; James 3:18). But here Paul's admonition specifically referred to the relationship between the Thessalonians and their pastors. For that relationship to be peaceful, the flock at Thessalonica needed to submit to its leaders. Such submission, if done in a God-honoring way, would eliminate conflict, strife, and discord and promote **peace,** harmony, and effective ministry within the church (cf. Rom. 12:18; 1 Cor. 14:33; Heb. 12:14; 1 Peter 3:10–11).

Nearly twenty years after Paul wrote to the Thessalonians, the writer of Hebrews further elaborated on the necessity for sheep to submit to their shepherds. First he commanded his readers, "Remember those who led you, who spoke the word of God to you; and considering the result of their conduct, imitate their faith" (13:7). "Remember" refers to remembering the shepherds with love and affection and considering how the Lord blessed the shepherds' lives and used them to proclaim His Word. Then that remembrance ought to prompt the sheep to emulate their shepherds' conduct. Imitating those who model righteous behavior is the central part of submission.

Hebrews 13:17 contains two additional exhortations regarding submission to elders. The first half of the verse says, "Obey your leaders and submit to them, for they keep watch over your souls as those who will give an account." Unless the shepherds ask the sheep to do something that is unscriptural or sinful, the sheep ought to obey and submit to the shepherds' leadership. Sheep should never disregard their shepherds' faithful teaching and oversight because such sinful disrespect only makes the leaders' accountability to God that much more difficult. The verse concludes by admonishing, "Let them do this with joy and not with grief, for this would be unprofitable for you." Stubborn, self-willed, and unsubmissive sheep steal the joy from their shepherds and give themselves and their leaders nothing but pain and an unprofitable relationship (cf. Jer. 9:1–6; Matt. 23:37–39). (For more complete commentary on Hebrews 13:7, 17, see *Hebrews,* The MacArthur New Testament Commentary [Chicago: Moody, 1983], chaps. 38–39.)

For the local church to function as God intended and receive His blessing, its pastors must be responsible to labor among the people, exercise authority over them, and provide instruction to them. At the same time, the people have obligations to appreciate the pastors, esteem them, and submit to them. When both fulfill their respective responsibilities, the church becomes the unified, joyful, peaceful, and healthy flock God intended it to be. Faithful pastors and faithful people ministering together bring honor to Christ, the head of the church, advance the kingdom of God, and give Him glory.

Growing a Healthy Flock—Part 2: Dealing with the Spiritually Needy (1 Thessalonians 5:14–15)

15

We urge you, brethren, admonish the unruly, encourage the faint-hearted, help the weak, be patient with everyone. See that no one repays another with evil for evil, but always seek after that which is good for one another and for all people. (5:14–15)

The closest any church has come to being what the Lord desires is the apostolic church in the book of Acts. Concerning the church's condition in the days and weeks following the dramatic events of Pentecost, Luke made these observations:

> They were continually devoting themselves to the apostles' teaching and to fellowship, to the breaking of bread and to prayer. Everyone kept feeling a sense of awe; and many wonders and signs were taking place through the apostles. And all those who had believed were together and had all things in common; and they began selling their property and possessions and were sharing them with all, as anyone might have need. Day by day continuing with one mind in the temple, and breaking bread from house to house, they were taking their meals together with gladness and sincerity of heart, praising God and having favor with all the people. And the Lord was adding to their number day by day those who were being saved. (Acts 2:42–47)

The apostolic church had a God-honoring response to every situation, including persecution. After the Jewish leaders apprehended Peter and John, interrogated them, warned them not to preach the gospel anymore, and released them, the church promptly prayed about the situation (4:24–30). As a result,

> the place where they had gathered together was shaken, and they were all filled with the Holy Spirit and began to speak the word of God with boldness. And the congregation of those who believed were of one heart and soul; and not one of them claimed that anything belonging to him was his own, but all things were common property to them. And with great power the apostles were giving testimony to the resurrection of the Lord Jesus, and abundant grace was upon them all. For there was not a needy person among them, for all who were owners of land or houses would sell them and bring the proceeds of the sales and lay them at the apostles' feet, and they would be distributed to each as any had need. (4:31–35)

There was another critical lesson, however, that the Lord had to teach the first church if it was to grow spiritually and be effective in reaching the lost. That lesson was the urgency of discipline for sinning members (cf. Acts 5:1–6). From Jesus' teaching (Matt. 18:15–18) and the Acts 5 events, the apostle Paul understood that principle well and realized that even the strongest churches, such as the one in Thessalonica, must be diligent to confront sin among the people (cf. 2 Cor. 12:20–13:2). He was thankful for the Thessalonians' spiritual health (1 Thess. 1:2–3, 9–10; 2:19–20; 3:9–10) but was eager for them to continue growing in grace (3:8, 12; 4:1, 10), and that meant directly ministering to people with problems, as this text indicates.

Paul's approach to church growth was in sharp contrast to present-day "church growth" experts' concerns about cultural demographics and homogeneity, subtle schemes to make the church more "seeker friendly," sophisticated entertainment methodologies to make worship services "more relevant," and glib marketing techniques to attract new members. Rather than relying on such man-made strategies or concepts, the apostle focused on the sinful obstacles to the Thessalonian church's spiritual growth. In so doing he identified five types of struggling sheep that the healthy sheep needed to deal with: the wayward, who needed to get back in line; the worried, who needed to have more courage, faith, boldness, and confidence; the weak, who needed to be more disciplined in holiness; the wearisome, who needed to keep pace in obedience; and the wicked, who needed to behave righteously. The church's lack of spiritual progress is usually due to the sinful behavior of people in those problem categories, and Paul earnestly desired that the Thessalonians know how to adequately deal with those in each category, as necessary.

DEALING WITH WAYWARD SHEEP

We urge you, brethren, admonish the unruly, (5:14*a*)

Paul's exhortation to the Thessalonians reflected his sense of urgency. **Urge** is from *parakaleō*, which literally means "to come along-side" and carries the idea of providing help to someone. The apostle zealously and eagerly encouraged the **brethren,** the spiritually healthy believers, to get involved in helping the needy. Although he recognized that the shepherds also had responsibility for troublesome sheep within the church, this exhortation, like the one in 5:12, was directed primarily at the **brethren,** or the congregation.

Paul identified the wayward by the term **unruly** (*ataktos*), which in extrabiblical Greek often occurred in a military context and referred to a soldier who was out of rank and behaved in a disorderly, insubordinate manner. The word came to refer to anyone who did not perform his duty or follow through on his responsibility. Some commentators say *ataktos* primarily referred to the idle, indolent, or apathetic (2 Thess. 3:6–7, 11; cf. 1 Tim. 5:13) in the Thessalonian church—those who were passive and shirked their duties. But the context suggests the term could also refer to those who had an actively rebellious attitude.

The unruly were those who were out of step with the direction everyone else was headed. Such are those who fail to serve the church with their spiritual gifts (cf. 1 Cor. 12:7; 14:12–13), give the church a portion of their wealth (cf. 1 Cor. 16:2; 2 Cor. 8:7; 9:6–12), or support the church's leadership (cf. 1 Thess. 5:12–13; 1 Tim. 5:17; Heb. 13:7, 17). They may have been unsupportive because they did not care, or because they were angry, rebellious, and contentious. Such people, if not dealt with, tend to become bitter. They can become criticizing benchwarmers and eventually rebels who undermine church leadership to justify their insubordination. Both are, obviously, divisive.

For Paul, helping the wayward did not involve some complex methodology or sophisticated psychological counseling program. Instead, other believers were to come alongside them and **admonish** (*noutheteō*) them. The King James Version translators rendered **admonish** "warn" (cf. Acts 20:31; 1 Cor. 4:14; Col. 1:28), a meaning that connotes putting sense into someone's head, or alerting him of the serious consequences of his actions. *Noutheteō* does not mean being judgmental or critical in a superior manner. Rather, it is the caring kind of warning against danger that

Paul gave to the Ephesian elders (Acts 20:31) and that he sought to bring to the Thessalonians.

DEALING WITH WORRIED SHEEP

encourage the fainthearted, (5:14*b*)

The second group of spiritually needy sheep Paul identified was **the fainthearted,** literally the "small souled" (*oligopsuchos*). Whereas the unruly were pushing on the edges of acceptable Christian behavior, these were the worried sheep, huddled in the middle and afraid to get near the edge. There are those in the church who are bold and courageous, unafraid of persecution or difficulty, and willing to put their lives on the line for a noble cause or principle of truth. In contrast, **the fainthearted** lack the boldness to accept a challenging new ministry, fear change and the unknown, and want a risk-free ministry that is traditional, safe, and absolutely secure.

Some of the Thessalonians were **fainthearted** because they did not deal well with persecution; apparently they had not understood or were unwilling to heed Paul's call for bold evangelism, fearing it might lead to suffering (1 Thess. 3:2–4; cf. Matt. 5:10–12; John 15:18–21; Phil. 1:29–30; 2 Tim. 3:12; 1 Peter 4:19; 5:10).

The apostle Paul's instruction for how the confident sheep should help the worried was simple: the confident should **encourage** the worried. **Encourage** (*paramutheomai*) literally means "to speak alongside" someone, and in so doing, to offer comfort and consolation. The confident need to become personal instructors and examples to the worried and teach them the biblical certainty that their Lord answers their prayers (1 John 5:14–15), secures their salvation (John 10:27–29), includes them in a final resurrection (John 11:24–27), loves them eternally (Rom. 8:38–39), and sovereignly fulfills His will for their lives (Prov. 19:21; Rom. 8:28–29). By such reminders the joyful, confident believer cheers up the joyless, timid one.

DEALING WITH WEAK SHEEP

help the weak, (5:14*c*)

The **weak** could be those who are fragile in faith, beset by doubts (Rom. 14:1–15:13; 1 Cor. 8:1–13; 9:19–23; 10:23–33). Their faith may not be strong enough to enjoy their freedom in Jesus Christ (cf. Gal. 5:1; Col.

2:16–23). They are certainly more susceptible to error (Eph. 4:14), temptation, and sin than stronger believers (cf. 1 Cor. 8:9–13). Some weaker believers have such sensitive consciences over their past sins that they perceive things as sin that are not sin at all (cf. 1 Cor. 8:7).

Weak (*asthenēs*) focuses on susceptibility to sin and applies to believers who struggle with abandoning sin and obeying God's will. Though modern English versions render *asthenēs* in James 5:14 "sick," it denotes sheep who are **weak**: "Is anyone among you sick? Then he must call for the elders of the church and they are to pray over him." The morally and spiritually weak one is to call the spiritually strong elders to come and intercede for him, and whatever sin has caused the weakness, they exhort him to repent of that sin. (For a full discussion of this verse and subsequent verses, see *James*, The MacArthur New Testament Commentary [Chicago: Moody, 1998], 276–90.) **The weak** are always impediments and stumbling blocks to growth and power in the church.

Paul urged those Thessalonians who were strong to **help the weak** (cf. Gal. 6:1–2). **Help** is a somewhat imprecise rendering of the Greek word *antechō,* which means "to hold firmly," "to cling to," "to support," "to hold up" (cf. Titus 1:9). Paul commanded the stronger sheep to come alongside the weaker sheep, establish close personal relationships with them, and provide them doctrinal instruction and encouragement toward righteousness and away from sin.

DEALING WITH WEARISOME SHEEP

be patient with everyone. (5:14*d*)

It is easy for healthy sheep to become frustrated, angry, or discouraged with some of the chronic problem sheep. It is always disappointing in a discipling relationship when a mature believer has taught, trained, exhorted, strengthened, and encouraged a less mature believer, only to have that person manifest little commitment to Christ or evidence of spiritual growth. Some in Thessalonica had heard the truth from Paul and other teachers and had numerous opportunities to apply it, but their spiritual progress was negligible. As a result, Paul exhorted the congregation to **be patient with everyone.**

By using the word **patient** (*makrothumeō*), Paul gave the injunction to be forbearing with those who struggled. By **everyone** Paul meant all those people with whom the strong Christians might easily have become impatient. Those sheep who grew so imperceptibly, never seemed to keep pace with the other sheep, were easily distracted, and were generally undisciplined in the means of grace could easily have tried the patience of the strong. Even Jesus was righteously exasperated with the disciples' slow growth and lack of understanding when on several occasions He called them "men of little faith" (Matt. 8:26; 16:8; Luke 12:28). But the Thessalonians were to have boundless patience with the wearisome sheep, even as God has great patience with all His sheep (Ex. 34:6; Num. 14:18; Ps. 86:15; Isa. 63:7–9; Rom. 3:25; 1 Tim. 1:16; cf. 1 Cor. 13:4–5; 2 Cor. 6:4–10; Gal. 5:22; Eph. 4:2; Col. 3:12–13; 2 Tim. 2:24; 4:2; Heb. 5:1–3).

In the following exchange with Peter, Jesus best summarized the magnitude to which believers ought to extend forgiving patience to others: "Then Peter came and said to Him, 'Lord, how often shall my brother sin against me and I forgive him? Up to seven times?' Jesus said to him, 'I do not say to you, up to seven times, but up to seventy times seven'" (Matt. 18:21–22; cf. vv. 23–35; Luke 17:3–4). Christ taught that there should be no arbitrary limit, no matter how generous that seemed, on the amount of times one forgives another. On the contrary, believers ought to extend patience and forgiveness unendingly to their brothers and sisters in Christ.

DEALING WITH WICKED SHEEP

See that no one repays another with evil for evil, but always seek after that which is good for one another and for all people. (5:15)

For Christians, the severest, most painful disappointments come not from the wickedness of the unbelieving world but from other sheep within the church. Sheep are definitely capable of harming other sheep, sinning against them in a variety of ways, such as attacking them with wicked words (cf. Prov. 13:2–3; 15:1, 4; 18:13, 21; 24:28; Matt. 5:22; James 3:1–12) that include gossip and slander (cf. Ex. 20:16; Prov. 11:13; 20:19; 24:28), ostracizing them from fellowship and ministry opportunities, or harming them more overtly by helping break up a marriage (cf. Ex. 20:14; 1 Thess. 4:6) or influencing someone toward sinful behavior (Matt. 18:6–10).

The apostle Paul instructed the Thessalonians on how to respond to such wickedness from others in the church: **see that no one repays another with evil for evil.** At some point, disobedient sheep had done **evil** ("baseness, meanness, wickedness") to the obedient ones. Paul's response—stated in the imperative—to those wronged was **that no one** should repay **with evil.** There is absolutely no place among Christians for retaliation or personal vengeance (Rom. 12:19). The only one who has the right to retaliate is God (Lev. 19:18; Deut. 32:35; Ps. 94:1; Prov. 20:22; Nah. 1:2; Heb. 10:30; Rev. 14:9–10, 14–20).

Therefore, the sheep's proper response when sinned against by fellow sheep is not to seek revenge, but to always **seek . . . that which is good**—to always pursue eagerly and zealously that which is beautiful, noble, and excellent (cf. 1 Cor. 13:4–7; 2 Cor. 8:21; Eph. 4:25; Phil. 4:8; James 3:17). "'But if your enemy is hungry, feed him, and if he is thirsty, give him a drink; for in so doing you will heap burning coals on his head.' Do not be overcome by evil, but overcome evil with good" (Rom. 12:20–21; cf. 2 Kings 6:22; Prov. 25:21–22; Matt. 5:43–44; Luke 6:27–38; 1 Cor. 4:12; 6:6–8; 1 Peter 2:19–23; 3:8–12).

Paul wanted the Thessalonians to respond to hostility with genuine acts of love. The welfare of **one another,** even those who had seriously offended them, was to be the Thessalonians' primary concern. That concern was also to extend beyond the church to **all people** (cf. Gal. 6:10; 1 Tim. 2:1; 2 Tim. 2:24; Titus 3:2, 8).

So a healthy flock is characterized by growth in faith, love, and purity, and progress toward the likeness of Christ. But spiritually needy and problem sheep within the flock can and do impede its growth. That means the healthy sheep must lovingly, patiently, but truthfully deal with the difficult sheep to remove sinful impediments and ensure real growth. The key is not finding some clever strategy to bypass the troubles, but addressing the issues directly, as shepherds and sheep alike admonish the wayward, encourage the worried, uphold the weak, bear with the wearisome, and render goodness to the wicked.

The Sheep's Responsibilities to the Great Shepherd— Part 1: Joyfulness, Prayerfulness, and Thankfulness (1 Thessalonians 5:16–18)

16

Rejoice always; pray without ceasing; in everything give thanks; for this is God's will for you in Christ Jesus. (5:16–18)

If God's flock is to be healthy, above all else the relationship between the sheep and the Great Shepherd, Jesus Christ the Son of God, must be right. For that to happen, believers must be mindful of their responsibilities to worship and serve the Lord their King. The words of the first three stanzas of Frances Havergal's classic hymn, "Take My Life, and Let It Be," perhaps capture the essence of those responsibilities better than any ordinary prose could:

> Take my life, and let it be Consecrated, Lord, to thee.
> Take my moments and my days; Let them flow in ceaseless praise.
>
> Take my hands, and let them move At the impulse of thy love.
> Take my feet, and let them be Swift and beautiful for thee.
>
> Take my voice, and let me sing, Always, only, for my King.
> Take my lips, and let them be Filled with messages from thee.

Explicitly and implicitly, that hymn contains the spirit of the first three of Paul's exhortations to the Thessalonians to strengthen their inner spiritual lives and thus be able to fulfill their responsibilities to God (1 Thess. 5:16–22). The three exhortations go right to the starting point of the believer's attitude: the exhortation to constant joyfulness, to constant prayerfulness, and to constant thankfulness.

The Exhortation to Constant Joyfulness

Rejoice always; (5:16)

A thorough and accurate understanding of Christian joy is essential for all believers. Paul's exhortation to the Thessalonians to **rejoice always** may seem absurd and impossible to obey given life's inevitable difficulties, but as a divinely inspired command, believers must heed it. Any failure to do so constitutes a disregard for Scripture's clear instructions and therefore sinful disobedience.

Many other statements throughout God's Word enjoin the believer to have joy in all situations (Deut. 12:18; Neh. 8:10; Pss. 2:11; 5:11; 32:11; 68:3; 100:2; 132:16; Isa. 29:19; Joel 2:23–24; Hab. 3:17–18; Matt. 5:10–12; Luke 6:22–23; 10:20; John 16:20–22; cf. Pss. 16:8–9; 21:6; 28:7; 132:16; Isa. 35:10; 55:12; 56:7; Zech. 9:9; Acts 5:41; Rom. 15:13; 2 Cor. 10:17; Eph. 5:9; Phil. 2:17–18; 4:4; Col. 1:24; James 1:2; 5:13; 1 Peter 1:6; 4:13). While he was aware of the many injunctions to rejoice, Paul also recognized the existence of negative human emotions like sorrow and distress (e.g., Acts 20:19, 37–38; Rom. 12:15; Phil. 3:18; cf. Isa. 32:11–12; Matt. 9:23; Mark 5:38–39). However, the apostle also knew believers must transcend their sorrows with a continual focus on true joy; they must be as he wrote of himself, "sorrowful yet always rejoicing" (2 Cor. 6:10). Such a focus is possible because biblical joy comes from God, not merely from a superficial emotional response to positive circumstances (cf. Phil. 3:3). Christian joy constantly flows from what the believer continually knows to be true about God and about his eternal, saving relationship to Him—regardless of circumstances (Pss. 16:11; 68:3; Luke 2:10–11; 24:52; Acts 16:34; Rom. 5:2, 11; 1 Peter 1:8). Supernatural joy is from the Holy Spirit; thus Paul listed it as an aspect of spiritual fruit (Gal. 5:22; cf. Rom. 14:17).

The phrase translated **rejoice always** literally reads "at all times be rejoicing" and emphasizes that truly joyful Christians will always have a deep-seated confidence in God's sovereign love and mighty power on behalf of His own, and in His providential working of all things according to His perfect plan (Matt. 6:33–34; Rom. 8:28–30; 11:33; Phil. 1:12; cf.

Gen. 50:20; Ps. 139:1–5). Therefore, no event or circumstance in the Christian's life, apart from sin, can or should diminish his true joy.

A proper perspective on biblical joy provides numerous reasons for believers to rejoice. First of all, they should **rejoice always** in appreciation for God's righteous character, which, even in trouble, He demonstrates so faithfully to believers. The psalmist declared, "The Lord is my strength and my shield; my heart trusts in Him, and I am helped; therefore my heart exults, and with my song I shall thank Him" (Ps. 28:7; cf. Neh. 8:10; Pss. 71:23; 89:16; Isa. 61:10). Second, they should have constant joy out of appreciation for Christ's redemptive work, which derives from a gracious, loving, merciful, and compassionate God (Luke 2:10; 10:20; Rom. 5:1–2, 11; 1 Peter 1:8–9), and for His infallible instruction (John 15:11; 16:30; 1 John 5:20). Third, they should rejoice in appreciation of the Holy Spirit's ministry on their behalf (Acts 10:44; Rom. 14:17; cf. 8:14–27). Fourth, believers should **rejoice always** because of the vast array of spiritual blessings they possess (cf. Eph. 1:3–4; Phil. 4:13, 19; Col. 2:9–14; 2 Peter 1:3). Fifth, they should have joy in God's providence as He orchestrates everything for their benefit (Rom. 8:28–30; James 1:2–4). Sixth, they should be joyful out of gratitude for the promise of future glory (cf. Ps. 16:8–11; Matt. 5:12; Luke 10:20; 1 Cor. 1:7; Phil. 1:18–21; 3:20; Jude 24). Seventh, answered prayer should always be a source of joy (Pss. 66:20; 116:1, 17; 118:21; John 16:24), as should an eighth reason, an appreciation for the gift of God's Word (Col. 3:16; cf. Pss. 19:7–11; 119:14, 111, 162; Jer. 15:16). Ninth, the privilege of genuine fellowship should bring continual joy to the believer (1 Thess. 3:9; 2 Tim. 1:4; Philem. 7; 2 John 12). And finally, true believers cannot help but express their joy at the saving proclamation of the gospel, as the early church did: "Therefore, being sent on their way by the church, they [Paul, Barnabas, and other believers] were passing through both Phoenicia and Samaria, describing in detail the conversion of the Gentiles, and were bringing great joy to all the brethren" (Acts 15:3; cf. Phil. 1:18).

The joyful Christian is more concerned about glorifying God than about avoiding temporal difficulties (Rom. 8:18; cf. Heb. 11:13–16, 25). He thinks more of his spiritual riches and eternal glory than he does any present pain or material poverty (1 Peter 1:6–7; 4:13; James 5:11; cf. 2 Cor. 6:4–10; 1 Peter 5:10). Believers who live like that will fulfill the command to **rejoice always.**

THE EXHORTATION TO CONSTANT PRAYERFULNESS

pray without ceasing; (5:17)

Joyful believers will also be prayerful believers. Those who live their Christian lives in joyful dependency on God will continually recognize their own insufficiency and therefore constantly be in an attitude of prayer. Paul's exhortation to the Thessalonians to **pray without ceasing** is thus a divine mandate to all believers. **Pray** is from *proseuchomai*, the most common New Testament word for prayer (e.g., Matt. 6:5–6; Mark 11:24; Luke 5:16; 11:1–2; Acts 10:9; Rom. 8:26; 1 Cor. 14:13–15; Eph. 6:18; Col. 1:9; 2 Thess. 3:1; James 5:13–14, 16). It encompasses all the aspects of prayer: submission, confession, petition, intercession, praise, and thanksgiving. **Without ceasing** means "constant" and defines prayer not as some perpetual activity of kneeling and interceding but as a way of life marked by a continual attitude of prayer.

One cannot begin to understand Paul's command to continual prayerfulness without considering how faithfully Jesus prayed during His earthly ministry. As the Son of God, He was in constant communion with the Father, and the Gospels provide many examples of the Lord's consistent prayer life (Matt. 14:23; Mark 1:35; 6:46; Luke 9:18, 28–29; cf. John 6:15; 17:1–26). During times when He went to the Mount of Olives to pray all night (Luke 21:37–38; John 8:1–2) He undoubtedly prayed with a kind of intensity that believers know little or nothing about. The classic example of such intensity is when Jesus prayed in the Garden of Gethsemane the night before His crucifixion. "And He withdrew from them about a stone's throw, and He knelt down and began to pray. . . . And being in agony He was praying very fervently; and His sweat became like drops of blood, falling down upon the ground" (Luke 22:41, 44). Matthew 26:38–46 records that Jesus' prayer in the garden was a prolonged experience in which He pleaded three times for the Father to spare Him from "this cup" (v. 39)—the divine wrath against sin, which He would have to bear the next day in His substitutionary death on the cross for sinners. (For a complete exposition of this passage, see *Matthew 24–28*, The MacArthur New Testament Commentary [Chicago: Moody, 1989], 167–78.) That level of intense agonizing is beyond anything Christians have to face, but it illustrates the persistence Jesus spoke of in the parables of the friend in need (Luke 11:5–10) and the relentless widow (Luke 18:1–8). It also uniquely exemplifies what the apostle Paul meant when he instructed the Thessalonians to **pray without ceasing.**

From its inception, the early church demonstrated a Christlike earnestness and constancy in its prayer life. Luke wrote how devoted Christ's followers were to prayer, even before the Day of Pentecost: "These all [the apostles] with one mind were continually devoting themselves to prayer, along with the women, and Mary the mother of Jesus, and with His brothers" (Acts 1:14). Later they gave themselves regularly to prayer (Acts 2:42). In their role as leaders of the young church, the apostles determined to devote themselves "to prayer and to the ministry of the word" (Acts 6:4). Also, diligent prayer by believers played a part in Peter's release from prison (Acts 12:11–16; cf. 4:23–31).

The New Testament emphasis on the importance of prayer cannot be overstated. Already in 1 Thessalonians, Paul had written, "As we night and day keep praying most earnestly that we may see your face" (3:10). Many of Paul's other epistles also indicate the importance of prayer (Rom. 12:12; 1 Cor. 7:5; Eph. 6:18–19; Phil. 4:6; Col. 4:2; 2 Thess. 3:1; 1 Tim. 2:8).

The strong scriptural emphasis on prayer suggests a substantial list of motivations for Christians to **pray without ceasing.** First of all— and the highest of all motives for believers—is their desire to glorify the Lord. Jesus taught the disciples in His model prayer, "Pray, then, in this way: 'Our Father who is in heaven, hallowed be Your name. Your kingdom come. Your will be done, on earth as it is in heaven'" (Matt. 6:9–10; cf. Dan. 9:4–19). Second, the desire for fellowship with God motivates believers to pray: "As the deer pants for the water brooks, so my soul pants for You, O God. My soul thirsts for God, for the living God; when shall I come and appear before God?" (Ps. 42:1–2; cf. 27:1, 4; 63:1–2; 84:1–2). Jesus said believers' prayers would be answered in order that "the Father may be glorified in the Son" (John 14:13; cf. v. 14).

Third, believers will pray for God to meet their needs: "Give us this day our daily bread" (Matt. 6:11; cf. Luke 11:9–13; 1 John 5:14–15). Fourth, Christians will pray persistently for God's wisdom as they live in the midst of a sinful world: "But if any of you lacks wisdom, let him ask of God, who gives to all generously and without reproach, and it will be given to him" (James 1:5; cf. Matt. 6:13; 1 Cor. 10:13). Fifth, the desire for deliverance from trouble motivates prayer. Jonah is a vivid example of such motivation: "Then Jonah prayed to the Lord his God from the stomach of the fish, and he said, 'I called out of my distress to the Lord, and He answered me. I cried for help from the depth of Sheol; You heard my voice'" (Jonah 2:1–2; cf. Ps. 20:1).

Sixth, all Christians desire relief from fear and worry. Paul encouraged the Philippians: "Be anxious for nothing, but in everything by prayer and supplication with thanksgiving let your requests be made known to God. And the peace of God, which surpasses all comprehension, will guard your hearts and your minds in Christ Jesus" (Phil. 4:6–7; cf. Ps. 4:1). A seventh motive is gratitude for past blessings, as the psalmist prayed:

> O God, we have heard with our ears, our fathers have told us the work that You did in their days, in the days of old. You with Your own hand drove out the nations; then You planted them; You afflicted the peoples, then You spread them abroad. For by their own sword they did not possess the land, and their own arm did not save them, but Your right hand

and Your arm and the light of Your presence, for You favored them. You are my King, O God. (Ps. 44:1–4*a*; cf. Phil. 1:3–5)

Eighth, believers pray to be freed from the guilt of sin. David expressed this when he wrote, "I acknowledged my sin to You, and my iniquity I did not hide; I said, 'I will confess my transgressions to the Lord'; and You forgave the guilt of my sin" (Ps. 32:5; cf. Prov. 28:13; 1 John 1:9). Ninth, believers' concern for salvation of the lost causes them to pray. Paul captured this motivation in his words to Timothy:

> First of all, then, I urge that entreaties and prayers, petitions and thanks-givings, be made on behalf of all men, for kings and all who are in authority, so that we may lead a tranquil and quiet life in all godliness and dignity. This is good and acceptable in the sight of God our Savior, who desires all men to be saved and to come to the knowledge of the truth. (1 Tim. 2:1–4; cf. Matt. 9:37–38; Rom. 10:1)

Finally, and certainly as important as any of the motivations for Christians to **pray without ceasing,** is their desire for spiritual growth—for themselves and for fellow believers. Paul's petition to the Lord for the Ephesians is a model in this regard:

> For this reason I bow my knees before the Father, from whom every family in heaven and on earth derives its name, that He would grant you, according to the riches of His glory, to be strengthened with power through His Spirit in the inner man, so that Christ may dwell in your hearts through faith; and that you, being rooted and grounded in love, may be able to comprehend with all the saints what is the breadth and length and height and depth, and to know the love of Christ which sur-passes knowledge, that you may be filled up to all the fullness of God. Now to Him who is able to do far more abundantly beyond all that we ask or think, according to the power that works within us, to Him be the glory in the church and in Christ Jesus to all generations forever and ever. Amen. (Eph. 3:14–21; cf. 1:15–19; Col. 1:9–12)

THE EXHORTATION TO CONSTANT THANKFULNESS

in everything give thanks; for this is God's will for you in Christ Jesus. (5:18)

Being unthankful is the very essence of the unregenerate heart. The apostle Paul identified unbelievers as ungrateful: "For even though they knew God [through conscience and general revelation], they did not honor Him as God or give thanks, but they became futile in their speculations, and their foolish heart was darkened" (Rom. 1:21). But when God regenerates an individual, He produces a new heart that longs to obey Paul's injunction and **in everything give thanks.** That simple, direct statement allows believers no excuses to be ungrateful. **In everything** (*en panti*) refers to *all* that occurs in life. No matter what struggles, trials, testings, or vicissitudes occur in the lives of Christians (with the obvious exception of personal sins), they are to **give thanks** (Acts 5:41; cf. James 1:2–3; 1 Peter 1:6–9). Thankfulness therefore should be part of the fabric of the regenerate life (Ps. 136:1–3; Dan. 6:10; Eph. 5:20; Col. 3:17; Heb. 13:15), a gracious fruit of the Holy Spirit's work within the believer's heart (cf. Col. 2:7).

It is spiritually abnormal for Christians to be unthankful. Unthankfulness disobeys the many Scripture texts that enjoin the believer to a life of gratitude. Romans 8:28 sets forth the overarching principle: "And we know that God causes all things to work together for good to those who love God, to those who are called according to His purpose." God's providence—His sovereign blending of all of life's contingencies for believers' ultimate blessing—causes them to be thankful for everything in life, knowing that it fits into His eternal purpose for them (cf. Gen. 50:20; Pss. 37:28; 91:3–4; 145:9; Prov. 19:21).

When the early church met, one of its main purposes was to give thanks to God. That is implicit even in Paul's instruction to the Corinthians concerning the proper use of tongues (languages) during their worship services.

> So also you, since you are zealous of spiritual gifts, seek to abound for the edification of the church. Therefore let one who speaks in a tongue pray that he may interpret. For if I pray in a tongue, my spirit prays, but my mind is unfruitful. What is the outcome then? I will pray with the spirit and I will pray with the mind also; I will sing with the spirit and I will sing with the mind also. Otherwise if you bless in the spirit only, how will the one who fills the place of the ungifted say the "Amen" at your giving of thanks, since he does not know what you are saying? For you are giving thanks well enough, but the other person is not edified. (1 Cor. 14:12–17)

Paul's other letters remind believers to express their thankfulness and thereby be distinct from the ungrateful, unbelieving culture around them. "But immorality or any impurity or greed must not even be named among you, as is proper among saints; and there must be no filthiness and silly talk, or coarse jesting, which are not fitting, but rather giving of thanks" (Eph. 5:3–4; cf. 2 Cor. 4:15; 9:11).

Ephesians 5:18–20 clearly affirms that Christians ought to be known by their constant thankfulness:

> And do not get drunk with wine, for that is dissipation, but be filled with the Spirit, speaking to one another in psalms and hymns and spiritual songs, singing and making melody with your heart to the Lord; always giving thanks for all things in the name of our Lord Jesus Christ to God, even the Father. (Cf. Col. 2:6–7; 3:15–17; 4:2.)

Even in times of great anxiety, fear, worry, and stress, a prayerful attitude of thanksgiving should characterize believers (Phil. 4:6–7).

Paul's statement, **for this is God's will for you in Christ Jesus,** attaches to all three commands in this passage. It **is God's will** that all those who are **in Christ Jesus** should express constant joy, constant prayer, and constant thanksgiving. And God not only mandates those expressions of righteousness, but He makes it possible for believers to articulate them (cf. Phil. 2:13)—and is pleased when they do.

The Sheep's Responsibilities to the Great Shepherd— Part 2: Do Not Quench the Spirit; Respond to God's Word; Be Discerning (1 Thessalonians 5:19–22)

17

Do not quench the Spirit; do not despise prophetic utterances. But examine everything carefully; hold fast to that which is good; abstain from every form of evil. (5:19–22)

Today much of the evangelical church has minimized the importance of the Holy Spirit and God's Word in the spiritual lives of believers. It is therefore guilty of the same kind of error Paul rebuked the Galatians for: "Are you so foolish? Having begun by the Spirit, are you now being perfected by the flesh?" (Gal. 3:3). The Holy Spirit's ministry and the Word's power become secondary to pragmatic, humanistic techniques and methodologies in dealing with people's emotional and spiritual needs. The church's current preoccupation with psychology, for example, substitutes man-centered approaches for biblical truth in dealing with problems. The common assertion is that the Holy Spirit and God's Word deal with problems simplistically and superficially, whereas psychotherapy gets at the hidden issues and effects genuine, deep-seated healing in an individual's life. But psychology's viewpoint turns the truth on its head. In reality, *it* is the superficial solution to spiritual needs; but the Spirit, utilizing the Word and prayer, provides deep, effective, and lasting spiritual solutions to believers' difficulties.

The contemporary charismatic movement, with its mystical under-tones, also misrepresents the true work of the Holy Spirit and quenches His sanctifying purposes. Charismatic religion focuses much of its atten-tion on the Holy Spirit, emphasizing His ministry and gifts and, in the case of the Word/Faith movement, expecting Him to constantly perform supernatural works at the "sovereign" behest of so-called faith claims. Ironically, however, those emphases actually misrepresent the Spirit, offering a counterfeit for His sanctifying work, and thereby disregarding Paul's warning to the Thessalonians not to quench Him. (For a complete look at the problems psychology and the charismatic movement pose for the church, see John MacArthur, *Our Sufficiency in Christ* [Dallas: Word, 1991] and *Charismatic Chaos* [Grand Rapids: Zondervan, 1992].)

The church's de-emphasis of the Holy Spirit's working through the Word has also led to a pronounced lack of spiritual discernment. One could cite many symptoms of this deficiency, but six basic ones come to mind immediately. First, there has been a general weakening of doctrinal clarity and conviction within the church. Many Christians no longer think biblically and theologically, and they consider it wrong and unloving to be dogmatic, even on the most basic doctrines such as the inerrancy of Scripture and the definition of the gospel. Second, much of the church is no longer antithetical in its thinking. It does not make sharp distinctions between true and false, right and wrong, but instead embraces subjectivity, relativity, and pragmatism. Third, image and influ-ence have replaced the proclamation of the truth as the essence of evan-gelization. The church is reluctant to risk offending unbelievers with a clear, convicting gospel message. Instead, it relies on marketing philoso-phy to present a seeker-friendly message that focuses on people's "felt needs." Fourth, the church has ceased valuing sound hermeneutics. Many preachers no longer work diligently at the careful and accurate interpretation of the Word. They have substituted anecdotes, psychology, and subjectivity for the objective exposition of Scripture. Fifth, the church has mostly ceased exercising church discipline against those members who persist in sin and error. As a result, the world's philosophy and practice enters the church and it stops being distinct from the sur-rounding pagan culture. Sixth, all of the preceding features produce and are characteristic of a spiritually immature church. The self-absorbed church, preoccupied with attaining personal comfort, success, and achiev-ing man-centered solutions to life's problems, possesses a superficial faith that cannot discern between good and evil, or truth and error. (For a fuller study of the church's drift from spiritual discernment in recent dec-ades and the keys to regaining such discernment, see John MacArthur, *Reckless Faith* [Wheaton, Ill.: Crossway], 1994.)

The widespread errors of psychology and charismatic doctrine and the church's alarming lack of discernment relentlessly threaten its spiritual health and effectiveness. But Paul's clear admonitions in 1 Thessalonians 5:19–22 direct believers toward their true responsibilities to not quench the Spirit, to respond to God's Word, and to be discerning in all things.

THE RESPONSIBILITY NOT TO QUENCH THE SPIRIT

Do not quench the Spirit; (5:19)

Some commentators believe this verse is connected to verses 20–22 and refers to forbidding the expression of the charismatic gifts in the Thessalonian church. They argue that Paul was warning the Thessalonians not to stifle the exercise of those gifts within their assembly. Those commentators go on to assert that the "prophetic utterances" (v. 20) are supernatural prophesyings that must be examined carefully to make sure they are good rather than evil (vv. 21–22). This view concludes that verses 19–22, in constituting Paul's attempt to correct the Thessalonians' underestimation of the miraculous gifts, are equivalent to an affirmation of the gifts' use in the church.

However, such arguments are not convincing for several reasons. First, there is no compelling reason in the text to make Paul's exhortation, **do not quench the Spirit,** or the other exhortations in verses 20–22, as anything other than separate statements of general exhortation. Readers ought to see them as principles for the Christian life and not read anything more into the text. Second, if the Thessalonian church had been abusing the charismatic gifts, Paul would have earnestly admonished the Thessalonians in detail, as he later did the Corinthians.

To appreciate this short command's true application and view it in its proper perspective, one must remember the Holy Spirit's role in believers' lives. By His sovereign power (cf. John 1:12–13; 6:37, 44; Acts 13:48; 16:14) God through the Spirit regenerates sinners (John 3:6, 8; Eph. 2:1, 5; Titus 3:5; cf. Ezek. 37:11–14), thereby effecting a complete transformation of their spiritual affections (Titus 3:5; cf. Ezek. 11:19; 36:27; Rom. 2:29; 2 Cor. 5:17). He frees them from slavery to habitual sin (Rom. 8:3–9), places them into the body of Christ (Rom. 8:15–17), takes up permanent residence within each new believer (John 14:17; Rom. 8:9, 11, 14; 1 Cor. 3:16; 1 John 2:27; 4:13; cf. 1 Cor. 6:19), pours the love of God into their hearts (Rom. 5:5; 2 Thess. 3:5; cf. 1 John 2:5), gifts them for spiritual service (1 Cor. 12:4–10, 28; cf. Rom. 12:4–13; 1 Cor. 2:12–13; 1 Tim. 4:14; 2 Tim. 1:6), seals them for eternity (2 Cor. 1:22; Eph. 1:13–14; 4:30), and sanctifies them (Rom. 15:16; 1 Cor. 6:11; 2 Thess. 2:13; Heb. 10:14–15; 1 Peter 1:2).

It is that process of progressive sanctification by the Spirit that Paul warned the Thessalonians **not** to **quench**. The metaphor **quench** means "to extinguish, stifle, or retard" the power or energy of something (cf. Matt. 25:8; Mark 9:48). Sometimes Scripture represents the presence of **the Spirit** as a fire (Acts 2:2–4; cf. Ex. 13:21; Mal. 3:2–3); thus the apostle warned the Thessalonians not to smother the Holy Spirit's work within them, comparing such quenching to extinguishing a fire (cf. Isa. 63:10; Acts 5:3–4; 7:51; Eph. 4:30; 2 Tim. 1:6).

That Jesus promised to send all believers the Holy Spirit—as a Helper to assist them in ministry and progressively sanctify them (John 14:16; 15:26; 16:7; Acts 1:4–5; cf. Prov. 1:23)—is another crucial reason **not** to **quench** Him. And that sanctification process comprises a variety of Spirit-initiated works.

First, the Holy Spirit illuminates the Word of God. "For to us God revealed them through the Spirit; for the Spirit searches all things, even the depths of God" (1 Cor. 2:10; cf. vv. 12–13; 2 Tim. 3:16; 2 Peter 1:20–21; 1 John 2:27). Believers grow spiritually only as they feed on the Word, when they "like newborn babies, long for the pure milk of the word, so that by it [they] may grow in respect to salvation" (1 Peter 2:2; cf. Ps. 19:7–14; Matt. 4:4). Believers can quench this aspect of the Spirit's work by failing to study Scripture or misinterpreting it (cf. 2 Tim. 2:15), by not receiving it with humility and applying it to their lives (cf. James 1:21–25), by failing to hide it in their hearts (cf. Ps. 119:11), by not searching it diligently (cf. John 5:39; 8:31–32), and by not letting it dwell richly within them (cf. Col. 3:16).

Second, the Holy Spirit brings believers into intimacy with God. "For you have not received a spirit of slavery leading to fear again, but you have received a spirit of adoption as sons by which we cry out, 'Abba! Father!' The Spirit Himself testifies with our spirit that we are children of God" (Rom. 8:15–16). The Spirit wants believers to have the joyful confidence that God loves them as His children (*Abba* means "Papa" or "Daddy," a term of intimacy and endearment) and that they are secure in His salvation. Paul told the Galatians, "Because you are sons, God has sent forth the Spirit of His Son into our hearts, crying, 'Abba! Father!'" (Gal. 4:6). The Spirit prompts believers to pray for divine resources (cf. Ps. 116:2; Matt. 6:33; 1 Cor. 14:15; Phil. 4:6; Heb. 4:16). If believers are growing in sanctification, they will have an increasingly deeper and more intimate knowledge of God (cf. Pss. 9:10; 25:4; 1 Cor. 2:2; Eph. 3:19; Phil. 3:10; 1 John 2:3). Believers can, however, quench that Spirit-prompted, intimate knowledge by not accepting God's purpose in life's difficulties (cf. Rom. 5:3; James 1:2–3, 12), by not being prayerful and worshipful (cf. John 4:24; Col. 4:2; 1 Thess. 5:17), by not casting their cares upon God (cf. 1 Peter 5:7), by operating in their own flesh rather than trusting God's strength (cf. Prov. 3:5–6), by not trusting God's supply (2 Cor. 9:8; Phil. 4:19), and by not trusting God's love (cf. Eph. 2:4–5; 1 John 3:1; 4:19).

Third, the Holy Spirit glorifies Christ to believers and makes them more like Him. "But we all, with unveiled face, beholding as in a mirror the glory of the Lord, are being transformed into the same image from glory to glory, just as from the Lord, the Spirit" (2 Cor. 3:18; cf. John 16:14–15; Gal. 4:19). Under the New Covenant, the veil is removed and believers can look into the mirror of the Word and see the glory of Christ (cf. Isa. 40:5; John 5:39). Genuine Christians affirm Christ's lordship and glorify His name (1 Cor. 12:3; cf. 1 John 2:6). But believers also can quench the Spirit's efforts to make them more Christlike; for instance, by neglecting the reading and studying of Scripture (cf. Ps. 119:130; Acts 17:11; 2 Tim. 2:15), or by merely reading the Bible for information rather than allowing it to reveal Christ to them. Or they can proudly refuse to admit that they need to see His glory and become more like Him (cf. James 1:22–25).

Fourth, the Holy Spirit helps believers know God's will (cf. Eph. 5:17; James 1:5; 1 John 5:14–15). He ensures, first, that they know and obey the scripturally revealed will of God. "I will put My Spirit within you and cause you to walk in My statutes, and you will be careful to observe My ordinances" (Ezek. 36:27; cf. Isa. 28:29; Jer. 10:23; John 10:4). Second, the Spirit leads believers more subjectively into God's will concerning issues that are not specifically revealed in Scripture. The Spirit provides believers with a level path of guidance (Ps. 143:10) as He operates through providence and helps them make decisions in accord with the Father's will (cf. Ps. 37:5; Prov. 16:3; James 4:15). Believers can quench this element of the Spirit's work in sanctification through self-will, stubbornness, pride, indifference, and insensitivity regarding God's will (cf. Prov. 26:12; Dan. 5:20; Luke 18:11–12; Rom. 12:3; Rev. 2:4; 3:16–17).

Finally, the Holy Spirit grants believers inward strength to help them stay on the path of progressive sanctification. Paul prayed for the Ephesians "that [God] would grant [them], according to the riches of His glory, to be strengthened with power through His Spirit in the inner man" (Eph. 3:16; cf. Zech. 4:6; 2 Cor. 12:9). In no respect can Christians walk obediently with Christ unless they rely on the Holy Spirit's strength by the indwelling Word (Gal. 5:16; cf. Eph. 5:8–10). Through the Spirit's sealing, they can know the security of their salvation (Eph. 1:13–14). Without the Spirit's strength, they could not have victory over sin and the flesh (Rom. 8:5, 13; Gal. 3:3; 6:8; cf. Matt. 26:41; Rom. 7:18). Unless they have the Spirit's power, believers cannot witness effectively (Acts 1:8; cf. Matt. 28:18–20; Acts 8:26–29). The Spirit's enabling and filling allows them to worship God from the heart and relate to everyone else in their lives in a God-honoring fashion. However, the empowering work of the Spirit can also be quenched through pride and overconfidence in human ability, both of which deny the believer's need to rely on the Spirit.

Isaiah 11:2 aptly summarizes how the Holy Spirit would assist Christ during His earthly ministry and suggests the kinds of empowerment all Christians have available: "The Spirit of the Lord will rest on Him [Christ], the spirit of wisdom and understanding, the spirit of counsel and strength, the spirit of knowledge and the fear of the Lord." But believers can utilize those resources only when they are filled with the Spirit (Eph. 5:18) and walk by the Spirit (Gal. 5:25)—two expressions of what it means to be Spirit-controlled. (For a complete study of the Holy Spirit's Person and work, see John MacArthur, *The Silent Shepherd* [Wheaton, Ill.: Scripture Press/Victor Books, 1996].)

THE RESPONSIBILITY TO RESPOND TO GOD'S WORD

do not despise prophetic utterances. (5:20)

The Word of God is infinitely superior to all the words of man. Jesus summarized its excellence when He quoted Deuteronomy 8:3, "'Man shall not live on bread alone, but on every word that proceeds out of the mouth of God'" (Matt. 4:4). Respect for the supremacy of the revelation of God in Scripture is what the apostle Paul had in mind when he cautioned the Thessalonians **not** to **despise prophetic utterances. Despise** (*exoutheneō*) carries the strong meaning, "to consider as absolutely nothing," "to treat with contempt," or "to look down on." In the New Testament, **prophetic utterances** (*prophēteia*) can refer either to spoken words or written words. The verb form (*prophēteuō*) means "to speak or proclaim publicly"; thus the gift of prophecy is the Spirit-endowed skill of publicly proclaiming God's Word (cf. Rom. 12:6). New Testament prophets sometimes delivered a brand-new revelation directly from God (Luke 2:29–32; cf. v. 38; Acts 15:23–29). At other times they merely reiterated a divine proclamation that was already recorded (cf. Luke 3:5–6; Acts 2:17–21, 25–28, 34–35; 4:25–26; 7:2–53).

The apostles and their associates received, spoke, and wrote the text of the New Testament, and other spokesmen delivered supernatural utterances of practical revelation for certain temporal matters (cf. Acts 11:27–30). In New Testament times, prophecy was routinely the proclamation of God's previously revealed word, as it is today, inasmuch as Scripture is complete. Romans 12:6 supports that contention: "if prophecy, according to the proportion of his faith." In the original, the latter phrase reads, "according to the proportion of the faith," which indicates one with the gift of prophecy had to speak in agreement with the divinely revealed body of Christian doctrine. The New Testament always considered the faith to be synonymous with the collection of previously revealed truth (Acts 6:7; Jude 3, 20). Thus Paul instructed the Romans that **prophetic utterances** must perfectly agree with "*the* faith," which is God's Word. Similarly, Revelation 19:10 concludes, "For the testimony of Jesus is the spirit of prophecy." Genuine prophecy reports God's own revelation of Christ and never deviates from Scripture.

Revelatory **prophetic utterances** (1 Cor. 12:10) were limited to the apostolic era. But the non-revelatory gift of prophecy is permanent, as preachers are called to "preach the word" (2 Tim. 4:2), that is, proclaim the divine record. When Paul preached in Berea, the believers were "examining the Scriptures daily" to see if what he said was true. That was a noble and excellent response (Acts 17:10–11). Prophecy is essential to the health of the church, which is why Paul urged the Thessalonians **not** to **despise** it. Later, in his first letter to the Corinthians, Paul stressed the importance of the prophetic gift, urging the entire flock to desire its use because it clearly edified, exhorted, and comforted (1 Cor. 14:1–3; cf. v. 6). He further elaborated on the significance of prophecy for the church, including its superiority over the ecstatic gifts, in the second part of chapter 14:

> Therefore if the whole church assembles together and all speak in tongues, and ungifted men or unbelievers enter, will they not say that you are mad? But if all prophesy, and an unbeliever or an ungifted man enters, he is convicted by all, he is called to account by all; the secrets of his heart are disclosed; and so he will fall on his face and worship God, declaring that God is certainly among you. What is the outcome then, brethren? When you assemble, each one has a psalm, has a teaching, has a revelation, has a tongue, has an interpretation. Let all things be done for edification. . . . If anyone thinks he is a prophet or spiritual, let him recognize that the things which I write to you are the Lord's commandment. But if anyone does not recognize this, he is not recognized. Therefore, my brethren, desire earnestly to prophesy, and do not forbid to speak in tongues. But all things must be done properly and in an orderly manner. (14:23–26, 37–40)

Prophecy, as a term, is actually used to refer to God's written Word. The apostle Peter wrote, "But know this first of all, that no prophecy of Scripture is a matter of one's own interpretation, for no prophecy was ever made by an act of the human will, but men moved by the Holy Spirit spoke from God" (2 Peter 1:20–21; cf. Matt. 13:14; Rom. 16:25–26). The apostle John added this statement: "Blessed is he who reads and those who hear the words of the prophecy [the book of Revelation], and heed the things which are written in it; for the time is near" (Rev. 1:3; cf. 22:10, 18–19).

Paul's reverence for the Word of God had its roots in the Old Testament (cf. Josh. 1:8; Job 23:12; Pss. 1:1–2; 119:1–8; Jer. 15:16). Such a great love and respect for the Word of God undoubtedly resulted from God's command to Moses and the Israelites:

> These words, which I am commanding you today, shall be on your heart. You shall teach them diligently to your sons and shall talk of them when you sit in your house and when you walk by the way and when you lie down and when you rise up. You shall bind them as a sign on your hand and they shall be as frontals on your forehead. You shall write them on the doorposts of your house and on your gates. (Deut. 6:6–9)

That passage also suggests two detailed lists of reasons that believers today should **not despise prophetic utterances:** (1) Because of Scripture's essential character. First, it is authoritative (Isa. 1:2); second, it is completely infallible (Ps. 19:7); third, it is inerrant in every part (Prov. 30:5–6; cf. Matt. 5:18); fourth, it is sufficient for all spiritual needs (Ps. 19:7–11; 2 Tim. 3:15–17); fifth, it is absolutely effective (Isa. 55:11); and sixth, it is determinative of one's spiritual condition (John 5:24). (2) Because of Scripture's generous benefits. First, it is the supreme source of truth (John 17:17); second, it is the source of all true happiness (Prov. 8:34; Luke 11:28); third, it is the source of victory over sin and the forces of evil (Ps. 119:9, 11; Matt. 4:1–11; Eph. 6:17); fourth, it is the ultimate source of spiritual growth (2 Tim. 3:16–17; 1 Peter 2:2); fifth, it is the only perfectly reliable source of guidance (Pss. 19:8; 119:105); and sixth, it is the source of hope (Ps. 119:116; Rom. 15:4).

THE RESPONSIBILITY TO BE DISCERNING

But examine everything carefully; hold fast to that which is good; abstain from every form of evil. (5:21–22)

The noted British expositor D. Martyn Lloyd-Jones correctly realized in the early 1970s that the church was drifting from spiritual discernment and explained how postmodern culture had contributed to that reality:

> There is a very obvious reaction at the present time against intellectualism. . . . This is found among the students in America, and increasingly in this country. Reason is being distrusted and set on one side. Following D. H. Lawrence many are saying that our troubles are due to the fact that we have over-developed our cerebrum. We must listen

more to our "blood" and go back to nature. And so turning against intellectualism, and deliberately espousing the creed of irrationality, they yield themselves to the desire for "experience", and place sensation above understanding. What matters is feeling and enjoyment; not thought. Pure thought leads nowhere. (Cited in Iain H. Murray, *D. Martyn Lloyd-Jones: The Fight of Faith, 1939–1981* [Edinburgh: Banner of Truth, 1990], 666)

If anything, such cultural tendencies have only become more pronounced and real discernment is now largely absent from most segments of the evangelical church.

Spiritual discernment is the ability to distinguish divine truth from error and half-truth (cf. Acts 17:11; 1 Tim. 4:1–6, 13, 16; 6:20–21; 2 Tim. 4:1–5; Titus 1:9) and is essential to the Christian life (1 Cor. 12:10; Eph. 4:14–15; Heb. 5:14; 1 John 4:1; cf. 1 Kings 3:9; Prov. 2:3; 14:15, 33; 16:21). That is why the apostle Paul exhorted the Thessalonians to **examine everything**. **Examine** translates *dokimazō*, a common New Testament word that often refers to testing something for authenticity. It entails distinguishing between true and false, right and wrong, or good and bad (cf. 2 Sam. 14:17). Sometimes the word denotes the process of distinguishing what is pleasing to the Lord (Eph. 5:10; cf. Rom. 12:2). **Everything** permits no exceptions; it includes every issue and idea that might confront believers.

Once they **examine everything,** believers must then **hold fast to that which is good. Hold fast** means "to embrace wholeheartedly," "to take possession of." **Good** (*kalos*) denotes what is inherently genuine, true, noble, and right (Rom. 7:16; 1 Tim. 1:8, 18; 2:3; 4:4; 6:12–13, 19; 2 Tim. 4:7; Titus 3:8), not just what might be beautiful in appearance. When believers find what is **good,** they must embrace it and make it their own (cf. Rom. 12:9; 16:19; Phil. 4:8).

Conversely, Paul in verse 22 warned the Thessalonians to **abstain from every form of evil. Abstain** (*apechō*) is a strong word that means "to hold oneself away from." The emphasis is on the believer's complete avoidance of any evil teaching or behavior. Nowhere does Scripture permit believers to expose themselves to the influences of what is false or evil; instead, they are to **abstain** from such things, even flee them (1 Cor. 6:18; 10:14; 1 Tim. 6:11; 2 Tim. 2:22; cf. Pss. 34:14; 37:27; 97:10; Prov. 3:7; 8:13; 14:16; 22:3).

Evil refers to something that is actively harmful or malignant. Such **evil,** which includes lies and distortions of truth as well as moral perversions, appears in many forms. Because of its many manifestations (cf. Matt. 5:11; 12:35; 15:19; Mark 7:23; John 3:19; Rom. 1:29–30; Col. 3:5; 1 Tim. 6:10; James 3:16), the apostle warned the Thessalonians to shun

every form of evil. Paul's exhortation was a general call for believers to discern truth from error, good from evil, righteousness from sin, and a command to shun any of the negative teachings, influences, or behaviors that would displease God.

Believers who yield to the Holy Spirit's complete control will appreciate Scripture's character, allow its power to sanctify their lives, and examine everything by its standards. Thus they will fulfill three more vital responsibilities all believers have to Jesus Christ—to honor His Spirit, obey His Word, and exercise spiritual discernment.

A Prayer for Complete Sanctification (1 Thessalonians 5:23–24)

18

Now may the God of peace Himself sanctify you entirely; and may your spirit and soul and body be preserved complete, without blame at the coming of our Lord Jesus Christ. Faithful is He who calls you, and He also will bring it to pass. (5:23–24)

Paul's concluding benediction points to the only source of power for obeying all the exhortations of 4:1–5:22—God, who alone sanctifies the obedient believer. Sanctification is inseparably linked to saving faith, because those whom God justifies He also sanctifies (cf. Rom. 8:28–29). The apostle Paul began this epistle with testimony that the Thessalonians had truly responded in saving faith to his gospel preaching and been justified (1:2–5; 2:1, 12–13), and here at the conclusion, he prayed for their complete sanctification. His prayerful benediction for them in these verses reveals several essential elements of sanctification: its nature, source, and extent; its human components; its goal and culmination; and its final security.

SANCTIFICATION'S NATURE, SOURCE, AND EXTENT

Now may the God of peace Himself sanctify you entirely; (5:23*a*)

Sanctify (*hagiazō*) means, "to set apart," "to separate" from sin to holiness. The optative mood here expresses a wish or desire. The noun form occurs several other times in this letter (4:3–4, 7) and the verb a number of times elsewhere in the New Testament (John 10:36; 17:17, 19; Acts 20:32; 26:18; Rom. 15:16; 1 Cor. 1:2; 6:11; 7:14; Eph. 5:26; 1 Tim. 4:5; 2 Tim. 2:21; Heb. 2:11; 9:13; 10:10, 14, 29; 13:12; 1 Peter 3:15). Sanctification is the ongoing spiritual process by which God increasingly sets believers apart from sin and moves them toward holiness. The apostle's entreaty for the Thessalonians parallels and reiterates the theme and form of his earlier prayer for their spiritual growth in 3:11–13:

> Now may our God and Father Himself and Jesus our Lord direct our way to you; and may the Lord cause you to increase and abound in love for one another, and for all people, just as we also do for you; so that He may establish your hearts without blame in holiness before our God and Father at the coming of our Lord Jesus with all His saints.

The concept of sanctification, setting things apart to God, is one of the oldest in Scripture. In Genesis 2:3 God Himself sanctified the seventh day and rested from His creative work. Job regularly made burnt offerings to God and consecrated his sons to Him (Job 1:5). At the Exodus, God set apart the firstborn of His people and their animals for His use (Ex. 13:1–2). Just prior to God's giving Moses the Ten Commandments, He set apart Israel as a holy nation (Ex. 19:5–6; cf. Ezek. 37:28) and a few days later sanctified Mount Sinai (Ex. 19:23), having already forbidden the Israelites from coming too near it (v. 12). Later in the wilderness, the Lord sanctified Aaron and his sons for the priestly office (Ex. 28:41 ff.) and set apart the tabernacle and its vessels for sacred purposes (chaps. 30–31; 35–40). Samuel sanctified Jesse and his son David (1 Sam. 16:5, 12–13). Many years later God sanctified the temple in Jerusalem (2 Chron. 7:16). Before the prophet Jeremiah was even born, God set him apart for prophetic ministry (Jer. 1:5).

New Testament narratives also contain examples of God's special sanctifying work. He set apart John the Baptist to be the forerunner of Jesus Christ (Luke 1:13–17). God the Father also set apart His Son the Messiah for the work of redemption (Matt. 1:20–23; Luke 1:31–33; cf. 2:29–35; Matt. 3:13–17; Acts 2:22–24). Jesus set apart the twelve apostles from the larger number of disciples who followed Him (Mark 3:13–19; Luke 6:12–16). The early church set apart for divine service the first deacons (Acts 6:1–6) and some for missionary service (13:1–3).

Three basic elements define believers' sanctification. First is the past, fixed aspect—positional sanctification—which God effected at the time He saved each believer. God secured positional sanctification through the death of His Son: "We have been sanctified through the offering of the body of Jesus Christ once for all. . . . For by one offering He has perfected for all time those who are sanctified" (Heb. 10:10, 14). By that atoning work, God rescued all believers from the dominion of sin and spiritual darkness and placed them into the dominion of His righteousness and spiritual light. Believers also receive a new nature at salvation: "Therefore if anyone is in Christ, he is a new creature; the old things passed away; behold, new things have come" (2 Cor. 5:17; cf. 2 Peter 1:4). The indwelling Holy Spirit signifies the believer's new nature (Rom. 8:9). God imputes Christ's righteousness to believers so that He sees them not as sinners, but as those sanctified, covered with the righteousness of Christ (cf. Rom. 3:21–25; 2 Cor. 5:21; 1 John 4:10). As a result, God declares them holy and calls them "holy ones" or "saints" (cf. Rom. 1:7; 1 Cor. 1:2; 2 Cor. 1:1; Eph. 1:1).

Sanctification has a second, future aspect—ultimate sanctification—when God actually makes believers sinless in body and spirit forever. Paul assured the Philippians, "For our citizenship is in heaven, from which also we eagerly wait for a Savior, the Lord Jesus Christ; who will transform the body of our humble state into conformity with the body of His glory" (Phil. 3:20–21; cf. Rom. 8:30; 1 Cor. 15:52–54; 1 John 3:2–3). In ultimate sanctification, God joins the new nature, then relieved of the debilitating flesh, to transformed and glorified bodies for all eternity. It is the promised realization of the church being presented as a bride without spot or blemish to her Bridegroom, Jesus Christ (Rev. 19:7–8; 21:2, 9; cf. Eph. 5:26–27; Col. 1:21–23).

The third element defining biblical sanctification is the experiential aspect, which concerns present Christian living and thus lies between the past/positional and future/ultimate aspects of sanctification. It is the process in which believers strive, by the Spirit's power, to be more and more conformed to the image of Christ. Paul summed it up in 2 Corinthians 3:18: "But we all, with unveiled face, beholding as in a mirror the glory of the Lord, are being transformed into the same image from glory to glory, just as from the Lord, the Spirit" (cf. Rom. 12:9–21; 15:4–7; 2 Cor. 9:6–12; Gal. 5:16–6:10; Eph. 4:1–6:18; Phil. 2:1–4, 14–15; 3:15–17; 4:4–9; Col. 3:1–4:6; 1 Thess. 3:11–13; 4:3–12; 2 Thess. 2:13–15; 3:7, 13; 1 Tim. 4:12–16; 6:11–14; 2 Tim. 1:6–10; Titus 3:1–8; Heb. 12:12–15; 13:1–9; James 1:2–27; 3:13–18; 1 Peter 3:1–12; 2 Peter 1:5–11; 1 John 1:5–9). Experiential sanctification is the pursuit of holiness (cf. Matt. 5:48; 1 Peter 1:14–16). The Puritan Thomas Watson stated it this way, "[Sanctification] is a principle of grace savingly wrought, whereby the heart becomes holy, and is made after God's own heart. A sanctified person bears not only God's name, but His image" (*Body of Divinity* [reprint; Grand Rapids: Baker, 1979], 167). In all of Paul's epistles, whenever he moves from doctrinal exposition to practical exhortation, he has this aspect of sanctification in mind. His passionate prayer for the Thessalonians and for all believers was that through experiential sanctification God would progressively conform them to holiness.

God is the source of sanctification. After giving the Thessalonians a series of commands and exhortations that called for them to put forth disciplined, devoted effort (5:12–22; see also 4:1–8, 11–12, 18; 5:6, 8, 11), Paul wanted them to recognize that ultimately it is God who enables believers to obey those admonitions and progress in sanctification (cf. Phil. 2:13). Centuries earlier the prophet Zechariah made that principle clear: "'Not by might nor by power, but by My Spirit,' says the Lord of hosts" (Zech. 4:6). Regarding his own ministry, Paul understood the principle well: "We proclaim Him, admonishing every man and teaching every man with all wisdom, so that we may present every man complete in Christ. For this purpose also I labor, striving according to His power, which mightily works within me" (Col. 1:28–29; cf. 1 Cor. 2:1–5; Eph. 3:20). However, Paul's assertion to the Colossians also reveals the inseparable link between human effort and divine power in living the Christian life. Believers must yield themselves to God (Rom. 6:19; 12:1–2) and diligently pursue holiness (1 Cor. 9:24–27; 2 Tim. 4:7; 2 Peter 1:5–11), yet always proceed in humble dependence on Him (cf. 1 Cor. 15:10; Gal. 2:20).

From a human standpoint, it is impossible to fully understand how this symbiosis works (cf. Deut. 29:29; Isa. 55:9). Paul summarized this unfathomable process best when he told the Philippians, "So then, my beloved, just as you have always obeyed, not as in my presence only, but now much more in my absence, work out your salvation with fear and trembling; for it is God who is at work in you, both to will and to work for His good pleasure" (Phil. 2:12–13; cf. Gal. 2:20). Christians are to live out in their daily lives the salvation God has wrought in them.

Paul chose to identify the Lord with the familiar scriptural expression **the God of peace** (cf. Rom. 15:33; 16:20; 1 Cor. 14:33; 2 Cor. 13:11; Phil. 4:9; Heb. 13:20). **Peace** (*eirēnē*) is the best word to summarize God's saving work, which is why the New Testament often uses it to describe Him (cf. Luke 19:38; John 14:27; Rom. 1:7; 1 Cor. 1:3; 2 Cor. 1:2; Eph. 2:14; 2 Thess. 3:16). It denotes not just some existence, situation, or state of mind free from conflict, but the composite of gospel blessing. Paul is not speaking of God's own tranquility, but the **peace** of salvation He provides through the cross of Christ for all who repent and believe (Isa. 53:5; Rom. 5:1; Eph. 2:14–15; Col. 1:20; cf. Luke 1:79; 2:14; John 14:27; Acts 10:36; Rom. 10:17).

To underscore that it is **God** who sanctifies, the apostle used **Himself** (*autos*) in the emphatic position. God does not delegate the sanctifying process to an angel or an apostle; neither does He accomplish it by some distant decree. Rather He accomplishes it by His own actions as He works directly in believers' lives.

Entirely is used only here in the New Testament and is a compound of two Greek words, *holos*, "whole," "complete," and *telēs*, "end," "finish." Paul asked that God would sanctify the Thessalonians "all the way through," or "through and through"—that sanctification would leave no part of their inner beings unaffected.

SANCTIFICATION'S HUMAN COMPONENTS

and may your spirit and soul and body (5:23*b*)

The sanctifying work of God includes not only the immaterial part of the believer (**spirit and soul**), but also the **body**. (Paul is not here referring to glorification, because he desired that the element of sanctification now mentioned be true of the Thessalonians when Christ comes, not after.) In view of the prevailing Greek culture, it is significant that Paul included the **body** in his benediction. That culture—influenced by a philosophical dualism which taught that man's spirit is inherently good and his body inherently evil—held the body in low esteem. That philosophy provided a convenient rationale for dismissing as inconsequential whatever immoral physical behavior people might have engaged in.

But such thinking was abhorrent to the apostle Paul; he later exhorted the Corinthians, "Do you not know that your body is a temple of the Holy Spirit who is in you, whom you have from God, and that you are not your own? For you have been bought with a price: therefore glorify God in your body" (1 Cor. 6:19–20; cf. Luke 11:36; Rom. 6:12–13; 8:13; 12:1; 1 Cor. 6:13, 15; 9:27; Col. 2:23; 3:5; James 3:2–3, 6). If sanctification is to be complete, it will extend to every part of the believer, especially the body, which thinks, feels, and acts in response to the holiness of the inner person.

There has been a significant debate over the years about the definition and usage of the terms **spirit and soul**. Some (historically called trichotomists) believe Paul was identifying two different, distinct categories of the nonmaterial essence of man. Those parts, along with the body, make man a three-part being. Others (historically called dichotomists) believe spirit and soul are interchangeable words denoting man's indivisible inner nature. Those interpreters therefore view man as a two-part being, composed simply of a nonmaterial nature (**spirit and soul**) and a material nature (**body**).

No Scripture text ascribes different, distinct substance and functions to the spirit and soul. Trichotomists nevertheless usually propose that **spirit** is man's Godward consciousness and **soul** is his earthward consciousness; however, neither the Greek usage of **spirit** (*pneuma*) nor of **soul** (*psuchē*) sustains that proposition. The nonmaterial part of man does have myriad capacities to respond to God, Satan, and the world's many stimuli, but it is untenable to arbitrarily separate the spirit from the soul. The two terms are used interchangeably in Scripture (cf. Heb. 6:19; 10:39; 1 Peter 2:11; 2 Peter 2:8). **Spirit and soul** are familiar and common synonyms that Paul used to emphasize the depth and scope of sanctification. Some suggest that an acceptable translation of this portion of Paul's prayer could be, "May your spirit, even soul and body," in which case "spirit" would refer to the whole person, and "soul and body" to the person's nonmaterial and material parts. References from Paul's other epistles provide clear evidence that he was a dichotomist (Rom. 8:10; 1 Cor. 2:11; 5:3, 5; 7:34; 2 Cor. 7:1; Gal. 6:18; Col. 2:5; 2 Tim. 4:22).

Some claim Hebrews 4:12, "For the word of God is living and active and sharper than any two-edged sword, and piercing as far as the division of soul and spirit, of both joints and marrow, and able to judge the thoughts and intentions of the heart," supports a trichotomist view of man's essence because it suggests splitting soul and spirit. But a careful look at the verse's language refutes that contention. The writer did not say the sword of the Word penetrates a person's inner being and separates his soul from his spirit. He said only that the sword cuts open the soul and the spirit of the person. He used a second metaphorical expression "piercing . . . both joints and marrow" to further depict the deep penetration God's Word makes into the inner person. This verse poses no special difficulty for the dichotomist position.

SANCTIFICATION'S GOAL AND CULMINATION

be preserved complete, without blame at the coming of our Lord Jesus Christ. (5:23c)

Complete (*holoklēros*) means "with integrity," "total," "intact," "undamaged," and perfectly conforms with Paul's and his Lord's desire for the church to be holy, without blemish or defect (Eph. 5:25–27; cf. 2 Cor. 6:16; 11:2; 1 Tim. 3:15; 1 Peter 2:5; Rev. 19:7–8; 21:2).

This portion of Paul's prayer is also consistent with the personal goal he later expressed to the Philippians: "I press on toward the goal for the prize of the upward call of God in Christ Jesus" (Phil. 3:14). The prize of being called up to heaven is eternal holiness and Christlikeness. And meanwhile the apostle had, as much as possible, the same earthly goal, which meant pursuing Christlikeness. He said it was the one thing he did (3:13). In the wondrous balance of diligent effort and divine power that is in every aspect of salvation, Paul prayed that the saints would **be preserved** ("kept"), that God would keep them in the path of holiness until they received their ultimate sanctification (cf. Matt. 24:13; Acts 13:43; 14:22; Eph. 6:18; Col. 1:21–23; Heb. 12:2–3). His desire was that God would bring them to that point **without blame. Without blame** (*amemptōs*) is the same word archeologists have found on Christian tombs from ancient Thessalonica. When people wanted to identify a deceased friend or loved one as a Christian, they inscribed "blameless" on his or her grave —and behavioral blamelessness (not just the imputed and forensic) is the Lord's desire for His church (cf. Eph. 5:26–27).

At the coming of the **Lord Jesus Christ,** God will make all believers sinless forever. First Corinthians 15:50–54 affirms that reality:

> Now I say this, brethren, that flesh and blood cannot inherit the kingdom of God; nor does the perishable inherit the imperishable. Behold, I tell you a mystery; we will not all sleep, but we will all be changed, in a moment, in the twinkling of an eye, at the last trumpet; for the trumpet will sound, and the dead will be raised imperishable, and we will be changed. For this perishable must put on the imperishable, and this mortal must put on immortality. But when this perishable will have put on the imperishable, and this mortal will have put on immortality, then will come about the saying that is written, "Death is swallowed up in victory."

This is the letter's fourth mention of His **coming** (*parousia*) and, as with the other occurrences (2:19; 3:13; 4:15), it is again a reference to the Rapture of the church. Paul prayed that when the **Lord Jesus Christ** comes for believers He will find them faithfully pursuing the goal of being as holy as their Lord and longing to receive the promised heavenly perfection.

SANCTIFICATION'S FINAL SECURITY

Faithful is He who calls you, and He also will bring it to pass. (5:24)

God **who calls** is also **faithful** to complete and **bring . . . to pass** His sanctifying purpose. Paul later expressed to the Philippians this confidence in God's faithfulness to believers: "For I am confident of this very thing, that He who began a good work in you will perfect it until the day of Christ Jesus" (Phil. 1:6). That is another pledge to all believers that God has the power to guarantee their ultimate sanctification. The salvation God grants is secure—He graciously and efficaciously **calls** individuals (John 6:37, 44–45, 64–65), supplies them the faith to repent and believe (Eph. 2:8–9; cf. 2 Tim. 2:25–26), and provides them the grace to persevere to the glory of ultimate sanctification (Jude 24–25; cf. 1 Cor. 10:13). Romans 8:28–30 also states this pledge:

> And we know that God causes all things to work together for good to those who love God, to those who are called according to His purpose. For those whom He foreknew, He also predestined to become conformed to the image of His Son, so that He would be the firstborn among many brethren; and these whom He predestined, He also called; and these whom He called, He also justified; and these whom He justified, He also glorified.

In summary, Paul's prayer for the Thessalonians suggests a number of essential principles that all Christians need to remember concerning the sanctification process. First, experiential sanctification is inherently both negative and positive. Negatively, it involves the purging out of sin (cf. Rom. 6:6; 8:13; 2 Tim. 2:19). Scripture compares sin to leaven (cf. Matt. 16:12; 1 Cor. 5:6–8; Gal. 5:8–9), which connotes the evil influence with which sin permeates humanity. Sanctification does not remove the presence of sin, but it purges from the believer his love for sin and decreases sin's frequency in his life (cf. Rom. 6:22; 7:21–25; Phil. 3:7–16; Titus 2:11–12). Positively, sanctification involves the renewing of the mind (cf. Rom. 12:2) and the putting on of Christlikeness (cf. Col. 3:5–17). The negative and positive changes occur as the Holy Spirit continually uses God's Word in believers' lives (John 17:17; 2 Tim. 3:16–17; cf. John 15:1–3).

Second, sanctification occurs chiefly in the heart, the mind, the inner being. It is not concerned with modifying one's outward behavior —even if that behavior were in line with God's law—apart from the changed heart (cf. Rom. 3:21–23, 28; 4:4–5; 5:1–2), nor is it circumscribing one's attitudes and actions to an arbitrary code of ethics (cf. Rom. 14:17; Col. 2:16–23). Sanctification does affect a Christian's outward actions (cf. John 15:4–5; Eph. 2:10), but it is essentially an inward grace. It is illustrated by what the apostle Peter wrote to believing wives: "Your adornment must not be merely external—braiding the hair, and wearing gold jewelry, or putting on dresses; but let it be the hidden person of the heart, with the imperishable quality of a gentle and quiet spirit, which is precious in the sight of God" (1 Peter 3:3–4).

Third, the Bible implicitly calls sanctification a beautiful reality (cf. Ps. 110:3 KJV). Holiness is the beautiful crown jewel of the Godhead, reflecting divine perfection, unmitigated virtue, absolute righteousness, and pure sinlessness (cf. Ex. 15:11; Pss. 47:8; 145:17; Isa. 57:15). Sanctification, then, is a noble experience, imparting to believers a measure of the majesty God intended for them when He created mankind in His image (cf. Gen. 1:26–27; Ps. 8:4–6).

Fourth, sanctification is an ongoing reality. At the new birth, God plants the seed of righteousness, the principle of divine life, into the believer's heart (cf. 1 Peter 1:23–25). That does not mean he will never sin again, but it does mean he will discontinue living in his previous unbroken pattern of sinfulness and begin to live in a new pattern of holiness (cf. Rom. 6:17–18; 1 John 3:9).

Fifth, believers must remember that people can counterfeit sanctification in a number of ways. First, moral virtue can substitute for true sanctification. People can exhibit character qualities such as fair-mindedness, loyalty, civility, kindness, generosity, diligence, and philanthropy and yet at heart be unbelievers (cf. Isa. 29:13). Second, religious activity can masquerade as sanctification. For example, devoutly religious people might spend years avoiding the most heinous sins and seeking to please God by adhering to their church's rituals and self-righteously engaging in good works (cf. Matt. 23:23–25; Luke 18:10–14). But they do it all because they are afraid of God and want to earn His forgiveness, not because they are His children who sincerely love Him for His grace. Third, outward Christian profession can appear to be genuine sanctification (cf. Matt. 23:27–28). It often parades a hypocritical type of piety that is merely superficial (cf. Matt. 7:21–23). Such false sanctification deceives not only those who witness it, but also those who practice it. Fourth, their conscience and fear of sin's consequences often restrain people from bad behavior. Most of the time they reject sin because they fear its negative physical, psychological, or even legal consequences. They may have grown up in a Christian family in which their parents taught them biblical principles and established a doctrinal foundation that informs their consciences with moral convictions. Such people are afraid to engage in overt sin and on the exterior appear to be righteous, but only because they do not want a guilty conscience to bother them. A saving love for Christ does not motivate their behavior; instead, human fear and a sensitive conscience drive their actions.

Sixth, sanctification keeps believers from polluting holy things. "To the pure, all things are pure; but to those who are defiled and unbelieving, nothing is pure, but both their mind and their conscience are defiled" (Titus 1:15). Unbelievers mock and blaspheme God and His Son (cf. Luke 22:65; Rom. 8:7; Col. 1:21; Rev. 16:9). They ridicule the things of God and the people of God (cf. Neh. 2:19; Ps. 38:12; 2 Tim. 3:3–4), which means they also ridicule and demean the Word of God (cf. Neh.

9:28–29). They pollute everything God has designed for His glory and mankind's blessing (cf. Rom. 1:21–32), such as the beauty of creation, marriage, and friendship. By contrast, when God is sanctifying believers, they consider the simplest, most mundane things in life as holy and respect all the things the unbeliever does not (cf. Ps. 1:1–6).

Finally, Christians must remember that sanctification is God's priority for their lives. It is His will for them (1 Thess. 4:3; cf. Heb. 12:14) and the result of Christ's death on their behalf—"who gave Himself for us to redeem us from every lawless deed, and to purify for Himself a people for His own possession, zealous for good deeds" (Titus 2:14). All believers are to live for sanctification. They have no other goal in life than to be like Jesus Christ: "The one who says he abides in Him ought himself to walk in the same manner as He walked" (1 John 2:6).

Paul's Final Requests (1 Thessalonians 5:25–28)

19

Brethren, pray for us. Greet all the brethren with a holy kiss. I adjure you by the Lord to have this letter read to all the brethren. The grace of our Lord Jesus Christ be with you. (5:25–28)

In this postscript, Paul conveys his personal requests directly and clearly for his beloved church in Thessalonica. Before closing with a benediction, he offers three pleas: (1) pray for him as pastor, (2) show affection for one another, and (3) submit to God's Word.

A Request for Prayer

Brethren, pray for us. (5:25)

Paul's simple request that the Thessalonian **brethren** would **pray for** him constitutes his first parting desire for them. As so often expressed to his churches, the burden of the apostle's heart was that his flock would intercede before the Lord for him (cf. Rom. 15:30; 2 Cor. 1:11; Eph. 6:18–20; Phil. 1:19; Col. 4:2–4; Philem. 22) and, by implication, that all believers would pray for their pastors.

Brethren (*adelphoi*), in an emphatic position, is used repeatedly (see also 1:4; 2:1, 9, 17; 3:7; 4:1, 10; 5:1, 12, 14) to underscore Paul's strong affection for the Thessalonians. **Brethren** left no one out and served as a basis for Paul's first request—because they were together in the family of God and he had the right to expect them to pray for him.

Us includes Paul's co-laborers Silas and Timothy. All three had been faithful in praying for the Thessalonians: "We give thanks to God always for all of you, making mention of you in our prayers" (1 Thess. 1:2; cf. Acts 6:4), and now Paul asked them to return the spiritual favor. **Pray** is in the present tense, indicating that Paul wanted the Thessalonians to make these prayers a habit.

That Paul would express his dependence on the prayers of other believers is consistent with the pleas he made in his other epistles. William Hendriksen comments:

> The man [Paul] who, in the midst of his herculean labors, in II Cor. 11:29 exclaims, "Who is weak, that I am not weak?" and who prefaces that remark with a long list of sufferings and hardships which he had to endure, feels the need of prayer. The circumstances which surround him at Corinth are by no means easy. . . . Besides, he (together with Silas and Timothy, of course) believes in the efficacy of prayer. It is therefore not surprising that here (and in several of the epistles) we find this stirring request, Brothers, do pray for us. Cf. II Thess. 3:1; Rom. 15:30; Eph. 6:19; Col. 4:3. (*New Testament Commentary. Exposition of Thessalonians, Timothy, and Titus* [Grand Rapids: Baker, 1981], 142)

Gardiner Spring, a nineteenth-century Presbyterian pastor in New York City, understood the vital role prayer has in spiritual warfare and made an impassioned plea for Christians to pray for their pastors:

> O it is at a fearful expense that ministers are ever allowed to enter the pulpit without being preceded, accompanied, and followed by the earnest prayers of the churches. It is no marvel that the pulpit is so powerless, and ministers so often disheartened when there are so few to hold up their hands. The consequence of neglecting this duty is seen and felt in the spiritual declension of the churches, and it will be seen and felt in the everlasting perdition of men; while the consequence of regarding it would be the ingathering of multitudes into the kingdom of God, and new glories to the Lamb that was slain!

> On his behalf therefore, and on the behalf of his beloved and respected brethren in the ministry, the writer would crave an interest in the prayers of all who love the Savior and the souls of men. We are the dispensers of God's truth and at best fall far below our mighty theme. The duties of our calling return upon us with every returning week and day. They often come upon us with many and conflicting demands. They

sometimes put a demand upon all our thoughts, and at the very time when we have lost the power of thinking; and sometimes they call for all the intensity and strength of our affections, just at the time we are the least capable of expressing them. There is also associated with these demands that pressing distress, and decaying anxiety, which exhausts our vigor, cripples our courage, and drinks up our spirits. And then, in addition to all this, there are so many disappointments in our work, that we desperately need the sympathy and comfort of the prayers of God's faithful people! ("A Plea to Pray for Pastors" [Amityville, N.Y.: Calvary, 1991], 5–6; excerpted from *The Power of the Pulpit* [reprint of 1848 edition; Edinburgh: Banner of Truth, n.d.])

Paul's requests for prayer suggest a number of matters that believers especially ought to remember when they **pray for** their pastor. First, it is important to pray for the pastor's safety. In his second letter to them, Paul told the Thessalonians, "Finally, brethren, pray for us that the word of the Lord will spread rapidly and be glorified, just as it did also with you; and that we will be rescued from perverse and evil men; for not all have faith" (2 Thess. 3:1–2; cf. Rom. 15:31*a*). "Perverse" refers to ones who were outrageously wicked, hostile to Paul, and sought to harm him (primarily unbelieving Jews). Potentially, the faithful pastor who consistently confronts the world's wicked system with spiritual truth could suffer harm (John 15:20; 2 Tim. 3:12; cf. Acts 4:3; 5:18; 13:50; 16:23) and therefore needs his people's prayers for safety.

Second, believers ought to pray for their pastor's wisdom in service. Paul asked the Romans to pray that his "service for Jerusalem may prove acceptable to the saints" (Rom. 15:31*b*). By "service" he was not referring to his preaching and teaching of doctrine. Rather, Paul was referring to his servant leadership as he collected money from the Gentile churches in Macedonia and Asia Minor for the financially poor members of the Jerusalem church (Acts 11:27–30; 1 Cor. 16:1–3; cf. 2 Cor. 8–9). Paul coveted believers' prayers for his wisdom to administer the plan effectively. As he undertook that special collection, the apostle had no guarantee that the Jews would receive it with loving gratitude and recognize that the Gentiles intended it as a gesture of brotherly kindness. His plea to the Romans illustrates simply and well why pastors need prayer to make good leadership decisions and exercise wise judgment in resolving potential conflicts.

Third, believers should pray that their pastor's future plans and priorities are consistent with God's will for him (James 4:13–15; cf. Matt. 6:10, 33; Acts 21:14; Rom. 1:10; 15:32; Eph. 6:6; 1 Peter 5:1–4). Paul asked the Romans to pray that God would direct his path "so that [he might] come to [them] in joy by the will of God and find refreshing rest in [their] company" (Rom. 15:32). Pastors have desires and visions for future ministry and, like Paul, they need the encouragement that can result from believing prayer—that God in His providence will fulfill those plans.

Fourth, Christians need to pray for their pastor's effectiveness in preaching the Word of God. Paul sought such prayer from the Ephesians: "Pray on my behalf, that utterance may be given to me in the opening of my mouth, to make known with boldness the mystery of the gospel" (Eph. 6:19; cf. Col. 4:2–4). Paul added those requests to what he earlier had asked the Thessalonians to pray: "that the word of the Lord will spread rapidly and be glorified" (2 Thess. 3:1). There his desire was that the Word would "run" from one place to another (as a sprinter would) and receive honor when people obeyed it.

Finally, the flock needs to pray that God would spiritually strengthen its pastor and allow him to minister with integrity. Gardiner Spring solicited prayer for spiritual strength this way:

> Brethren, *pray for us*, that we may be kept from sin; that we may walk carefully, not as fools, but as wise, redeeming the time [Eph. 5:16]; that our hearts may be more devoted to God, and our lives a more impressive example of the Gospel we preach; that we may be more completely furnished for our work and our conflicts, and put on the whole armor of God [6:10–17]; that we may be more faithful and wise to win souls, and that we may discipline our body, and bring it into subjection, lest having preached to others, we ourselves be cast away [1 Cor. 9:27]. ("A Plea to Pray for Pastors," 9; emphasis in original)

The writer of Hebrews urged his people to pray that his integrity would remain evident: "Pray for us, for we are sure that we have a good conscience, desiring to conduct ourselves honorably in all things" (Heb. 13:18).

A REQUEST FOR AFFECTION

Greet all the brethren with a holy kiss. (5:26)

Paul's second parting desire for the Thessalonians was that they would display loving affection for one another. This wish that his readers would **greet** one another **with a holy kiss** was a common conclusion for Paul's letters (Rom. 16:16; 1 Cor. 16:20; 2 Cor. 13:12; cf. 1 Peter 5:14). **Greet** conveys the intention of a friendly and righteous gesture, as opposed to a formal, reserved acknowledgement.

All the brethren leaves out none of the Thessalonian believers, not even the unruly ones of 5:14. When the elders received this letter they were to begin passing along to the entire congregation, by means of

a holy kiss, the apostle's love for the church. As members kissed, they would tangibly demonstrate love for one another as well. In Paul's day, it was customary for people to greet a superior with a kiss on the foot, knee, elbow, or hand; but friends kissed one another on the cheek. (The wretched hypocrisy of Judas Iscariot's kiss is the most twisted illustration of this custom [cf. Matt. 26:49].) Among believers, the **holy kiss** became a symbol of genuine love and affection; but it was more than a liturgical sign or ritual gesture performed only during worship services—it was a spontaneous, personal display of affection practiced whenever believing friends met.

Eventually people in the church began to abuse the holy kiss and by the thirteenth century the Western church abandoned the custom. Christians in Western culture now generally express affection by shaking hands or embracing one another. In whatever appropriate form the affection might take, however, the apostle Paul commanded believers to love one another in a demonstrable fashion.

A REQUEST FOR SUBMISSION

I adjure you by the Lord to have this letter read to all the brethren. (5:27)

Paul declared, in the strongest of terms, his third parting desire for the Thessalonians—that they would submit to God's Word. Because the contents of **this letter** were divinely inspired, Paul could **adjure** the Thessalonians **to have** it **read to all the brethren.**

Adjure (*enorkizō*) is a strong word that means "to bind with an oath." Paul was so intent that all the Thessalonians receive his letter's contents that he imposed a solemn oath (**by the Lord**) on the elders. The Holy Spirit through Paul thus obligated them to make sure everyone heard the letter (cf. Rev. 2:7, 17, 29; 3:6, 13, 22).

Read connotes a reading aloud in the public worship service. Public reading of Scripture was essential to the spiritual accountability of the people of God (2 Thess. 3:14; 1 Tim. 4:13; cf. Gal. 4:16). The apostle was concerned that the Thessalonians might be disappointed at his not having come in person and therefore neglect this letter. So he urged that the elders have it read when the church met so that all would hear the letter's contents. Paul especially wanted them to hear his words of comfort and clarification concerning eschatology (4:13–5:11).

Initially, there was only one treasured copy of the epistle, which made it impossible for everyone to read it individually. Most of the church members would likely have been unable to read it because of illiteracy. The letter was to be read as God's Word, a revelation from heaven that was true and authoritative, requiring belief and obedience.

PAUL GIVES HIS BENEDICTION TO THE THESSALONIANS

The grace of our Lord Jesus Christ be with you. (5:28)

The apostle Paul summed up his correspondence with a benediction, praying that they would experience **the grace of** the **Lord Jesus Christ.** Paul began and ended all his epistles with a mention of divine **grace** (e.g., Rom. 1:7; 16:20; 1 Cor. 1:3; 16:23; Gal. 1:3; 6:18) because grace is at the heart of Christian theology (John 1:14, 17; Rom. 3:24; Eph. 1:7; 2:5; Titus 3:7). Grace summarizes all that God provides believers **in Jesus Christ** (Rom. 4:16; 1 Cor. 15:10; 2 Cor. 9:8; 2 Thess. 1:11–12; 2 Peter 3:18). Regarding Paul's use of the term **grace** in the openings and closings of his letters, Leon Morris observed:

> Grace fundamentally means "that which causes joy," a shade of meaning we may still discern when we speak of a graceful action or the social graces. It comes to mean "favor," "kindness," and then especially God's kindness to man in providing for his spiritual needs in Christ. Thence it comes to signify what is due to grace, namely, God's good gifts to men, and finally the attitude of thankfulness which all this awakes within the Christian. As used in greetings it is the free gift of God that is meant, but the word necessarily evokes memories of the free gift on Calvary. . . . It is the grace of the Lord which lingers in the Apostle's thoughts [as he closes his letters], just as it is the grace of the Lord with which he begins his letters. (*The First and Second Epistles to the Thessalonians*, The New International Commentary on the New Testament [Grand Rapids: Eerdmans, 1989], 49, 187)

The closing requests Paul made to the Thessalonians match what all dedicated pastors desire from their own churches: that their people pray for them, that their people demonstrate affection to them and to one another, and that their people hear, read, study, and apply God's Word. The evangelical church now resides in a time when so many people assume that it can accomplish its mission by man-centered methods, programs, and strategies. Those same people minimize the need to seriously and faithfully pray for their pastors, or the necessity to regularly rely on the divine, all-sufficient resources contained in Scripture. It is a lie from Satan that pastors can do without the divinely energized prayers of their people, but it is God's truth that, through those prayers, He will powerfully enable pastors to fulfill their callings and help build His church.

Introduction to
2 Thessalonians

THE CITY OF THESSALONICA

See the Introduction to 1 Thessalonians.

THE FOUNDING OF THE CHURCH AT THESSALONICA

See the Introduction to 1 Thessalonians.

THE OCCASION OF 2 THESSALONIANS

A few months had passed since Paul wrote 1 Thessalonians. Though unable to visit them (1 Thess. 2:18), the apostle had maintained contact with the church. He was generally pleased with their progress (2 Thess. 1:3–4), yet there were still some issues that needed to be resolved. In his second inspired letter, Paul addressed three essential matters. The persecution, which had begun while Paul was there, was still ongoing. In chapter 1, he encouraged the Thessalonians to stand firm and remain faithful to the Lord despite their suffering.

Paul had instructed the Thessalonians about the end times while he was with them (2 Thess. 2:5), and in 1 Thessalonians (4:13–5:11). Yet they were still confused, fearing they had missed the Rapture and were in the Day of the Lord. Though the severity of the persecution they were undergoing contributed to that mistaken belief, the main reason for their confusion came from some false teachers who taught that the Day of the Lord had arrived. Those lying deceivers claimed Paul, Silas, and Timothy now taught that, even producing a forged letter supposedly from the apostle Paul to support their claim. Paul wrote chapter 2 to calm the Thessalonians' fears, clarify his teaching, and thus reassure them that the Day of the Lord had not arrived.

Finally, the problem of idleness Paul had addressed in his first epistle (1 Thess. 4:11–12) had escalated. Some, expecting the Lord to return at any moment, had stopped working altogether. The apostle sternly dealt with those idle loafers and the related issue of church discipline in chapter 3.

THE AUTHOR OF 2 THESSALONIANS

As he did in 1 Thessalonians, Paul twice identified himself as the author of this epistle (1:1; 3:17). Despite the clear statement of the inspired text, some have challenged Paul's authorship of 2 Thessalonians. Critics claim that there is a contradiction between the eschatological teaching of the two epistles. They argue that while 1 Thessalonians stresses the suddenness and unexpectedness of the Lord's return, 2 Thessalonians teaches that signs will precede it. But Paul had in mind two distinct phases of the Lord's return: 1 Thessalonians points out that the Rapture will come suddenly and unexpectedly. Second Thessalonians, written to counter the false teaching that the Day of the Lord had already arrived, notes that a specific event will precede that Day. That event, the arrival and unveiling of the final Antichrist, does not obviate the unexpectedness of the Day of the Lord. Despite its precursors, "the day of the Lord will come just like a thief in the night" (1 Thess. 5:2).

Equally gratuitous is the assertion that Paul could not have written 2 Thessalonians because he does not mention the man of lawlessness (2 Thess. 2:3) elsewhere in his writings. But why should a writer's veracity be questioned merely because he mentions a topic only once? Further, Paul taught the Thessalonians about the man of lawlessness while he was in Thessalonica (2 Thess. 2:5). Finally, Paul's teaching on the man of lawlessness (the Antichrist) is in harmony with that of both the Old Testament prophets and the Lord Jesus Christ (see the discussion of this point in chapter 23 of this volume).

Second Thessalonians was widely accepted by the early church as an inspired writing of Paul. In addition to the witnesses to the Pauline authorship of 1 Thessalonians (see the Introduction to 1 Thessalonians in this volume), Polycarp, Justin Martyr, and possibly the *Didache* and Ignatius affirm that Paul wrote 2 Thessalonians.

As with 1 Thessalonians, the style and vocabulary of 2 Thessalonians are consistent with Paul's other inspired writings.

THE DATE AND PLACE OF THE WRITING OF 2 THESSALONIANS

Second Thessalonians was written from Corinth a few months after 1 Thessalonians (see discussion of the date and place of the writing of 1 Thessalonians in the Introduction to 1 Thessalonians in this volume).

OUTLINE

I. Salutation (1:1–2)
II. Comfort in Persecution (1:3–12)
   A. Encouragement (1:3–4)
   B. Exhortation (1:5–12)
III. Correction of Prophetic Error (2:1–17)
   A. Crisis (2:1–2)
   B. Correction (2:3–12)
   C. Comfort (2:13–17)
IV. Practical Exhortations (3:1–15)
   A. Regarding Prayer (3:1–5)
   B. Regarding Undisciplined Living (3:6–15)
V. Benediction (3:16–18)

A Church
to Be Proud Of
(2 Thessalonians 1:1–5)

20

Paul and Silvanus and Timothy, to the church of the Thessalonians in God our Father and the Lord Jesus Christ: Grace to you and peace from God the Father and the Lord Jesus Christ. We ought always to give thanks to God for you, brethren, as is only fitting, because your faith is greatly enlarged, and the love of each one of you toward one another grows ever greater; therefore, we ourselves speak proudly of you among the churches of God for your perseverance and faith in the midst of all your persecutions and afflictions which you endure. This is a plain indication of God's righteous judgment so that you will be considered worthy of the kingdom of God, for which indeed you are suffering. (1:1–5)

Churches take pride in many things: their large membership roll or attendance, the size of their campus, the design of their buildings, their wealth, their music, the social status of their members, the prominence of their pastor, their political clout, their influence in the community, or their zeal for a particular theological cause. Others celebrate their creativity and freedom from traditional modes of worship, trading theology for psychology, choirs and organs for rock bands, and replacing sermons with skits, musicals, and other forms of entertainment in an effort to create an inoffensive, nonthreatening atmosphere for the unbelievers and nominal Christians in their congregations. They have become the model churches many seek to emulate. (For a critique of the contemporary church growth movement, see John MacArthur, *Ashamed of the Gospel* [Wheaton, Ill.: Crossway, 1993].)

Judged by the superficial standards mentioned above, the Thessalonian church certainly had little to commend it. It had no buildings (the earliest known church building dates from the third century A.D.), programs, performers, or publications. It was not a large or wealthy church (most of the early Christians were from the lower social classes; cf. 1 Cor. 1:26); the congregation lacked social and political influence (Christians were despised outcasts in Roman society); nor did they have a famous pastor (the names of the elders are not even mentioned). They could not offer prospective converts the comfortable, entertaining, nonthreatening environment of a modern "user-friendly" church but merely "persecutions and afflictions" (1:4). Yet they were a church to which the apostle Paul could write, "We ought always to give thanks to God for you, brethren, as is only fitting. . . . We ourselves speak proudly of you among the churches of God" (2 Thess. 1:3–4). The opening verses of this epistle list several reasons for Paul's grateful boasting about this church.

Though **Paul** mentioned his beloved coworkers **Silvanus** and **Timothy** in his greeting, he was the sole author of the epistle. As they had been when the church was founded (Acts 17:4; cf. 16:1–3), the three were together when this letter was written. (For more information on the founding of the Thessalonian church, see the Introduction to 1 Thessalonians.) They had been in Corinth for some time, since they were there when 1 Thessalonians was written several months earlier (1 Thess. 1:1).

Only in the Thessalonian epistles does **Paul** fail to add a title (such as "apostle," or "bond-servant") to his name. Evidently, these believers did not question his apostolic authority. In his first letter to them, Paul alluded to attacks against him from outside the church (2:14–16; cf. Acts 17:5–10); but there were apparently no challenges to his authority or integrity from anyone in the church. This absence of the usual formal title gives the introduction a more endearing and intimate tone, which is fitting for this encouraging letter.

Silvanus, known in Acts as Silas, was Paul's faithful partner in ministry. Like the apostle, he was a Jew who held Roman citizenship (Acts 16:37); so also like Paul he had both a Jewish (Aramaic) name, Silas, and a Roman name, **Silvanus.** That he was chosen to take the decision of the Jerusalem council to the believers in Antioch (Acts 15:27) confirms his status as one of the "leading men among the brethren" (Acts 15:22). Acts 15:32 notes that he was a prophet, hence a preacher of the gospel. He became Paul's missionary partner after the apostle split with Barnabas over John Mark (Acts 15:40), and was with Paul in the Philippian jail, where he witnessed the jailer's dramatic conversion after the earthquake (Acts 16:19–34). He ministered with Paul in many other places, including Berea (Acts 17:10) and Corinth (Acts 18:5; 2 Cor. 1:19). Later, he became Peter's amanuensis and likely carried 1 Peter to its readers (1 Peter 5:12).

Timothy was Paul's protégé and beloved son in the faith (2 Tim. 1:2; cf. 1 Tim. 1:18). A native of Lystra, a city in Asia Minor, Timothy was the son and grandson of believing Jewish women (2 Tim. 1:5) but had a Gentile father (Acts 16:1). Paul met Timothy on his second missionary journey and was impressed enough with him to add him to his missionary team (Acts 16:1–3). Though Timothy was younger than either Paul or Silas (cf. 1 Tim. 4:12), he quickly became Paul's most valuable assistant. So great was Paul's trust in Timothy as a faithful reflection of the apostle that he frequently served as his emissary and representative (1 Thess. 3:2; Acts 19:22; 1 Cor. 4:17; 16:10; Phil. 2:19–24; 1 Tim. 1:3). Paul wrote two inspired epistles to him and mentioned him in eight others.

As noted in the Introduction to 1 Thessalonians, Thessalonica was a city of a quarter of a million people and the capital of Macedonia (the northern region of Greece). A bustling seaport located along the important Roman highway known as the Egnatian Way, the city was a busy center of trade and commerce.

Paul and his companions founded the **church** on his second missionary journey (Acts 17:1–9). Their success in evangelizing the city (Acts 17:4) enraged the unbelieving Jews, and the ensuing uproar forced the missionary team to leave (Acts 17:10, 14). After stops in Berea and Athens, Paul eventually made his way to Corinth, from which he wrote the first letter. A few months later, Paul penned this letter, prompted by a further report about the situation in Thessalonica.

Though the source of that report is unknown, its contents can be deduced from the issues discussed in this epistle. First, the report must have indicated that the persecution the Thessalonians were undergoing had intensified, prompting Paul to exhort them to endurance (1:4–10). Second, despite Paul's teaching in the first letter (4:13–5:11), he learned that the Thessalonians were still confused about the Rapture and the Day of the Lord. False teachers had prompted the confusion when they produced a forged letter—allegedly from Paul—with which they bolstered their claim that the Day of the Lord had arrived (2:1–2). In response, Paul reiterated that the Day of the Lord had not arrived because its precursors had not yet appeared (2:3–12). Finally, there was information in the report that some, believing Jesus would return very soon, had stopped working and were sponging off the rest of the congregation. Paul sternly rebuked them for their idleness and instructed them to work and provide for their own needs (3:6–15). Although those issues were serious, and addressed appropriately, Paul did not write only with an authoritative tone. For example, as he concluded the letter, Paul charged them, "If anyone does not obey our instruction in this letter, take special note of that person and do not associate with him, so that he will be put to shame" (3:14). Yet he immediately tempered that strong exhortation by urging them, "Do not regard him as an enemy, but admonish him as a brother" (3:15). The gentle, loving tone Paul adopted in this epistle suggests that the issues reported to him needed clarification and correction but did not threaten the church's life and testimony.

Nor did those issues keep Paul from being immensely thankful for the strong spiritual character of the church. It was, in reality, a church to be proud of, for five reasons: genuine conversion, increasing faith, growing love, persevering hope, and a kingdom attitude.

GENUINE CONVERSION

in God our Father and the Lord Jesus Christ: Grace to you and peace from God the Father and the Lord Jesus Christ. (1:1b–2)

The key word **in** emphasizes the believers' eternal life with **God** the **Father** and **the Lord Jesus Christ.** Paul's simple greeting identifies the church as a regenerate church. It is the same greeting the apostle used in his first letter except for the addition of the personal possessive pronoun **our**, which emphasizes that **God** is the **Father** of believers (cf. 1 Thess. 1:3; 3:11, 13; Rom. 1:7; 1 Cor. 1:3; 2 Cor. 1:2; Gal. 1:3, 4; Eph. 1:2; Phil. 1:2; 4:20; Col. 1:2; 2 Thess. 2:16; Philem. 3). But though Paul frequently speaks of believers as being in Christ, only here and in the first verse of the first letter does he describe them as being **in God** the **Father.** It is, however, an appropriate reminder of the Father's care for a church undergoing severe persecution.

The truth that Christians are **in** personal, spiritual, and eternal union with **God** is unique to Christianity; adherents of other religions do not speak of being **in** their god. But the Bible teaches that those who put their faith in Christ "become partakers of the divine nature" (2 Peter 1:4), sharing eternal life with God through faith and identification with His Son. "I have been crucified with Christ," Paul wrote, "and it is no longer I who live, but Christ lives in me; and the life which I now live in the flesh I live by faith in the Son of God, who loved me and gave Himself up for me" (Gal. 2:20; cf. John 14:23; Rom. 6:11; 8:1; 12:5; 16:7, 9, 10; 1 Cor. 1:2;

6:17; 15:22; 2 Cor. 5:17; Eph. 1:1–3; 2:10; Phil. 1:1; Col. 1:2; 3:3; 2 Peter 1:4). Out of that living union flows **grace** and **peace.** Those two wonderful words sum up the gospel; **grace** is God's unmerited favor to the sinner, and **peace** is the result of that favor. It is no wonder that they appear in the greetings of all of Paul's epistles.

That Paul placed the **Lord Jesus Christ** alongside **God the Father** without comment or defense clearly affirms Christ's deity and full equality with the Father. If that were not true, Paul would have needed to explain how believers could be spiritually united with both Christ and the Father. He would also have needed to explain how Jesus, along with the Father, could be the source of **grace** and **peace** if He is not God.

Unlike the dead church at Sardis (Rev. 3:1–6) or the nauseatingly lukewarm church at Laodicea (Rev. 3:14–22), the Thessalonian church was a genuinely converted church, as 2:13–14 proves:

> But we should always give thanks to God for you, brethren beloved by the Lord, because God has chosen you from the beginning for salvation through sanctification by the Spirit and faith in the truth. It was for this He called you through our gospel, that you may gain the glory of our Lord Jesus Christ.

INCREASING FAITH

We ought always to give thanks to God for you, brethren, as is only fitting, because your faith is greatly enlarged, (1:3a)

Opheilō (**ought**) refers to a deep obligation, debt, or responsibility. Paul had no choice but **always to give thanks to God for** the Thessalonians; he was bound under compulsion to do so. God deservedly received all of the apostle's gratitude, for His grace alone made the Thessalonians what they were.

What made Paul most grateful was not the size of the Thessalonians' congregation, buildings, budget, or popularity. The apostle praised God most of all because their **faith** was **greatly enlarged.** *Huperauxanō* (**greatly enlarged**) is an intense compound word and could be translated "increased beyond measure," or "grown beyond what could be expected." Paul's joy was deeply satisfying, because though confident that their faith was genuine and growing (cf. the discussion of 1 Thess. 1:3 in chapter 1 of this volume), he nevertheless had prayed that God would permit him to "complete what [was] lacking in [their] faith" (1 Thess. 3:10). Timothy's report (1 Thess. 3:2, 6) revealed that Paul's prayer for the Thessalonians had been answered.

The Thessalonians' faith had grown not only despite the persecution they were undergoing but also because of it. Persecution destroys false faith. In the parable of the soils, Jesus said, "The one on whom seed was sown on the rocky places, this is the man who hears the word and immediately receives it with joy; yet he has no firm root in himself, but is only temporary, and when affliction or persecution arises because of the word, immediately he falls away" (Matt. 13:20–21). True faith, on the other hand, is indestructible, because the Lord Jesus Christ will not allow it to be destroyed. He warned Peter, "Simon, Simon, behold, Satan has demanded permission to sift you like wheat" (Luke 22:31). But though Peter's faith would be severely shaken (cf. Matt. 26:69–75), it would not be destroyed because, as Jesus went on to say, "I have prayed for you, that your faith may not fail; and you, when once you have turned again, strengthen your brothers" (Luke 22:32; cf. John 21:18–19). Perhaps reflecting on his own experience, Peter later wrote:

> In this you greatly rejoice, even though now for a little while, if necessary, you have been distressed by various trials, so that the proof of your faith, being more precious than gold which is perishable, even though tested by fire, may be found to result in praise and glory and honor at the revelation of Jesus Christ. (1 Peter 1:6–7)

After enduring unspeakable suffering, Job reaffirmed his faith in God:

> Then Job answered the Lord and said, "I know that You can do all things, and that no purpose of Yours can be thwarted. 'Who is this that hides counsel without knowledge?' Therefore I have declared that which I did not understand, things too wonderful for me, which I did not know. 'Hear, now, and I will speak; I will ask You, and You instruct me.' I have heard of You by the hearing of the ear; but now my eye sees You; Therefore I retract, and I repent in dust and ashes." (Job 42:1–6)

In Romans 8:35–39 Paul expressed the utter impossibility that even the most severe suffering could destroy genuine saving faith:

> Who will separate us from the love of Christ? Will tribulation, or distress, or persecution, or famine, or nakedness, or peril, or sword? Just as it is written, "For Your sake we are being put to death all day long; we were considered as sheep to be slaughtered." But in all these things we overwhelmingly conquer through Him who loved us. For I am convinced that neither death, nor life, nor angels, nor principalities, nor things present, nor things to come, nor powers, nor height, nor depth, nor any other created thing, will be able to separate us from the love of God, which is in Christ Jesus our Lord.

Persecution strengthens believers' faith by driving them to God. Facing a painful, difficult trial, Paul "implored the Lord three times that it might leave [him]" (2 Cor. 12:8). Trouble, distress, affliction, pain, and suffering drive those with genuine faith to a greater dependence on the Lord. That increases their knowledge of Him, which in turn increases their ability to trust Him. Therefore, the psalmist could confidently declare, "Before I was afflicted I went astray, but now I keep Your word. . . . It is good for me that I was afflicted, that I may learn Your statutes. . . . I know, O Lord, that Your judgments are righteous, and that in faithfulness You have afflicted me" (Ps. 119:67, 71, 75).

The blasphemous notion suggested by some that Christians need to forgive God for allowing them to suffer completely misses the point. According to that view, believers suffer because though God is well meaning, He is unable to work out all of life's contingencies. Nothing could be further from the truth. For the reasons noted above, suffering is part of God's wise, loving, perfect, sovereign plan for His children; they "suffer according to the will of God" (1 Peter 4:19). "Consider it all joy, my brethren," wrote James, "when you encounter various trials, knowing that the testing of your faith produces endurance. And let endurance have its perfect result, so that you may be perfect and complete, lacking in nothing" (James 1:2–4). Peter reminded suffering believers, "After you have suffered for a little while, the God of all grace, who called you to His eternal glory in Christ, will Himself perfect, confirm, strengthen and establish you" (1 Peter 5:10).

The Thessalonians' increasing faith in the face of persecution affirmed their genuine conversion.

GROWING LOVE

and the love of each one of you toward one another grows ever greater; (1:3*b*)

As he had with their faith, Paul commended the church for their **love** in the first epistle (1 Thess. 1:3; 4:9–10). Yet that did not stop him from praying that "the Lord [would] cause [them] to increase and abound in love for one another" (1 Thess. 3:12). To his great joy, Timothy's report indicated that the **love** of **each one** of the believers **toward one another** was gaining strength, like a healthy plant. Love permeated the entire congregation despite the persecution.

Love, not as fuzzy sentimentality or emotional feeling but as eager, sacrificial service, marks true believers. In John 13:34–35 Jesus said, "A new commandment I give to you, that you love one another, even as I have loved you, that you also love one another. By this all men will know that you are My disciples, if you have love for one another." To the Romans Paul wrote, "The love of God has been poured out within our hearts through the Holy Spirit who was given to us" (Rom. 5:5). In 1 Thessalonians 4:9 Paul reminded the Thessalonians, "Now as to the love of the brethren, you have no need for anyone to write to you, for you yourselves are taught by God to love one another." John affirmed that "the one who loves his brother abides in the Light and there is no cause for stumbling in him" (1 John 2:10).

Increasing faith in God and love for others are essential elements of the redeemed nature (2 Cor. 8:7; Gal. 5:6; Eph. 1:15; 6:23). To Paul's immense joy and satisfaction, they were evident in this church.

PERSEVERING HOPE

therefore, we ourselves speak proudly of you among the churches of God for your perseverance and faith in the midst of all your persecutions and afflictions which you endure. (1:4)

Paul praised them in 1 Thessalonians 1:3 for being strong in hope when he wrote of their "steadfastness of hope in our Lord Jesus Christ in the presence of our God and Father." Yet as he did with their faith and love, Paul desired for their hope to increase. Because of that, he expressed concern in his first letter (3:3–5) that affliction might cause the Thessalonians to lose hope. Timothy's report that they were standing firm amidst the storm of persecution was for Paul yet another answer to prayer.

The emphatic phrase **we ourselves** introduces a subtle nuance in the text. The humble Christians were no doubt overwhelmed by the lavish praise Paul gave them in the first epistle (cf. 1 Thess. 1:8). They probably felt unworthy of such grandiose affection from the noble apostle, and may have been uncomfortable accepting the role of a model church. So it was Paul and his companions, knowing they would never do so on their own behalf (cf. Prov. 27:2; 2 Cor. 10:18), who took it upon themselves to **speak proudly of** them **among the churches of God.** Further, it was Paul, Silas, and Timothy—three of the leading figures in the early church—who expressed that pride because they were greatly encouraged by the Thessalonians' spiritual growth and the absence of significant problems in the congregation. Ironically, Paul wrote **proudly** of the Thessalonians from Corinth, site of the most troubled, spiritually immature of all Paul's churches.

Specifically, Paul, Silas, and Timothy were thankful for the saints' **perseverance and faith in the midst of all** the **persecutions and**

afflictions which they **endured. Perseverance** (*hupomonē*) is not resigned, stoic acquiescence but patient, courageous enduring of trouble. The word literally speaks of "remaining under," or sustaining hope under difficulty. It is not a grim waiting but a joyful hoping. As it does in Romans 3:3, Galatians 5:22, and Titus 2:10, *pistis* (**faith**) has the sense of "faithfulness." Paul was thankful for and proud of how the church remained faithful to the Lord despite the **persecutions** (hostility from enemies of the gospel) and **afflictions** (suffering resulting from persecution) they endured. They refused to renounce their faith, let their love grow cold, or abandon their hope.

A KINGDOM ATTITUDE

This is a plain indication of God's righteous judgment so that you will be considered worthy of the kingdom of God, for which indeed you are suffering. (1:5)

In contrast to the man-centered atmosphere that pervades many churches today, this young church had only a God-centered outlook. Instead of being consumed with personal happiness, fulfillment, comfort, success, or prosperity, they were living out Jesus' command to "seek first His kingdom and His righteousness" (Matt. 6:33). That perspective enabled them to successfully endure the inevitable persecution that comes to the bold faithful.

That kingdom attitude was **a plain indication of God's righteous judgment.** *Endeigma* (**plain indication**) refers to evidence or proof; **God's righteous judgment** to His chastening **so that** they would be considered **worthy of the kingdom of God, for which indeed** they were **suffering** (cf. Heb. 12:10). God's chastening of His own proved they were His children, for "God deals with [believers] as with sons; for what son is there whom his father does not discipline? But [those] without discipline . . . are illegitimate children and not sons" (Heb. 12:7–8). Their **suffering** was not, of course, the basis of the Thessalonians' salvation but the evidence of it. Through His purging, chastening, purifying work in their lives, God prepared them to be **worthy of the kingdom,** for "through many tribulations we must enter the kingdom of God" (Acts 14:22; cf. 1 Thess. 2:12; 1 Peter 5:10).

Believers can face trials joyfully, knowing that God is equipping them for eternal glory. Leon Morris insightfully observes:

> The New Testament does not look on suffering in quite the same way as do most modern people. To us it is in itself an evil, something to be avoided at all costs. Now while the New Testament does not gloss over

this aspect of suffering it does not lose sight either of the fact that in the good providence of God suffering is often the means of working out God's eternal purpose. It develops in the sufferers qualities of character. It teaches valuable lessons. Suffering is not thought of as something which may possibly be avoided by the Christian. For him it is inevitable. He is ordained to it (1 Thess. 3:3). He must live out his life and develop his Christian character in a world which is dominated by non-Christian ideas. His faith is not some fragile thing, to be kept in a kind of spiritual cotton wool, insulated from all shocks. It is robust. It is to be manifested in the fires of trouble, and in the furnace of affliction. And not only is it to be manifested there, but in part at any rate, it is to be fashioned in such places. The very troubles and afflictions which the world heaps on the believer become, under God, the means of making him what he ought to be. Suffering, when we have come to regard it in this light, is not to be thought of as evidence that God has forsaken us, but as evidence that God is with us. Paul can rejoice that he fills up "that which is lacking of the afflictions of Christ in my flesh for his body's sake, which is the church" (Col. 1:24). Such suffering is a vivid token of the presence of God. (*The First and Second Epistles to the Thessalonians,* The New International Commentary on the New Testament [Grand Rapids: Eerdmans, 1989], 197–98)

Again, God never evaluates a church based on external features (cf. 1 Sam. 16:7). He is not impressed with innovative, clever repackaging of the gospel to make it more palatable for unbelievers. Nor are a church's elaborately staged worship services, political awareness, social prominence, or size reasons to boast before God. A church to be proud of is a place where the genuinely converted see their faith increase, their love grow, their hope endure despite persecution, and their focus remain singularly on God's kingdom.

The Vengeance of the Lord Jesus (2 Thessalonians 1:6–10)

21

For after all it is only just for God to repay with affliction those who afflict you, and to give relief to you who are afflicted and to us as well when the Lord Jesus will be revealed from heaven with His mighty angels in flaming fire, dealing out retribution to those who do not know God and to those who do not obey the gospel of our Lord Jesus. These will pay the penalty of eternal destruction, away from the presence of the Lord and from the glory of His power, when He comes to be glorified in His saints on that day, and to be marveled at among all who have believed—for our testimony to you was believed. (1:6–10)

The second coming of the Lord Jesus Christ is the climax of history. Though now in heaven where, having been exalted to the right hand of God since His ascension, He serves as the faithful High Priest for His people, Jesus Christ will one day return to earth in full glory (cf. Matt. 24:30; 25:31; Acts 1:11; 1 Thess. 1:10; Rev. 1:7; 19:11–21; 22:20).

The return of the Lord Jesus Christ to establish His kingdom is a vital theme in Scripture:

> This crucial component of Scripture brings the whole story to its God-ordained consummation. Redemptive history is controlled by God, so

as to culminate in His eternal glory. Redemptive history will end with the same precision and exactness with which it began. The truths of eschatology are neither vague nor unclear—nor are they unimportant. As in any book, how the story ends is the most crucial and compelling part—so with the Bible. Scripture notes several very specific features of the end planned by God.

In the OT, there is repeated mention of an earthly kingdom ruled by the Messiah, Lord Savior, who will come to reign. Associated with that kingdom will be the salvation of Israel, the salvation of Gentiles, the renewal of the earth from the effects of the curse, and the bodily resurrection of God's people who have died. Finally, the OT predicts that there will be the "uncreation" or dissolution of the universe, and the creation of a new heaven and new earth—which will be the eternal state of the godly—and a final hell for the ungodly.

In the NT, these features are clarified and expanded. The King was rejected and executed, but He promised to come back in glory, bringing judgment, resurrection, and His kingdom for all who believe. Innumerable Gentiles from every nation will be included among the redeemed. Israel will be saved and grafted back into the root of blessing from which she has been temporarily excised.

Israel's promised kingdom will be enjoyed, with the Lord Savior reigning on the throne, in the renewed earth, exercising power over the whole world, having taken back His rightful authority, and receiving due honor and worship. Following that kingdom will come the dissolution of the renewed, but still sin-stained creation, and the subsequent creation of a new heaven and new earth—which will be the eternal state, separate forever from the ungodly in hell. (John MacArthur, *The MacArthur Study Bible* [Nashville: Word, 1997], x)

There are several more motives for Christ to return. The church is His bride, and He must return to take her to the wedding feast. Nor will the true King permit the usurper, Satan, to rule the world forever; Christ will return to take back what is rightfully His. Christ's humiliation in His first coming also demands that He return in glory; the last view the world has of Him cannot be as a victim dying on the cross.

The return of Jesus Christ is therefore the climax of all redemptive history and brings God's purpose to culmination. Paul reminded the Thessalonians of this great hope to encourage them to stand firm despite the severe persecution they were undergoing. Their hope—like that of all suffering Christians—was that Jesus would return and bring them relief.

Currently, the glory of our Lord is hidden, and most people believe He is dead (cf. Acts 25:19). Even believers do not experience the fullness of His glorious presence, for as Peter writes, "Though you have not seen Him, you love Him, and though you do not see Him now, but believe in Him, you greatly rejoice with joy inexpressible and full of glory" (1 Peter 1:8). But the day is coming when He will be revealed, both to believers and to unbelievers.

When Paul referred to the Second Coming in relation to believers, he favored the word *parousia* ("presence"; "coming"). For believers, Christ's return is the presence of One they know and have an eternal relationship with. They know Him as revealed in the Old Testament prophecies, the New Testament gospel records of His life, and the elucidation of His life, death, and resurrection in the epistles. But in verse 7 when Paul wrote **the Lord Jesus will be revealed,** he used a different word, *apokalupsis* ("revelation"; "unveiling"; "uncovering"). That word, which has the idea of manifesting what was previously hidden or secret (cf. Rom. 2:5; 16:25; 1 Cor. 14:6; 2 Cor. 12:1, 7; Gal. 1:12; Eph. 3:3), views the return of Christ in relation to unbelievers. The One who has been hidden will be revealed in all His sovereign glory to a world that does not know or worship Him. He will be unveiled as Judge (v. 8). This will be the Day of the Lord (see the discussion in chapter 12 of this volume).

At His first coming, the reality of His deity was hidden; though Jesus was God incarnate, He was veiled in human flesh. As a result, "He was in the world, and the world was made through Him, and the world did not know Him" (John 1:10). But there will be no mistaking the reality of who Jesus is at His second coming, for the whole world will "see the Son of Man coming on the clouds of the sky with power and great glory" (Matt. 24:30). Throughout history there have been (and will continue to be) false christs (cf. Matt. 24:24). But nothing they can do comes remotely close to matching the dazzling Shekinah glory that will be manifested when Christ returns.

Paul described the *apokalupsis* of the Lord Jesus Christ by using three prepositional phrases. First, **from heaven.** Just as He ascended visibly, bodily into heaven, so Jesus will return from heaven visibly, bodily to earth:

> And after He had said these things, He was lifted up while they were looking on, and a cloud received Him out of their sight. And as they were gazing intently into the sky while He was going, behold, two men in white clothing stood beside them. They also said, "Men of Galilee, why do you stand looking into the sky? This Jesus, who has been taken up from you into heaven, will come in just the same way as you have watched Him go into heaven." (Acts 1:9–11)

Having ascended into heaven, Jesus has now "taken His seat at the right hand of the throne of the Majesty in the heavens" (Heb. 8:1; cf. 1:3; 10:12;

12:2; Acts 2:33; 7:55–56; Rom. 8:34; Eph. 1:20; Col. 3:1; 1 Peter 3:22). From that exalted position of power and honor, Jesus intercedes for His people (Rom. 8:34; cf. Isa. 53:12; Heb. 7:25; 9:24; 1 John 2:1), and from that heavenly throne He will one day return to judge His enemies (Matt. 16:27; Acts 10:42; 17:31; Rom. 2:16; 2 Tim. 4:1).

Jesus will not return solo on the Day of the Lord, but **with His mighty angels** (lit., "the angels of His power"). **Angels** are instruments through whom the Son's power is delegated to accomplish His purposes, in that case, judgment.

Angels often appeared with God in the Old Testament. In a probable reference to the giving of the Law at Mount Sinai, Moses declared, "The Lord . . . came from the midst of ten thousand holy ones; at His right hand there was flashing lightning for them" (Deut. 33:2; cf. Acts 7:53; Gal. 3:19; Heb. 2:2). In Psalm 68:17 David wrote, "The chariots of God are myriads, thousands upon thousands [poetic language denoting a vast, uncountable multitude]; the Lord is among them as at Sinai, in holiness." In Psalm 89:5–7 the psalmist affirmed,

> The heavens will praise Your wonders, O Lord; Your faithfulness also in the assembly of the holy ones. For who in the skies is comparable to the Lord? Who among the sons of the mighty is like the Lord, a God greatly feared in the council of the holy ones, and awesome above all those who are around Him?

The New Testament reveals that angels will accompany Jesus when He returns, just as He predicted in Matthew 16:27: "For the Son of Man is going to come in the glory of His Father with His angels, and will then repay every man according to his deeds." In another description of the Second Coming, Jesus said, "But when the Son of Man comes in His glory, and all the angels with Him . . ." (Matt. 25:31; cf. Mark 8:38). When Jesus returns, "He will send forth His angels with a great trumpet and they will gather together His elect from the four winds, from one end of the sky to the other" (Matt. 24:31). Angels will not only gather the elect for blessing but also unbelievers for judgment:

> The Son of Man will send forth His angels, and they will gather out of His kingdom all stumbling blocks, and those who commit lawlessness, and will throw them into the furnace of fire; in that place there will be weeping and gnashing of teeth. . . . So it will be at the end of the age; the angels will come forth and take out the wicked from among the righteous, and will throw them into the furnace of fire; in that place there will be weeping and gnashing of teeth. (Matt. 13:41–42, 49–50)

Finally, when the Lord Jesus Christ returns from heaven with the holy angels He will return **in flaming fire.** The **fire** described here is the fire of judgment (as in Isa. 66:16; Matt. 3:12; 13:30; Heb. 10:27; 2 Peter 3:7, 10). It was the **fire** Moses saw when "the angel of the Lord appeared to him in a blazing fire from the midst of a bush; and he looked, and behold, the bush was burning with fire, yet the bush was not consumed" (Ex. 3:2). When God appeared to give the Law to Israel, "Mount Sinai was all in smoke because the Lord descended upon it in fire; and its smoke ascended like the smoke of a furnace, and the whole mountain quaked violently" (Ex. 19:18; cf. Deut. 4:33; 5:4, 24–26; 18:16). The **fire** of God's judgment is so closely associated with God's nature that Scripture declares, "The Lord your God is a consuming fire" (Deut. 4:24; cf. 9:3; Heb. 12:29).

These three modifying phrases provide striking confirmation of the deity of the Lord Jesus Christ. He will return **from heaven,** where He is seated on the throne of God (Rev. 3:21). He will return with the same **mighty angels** who attend and serve only God; they are also **His** angels. Finally, Jesus Christ will return **in** the same **flaming fire** that marked God's glorious judgment presence. By associating with the Son the realities characteristic of the Father, the apostle affirms His deity as the Second Person of the Trinity.

Paul's description of the twofold nature of Christ's return—relief, rest, refreshment, and peace for believers; retribution, judgment, punishment, and vengeance for unbelievers—was not new teaching. Christ, Himself God, taught that His second coming would impact believers and unbelievers differently. "At the end of the age," He declared, "the Son of Man will send forth His angels, and they will gather out of His kingdom all stumbling blocks, and those who commit lawlessness, and will throw them into the furnace of fire; in that place there will be weeping and gnashing of teeth" (Matt. 13:40–42). On the other hand, when the Lord returns "He will send forth His angels with a great trumpet and they will gather together His elect from the four winds, from one end of the sky to the other" (Matt. 24:31).

Christ's return will thus produce two radically different results. Like the little book described in Revelation 10:9–10, those results will be both bitter and sweet:

So I went to the angel, telling him to give me the little book. And he said to me, "Take it and eat it; it will make your stomach bitter, but in your mouth it will be sweet as honey." I took the little book out of the angel's hand and ate it, and in my mouth it was sweet as honey; and when I had eaten it, my stomach was made bitter.

For unbelievers, the Second Coming will bring bitter retribution; for believers, sweet relief.

For after all it is only just for God to repay with affliction those who afflict you . . . dealing out retribution to those who do not know God and to those who do not obey the gospel of our Lord Jesus. These will pay the penalty of eternal destruction, away from the presence of the Lord and from the glory of His power, (1:6, 8–9)

Ekdikēsis (**retribution**), meaning "to give full punishment," is variously translated "justice," "punishment," "retribution," "vengeance," and "avenging of wrong." In his defense before the Sanhedrin, Stephen said, "And when he [Moses] saw one of them being treated unjustly, he defended him and took vengeance [*ekdikēsis*] for the oppressed by striking down the Egyptian" (Acts 7:24). Just as Moses brought retribution to the Egyptian for mistreating his fellow Israelites, so also will God bring **retribution** to those who reject Him and mistreat His people.

God's **retribution**, however, is not like the unruly, hostile, selfish, sinful passion that causes people to retaliate against others, since "the God who inflicts wrath is not unrighteous" (Rom. 3:5). But because sinful humans are not perfectly holy, completely just, and omniscient, they cannot render perfect judgment. Therefore, God reserves vengeance for Himself. In the Sermon on the Mount, Jesus forbade personal vengeance (Matt. 5:38–48), and Paul wrote in Romans 12:19, "Never take your own revenge, beloved, but leave room for the wrath of God, for it is written, 'Vengeance is Mine, I will repay,' says the Lord" (cf. Deut. 32:35; Isa. 66:15–16; Heb. 10:30).

The Bible repeatedly teaches that God will deal out retribution to sinners. The imprecatory Psalms (7; 35; 40; 55; 58; 59; 69; 79; 109; 137; 139; 144) presuppose and even exalt God's retribution. In strong, even shocking language, the psalmists cry out for God to take vengeance on their enemies:

The righteous will rejoice when he sees the vengeance;
He will wash his feet in the blood of the wicked. (Ps. 58:10)

Surely God will shatter the head of His enemies,
The hairy crown of him who goes on in his guilty deeds. (Ps. 68:21)

Add iniquity to their iniquity,
And may they not come into Your righteousness. (Ps. 69:27)

And return to our neighbors sevenfold into their bosom
The reproach with which they have reproached You, O Lord. (Ps. 79:12)

Let there be none to extend lovingkindness to him,
Nor any to be gracious to his fatherless children. (Ps. 109:12)

How blessed will be the one who seizes and dashes your little ones
Against the rock. (Ps. 137:9)

Do I not hate those who hate You, O Lord?
And do I not loathe those who rise up against You?
I hate them with the utmost hatred;
They have become my enemies. (Ps. 139:21–22)

Such forceful calls for God's just vengeance on His enemies disturb some, as John Wenham notes:

> Earlier this year [1962] 14 church study groups in Woodford looked at the Old Testament psalms and concluded that 84 of them were "not fit for Christians to sing"; and J. C. Wansey, compiler of the useful collection of New Testament passages which have been printed for congregational chanting under the title *A New Testament Psalter*, commented: "These psalms and parts of many others are full of tribal jealousies, bloodthirsty threats and curses, whinings and moanings, which are shocking in themselves and time-wasting to God and man. The New Testament psalms are Christian through and through." But to jettison half the Psalter is a dubious expedient, for, as C. S. Lewis realizes, the harsh passages and the tender passages are hopelessly mixed up, and it is not possible just to ignore the unpleasant sections. (*The Goodness of God* [Downers Grove, Ill: InterVarsity, 1975], 149)

But imprecatory language is not restricted to the Psalms. Warned by God that the men of his hometown sought his life (Jer. 11:18, 21), Jeremiah prayed, "O Lord of hosts, who judges righteously, who tries the feelings and the heart, let me see Your vengeance on them, for to You have I committed my cause" (11:20). In response, God promised, "Behold, I am about to punish them! The young men will die by the sword, their sons and daughters will die by famine; and a remnant will not be left to them, for I will bring disaster on the men of Anathoth—the year of their punishment" (Jer. 11:22–23).

Later, in an even more forcefully worded prayer, Jeremiah cried out,

Do give heed to me, O Lord, and listen to what my opponents are saying! Should good be repaid with evil? For they have dug a pit for me. Remember how I stood before You to speak good on their behalf, so as to turn away Your wrath from them. Therefore, give their children over to famine and deliver them up to the power of the sword; and let their wives become childless and widowed. Let their men also be smitten to death, their young men struck down by the sword in battle. May an outcry be heard from their houses, when You suddenly bring raiders upon them; for they have dug a pit to capture me and hidden snares for my feet. Yet You, O Lord, know all their deadly designs against me; do not forgive their iniquity or blot out their sin from Your sight. But may they be overthrown before You; deal with them in the time of Your anger! (Jer. 18:19–23)

In Jeremiah 19:3–9 God answered the prophet's prayer:

Thus says the Lord of hosts, the God of Israel, "Behold I am about to bring a calamity upon this place, at which the ears of everyone that hears of it will tingle. Because they have forsaken Me and have made this an alien place and have burned sacrifices in it to other gods, that neither they nor their forefathers nor the kings of Judah had ever known, and because they have filled this place with the blood of the innocent and have built the high places of Baal to burn their sons in the fire as burnt offerings to Baal, a thing which I never commanded or spoke of, nor did it ever enter My mind; therefore, behold, days are coming," declares the Lord, "when this place will no longer be called Topheth or the valley of Ben-hinnom, but rather the valley of Slaughter. I will make void the counsel of Judah and Jerusalem in this place, and I will cause them to fall by the sword before their enemies and by the hand of those who seek their life; and I will give over their carcasses as food for the birds of the sky and the beasts of the earth. I will also make this city a desolation and an object of hissing; everyone who passes by it will be astonished and hiss because of all its disasters. I will make them eat the flesh of their sons and the flesh of their daughters, and they will eat one another's flesh in the siege and in the distress with which their enemies and those who seek their life will distress them."

Some, hearkening back to liberal theology's false dichotomy between the supposedly harsh, cruel God of the Old Testament and the gentle, meek, loving Jesus of the New Testament, might be tempted to reject such strongly worded language as uncharacteristic of Jesus. But Jesus and the New Testament writers used equally strong language. Paul wrote to Timothy, "Alexander the coppersmith did me much harm; the Lord will repay him according to his deeds" (2 Tim. 4:14), while in Revelation 6:10 the Tribulation martyrs cry out, "How long, O Lord, holy and true, will You refrain from judging and avenging our blood on those who dwell on the earth?" In Matthew 3:12 John the Baptist said of Jesus, "His winnowing fork is in His hand, and He will thoroughly clear His threshing floor; and He will gather His wheat into the barn, but He will burn up the chaff with unquenchable fire." In contrast to a popular evangelical cliché, Jesus has a horrible plan for the lives of those who reject Him.

In the parable of the wicked vinedressers (Luke 20:9–19), which pictures God's judgment on those who reject His Son, Jesus declared,

> "What, then, will the owner of the vineyard do to them? He will come and destroy these vine-growers and will give the vineyard to others." When they heard it, they said, "May it never be!" But Jesus looked at them and said, "What then is this that is written: 'The stone which the builders rejected, this became the chief corner stone'? Everyone who falls on that stone will be broken to pieces; but on whomever it falls, it will scatter him like dust." (Luke 20:15–18)

In Matthew 23:13–36 Jesus denounced the scribes and Pharisees and declared that they would be condemned to hell (v. 33). He promised Chorazin and Bethsaida a more fearful judgment than Tyre and Sidon (Matt. 11:20–22), whose destruction God decreed in the Old Testament (cf. Ezek. 26–28). He threatened Capernaum with a stricter judgment than even the grossly wicked city of Sodom (Matt. 11:24). Jesus declared of those who cause believers to sin, "Whoever causes one of these little ones who believe to stumble, it would be better for him if, with a heavy millstone hung around his neck, he had been cast into the sea" (Mark 9:42). In Mark 14:21 Jesus pronounced His own curse on Judas Iscariot: "For the Son of Man is to go just as it is written of Him; but woe to that man by whom the Son of Man is betrayed! It would have been good for that man if he had not been born."

Jesus referred to the events surrounding His second coming as the "days of vengeance" (Luke 21:22), when He will say to those who reject Him, "Depart from Me, accursed ones, into the eternal fire which has been prepared for the devil and his angels. . . . These will go away into eternal punishment" (Matt. 25:41, 46). In John 5:29 He taught that there will eventually be a resurrection to judgment for all unbelievers. No passage outside of Revelation portrays so poignantly and powerfully the retribution that awaits sinners at the Second Coming as does that final New Testament book.

There is, then, no contradiction between God the Father and Jesus the Son, or between the Old and New Testaments concerning the vengeance of God; Jesus and the apostles strongly reiterated it. The subject of divine retribution leads to three questions: why will Jesus deal out retribution, to whom will He deal it out, and how will He deal it out.

WHY?

For after all it is only just for God to repay (1:6a)

Every culture, no matter what its laws, ethics, or morals, punishes criminals. People have a sense of justice, including capital punishment, because they are made in God's image. What is imperfectly true in the human realm is perfectly true in God's realm. When Paul wrote that **after all it is only just,** fitting, and proper for God to repay with retribution those who violate His law (as it is right for God to reward believers with the kingdom; v. 5), he was stating a self-evident truth. In fact, the word translated "retribution" in verse 8 is related to a word that means "just," or "right." God's retribution is not petty vindictiveness or an emotional frenzy; God does not reach a certain level of exasperation or frustration, lose self-control, and explode in rage against wrongdoers. His retribution is the calm, controlled, just punishment meted out by the perfectly righteous Judge to those who have willfully violated His perfect law. It is not possible for God to be unjust, for "shall not the Judge of all the earth deal justly?" (Gen. 18:25).

Isaiah 45:20–25 illustrates God's just dealing with those who reject Him:

> Gather yourselves and come; draw near together, you fugitives of the nations; they have no knowledge, who carry about their wooden idol and pray to a god who cannot save. Declare and set forth your case; indeed, let them consult together. Who has announced this from of old? Who has long since declared it? Is it not I, the Lord? And there is no other God besides Me, a righteous God and a Savior; there is none except Me. Turn to Me and be saved, all the ends of the earth; for I am God, and there is no other. I have sworn by Myself, the word has gone forth from My mouth in righteousness and will not turn back, that to Me every knee will bow, every tongue will swear allegiance. They will say of Me, "Only in the Lord are righteousness and strength." Men will come to Him, and all who were angry at Him will be put to shame. In the Lord all the offspring of Israel will be justified and will glory.

God, as it were, summons people into court and demands to know why they should not be punished for violating His law and rejecting His commandment to repent and seek His gracious forgiveness (Isa. 55:6–7). No one, of course, can offer any viable reason for having done so. Therefore,

God's judgment is just and sinners are justly condemned for rejecting Him.

Ezekiel 33:17–20 also declares God to be just when He condemns unrepentant sinners:

> Yet your fellow citizens say, "The way of the Lord is not right," when it is their own way that is not right. When the righteous turns from his righteousness and commits iniquity, then he shall die in it. But when the wicked turns from his wickedness and practices justice and righteousness, he will live by them. Yet you say, "The way of the Lord is not right." O house of Israel, I will judge each of you according to his ways.

God cannot be unjust in dealing out retribution to sinners, for "the Almighty . . . will not do violence to justice and abundant righteousness" (Job 37:23); He is "great in counsel and mighty in deed, whose eyes are open to all the ways of the sons of men, giving to everyone according to his ways and according to the fruit of his deeds" (Jer. 32:19).

When the Lord Jesus Christ brings vengeance on those who reject Him, He will be acting in perfect harmony with God's pure justice, for He is "Faithful and True, and in righteousness He judges and wages war" (Rev. 19:11). Those who accuse the absolutely holy God of being unjust are in fact unjust themselves. He has given His law and called people to obey it and will judge those who do not. The truth is that God would not be righteous if He did not.

Antapodidōmi (**repay**) means "to give back," or "recompense." It is a strong, compound word that conveys the idea of a full and complete repayment. The God who said, "Vengeance is Mine, and retribution" (Deut. 32:35), will justly **repay** sinners for violating His law.

An incident in Luke 13 illustrates that principle. Some people told Jesus "about the Galileans whose blood Pilate had mixed with their sacrifices" (v. 1). Apparently, Pilate had chosen to execute some Jewish rebels at a most inopportune time—while they were offering sacrifices. Naturally, that act outraged the Jews, hence their comment to Jesus. But His reply was startling. Instead of commiserating with them or expounding on why bad things happen to good people, He solemnly warned them,

> Do you suppose that these Galileans were greater sinners than all other Galileans because they suffered this fate? I tell you, no, but unless you repent, you will all likewise perish. Or do you suppose that those eighteen on whom the tower in Siloam fell and killed them were worse culprits than all the men who live in Jerusalem? I tell you, no, but unless you repent, you will all likewise perish. (vv. 2–5)

The fate of the victims was exactly that which all sinners deserve—divine judgment. All sinners deserve death and hell; therefore, Jesus twice warned His hearers that they would suffer a similar fate unless they repented. The threat of God's vengeance, retribution, and judgment is not only just but also a deterrent, a roadblock on the way to hell. Those who ignore that roadblock are without excuse (Rom. 1:18–20).

WHO?

with affliction those who afflict you . . . to those who do not know God and to those who do not obey the gospel of our Lord Jesus. (1:6*c*, 8*b*)

Those who afflict believers is a broad category, including all who attack the people of God. In Genesis 12:3 God promised Abraham, "The one who curses you I will curse," while Zechariah 2:8 warns that "he who touches [God's people], touches the apple of His eye." Those who trouble God's people in effect poke a finger in His eye. In Matthew 18:6–10 Jesus warned:

> Whoever causes one of these little ones who believe in Me to stumble, it would be better for him to have a heavy millstone hung around his neck, and to be drowned in the depth of the sea. Woe to the world because of its stumbling blocks! For it is inevitable that stumbling blocks come; but woe to that man through whom the stumbling block comes! If your hand or your foot causes you to stumble, cut it off and throw it from you; it is better for you to enter life crippled or lame, than to have two hands or two feet and be cast into the eternal fire. If your eye causes you to stumble, pluck it out and throw it from you. It is better for you to enter life with one eye, than to have two eyes and be cast into the fiery hell. See that you do not despise one of these little ones, for I say to you that their angels in heaven continually see the face of My Father who is in heaven.

Paul further describes those who will face God's retribution by using two phrases. First, he describes them as **those who do not know God** (cf. Judg. 2:10; 1 Sam. 2:12; Job 18:21; Ps. 9:17; Jer. 2:8; 9:3, 6; 10:25; Hos. 4:1, 6; 5:4; John 7:28; 8:54–55; Gal. 4:8; 1 Thess. 4:5; 1 John 4:8); that is, they do not have a personal relationship with Him (cf. John 17:3; Eph. 2:12; 4:17–18; Titus 1:16). They may know the facts about Him, and even imagine that they are serving Him by persecuting His people (cf. John 16:2), but they are in reality "separate from Christ . . . having no hope and without God in the world" (Eph. 2:12).

The reason they do not know God is not ignorance but wickedness that causes them to suppress the truth that they do know:

For the wrath of God is revealed from heaven against all ungodliness and unrighteousness of men who suppress the truth in unrighteousness, because that which is known about God is evident within them; for God made it evident to them. For since the creation of the world His invisible attributes, His eternal power and divine nature, have been clearly seen, being understood through what has been made, so that they are without excuse. For even though they knew God, they did not honor Him as God or give thanks, but they became futile in their speculations, and their foolish heart was darkened. (Rom. 1:18–21)

God has planted the knowledge of Himself around and within every person, so that all are without excuse (Rom. 1:20–21). He has written His law on every heart and in every conscience (Rom. 2:14–15). As a consequence of their sin-darkened hearts, unbelievers, though "professing to be wise," in fact "became fools, and exchanged the glory of the incorruptible God for an image in the form of corruptible man and of birds and four-footed animals and crawling creatures" (Rom. 1:22–23). Despite the abundant evidence all around them (and within them) that should lead them to a true knowledge of God, people refuse to believe. Hell will be populated by the willfully ignorant. The last words those who reject God will hear will be the Lord Jesus Christ's chilling, terrifying pronouncement, "I never knew you; depart from Me, you who practice lawlessness" (Matt. 7:23).

Paul further defines those who will face God's retribution as **those who do not obey the gospel of our Lord Jesus.** This description intensifies their guilt. It is damning to reject an innate knowledge of God; it is to incur severer judgment to openly reject **the gospel.** The hottest hell, the severest punishment, is reserved for those who **do not obey the gospel.** In Luke 12:47–48 Jesus taught that there are varying degrees of punishment:

That slave who knew his master's will and did not get ready or act in accord with his will, will receive many lashes, but the one who did not know it, and committed deeds worthy of a flogging, will receive but few. From everyone who has been given much, much will be required; and to whom they entrusted much, of him they will ask all the more.

The writer of Hebrews clearly states that rejecting the gospel intensifies unbelievers' guilt:

If we go on sinning willfully after receiving the knowledge of the truth, there no longer remains a sacrifice for sins, but a terrifying expectation of judgment and the fury of a fire which will consume the adversaries. Anyone who has set aside the Law of Moses dies without mercy on the testimony of two or three witnesses. How much severer punishment do you think he will deserve who has trampled under foot the Son of God, and has regarded as unclean the blood of the covenant by which he was sanctified, and has insulted the Spirit of grace? For we know Him who said, "Vengeance is Mine, I will repay." And again, "The Lord will judge His people." It is a terrifying thing to fall into the hands of the living God. (Heb. 10:26–31)

Whereas salvation is a gift to be received, the **gospel** is a command to be obeyed. "Therefore having overlooked the times of ignorance," Paul declared, "God is now declaring to men that all people everywhere should repent" (Acts 17:30; cf. 26:20). For that reason, Paul wrote that his apostolic mission was "to bring about the obedience of faith among all the Gentiles for His name's sake" (Rom. 1:5; cf. 15:18; 16:19, 26; 1 Peter 1:22). Therefore, those who remain disobedient to the command to believe the gospel will face God's retribution.

This judgment is not rendered by God because He is angry at unbelievers for hurting His children but rather because the persecutors did not come to the Lord Jesus Christ and embrace the gospel. Specifically, this Day of the Lord judgment comes in two phases on the ungodly: First, at the close of the seven-year Tribulation (Rev. 19:11–21), and second, at the end of the millennial kingdom (Rev. 20:7–10). It will then be the fate of all the ungodly of all ages to be judged at the Great White Throne and sentenced forever to the lake of fire (Rev. 20:11–15).

HOW?

with affliction. . . . These will pay the penalty of eternal destruction, away from the presence of the Lord and from the glory of His power, (1:6b, 9)

Fittingly, God will repay the disobedient unbelievers who afflict His people with **affliction.** *Thlipsis* (**affliction**) can mean "trouble," "distress," "difficult circumstances," or "suffering." Paul specifically defined it in this passage as **the penalty of eternal destruction.** *Aiōnios* (**eternal**) refers in the overwhelming majority of its New Testament uses to things of endless duration, such as God (Rom. 16:26), the Holy Spirit (Heb. 9:14), heaven (Luke 16:9), salvation (Heb. 5:9), redemption (Heb. 9:12), the covenant (Heb. 13:20), the gospel (Rev. 14:6), God's kingdom

(2 Peter 1:11), hell (Matt. 18:8; 25:41, 46; Heb. 6:2; Jude 7), and, most frequently, eternal life (Matt. 19:16, 29; 25:46; Mark 10:17, 30; Luke 10:25; 18:18, 30; John 3:15, 16, 36; 4:14, 36; 5:24, 39; 6:27, 40, 47, 54, 68; 10:28; 12:25, 50; 17:2, 3; Acts 13:46, 48; Rom. 2:7; 5:21; 6:22, 23; Gal. 6:8; 1 Tim. 1:16; 6:12; Titus 1:2; 3:7; 1 John 1:2; 2:25; 3:15; 5:11, 13, 20; Jude 21). Like all of the above-mentioned things, the **destruction** of the wicked will have no end but will last forever.

Olethros (**destruction**) does not refer to annihilation, but to ruination. It does not mean the cessation of existence but rather the loss of all that makes existence worthwhile (cf. 1 Tim. 6:9). The lost will not cease to exist but will experience forever a life of uselessness, hopelessness, emptiness, and meaninglessness, with no value, worth, accomplishment, purpose, goal, or hope. They will be ruined forever; "They pass into a night on which no morning dawns" (Leon Morris, *The Epistles of Paul to the Thessalonians*, Tyndale New Testament Commentaries [Grand Rapids: Eerdmans, 1976], 120).

Two conditions under which the lost will serve their eternal sentence reinforce the horror of their punishment. First, they will be forever **away from the presence of the Lord** (cf. Matt. 7:23; 25:41; Luke 13:27; Rev. 22:15). There is a great chasm fixed between the eternal realms of the blessed and the cursed (cf. Luke 16:26), separating the cursed from all that represents God's presence. And since "every good thing given and every perfect gift is from above, coming down from the Father of lights" (James 1:17), there will be no vestige of goodness in hell.

The lost will also serve their eternal sentence **away . . . from the glory of His power.** Jesus described hell as a place of darkness (Matt. 8:12; 22:13; 25:30; cf. 2 Peter 2:4, 17; Jude 13), cut off from the visible display of God's splendor and majesty. There will be no relief from hell's horrors; nothing of God's glorious presence to bring any shred of beauty, pleasure, joy, or peace. The lost will share hell with the devil and his angels; it will be a place of "weeping and gnashing of teeth" (Matt. 8:12; 13:42, 50; 22:13; 24:51; 25:30; Luke 13:28), where "the smoke of their torment goes up forever and ever; they have no rest day and night" (Rev. 14:11). Yet no words can adequately express the misery of this reality.

RELIEF

it is only just for God . . . to give relief to you who are afflicted and to us as well . . . when He comes to be glorified in His saints on that day, and to be marveled at among all who have believed —for our testimony to you was believed. (1:*6a, 7a–b,* 10)

Not only will Christ return to bring retribution to unbelievers but also **to give relief** to believers. *Anesis* (**relief**) expresses the idea of relaxation, loosening, easing, freedom, refreshment, restoration, and rest. The Bible promises three kinds of rest to believers. First, there is the rest that salvation brings. In Matthew 11:28–29 Jesus promised, "Come to Me, all who are weary and heavy-laden, and I will give you rest. Take My yoke upon you and learn from Me, for I am gentle and humble in heart, and you will find rest for your souls." Salvation brings rest from the crushing burden of sin. The writer of Hebrews described salvation rest in Hebrews 4:9–11:

> So there remains a Sabbath rest for the people of God. For the one who has entered His rest has himself also rested from his works, as God did from His. Therefore let us be diligent to enter that rest, so that no one will fall, through following the same example of disobedience.

But salvation rest is not in view in this passage. Paul has two other kinds of rest in mind—the second two kinds of rest promised in Scripture. In addition to salvation rest, the Bible promises millennial rest. When Jesus returns at the end of the seven-year Tribulation (Rev. 19:11–20:7), He will establish His earthly kingdom, in which His subjects will enjoy rest and peace. In Acts 3:19–21 Peter spoke of that millennial rest:

> Therefore repent and return, so that your sins may be wiped away, in order that times of refreshing may come from the presence of the Lord; and that He may send Jesus, the Christ appointed for you, whom heaven must receive until the period of restoration of all things about which God spoke by the mouth of His holy prophets from ancient time.

Paradise will be restored, and the world will be somewhat as God originally intended it to be. The authority of Jesus Christ will be absolute, and rebels will be instantly and devastatingly dealt with (Ps. 2:8–9; Rev. 12:5; 19:15).

A final rest promised in Scripture is the eternal rest the redeemed enter into at death. In the presence of God believers will find rest forever—from sin, temptation, trials, sorrows, and any other form of suffering—because "He will wipe away every tear from their eyes; and there will no longer be any death; there will no longer be any mourning, or crying, or pain" (Rev. 21:4).

As did the issue of retribution, the issue of rest and relief poses three questions: why, who, and how.

WHY?

it is only just for God . . . to give relief (1:6a, 7a)

Just as God's justice demands that He bring retribution on unbelievers, so also **it is only just for** Him **to give relief** to the redeemed. "If we confess our sins," John wrote, "He is faithful and righteous to forgive us our sins and to cleanse us from all unrighteousness" (1 John 1:9). Why? Because Jesus paid for our sins on the cross, suffering the just judgment of God in our place (cf. Isa. 53:4–6, 12; 2 Cor. 5:21; 1 Peter 2:24). God is "just and the justifier of the one who has faith in Jesus" (Rom. 3:26). Addressing the question of how a just God can still be merciful and forgive sinners, A. W. Tozer wrote:

> [The] solution for the problem of how God can be just and still justify the unjust is found in the Christian doctrine of redemption. It is that, through the work of Christ in atonement, justice is not violated but satisfied when God spares a sinner. Redemptive theology teaches that mercy does not become effective toward a man until justice has done its work. The just penalty for sin was exacted when Christ our Substitute died for us on the cross. However unpleasant this may sound to the ear of the natural man, it has ever been sweet to the ear of faith. (*The Knowledge of the Holy* [New York: Harper & Row, 1975], 94)

The due penalty for sin has been paid by the Lamb of God; divine justice has been satisfied by His death for sinners; believers' eternal rest is secure.

That believers' final rest is still future does not mean they will enjoy no relief from affliction in this life. Peter wrote, "After you have suffered for a little while, the God of all grace, who called you to His eternal glory in Christ, will Himself perfect, confirm, strengthen and establish you" (1 Peter 5:10). Believers can "Consider it all joy . . . when [they] encounter various trials, knowing that the testing of [their] faith produces endurance. And . . . endurance [will] have [as] its perfect result . . . that [they will] be perfect and complete, lacking in nothing" (James 1:2–4). Paul could exult in the midst of the most severe trials, "I am well content with weaknesses, with insults, with distresses, with persecutions, with difficulties, for Christ's sake; for when I am weak, then I am strong" (2 Cor. 12:10). In Romans 8:18 he wrote, "For I consider that the sufferings of this present time are not worthy to be compared with the glory that is to be revealed to us," while in 2 Corinthians 4:17 he added, "For momentary, light affliction is producing for us an eternal weight of glory far beyond all comparison."

WHO?

to you who are afflicted and to us as well (1:7*b*)

God promises eternal rest to all believers, for all believers can expect to be **afflicted.** To Timothy Paul wrote, "Indeed, all who desire to live godly in Christ Jesus will be persecuted" (2 Tim. 3:12; cf. Acts 14:22). Suffering for Christ is a mark of a true Christian; those whose faith is not genuine will not survive persecution (Matt. 13:20–21). Eternal rest comes to those who counted the cost of following Christ, and willingly took up their crosses to follow Him (Luke 9:23). They are the little flock to whom the Father has gladly chosen to give the kingdom (Luke 12:32).

HOW?

when He comes to be glorified in His saints on that day, and to be marveled at among all who have believed—for our testimony to you was believed. (1:10)

When He comes, two things will happen that will bring relief to believers. First, Christ will **be glorified in His saints on that day.** There is coming a day in which God will be glorified through believers in a manner never before seen. Believers are called in this life to make manifest the glory of the indwelling Christ by doing "all to the glory of God" (1 Cor. 10:31; cf. Phil. 1:11). They are to obey Jesus' injunction, "Let your light shine before men in such a way that they may see your good works, and glorify your Father who is in heaven" (Matt. 5:16). In this life, believers can only do so imperfectly, but when Christ returns, He "will transform the body of [their] humble state into conformity with the body of His glory, by the exertion of the power that He has even to subject all things to Himself" (Phil. 3:21; cf. 1 John 3:2). They will then be pure vessels through which the glory of God shines.

This is the glorious manifestation of believers that Paul wrote about in Romans 8:18–19: "For I consider that the sufferings of this present time are not worthy to be compared with the glory that is to be revealed to us. For the anxious longing of the creation waits eagerly for the revealing of the sons of God." This glorification will be the final and full redemption of all believers alive when Jesus Christ comes in glory. That requires some explanation. Some believers will already be in the glorified condition, having been raptured before the Tribulation. They will have been in heaven since then in the place prepared for them (John 14:1–3) in resurrection glory enjoying their rewards and fellowship with their Lord. They will return with Christ (Rev. 19:14) to the earth for the Millennium, to join the saints still alive on earth who will receive the earthly kingdom and reign of the Savior. Apparently at the time of Christ's return, Tribulation saints and Old Testament saints, whose spirits have been with the Lord, will be raised and fully glorified to join those descending from heaven. This is the resurrection spoken of by Daniel:

> Now at that time Michael, the great prince who stands guard over the sons of your people, will arise. And there will be a time of distress such as never occurred since there was a nation until that time; and at that time your people, everyone who is found written in the book, will be rescued. Many of those who sleep in the dust of the ground will awake, these to everlasting life, but the others to disgrace and everlasting contempt. Those who have insight will shine brightly like the brightness of the expanse of heaven, and those who lead the many to righteousness, like the stars forever and ever. (Dan. 12:1–3)

All the living believers who enter the kingdom will see the glorified saints.

Second, believers will be **marveled at among all who have believed.** Since only believers enter the kingdom, as the judgment of the sheep and goats makes clear (cf. Matt. 25:31–46; Rev. 20:6), the redeemed will wonder at the glory of Christ that is fully revealed in the resurrected saints.

Lest the Thessalonians fear that they might miss out on the relief Christ will bring when He returns, Paul reminded them that they would be among the glorified saints because **our testimony to you was believed.** Since they **believed** Paul, Silas, and Timothy's preaching of the gospel they will never face retribution but will experience the blessed relief of glory that awaits the redeemed.

Praying for the Right Things (2 Thessalonians 1:11–12)

22

To this end also we pray for you always, that our God will count you worthy of your calling, and fulfill every desire for goodness and the work of faith with power, so that the name of our Lord Jesus will be glorified in you, and you in Him, according to the grace of our God and the Lord Jesus Christ. (1:11–12)

Among the more unusual religious movements in the world are the cargo cults of the South Pacific. Though their origins date back to the nineteenth century, they experienced an upsurge in popularity during World War II. As part of their island-hopping campaign against the Japanese forces, the Americans often used remote islands as supply depots and air bases. The dazzling array of modern technological devices they brought with them, such as airplanes, jeeps, modern weapons, refrigerators, radios, power tools, even cigarette lighters that magically produced fire, appeared supernatural to the islanders. As a result, some of them concluded that the white men must be gods who flew in out of the sky bearing all these amazing things.

Eventually, the island bases were abandoned as the fighting drew ever closer to the Japanese home islands. But the tribesmen found their way of life permanently changed by their exposure to the "cargo gods" and the materialistic bounty they brought. They built shrines to the cargo gods, often weaving perfect replicas of planes, control towers, and hangers, and venerated such holy relics as cigarette lighters, cameras, eyeglasses, pens, and nuts and bolts. Vainly hoping to bring back the cargo gods, their chiefs "utter[ed] 'magic' phrases, such as 'Roger ... over and out ...you have landing clearance ... come in'" (Ted Daniels, "John Frum: Cargo and Catastrophe" [http://www.channel1.com/mpr/current/63-frum.html], vol. 3, no. 6, Oct. 1997). The cargo cults still thrive to this day, the best known one being the John Frum (possibly John "Frum" America) cult headquartered on the island of Tanna in Vanuatu (formerly the New Hebrides). Followers of the cargo cults are so passionately consumed with materialism that missionaries find it difficult to evangelize them; they are interested in cargo, not the gospel.

Incredibly, the cargo cults find a parallel in contemporary Christianity, in the movement variously known as Word/Faith, Positive Confession, Name It and Claim It, and the Prosperity or Health and Wealth gospel. The Word Faith movement is in effect a Western cargo cult, teaching that God delivers tangible, consumable products on demand. Its proponents unabashedly teach that prayer is a means of self-gratification; a tool for getting houses, cars, clothes, and other cargo. The god of the Word Faith movement is little more than a utilitarian genie who exists to grant the materialistic wishes of his followers.

Though they may not go to the extremes of the cargo cults or the Word Faith movement, Christians can still pray for the wrong things. Their prayers are too often shallow, shortsighted, misdirected, and, frankly, selfish. They pray for health, wealth, happiness, comfort, success, a house, a job, a wife or husband, a promotion, or a raise. While those things are not necessarily wrong, they were not high on either Jesus' (Matt. 6:25–34) or Paul's (Phil. 4:11–12, 19) priority list. The problem of praying for the wrong things is compounded when believers pray for the wrong reason. James warned: "You ask and do not receive, because you ask with wrong motives, so that you may spend it on your pleasures" (James 4:3).

The essence of prayer is not demanding things from God but listening to discern His will. The deeper believers' prayer lives become, the more they line up with God's will as revealed in Scripture, the less inclined they are to ask for trivial things. As they learn to desire what He desires, love what He loves, and hate what He hates, they pray, "Our Father who is in heaven, hallowed be Your name. Your kingdom come. Your will be done, on earth as it is in heaven" (Matt. 6:9–10).

Verses 11 and 12 do not record one of the many prayers that mark Paul's epistles, but rather are a general report of how he habitually prayed. The passage shows that he prayed for the right things with the right motives. It also reveals that for Paul prayer was not a ritual or a routine but a way of life. Beneath the surface of his teaching, preaching, planning, writing, working, exhorting, discipling, traveling, and suffering was the deeper level of Paul's spiritual life. Those external activities demanded his constant attention, but at the same time, he was in unbroken communion with God. Paul's example demonstrates that prayer is the unending preoccupation of those who know God intimately.

The apostle's spiritual life could be likened to a volcano. Beneath the thin outer crust of his life was a burning, passionate heart for God. Frequently, the volcanic heat of his heart would cause prayer to burst through the veneer of routine, surface activities. This passage describes those eruptions; these two verses reveal the passionate heart of a man on fire for God.

This brief section on prayer follows logically Paul's discussion of Christ's return in verses 5–10. The Second Coming is not only the believer's future hope but also has practical implications in the present. Peter illustrated this principle in 2 Peter 3 when he followed an eschatological discussion (vv. 3–10) with exhortations to practical living:"Since all these things are to be destroyed in this way, what sort of people ought you to be in holy conduct and godliness. . . . Therefore, beloved, since you look for these things, be diligent to be found by Him in peace, spotless and blameless"(vv. 11, 14).The apostle John reminded believers in 1 John 3:3 that"everyone who has this hope [the Second Coming; v. 2] fixed on Him purifies himself, just as He is pure."Hope in Christ's return affects not only our understanding of the future but also our present living.

Three important features emerge from Paul's brief prayer report: the resource of prayer, the requests Paul made for the Thessalonians, and the reason or goal of his prayers for them.

THE RESOURCE

To this end also we pray for you always, (1:11a)

Paul understood that one of the primary responsibilities of a faithful pastor is to **pray** for his flock **always** and thereby reach into the divine resource of God's power and purpose (Acts 6:4).Though the time a pastor can spend teaching his people is limited to meetings, he can pray for them constantly. The **end** or goal of the apostle's prayers for believers was their spiritual growth. His prayers were therefore not aimless, not couched in meaningless generalities, but direct and to the point. Not surprisingly, this kind of prayer permeates Paul's epistles (cf. Rom. 1:9–10; 2 Cor. 13:7, 9; Eph. 1:15–17; 3:14–21; Phil. 1:4, 9–11; Col. 1:3, 9–11; 1 Thess. 1:2; 3:10, 11–13; 5:23; 2 Tim. 1:3; Philem. 4, 6).

Paul petitioned the Lord for his people's maturity because he understood that sanctification, like justification, comes only through God's sovereign grace, though not apart from human obedience. So his epistles are also filled with specific commands, prohibitions, and exhortations. God's sovereign purposes, prayer, and obedience are all necessary elements of sanctification. That apparent paradox introduces the deeper issue of the relationship between prayer and the sovereignty of God.

The basic question is this: If God sovereignly controls everything that happens, why pray? This question is similar to others that inevitably arise when the infinite God interacts with finite human beings. For instance, God inspired every word of the Bible (2 Tim. 3:16). Yet He did not dictate it (as the Koran was supposedly dictated to Mohammed), but used the personalities, life experiences, and vocabulary of the human authors of Scripture. The Bible was written by "men moved by the Holy Spirit [who] spoke from God" (2 Peter 1:21). The finite human mind also finds it difficult to comprehend that Jesus Christ is both fully God and fully man; both "our God and Savior, Jesus Christ" (2 Peter 1:1; cf. Titus 2:13) and "the man Christ Jesus" (1 Tim. 2:5).

A strong, confident, biblical view of the sovereignty of God does not preclude prayer. Any theological perspective that holds otherwise is simply bad theology. And any view that strips believers of the passion to pray is disobedient Christianity.

The Bible strongly affirms God's absolute sovereignty. Humbled by God's rebuke, Job declared, "I know that You can do all things, and that no purpose of Yours can be thwarted" (Job 42:2). In one of the clearest, most direct statements of God's sovereignty anywhere in Scripture, David wrote, "The Lord has established His throne in the heavens, and His sovereignty rules over all" (Ps. 103:19). Proverbs 16:33 notes that "the lot is cast into the lap, but its every decision is from the Lord." In Isaiah 46:9–11 God declared,

> Remember the former things long past, for I am God, and there is no other; I am God, and there is no one like Me, declaring the end from the beginning, and from ancient times things which have not been done, saying, "My purpose will be established, and I will accomplish all My good pleasure"; calling a bird of prey from the east, the man of My purpose from a far country. Truly I have spoken; truly I will bring it to pass. I have planned it, surely I will do it.

The Lord Jesus Christ, Paul wrote to Timothy, "is the blessed and only Sovereign, the King of kings and Lord of lords" (1 Tim. 6:15; cf. Pss. 22:28; 47:2, 7; 95:3; Dan. 7:13–14; Mal. 1:14; Matt. 28:18; Rev. 17:14; 19:16).

But the Bible also teaches that God's sovereignty does not negate human responsibility. Acknowledging their sin in demanding a king, the people of Israel begged Samuel, "Pray for your servants to the Lord your God, so that we may not die, for we have added to all our sins this evil by asking for ourselves a king" (1 Sam. 12:19). Calming their fears, "Samuel said to the people, 'Do not fear. . . . For the Lord will not abandon His people on account of His great name, because the Lord has been pleased to make you a people for Himself'" (vv. 20, 22). Samuel reassured the frightened people that God would not forsake them because of His sovereign plan for the nation. But Samuel went on to say, "Moreover, as for me, far be it from me that I should sin against the Lord by ceasing to pray for you; but I will instruct you in the good and right way" (v. 23). Though he understood that God's sovereign choice of Israel was irrevocable (cf. Rom. 11:29), Samuel nevertheless acknowledged his responsibility to pray for the people and instruct them in divine truth. His prayers not only expressed Samuel's affirmation of God's will but also became part of the instrumentality by which God effected His sovereign plan.

Daniel understood from Jeremiah's prophecy that the Babylonian Captivity would last seventy years (Dan. 9:2). Yet that did not deter him from praying eloquently for God to restore Israel from captivity (Dan. 9:3–19). Daniel's prayer expressed the cry of his heart for God's will to be done (cf. Matt. 6:10). Knowing that God sovereignly chose those who will be saved (Rom. 9:16, 18, 24) did not stop Paul from crying out, "Brethren, my heart's desire and my prayer to God for them is for their salvation" (Rom. 10:1). In Luke 22:31 Jesus warned Peter, "Simon, Simon, behold, Satan has demanded permission to sift you like wheat." Though the Lord knew it was impossible for Peter to lose his salvation, He nevertheless told him, "I have prayed for you, that your faith may not fail" (v. 32). If Jesus, the sovereign God in human flesh, prayed that God's sovereign plan would come about, how can believers do any less? A final illustration comes from the last chapter of the Bible. Though the return of Jesus Christ is promised by God and is a major theme in Revelation, John nevertheless cried out, "Come, Lord Jesus" (Rev. 22:20).

Not only does prayer align the heart with the sovereign plan of God, but God also works prayer into bringing about His plan, as James says: "The effective prayer of a righteous man can accomplish much" (James 5:16). This is parallel to God's electing a person to salvation but using someone's faithful witness to bring about that salvation. A striking demonstration of the interaction between prayer and God's sovereignty comes from the life of godly King Hezekiah of Judah. After being informed by Isaiah the prophet that he would die from his illness (2 Kings 20:1), Hezekiah pleaded with God to spare his life (vv. 2–3). In response, God extended the king's life by fifteen years (vv. 4–6). Though it was not necessarily beneficial to the king, God fit it perfectly into His purpose (vv. 12–17). That incident demonstrates that a proper understanding of God's sovereignty does not lead to passive resignation but to active petition, which God may choose to hear and change the course of events, without altering His sovereign purpose. Indeed, the amazing, incomprehensible reality of such providence is that it was God's will all along.

THE REQUESTS

that our God will count you worthy of your calling, and fulfill every desire for goodness and the work of faith with power, (1:11b–d)

Knowing that prayer fits in harmoniously with God's sovereign will to bring about the spiritual ends He desires, Paul listed three specific requests he made on behalf of the Thessalonians: worthiness, fulfillment, and power.

WORTHINESS

that our God will count you worthy of your calling, (1:11b)

This comprehensive request encompasses the entire spectrum of Christian character. Paul prayed that God would enable the Thessalonians to honor the name of Christ. The intimate phrase **our God** reminds his readers that God is not a distant, indifferent tyrant, but a tender, caring Father. *Axioō* (**count . . . worthy**) can also be translated "make worthy." Either sense is appropriate here, for God makes worthy those whom He counts worthy. As is always the case in the New Testament epistles, the **calling** in view here is the irresistible call that infallibly results in salvation (cf. 2:14; Rom. 1:6, 7; 8:28, 30; 9:24; 11:29; 1 Cor. 1:2, 9, 24, 26; 7:17, 18, 20, 21, 22, 24; Gal. 1:6, 15; 5:8; Eph. 1:18; 4:1, 4; Col. 3:15; 1 Thess. 2:12; 4:7; 5:24; 1 Tim. 6:12; 2 Tim. 1:9; Heb. 3:1; 9:15; James 2:7; 1 Peter 1:15; 2:9, 21; 3:9; 5:10; 2 Peter 1:3, 10; Jude 1). Theologians refer to it as the effectual or saving call, as opposed to the general call which is the open invitation to salvation (cf. Matt. 22:14). Jesus referred to it when He said, "No one can come to Me unless the Father who sent Me draws him" (John 6:44). God's effectual call activates in time His election of the redeemed in eternity; He "called us with a holy calling . . . according to His own purpose and grace which was granted us in Christ Jesus from all eternity" (2 Tim. 1:9).

God takes sinners, worthy only of death (Rom. 1:32), and makes them **worthy** of His kingdom by imputing Christ's righteousness to them (2 Cor. 5:21). But Paul prayed that the Thessalonians would also prove **worthy** in practice through Holy Spirit sanctification, that they would "walk in a manner worthy of the God who calls [them] into His own kingdom and glory" (1 Thess. 2:12; cf. Eph. 4:1; Col. 1:10). As they become more like Jesus Christ, Christians become more deserving to bear His name. One important way God makes believers more **worthy** of their **calling** is through suffering (1:5).

As is sadly the case in every church, some in the Thessalonian congregation were not walking worthy. Paul rebuked them in chapter 3 of this epistle:

> Now we command you, brethren, in the name of our Lord Jesus Christ, that you keep away from every brother who leads an unruly life and not according to the tradition which you received from us.
>
> For we hear that some among you are leading an undisciplined life, doing no work at all, but acting like busybodies. (3:6, 11)

They were like the Jews of whom Paul wrote, "The name of God is blasphemed among the Gentiles because of you" (Rom. 2:24). Though made eternally worthy by Christ's imputed righteousness, their disobedient lives made them unworthy to be called Christians.

The Bible lists several components of the worthy walk. A worthy walk is a walk in the Holy Spirit (Rom. 8:4; Gal. 5:16, 25), humility (Eph. 4:2), purity (Rom. 13:13; Eph. 5:3), contentment (1 Cor. 7:17), faith (2 Cor. 5:7), righteousness (Eph. 2:10), unity (Eph. 4:3; Phil. 1:27), gentleness (Eph. 4:2), patience (Col. 1:11), love (Eph. 5:2), joy (Col. 1:11), thankfulness (Col. 1:12), light (Eph. 5:8–9), knowledge (Col. 1:10), wisdom (Eph. 5:15), truth (3 John 3, 4), and fruitfulness (Col. 1:10). In short, "The one who says he abides in Him ought himself to walk in the same manner as He walked" (1 John 2:6), because that pleases God (1 Thess. 4:1). Paul prayed that God would enable them to manifest the spiritual virtues that would make them worthy to be called Christians.

FULFILLMENT

and fulfill every desire for goodness (1:11*c*)

Paul also prayed that God would **fulfill every** noble, righteous **desire** of their hearts. *Plēroō* (**fulfill**) could also be translated "complete," or "accomplish"; *eudokia* (**desire**) could be translated "purpose," or "choice." Paul asked that the Lord would bring about all their longings for **goodness** (cf. Rom. 7:14–25; 15:14; Gal. 5:22; Eph. 5:9). Since God alone is good (Mark 10:18), Paul knew such a prayer was consistent with God's will. His definition of what is good and good for His people is the inevitable action He takes in answer to this prayer.

In Psalm 21:2–3 David wrote, "You have given him his heart's desire, and You have not withheld the request of his lips. For You meet him with the blessings of good things; You set a crown of fine gold on his head." God gave David what he asked for because He saw that it was good. Reinforcing that principle, David wrote in Psalm 37:4, "Delight yourself in the Lord; and He will give you the desires of your heart." Because those who delight in God desire what He desires, He will grant their requests. Those who make God's agenda their own can exclaim confidently with David, "The Lord will accomplish what concerns me" (Ps. 138:8). The Lord Jesus Christ promised, "If you abide in Me, and My words abide in you, ask whatever you wish, and it will be done for you" (John 15:7; cf. v. 16), while John wrote, "This is the confidence which we have before Him, that, if we ask anything according to His will, He hears us. And if we know that He hears us in whatever we ask, we know that we have the requests which we have asked from Him" (1 John 5:14–15). In contrast, James warns those with selfish agendas, "You ask and do not receive, because you ask with wrong motives, so that you may spend it on your pleasures" (James 4:3).

Far from being a cosmic killjoy, God is generous and gracious. In Psalm 107:9 the psalmist wrote that God "has satisfied the thirsty soul, and the hungry soul He has filled with what is good." In the same way David exulted, "You open Your hand and satisfy the desire of every living thing" (Ps. 145:16; cf. 104:28), while Isaiah added, "The Lord longs to be gracious to you" (Isa. 30:18). Those whose desires are in tune with God's will can say with Moses, "O satisfy us in the morning with Your lovingkindness, that we may sing for joy and be glad all our days" (Ps. 90:14).

POWER

and the work of faith with power, (1:11*d*)

The verb "fulfill" in the preceding phrase also governs this phrase. Paul's final request for the Thessalonians was that God would complete the **work of faith** He had begun in them (1 Thess. 1:3) **with power.** No one taught more clearly than Paul the glorious truth that salvation is by faith alone, entirely apart from human works (cf. Rom. 3:20–30; 4:4–5; 5:1; Gal. 2:16; 3:8, 11–14, 24; Phil. 3:9). But Paul also knew that genuine saving faith works inevitably to produce spiritual fruit (cf. Eph. 2:10; Titus 2:7, 14; 3:1, 8, 14)—a truth forcefully stated by James:

> What use is it, my brethren, if someone says he has faith but he has no works? Can that faith save him? If a brother or sister is without clothing and in need of daily food, and one of you says to them, "Go in peace, be warmed and be filled," and yet you do not give them what is necessary for their body, what use is that? Even so faith, if it has no works, is dead, being by itself.
>
> But someone may well say, "You have faith and I have works; show me your faith without the works, and I will show you my faith by my works." You believe that God is one. You do well; the demons also believe, and shudder. But are you willing to recognize, you foolish fellow, that faith without works is useless? Was not Abraham our father justified by works when he offered up Isaac his son on the altar? You see that faith was working with his works, and as a result of the works, faith was perfected; and the Scripture was fulfilled which says, "And Abraham believed God, and it was reckoned to him as righteousness," and he was called the friend of God. You see that a man is justified by works and not by faith alone. In the same way, was not Rahab the harlot also justified by works when she received the messengers and sent them out by another way? For just as the body without the spirit is dead, so also faith without works is dead. (James 2:14–26)

Paul knew the Thessalonians' faith was genuine because it produced such works (1 Thess. 1:3; see the discussion of this verse in chapter 1 of this volume). Yet he wanted their **work of faith** to increase in **power,** so that there would be more righteous deeds. He sought for them what he wanted for the Philippians: that they would be "filled with the fruit of righteousness which comes through Jesus Christ, to the glory and praise of God" (Phil. 1:11). That happens only through the filling of the Holy Spirit (Eph. 3:16; cf. Zech. 4:6) and the rich indwelling of the Word (Col. 3:16).

THE REASON

so that the name of our Lord Jesus will be glorified in you, and you in Him, according to the grace of our God and the Lord Jesus Christ. (1:12)

The ultimate purpose of Paul's prayer was not for them, but for **the name of our Lord Jesus** to **be glorified** in their lives. The phrase **the name of our Lord,** reminiscent of the familiar Old Testament phrase "the name of the Lord" (cf. Gen. 4:26; Ex. 33:19; Deut. 5:11; Isa. 42:8), clearly and unequivocally identifies Jesus as Yahweh of the Old Testament. To glorify the **name of** the **Lord** means to honor and exalt all that He is.

To do so should be the deepest desire of His people. At the end of his magnificent prayer for Israel's restoration from captivity, Daniel cried out, "O Lord, hear! O Lord, forgive! O Lord, listen and take action! For Your own sake, O my God, do not delay, because Your city and Your people are called by Your name" (Dan. 9:19). Daniel's primary concern was not the misery of his people, but the reputation of his God. Paul's concern was that those who bear the name of the Lord Jesus should honor it; that they "do all to the glory of God" (1 Cor. 10:31). Jesus instructed believers, "Let your light shine before men in such a way that they may see your good works, and glorify your Father who is in heaven" (Matt. 5:16). Paul described Titus and the men who accompanied him as "a glory to Christ" (2 Cor. 8:23).

When believers glorify the Lord Jesus Christ, they in turn will be glorified **in Him.** Paul has in view here both eternal glory and temporal honor. First Samuel 2:30 expresses this same spiritual principle: "The Lord declares . . . 'Those who honor Me I will honor.'" In John 12:26 Jesus promised, "If anyone serves Me, the Father will honor him." Christ will honor those whose lives honor Him.

Paul closed the passage by reminding his readers that the ability to glorify Jesus Christ comes only through **the grace of our God and the Lord Jesus Christ.** Like salvation itself, everything in the Christian life comes by **grace**—God's unmerited favor (cf. Gal. 3:3). It is grammatically possible to translate this final phrase "our God and Lord Jesus Christ," which would indicate Paul had only the Second Person of the Trinity in view. Both translations affirm Christ's deity; He is either called God or put on an equal footing with the Father.

Praying for the right things is inseparably linked with holy living. The godly Puritan John Owen noted, "He who prays as he ought, will endeavor to live as he prays" (*The Grace and Duty of Being Spiritually Minded* [reprint; Grand Rapids: Baker, 1977], 59). The dedication such prayer should engender in the believer's life is illustrated by one of most fabled organizations in American history—the Pony Express:

> The Pony Express was a private express company that carried mail by an organized relay of horseback riders. The eastern end was St. Joseph, Missouri, and the western terminal was in Sacramento, California. The cost of sending a letter by Pony Express was $2.50 an ounce. If the weather and horses held out and the Indians held off, that letter would complete the entire two-thousand-mile journey in a speedy ten days, as did the report of Lincoln's Inaugural Address.

It may surprise you that the Pony Express was only in operation from April 3, 1860, until November 18, 1861—just seventeen months. When the telegraph line was completed between two cities, the service was no longer needed.

Being a rider for the Pony Express was a tough job. You were expected to ride seventy-five to one hundred miles a day, changing horses every fifteen to twenty-five miles. Other than the mail, the only baggage you carried contained a few provisions, including a kit of flour, cornmeal, and bacon. In case of danger, you also had a medical pack of turpentine, borax, and cream of tartar. In order to travel light and to increase speed of mobility during Indian attacks, the men always rode in shirtsleeves, even during the fierce winter weather.

How would you recruit volunteers for this hazardous job? An 1860 San Francisco newspaper printed this ad for the Pony Express: "Wanted: Young, skinny, wiry fellows not over 18. Must be expert riders willing to risk [death] daily. Orphans preferred."

Those were the honest facts of the service required, but the Pony Express *never* had a shortage of riders. . . .

Like the Pony Express, serving God is not a job for the casually interested. It's costly service. He asks for your life. He asks for service to Him to become a priority, not a pastime. (Donald S. Whitney, *Spiritual Disciplines for the Christian Life* [Colorado Springs, Colo.: NavPress, 1991], 109–10. Italics in the original.)

How to Be Ready for the End Times— Part 1: Remember What You Know
(2 Thessalonians 2:1–5)

23

Now we request you, brethren, with regard to the coming of our Lord Jesus Christ and our gathering together to Him, that you not be quickly shaken from your composure or be disturbed either by a spirit or a message or a letter as if from us, to the effect that the day of the Lord has come. Let no one in any way deceive you, for it will not come unless the apostasy comes first, and the man of lawlessness is revealed, the son of destruction, who opposes and exalts himself above every so-called god or object of worship, so that he takes his seat in the temple of God, displaying himself as being God. Do you not remember that while I was still with you, I was telling you these things? (2:1–5)

Human history has had its share of evil leaders. The first century saw cruel Roman emperors, such as the mad Nero of Paul's day or the paranoid Domitian of John's later years. The twentieth century witnessed a host of evil dictators, most notoriously Stalin and Hitler. Man's religious history has also been plagued by false christs, false teachers, cult leaders, swamis, gurus, and countless other charlatans and wolves in sheep's clothing.

But one is coming who will surpass them all, both in the extent of his power and the evil of his person. He will be the most fiendish, wicked, powerful man ever to walk the earth. He is known in Scripture by many names; he is "Gog of the land of Magog, the prince of Rosh, Meshech and Tubal" (Ezek. 38:2); the little horn of Daniel 7:8, 24; 8:9; the "prince who is to come" (Dan. 9:26); the king who does as he pleases (Dan. 11:36); the foolish, worthless shepherd (Zech. 11:15–17); the beast (Rev. 11:7; 13:1; 14:9; 19:20; etc.). In this chapter, Paul describes him as "the man of lawlessness" (v. 3), the "son of destruction" (v. 3), "that lawless one" (v. 8), and "the one whose coming is in accord with the activity of Satan" (v. 9). But he is best known as the Antichrist (1 John 2:18). *Antichristos* ("Antichrist") is a compound Greek word, made up of the preposition *anti* and the noun *Christos. Anti* can mean both "against" and "in the place of." Both meanings are appropriate, for the Antichrist will both oppose the true Christ, and seek to usurp His place.

Anyone who opposes the Person and work of Christ manifests the Antichrist's spirit: "This is the antichrist," wrote John, "the one who denies the Father and the Son" (1 John 2:22; cf. 4:3; 2 John 7). For that reason John could write that "many antichrists have appeared" (1 John 2:18). The final Antichrist will be the culmination of all the antichrists who have gone before him (1 John 2:18); he will be the consummate and ultimate manifestation of the antichrist spirit.

The spirit of Antichrist has been at work since the fall of humanity and God's promise of a man to bruise the head of Satan and redeem man from sin and death (Gen. 3:14–15). Since then, Satan has opposed God's plan of redemption and attempted to thwart the work of the Redeemer. Genesis 6 records that the world had become so totally under his control that when God saw its unmitigated wickedness, He drowned the entire world, sparing only Noah and his seven family members. Later, hoping to destroy the line of messianic promise, Satan incited the Egyptians to attempt to murder all the male Hebrew babies (Ex. 1). Some six hundred years later, the family of Messiah was reduced to a single child (cf. 2 Chron. 21, 22), but Satan was unable to extinguish it. Nor did Satan's tool, Haman, succeed some four hundred years later in his plot to massacre the Jewish people (Est. 3). God saved them through the courage and wisdom of Esther and Mordecai (Est. 4–9). Those are only highlights of Satan's relentless efforts to thwart the redeeming work of the Messiah, Christ.

After the Messiah's birth, Satan, having failed to destroy His forbears, redoubled his futile efforts to eliminate Him. Herod's barbarous attempt to kill the Lord Jesus by slaughtering the male babies in Bethlehem failed when He and His parents escaped to Egypt (Matt. 2:7–18). In an attempt to kill Jesus at the hands of His own townspeople, Satan incited the synagogue crowd in Nazareth to throw Him off a cliff (Luke

4:28–30), but they did not succeed because Jesus disappeared. Satan's temptation of Christ (Matt. 4:1–11) and his attempt to use Peter to keep Jesus from the cross (Matt. 16:21–23) also failed. And even when the Jews and Romans cooperated (if only reluctantly by the Romans) to have Jesus killed, they were only doing God's will. Satan's brief satisfaction was cut short by the Resurrection (Acts 2:22–24).

Throughout history since then, Satan also has inspired hatred of Messiah's people, the Jews, through whom (Rev. 7:4–10; 14:1–5) and for whom (Rom. 11:25–27) salvation will come. The persecution, oppression, and pogroms they have endured culminated in the Holocaust brought on by the Nazis in the mid-twentieth century. Islamic animosity and desire to obliterate the Jews is the latest evidence of Satan's hatred of God's purpose to redeem the Jews and make His Son their King. But the Antichrist will be the Jews' worst persecutor as he attempts to thwart the fulfillment of God's pledge of salvation and a kingdom for Israel. After posing as their protector for the first half of the time of tribulation, he will break his covenant with them (Dan. 9:27). He will then unleash a persecution unparalleled in history—one that will see the eradication of two-thirds of the Jewish people (Zech. 13:8). For pastoral purpose, this unspeakably vile man is the subject of Paul's second chapter in this letter.

The apostle wrote this section to deal with the Thessalonians' loss of hope and joy through confusion about the end times. He had already given them explicit instruction about both the Rapture (1 Thess. 4:13–18) and the Day of the Lord (1 Thess. 5:1–11). Yet only a few months later, they had become confused, again fearing that they had missed the Rapture and were in the Day of the Lord. They knew that the Day of the Lord is God's final judgment on the sinful world (see the discussion of the Day of the Lord in chapter 12 of this volume). Apparently, even with the apostle's correctives in the first letter, the intensity of the persecution they were undergoing made them unable to shake the possibility that it had arrived. They were also directly assaulted by the deception of some false teachers. Playing off their confusion, they deceived the believers into thinking that Paul actually taught that the Day of the Lord had come and sought to prove it by producing a forged letter purporting to be from him in support of their teaching. Paul had explained in his first epistle why they could not be in the Day of the Lord (the Day of the Lord is for unbelievers; cf. 1 Thess. 5:4–9). Here, recognizing that due to the efforts of false teachers the truth does not yet prevail, he adds strong evidence to prove that they are not in the Day of the Lord: Antichrist had not appeared, and his coming will occur just before that Day comes.

That Antichrist was to come was common knowledge among the early Christians. John's readers had "heard that antichrist is coming" (1 John 2:18), and, as previously noted, Paul had taught that same truth to the Thessalonians (2:5). Believers were already experiencing persecution from his forerunners, those who manifested the antichrist spirit.

Besides Paul's teaching, the Thessalonians knew the final Antichrist had been prophesied in the Old Testament (e.g., Dan. 7, 9, 11) and predicted by the teaching of the Lord Jesus Himself (Matt. 24:15–31).

The final archenemy of the Savior first appears in Daniel 7:8, which describes him as a "little horn" who rises from obscurity to a place of prominence. That same verse describes him as having "eyes like the eyes of a man," indicating his intelligence, and "a mouth uttering great boasts," a reference to his oratorical skills and arrogant pride. Verse 21 reveals his relentless hostility against God's people; the prophet saw him "waging war with the saints and overpowering them." Verse 23 notes that his kingdom "will be different from all the other kingdoms and will devour the whole earth and tread it down and crush it." His empire, unlike any other in human history, will be worldwide. Verse 25 depicts him as a blasphemer who "will speak out against the Most High." He also will "make alterations in times and in law," replacing the world's religious ceremonies and observances with new ones in honor of himself and introducing a satanically inspired morality.

But Antichrist's oppression will be divinely limited to "a time, times, and half a time" (v. 25; cf. 9:27; Rev. 11:2, 3; 12:14; 13:5), the last three and a half years of the Tribulation when his reign of terror is in full swing. After that, "[God's] court will sit for judgment, and [Antichrist's] dominion will be taken away, annihilated and destroyed forever" (v. 26), and "the sovereignty, the dominion and the greatness of all the kingdoms under the whole heaven will be given to the people of the saints of the Highest One; His kingdom will be an everlasting kingdom, and all the dominions will serve and obey Him" (v. 27).

Daniel 8:23 describes Antichrist as "insolent." The Hebrew expression literally means that he has a fierce face, indicating that he will intimidate people into submission. That verse also notes that he will be "skilled in intrigue" (cf. v. 25, which also speaks of his shrewdness and deceit); Antichrist will be a deceiver, like his evil master Satan (Gen. 3:13; 2 Cor. 11:3; Rev. 12:9; 20:2–3, 8, 10). Verse 24 indicates that Antichrist will derive his power from Satan (cf. Rev. 13:2). Verse 25 adds that "he will magnify himself in his heart," speaking again of his arrogant pride; that "he will destroy many while they are at ease," indicating that he will be ruthless; that "he will even oppose the Prince of princes," revealing him to be a blasphemer of the Lord Jesus Christ (cf. Dan. 7:25); and that "he will be broken without human agency," indicating that God will judge and destroy him (cf. Dan. 7:26).

In Daniel's prophecy of the seventy weeks (9:24–27), Antichrist is "the prince who is to come" (v. 26). He "will make a firm covenant with the many [Israel] for one week" (v. 27), the seventieth week of years in Daniel's prophecy; the seven-year Tribulation period. He will pretend to be Israel's benefactor and protector. However, "in the middle of the week he will put a stop to sacrifice and grain offering; and on the wing of abominations will come one who makes desolate" (v. 27). Halfway through the Tribulation, Antichrist will show his true colors. He will turn on the Jewish people and commit the defiling act Jesus called the "abomination of desolation" (Matt. 24:15). This will launch the "great tribulation" (Matt. 24:21). But his reign will be short-lived (three and one half years), lasting only "until a complete destruction, one that is decreed, is poured out on the one who makes desolate" (v. 27). As Daniel 7:26 indicates, God will destroy Antichrist and his kingdom. Revelation 19:11ff. describes that destruction by the returning Lord Jesus Christ.

Daniel gives more details of Antichrist's career in chapter 11. He describes him as a ruthless, arrogant, proud "king [who] will do as he pleases" (v. 36). As he did earlier (cf. 7:25), Daniel depicts him as a blasphemer without parallel in human history who will "magnify himself above every god and will speak monstrous things against the God of gods" (v. 36). He also "will show no regard for the gods of his fathers" but will forsake the traditional religion of his ancestors. "Nor will he show regard for any other god; for he will magnify himself above them all" (v. 37); he will ultimately set himself up as an object of worship. That he will show no interest in "the desire of women" could mean he will be a homosexual; at least he will be heterosexually celibate. Some believe this probability, along with many other features, such as his world power and influence, unequalled religious ecumenical power, claim to rule in the place of Christ, and seeking of worship, seals the fact that he will be a pope. But once again Daniel stresses that God will judge him; he "will come to his end, and no one will help him" (v. 45).

This final Antichrist, as Scripture depicts him, has yet to appear on the world's stage. And since he must appear before the Day of the Lord begins, the Thessalonians' fears that they were already in that terrible time of judgment were groundless. Based on that truth, Paul made an urgent **request** of them to properly comprehend the events surrounding the Second Coming. It was to that subject that the apostle turned; the particle *de* (**now**) marks a transition from Paul's prayer report in 1:11–12 to the doctrinal issue of the epistle.

Unlike much contemporary teaching on eschatology, Paul's motive was not sensational but pastoral. His goal was not to gratify curiosity about the end times but to comfort confused Christians. Therefore, he limited his instruction to what was necessary to correct the error that robbed them of their joy, hope, and peace. And he did so tenderly, kindly, and patiently. He humbly called the Thessalonians his **brethren** and used the gentle term *erōtaō* (**request**), a verb that means "to plead," "implore," or even "to beg." Instead of coming across as authoritarian, intolerant, or overbearing, Paul gently corrected those struggling under this error.

The struggle came, Paul indicates once again (cf. 1 Thess. 4:13– 5:11), because they were confused with regard **to the coming of** the **Lord Jesus Christ** and believers' **gathering together to Him.** Though Paul used two expressions, he actually had one event in mind, not two. The Greek syntax uses only one article with the two nouns, making it clear that two complementary elements of one event are in view. This is the seventh mention in these two letters of Christ's coming (cf. 1 Thess. 1:10; 2:19; 3:13; 4:15; 5:23; 2 Thess. 1:10). Of the many aspects of the *parousia* (**coming**) **of our Lord Jesus Christ,** Paul focused specifically on the first event, the **gathering together** of believers **to Him** in the Rapture (1 Thess. 4:13–18). He zeroed in on that event because, as noted earlier, the confused Thessalonians, expecting relief (1:7), instead were suffering severe persecution. That caused them to believe they had missed the Rapture and were in the Day of the Lord.

In verse 2 Paul expressed his concern **that** the Thessalonians **not be quickly shaken from** their **composure or be disturbed either by a spirit or a message or a letter as if from** Paul and his companions, **to the effect that the day of the Lord has come. Spirit** likely refers to a false prophet who supposedly received divine revelation (cf. 1 John 4:1–3). **Message** refers to a sermon or teaching, and **letter** to a written authority for this doctrine. Taken together, these words indicate the careful and extensive way that this false teaching was presented; it had all the marks of authenticity—divine revelation, proclamation, and the authority of apostolic writing. It is important to see that the Thessalonians' fear indicates that Paul had taught them that the Rapture of the church precedes the final wrath of God, including the Tribulation and the Day of the Lord (1 Thess. 5:2–5; cf. Rev. 3:10). If he had taught them that they were to go through those judgment periods, they would have been rejoicing because being in them meant that the Lord's coming was near. Clearly, Paul had taught them that they would be taken up before those times, thus their confusion when they felt like they were in them.

Actually, false teachers had come to Thessalonica with teaching that reinforced their confusion in order to minimize the glory of Christ's coming for believers and destroy their hope and joy as well as to build distrust in God's love, grace, and goodness to His saints. What reinforced convincingly their feelings was that this teaching appeared to have apostolic sanction. It seemed to have been received supernaturally through direct revelation from God via a **spirit** (prophetic utterance), preached as God's **message,** and most convincing of all, written in an authentic apostolic **letter.** All that supposedly was from Paul himself, and attested by his partners Silas, and Timothy (**us**). Such forgeries and counterfeit apostolic documents (pseudepigrapha) continued in existence early in the life of the church, crafted and used to deceive many in the following centuries. Accordingly, Paul took special care to verify this letter's apostolic authenticity by closing it with his own distinctive handwriting (3:17; cf. Gal. 6:11).

This false teaching about the Rapture and the Day of the Lord had a devastating impact on the already jittery Thessalonians, as Paul's strong, graphic terminology reveals. Having become convinced that the Day of the Lord had arrived, they were **quickly shaken from** their **composure** and **disturbed**. Shaken translates a form of the verb *saleuō*, which describes a reed blown about in the wind (Matt. 11:7), the shaking of the powers of heaven in the end times (Matt. 24:29), the shaking of the building when the Holy Spirit came (Acts 4:31), the shaking of the prison at Philippi during the earthquake (Acts 16:26), and the agitating of the crowds at Berea by unbelieving Jews (Acts 17:13). *Nous* (**composure**) literally means "mind," while *throeō* (**disturbed**) is translated "frightened" in its only other New Testament uses (Matt. 24:6; Mark 13:7). The young believers had been shaken loose from their mental moorings and were adrift on a tossing sea of anxiety and fear, their faith, hope, and joy devastated by deception.

To end the Thessalonians' confusion, Paul needed to refute the lies of the false teachers. And to allay the Thessalonians' fears, he needed to correct their misunderstandings about the Day of the Lord. The apostle accomplished both objectives simply by proving that the Day of the Lord could not have arrived. His unarguable point was that God has fixed in the future an unmistakable event that must take place before the Day of the Lord arrives. That event still has not happened. Paul wove that truth into an exhortation to the Thessalonians to be ready for the end times by not being deceived, forgetful, ignorant, unbelieving, insecure, or weak.

Do Not Be Deceived

Let no one in any way deceive you, (2:3*a*)

Deception easily leads to anxiety and fear, and that was certainly the case with the Thessalonians. As noted above, when false teachers misled them into thinking they were in the Day of the Lord, they panicked. Unfortunately, deception in the church is commonplace, including the countless charlatans who have disturbed many over the centuries with false predictions about the Lord's return. Of such deceivers Jesus warned, "See to it that no one misleads you" (Matt. 24:4; Mark 13:5; cf. Luke 21:8).

The church faces the constant threat of deception because "Satan disguises himself as an angel of light.... His servants also disguise themselves as servants of righteousness" (2 Cor. 11:14–15). To avoid being deceived by this constant barrage of demonic lies, believers are "no longer to be children, tossed here and there by waves and carried about by every wind of doctrine, by the trickery of men, by craftiness in deceitful scheming" (Eph. 4:14). They must be alert for those guilty of "adulterating the word of God" (2 Cor. 4:2), who "deceive the hearts of the unsuspecting" (Rom. 16:18), knowing that as Christ's return draws near "evil men and impostors will proceed from bad to worse, deceiving and being deceived" (2 Tim. 3:13), and that already "many deceivers have gone out into the world" (2 John 7; cf. 1 John 2:26; 3:7).

Paul's command is a strong prohibition. The compound verb *exapataō* (**deceive**), a strengthened form of the verb *apataō,* means "to deceive completely," or "to delude." The apostle also used a double negative (*mē tis; mēdena*), saying in effect, "Do not let anyone by any means or any method lead you astray in any way." There was really no excuse for the Thessalonians to have been so gullible, despite the seemingly convincing forged letter. They should have realized that Paul would not abruptly contradict in a letter what he had so recently taught them in person and in his first epistle. The Thessalonians' gullibility was an emotional reaction to the stress of their situation. However, truth is not determined by emotions or circumstances, but by Scripture. Believers must allow biblical truth and theology to rise above every situation.

To be deceived about the Second Coming has serious practical consequences, making it essential to understand the truth about the return of Jesus Christ. Such knowledge is important because it produces accountability. Having described the cataclysmic destruction of the heavens and the earth, Peter exhorted his readers, "Since all these things are to be destroyed in this way, what sort of people ought you to be in holy conduct and godliness. ... Therefore, beloved, since you look for these things, be diligent to be found by Him in peace, spotless and blameless" (2 Peter 3:11, 14). The apostle John also wrote of the purifying effect of a proper view of Christ's return: "We know that when He appears, we will be like Him, because we will see Him just as He is. And everyone who has this hope fixed on Him purifies himself, just as He is pure" (1 John 3:2–3).

A correct hope in the Lord's return produces not only accountability and purity but also joy. Fearing that they would experience the horrors of the Day of the Lord robbed the Thessalonians of joy. That fear also robbed them of the hope of the Lord's promise to "keep [them] from the hour of testing, that hour which is about to come upon the whole world, to test those who dwell on the earth" (Rev. 3:10). To avoid losing the purity and joy of true hope the Thessalonians needed to remember the truths Paul had taught them.

DO NOT BE FORGETFUL

for it will not come unless the apostasy comes first, and the man of lawlessness is revealed, the son of destruction, who opposes and exalts himself above every so-called god or object of worship, so that he takes his seat in the temple of God, displaying himself as being God. Do you not remember that while I was still with you, I was telling you these things? (2:3b–5)

This point is closely tied to the first one, since forgetting the truth leaves believers vulnerable to deception. The key to this section is in the last sentence: **Do you not remember that while I was still with you, I was telling you these things?** The imperfect tense of the Greek verb (noting repeated action in past time) translated **was telling** indicates that teaching about end-time events was a continual theme during Paul's ministry in Thessalonica. Therefore, what the apostle wrote in this section was not new to the church; he merely reiterated what he had already taught them (cf. 2 Peter 1:12–15). That he taught prophetic truth in the few months he had with the new believers in Thessalonica shows that biblical eschatology, including the sequence of events, is not unimportant, as some think, but is foundational to the Christian faith. As noted above, its purpose was not sensational but practical; had the Thessalonians remembered Paul's teaching, they would not have lost their joy and hope.

The Thessalonians had forgotten that Paul told them when he was there that the Day of the Lord **will not come unless the apostasy comes first.** Out of all the precursors of the Day of the Lord (e.g., Joel 2:31; 3:14; Mal. 4:5), Paul singled out the **apostasy.** He was not, of course, setting a posttribulational date for the Rapture (cf. the discussion of 1 Thess. 4:13–18 in chapter 11 and 1 Thess. 5:1 in chapter 12 of this volume); he did not tell his readers that they would live to experience the **apostasy** and the unveiling of the man of lawlessness. Paul's point was merely that the **apostasy** will precede the Day of the Lord. And since the **apostasy** has not yet taken place, the Day of the Lord could not have arrived.

The basic meaning of *apostasia* (**apostasy**) is "revolt," or "rebellion." In its only other New Testament appearance it refers to forsaking

the Law of Moses (Acts 21:21). The Septuagint, the Greek translation of
the Old Testament, uses it three times to express rebellion against God
(Josh. 22:22; 2 Chron. 29:19; Jer. 2:19). Thus, the word marks a deliberate
defection from a formerly held religious position.

Paul was not referring here to apostasy (defection from the
gospel truth) in the general sense. There have always been apostate
churches, like that at Laodicea (Rev. 3:14–22), as well as apostate individuals (Heb. 10:25–31; 2 Peter 2:20–22). Such generalized apostasy,
because it is always present, cannot signify a particular time period.
Therefore, it cannot be the specific event Paul has in mind.

Apostasy will reach its peak in the end times:

> But realize this, that in the last days difficult times will come. For men
> will be lovers of self, lovers of money, boastful, arrogant, revilers, dis-
> obedient to parents, ungrateful, unholy, unloving, irreconcilable, mali-
> cious gossips, without self-control, brutal, haters of good, treacherous,
> reckless, conceited, lovers of pleasure rather than lovers of God, hold-
> ing to a form of godliness, although they have denied its power; avoid
> such men as these.... But evil men and impostors will proceed from
> bad to worse, deceiving and being deceived. (2 Tim. 3:1–5, 13; cf. 1 Tim.
> 4:1; 2 Peter 3:3–4; Jude 17–18)

But the heightened apostasy of the end times, like the apostasy that has
plagued the church throughout its history, is not the specific event Paul
has in mind.

Nor does Paul have in mind the apostasy during the Tribulation,
of which Jesus warned: "Many false prophets will arise and will mislead
many. Because lawlessness is increased, most people's love will grow
cold.... For false Christs and false prophets will arise and will show great
signs and wonders, so as to mislead, if possible, even the elect" (Matt.
24:11–12, 24).

Paul's use of the definite article reveals that he had in mind not a
general flow or trend, but a specific, identifiable act of apostasy. **The
apostasy** will be a blasphemous act of unprecedented magnitude. The
apostle identified the apostasy by naming the key character connected
with it: **the man of lawlessness.** Understanding who that key person is
is a prerequisite to identifying the **apostasy** event. *Anomia* (**lawlessness**) literally means "without law" (cf. 1 John 3:4). This person will be
the consummate lawless one; a blasphemous sinner, who will live in
open defiance of God's law. Of all the billions of godless, evil, lawless sinners in human history, his evil influence will be greater than any other's.
Even in the end times, when "lawlessness is increased" (Matt. 24:12), this
Satan-energized leader will stand out as the one whose depraved, wicked,

lawless leadership sweeps over the whole world—with influence never before seen.

The aorist tense of the verb translated **revealed** points to a definite time when this man will appear. It implies that he was previously present and known, but his act of apostasy will unveil his true evil identity; he will drop all pretense and the previously hidden wickedness of his character will be fully disclosed. God and the Lord Jesus will not have appeared as his enemies until the time he is **revealed.**

The title **man of lawlessness** has been identified with many different individuals, including Antiochus Epiphanes, Caligula, Nero, and in the last century, Hitler, Stalin, and others. But the close association of the **man of lawlessness** with the Day of the Lord rules out past historical persons; otherwise, the Day of the Lord might have come centuries ago. The **man of lawlessness** cannot be Satan, for he is distinguished from the devil in verse 9. Nor can this be a reference to a principle of evil, for the text specifically identifies him as a **man.** He can be none other than the final Antichrist.

Paul further described the **man of lawlessness** as the **son of destruction.** The expression **son of** is a Hebraism indicating a close association, or of the same kind, just as a son shares his father's nature. The Antichrist will be so completely devoted to the **destruction** of all that relates to God's purpose and plan that he can be said to be **destruction** personified. He, however, belongs to **destruction** (*apōleia;* "ruin," not "annihilation") as the one to be destroyed. He is fixed for punishment and judgment; he is human trash for the garbage dump of hell.

Only one other individual in Scripture shares the dubious distinction of being named **son of destruction:** Judas (John 17:12; the NASB translates the same Greek phrase "son of perdition"). The title is thus reserved for the two vilest people in human history, controlled by Satan (John 13:2; Rev. 13:2) and guilty of the two most heinous acts of apostasy. Judas lived and ministered intimately with the incarnate Son of God for more than three years—a privilege granted to only eleven others. Yet after observing Jesus' sinless life, hearing His wisdom, and experiencing His divine power and gracious love, Judas betrayed Him. Amazingly, he was so much a **son of destruction** that the glories of Christ that softened the eleven hardened him.

Monstrous as that apostasy was, it pales in comparison to the act of future apostasy Antichrist will commit. Judas betrayed the Son of God; Antichrist will proclaim himself God. Judas desecrated the temple with the money he received for betraying Christ (Matt. 27:5); Antichrist will desecrate the temple by committing the abomination of desolation (Matt. 24:15). Judas, apparently without influencing others, went astray, a tragic, solitary disaster (Acts 1:18–19); Antichrist will lead the world astray into destruction (Rev. 13:5–8).

After initially posing as the friend of religion (cf. Rev. 17:13), Antichrist will suddenly reveal his true nature when he commits blasphemy against God and **opposes and exalts himself above every so-called god or object of worship** (cf. Rev. 13:15–16). Energized by Satan and aided by the false prophet, Antichrist will have immense power to successfully demand that the world worship him (cf. Rev. 13:1–17). Satan, who has always longed to be worshiped (cf. Isa. 14:13–14), will fulfill that desire vicariously through the worship accorded Antichrist. Antichrist will exalt himself by taking **his seat in the temple of God, displaying himself as being God.** The **temple,** the symbol of God's presence, is the most fitting place for Satan to orchestrate the ultimate act of blasphemy—a wicked man **displaying himself as being God.** This apostasy, to which Paul refers here and which Jesus called the "abomination of desolation" (Matt. 24:15), referring to Daniel's prophecy, will take place at the midpoint of the Tribulation (Dan. 9:27). It will initiate God's judgment on the world through Antichrist's reign of terror during the second half of the Tribulation. At the end of that three-and-a-half-year period, Christ will return in glory to destroy Antichrist's kingdom and all the ungodly. The Lord Jesus will cast him into the lake of fire along with his false prophet (Rev. 19:11–21).

Paul's point is clear. **The apostasy,** Antichrist's blasphemous self-deification and desecration of the Temple, is a unique, unmistakable event that precedes the Day of the Lord. Since that clearly has not happened, the Day of the Lord cannot have arrived. And it never will for believers.

We need not fear the judgment of that Day. Believers are "not in darkness, that the day would overtake [them] like a thief" (1 Thess. 5:4). We are waiting for Jesus to return from heaven (1 Thess. 1:10) and gather us to Himself (2 Thess. 2:1; cf. John 14:1–3). We look for the true Christ, not the Antichrist. Only those who are deceived and forgetful risk losing the confident hope and expectant joy of Christ's return before the Day of the Lord.

How to Be Ready for the End Times— Part 2: Be Strong and Courageous (2 Thessalonians 2:6-17)

24

And you know what restrains him now, so that in his time he will be revealed. For the mystery of lawlessness is already at work; only he who now restrains will do so until he is taken out of the way. Then that lawless one will be revealed whom the Lord will slay with the breath of His mouth and bring to an end by the appearance of His coming; that is, the one whose coming is in accord with the activity of Satan, with all power and signs and false wonders, and with all the deception of wickedness for those who perish, because they did not receive the love of the truth so as to be saved. For this reason God will send upon them a deluding influence so that they will believe what is false, in order that they all may be judged who did not believe the truth, but took pleasure in wickedness. But we should always give thanks to God for you, brethren beloved by the Lord, because God has chosen you from the beginning for salvation through sanctification by the Spirit and faith in the truth. It was for this He called you through our gospel, that you may gain the glory of our Lord Jesus Christ. So then, brethren, stand firm and hold to the traditions which you were taught, whether by word of mouth or by letter from us. Now may our Lord Jesus Christ Himself and God our

Father, who has loved us and given us eternal comfort and good hope by grace, comfort and strengthen your hearts in every good work and word. (2:6–17)

A hallmark of false doctrine is its attack on the Person and work of the Lord Jesus Christ. Throughout history, mystics, rationalists, legalists, cultists, and other heretics have assaulted Christ's deity, humanity, and the singular efficacy and sufficiency of His saving work. The Reformation definition of salvation by grace alone through faith alone in Christ alone was affirmed against the backdrop of attacks on biblical soteriology. Satan apparently devotes his personal efforts not to tempting individual Christians but to devising false systems of religion, which teach lies about Christ (1 John 2:22; 4:3; 2 John 7). He is disguised as an "angel of light" (2 Cor. 11:14). His demon doctrines deceive countless millions, keeping them from the life-giving gospel of the Lord Jesus Christ.

There is coming a satanic false religion that will dominate the world like no other in history (cf. Rev. 17). Its object of worship will be the most powerful, evil, deceitful person to ever live: the man of lawlessness, the Antichrist. He will be the culmination of Satan's long war against God, the last and most malevolent manifestation of the antichrist spirit (1 John 4:3). Like his evil master, Antichrist will disguise himself as an "angel of light" and deceive the whole lost world (Rev. 12:9; 13:14).

As noted in the previous chapter of this volume, Paul wrote about Antichrist, called the man of lawlessness and son of destruction, because the Thessalonians had been deceived by the lie that their fears were true, that they had missed the Rapture and were in the judgment of the Day of the Lord. Seeking to correct their error, Paul called on them to remember what he had previously taught them, reassuring them that the Day of the Lord had not come. His argument was simple and irrefutable: Antichrist has not appeared, and his appearance is a necessary precursor to the Day of the Lord. He must appear and commit the ultimate act of apostasy, the abomination of desolation, before the Day of the Lord arrives.

Paul gave six specific exhortations to avoid fear about the end times. Believers must not be deceived, forgetful, ignorant, unbelieving, insecure, or weak. The previous chapter of this volume covered the first two exhortations; this chapter will discuss the last four.

Do Not Be Ignorant

And you know what restrains him now, so that in his time he will be revealed. For the mystery of lawlessness is already at work; only he who now restrains will do so until he is taken out of the

way. Then that lawless one will be revealed whom the Lord will slay with the breath of His mouth and bring to an end by the appearance of His coming; that is, the one whose coming is in accord with the activity of Satan, with all power and signs and false wonders, and with all the deception of wickedness for those who perish, (2:6–10*b*)

Having discussed the act of apostasy by which the Antichrist will reveal himself for who he really is, Paul takes a deeper look at the man himself. He lists four aspects of Antichrist's career: his revelation, destruction, power, and influence.

HIS REVELATION

And you know what restrains him now, so that in his time he will be revealed. For the mystery of lawlessness is already at work; only he who now restrains will do so until he is taken out of the way. Then that lawless one will be revealed (2:6–8*a*)

As the phrase **and you know** indicates, the Thessalonians understood **what** force currently **restrains** Antichrist because Paul had told them when he was with them. Therefore, he did not repeat it here—a fact that has led to endless speculation as to what it is. The Greek verb translated **restrains** (*katechō*; "to hold back," "to hold down," "to suppress") appears in this text as a neuter participle, prompting commentators to suggest numerous options as to the identity of that restraining force.

Some believe that the preaching of the gospel keeps Antichrist in check. Eventually, they argue, the gospel will be fully proclaimed (cf. Matt. 24:14) and the restraint will be removed. Other suggestions for the restrainer include the nation of Israel, the alleged binding of Satan by believers, the church's influence as salt and light in the world (cf. Matt. 5:13–14), human government (cf. Rom. 13:1–4), the general principle of law and morality in the world, the Roman Empire, and even Michael the archangel (cf. Dan. 10:21).

But none of those opinions is satisfactory. The most significant problem with all of them (except the last) is that they are human forces. Humans preach the gospel; humans make up the nation of Israel; humans attempt to bind Satan; humans comprise the church; humans run the world's governments; humans agree on principles of law and morality; and humans made up the Roman Empire. But human power, ingenuity, and institutions cannot restrain the supernatural power of

Satan that seeks to release Antichrist. And the one supernatural person in the list, Michael, does not have the power to restrain Satan (Jude 9). The most logical of those choices, the church, has never been able to restrain even human evil. It may do so to some extent in the lives of its members, but the outside world continues to grow worse and worse—a situation that will especially characterize the end times (2 Tim. 3:13). If no human or angelic power restrains, that leaves only the power of God to hold back the purpose of Satan for his Antichrist.

And God does the restraining **so that in his time he will be revealed.** Satan, of course, does not want to operate on God's timetable. If he could, he would have revealed Antichrist long before now. He longs for the false messiah, through whom he will rule the earth, to appear. But nothing—not even the purposes of hell—operates independently of God's sovereign timetable. Job confessed, "I know that You can do all things, and that no purpose of Yours can be thwarted" (Job 42:2). In Isaiah 46:10 God declares, "My purpose will be established, and I will accomplish all My good pleasure." Therefore, the man of lawlessness will not appear until the **time** predetermined by God.

God will not allow Antichrist to **be revealed** until all the redeemed, whom He chose for salvation in eternity past up to that time (2:13; cf. Matt. 25:34; Eph. 1:4; 2 Tim. 1:9; Rev. 13:8; 17:8), are gathered into the kingdom (cf. Rom. 11:25). Evil will not overstep its divinely ordained bounds. The true Messiah was revealed "when the fullness of the time came, [and] God sent forth His Son" (Gal. 4:4); the ultimate false messiah will likewise **be revealed** in God's perfect time.

Though Antichrist may be restrained, evil will not be; in fact, **the mystery of lawlessness is already at work.** *Mustērion* (**mystery**) describes something "which has been kept secret for long ages past" (Rom. 16:25) and is incapable of being known unless revealed by God. The true character of **lawlessness** is already at work (cf. 1 John 3:4); and "even now many antichrists have appeared" (1 John 2:18; cf. 4:3). Evil, lies, hypocrisy, immorality, and false religion permeate the world and grow increasingly worse, so that every generation is more wicked than those before (2 Tim. 3:13), but sin's ultimate manifestation is yet to come. When the restraint is removed and Antichrist appears, the true character of evil will be manifested. It should be noted that not only will the man of lawlessness be revealed, but God will also release demons from being bound in hell to inundate the earth (Rev. 9:1–19).

The change in gender from the neuter participle translated "what restrains" in verse 6 to the masculine participle rendered **he who . . . restrains** is significant. The sovereign, divine force that currently restrains Antichrist is exerted by a person—the Holy Spirit (cf. John 14:26; 15:26; 16:13 where Jesus used a masculine pronoun with the neuter noun translated "Spirit"). Only He has the supernatural power to hold Satan in check. The Holy Spirit has always battled wickedness in the world. Addressing the wicked pre-Flood generation, God declared, "My Spirit shall not strive with man forever" (Gen. 6:3). Stephen issued this stinging rebuke to the leaders of Israel: "You men who are stiff-necked and uncircumcised in heart and ears are always resisting the Holy Spirit; you are doing just as your fathers did" (Acts 7:51). The Holy Spirit also opposes evil by "convict[ing] the world concerning sin and righteousness and judgment" (John 16:8). He will continue His restraining work until the midpoint of the Tribulation. The removal of the Holy Spirit's restraint therefore cannot be identified with the Rapture of the church, since that event takes place three and a half years earlier, before the Tribulation.

The phrase **taken out of the way** must not be interpreted to mean that the Holy Spirit will be removed from the world. That is impossible, since He is omnipresent. Nor could anyone be saved during the Tribulation (cf. Rev. 7:14) apart from His regenerating work (John 3:3–8; Titus 3:5). The phrase refers not to the removal of the Holy Spirit from the world, but rather to the cessation of His restraining work.

Summarizing Paul's teaching on this issue, William Hendriksen wrote:

> Accordingly, the sense of the entire passage (verses 6 and 7) seems to be this: Satan, while perfectly aware of the fact that he cannot himself become incarnate, nevertheless would like to imitate the second person of the Trinity also in this respect as far as possible. He yearns for a man over whom he will have complete control, and who will perform his will as thoroughly as Jesus performed the will of the Father. It will have to be a man of outstanding talents. But as yet the devil is being frustrated in his attempt to put this plan into operation. Someone and something is always "holding back" the deceiver's man of lawlessness. This, of course, happens under God's direction. Hence, for the time being, *the worst* Satan can do is to promote the spirit of lawlessness. But this does not satisfy him. It is as if he and his man of sin bide their time. At the divinely decreed moment ("the appropriate season") when, as a punishment for man's willingness to cooperate with this spirit, the "some one" and "something" that now holds back is removed, Satan will begin to carry out his plans. (*New Testament Commentary: Exposition of Thessalonians, Timothy and Titus* [Grand Rapids: Baker, 1981], 182–83. Emphasis in the original.)

Romans 1:18–25 gives a clear and oft-repeated historical example of the removal of restraint so that sin is unleashed:

For the wrath of God is revealed from heaven against all ungodliness and unrighteousness of men who suppress the truth in unrighteousness, because that which is known about God is evident within them; for God made it evident to them. For since the creation of the world His invisible attributes, His eternal power and divine nature, have been clearly seen, being understood through what has been made, so that they are without excuse. For even though they knew God, they did not honor Him as God or give thanks, but they became futile in their speculations, and their foolish heart was darkened. Professing to be wise, they became fools, and exchanged the glory of the incorruptible God for an image in the form of corruptible man and of birds and four-footed animals and crawling creatures.

Therefore God gave them over in the lusts of their hearts to impurity, so that their bodies would be dishonored among them. For they exchanged the truth of God for a lie, and worshiped and served the creature rather than the Creator, who is blessed forever. Amen.

The three statements that "God gave them up" or "over" (vv. 24, 26, 28) describe the removal of divine restraint and the flood of immorality, homosexuality, and perverted thinking and behaving that drowns those so judged (cf. Ps. 81:11–12; Prov. 1:23–31; Hos. 4:17).

For the third time in this passage (cf. vv. 3, 6), Paul notes that the **lawless one will be revealed** when the Holy Spirit's restraint ceases. Antichrist will expose the depths of his evil nature by desecrating the temple and proclaiming himself to be God. God's judgments, which will begin during the first half of the Tribulation, will intensify dramatically as the Day of the Lord arrives in all its judgmental fury (cf. Rev. 4–19). But Antichrist's reign of terror will be short-lived.

HIS DESTRUCTION

whom the Lord will slay with the breath of His mouth and bring to an end by the appearance of His coming; (2:8b)

Just as Antichrist will be revealed at God's appointed time, so also is the moment of his destruction divinely ordained. At the height of his power, when he seems invincible, he will meet his end. Daniel 7:26 says, "His dominion will be taken away, annihilated and destroyed forever"; Daniel 11:45 notes that "he will come to his end, and no one will help him." Revelation 17:11 declares that Antichrist "goes to destruction," and that destruction is graphically described in Revelation 19:20: "And the beast was seized, and with him the false prophet who performed the signs in his presence, by which he deceived those who had received the mark of the beast and those who worshiped his image; these two were thrown alive into the lake of fire which burns with brimstone." The most hellish and powerful ruler in human history will be effortlessly crushed; **the Lord will slay** him **with the** mere **breath of His mouth.** The term **slay** does not mean that the Lord will kill Antichrist (the NIV translates it "overthrow"), since Revelation 19:20 says that he will still be alive when he is cast into the lake of fire. Robert L. Thomas notes:

> Some have supposed a discrepancy between the fate of these two [the beast (Antichrist) and the false prophet] and that of the man of lawlessness in 2 Thess. 2:8 . . . , but harmonization of the two accounts of Christ's return is quite easy. The verb . . . *anelei,* "destroy" used by Paul [in 2 Thess. 2:8] does not necessarily mean physical death. It can also refer to relegation to the lake of fire because the literal force of . . . *anaireō* [the root form of *anelei*] is "I make an end of." (*Revelation 8–22: An Exegetical Commentary* [Chicago: Moody, 1995], 397)

The concept that the Lord will destroy His enemies with **the breath of His mouth** stems from the Old Testament. Isaiah 11:4 says that the Lord "will strike the earth with the rod of His mouth, and with the breath of His lips He will slay the wicked." Isaiah 30:33 adds, "For Topheth has long been ready, indeed, it has been prepared for the king. He has made it deep and large, a pyre of fire with plenty of wood; the breath of the Lord, like a torrent of brimstone, sets it afire" (cf. Hos. 6:5). Revelation uses the similar picture of a sword coming out of the Lord's mouth to destroy His enemies (1:16; 2:16; 19:15,21).

The parallel statement **and bring to an end by the appearance of His coming** adds a slightly different dimension to Antichrist's destruction. *Katargeō* (**bring to an end**) literally means, "to render inoperative," "to abolish," or "to render ineffective." Not only will the Lord **slay** (destroy) Antichrist's person, He will also **bring to an end** his empire. Christ will annihilate both the man and his enterprise **by the appearance of His coming,** a reference to the visible manifestation of Christ at His second coming (Rev. 19:11–21).

So Antichrist will rule from the midpoint of the Tribulation until Christ's return—1,260 days (Rev. 12:6), or forty-two months (Rev. 13:5), both of which equal three and a half years (cf. Dan. 9:27). During that brief reign, so suddenly ended, he will exercise power unparalleled in human history.

HIS POWER

that is, the one whose coming is in accord with the activity of Satan, with all power and signs and false wonders, and with all the deception of wickedness (2:9–10a)

Antichrist's great power will not be his own but will be **in accord with the activity of Satan.** *Energeia* (**activity**), the root of the English word "energy," describes power in action. It usually refers to God's power (e. g., Eph. 1:19; 3:7; Phil. 3:21; Col. 1:29; 2:12), but here it describes Satan's power. Antichrist's **power and signs and false wonders** will not only be deceptive tricks, like falsifying his own death and resurrection (Rev. 13:3, 12, 14; 17:8, 11), but also actual manifestations of Satan's supernatural power. **Power** (miracles; cf. Matt. 7:22; 11:20, 21, 23, etc.) refers to supernatural acts; **signs** point to the one who performs them; **wonders** describes the astonishing results. Antichrist's miracles will reveal his supernatural power and create wonder, shock, and astonishment. *Pseudos* (**false**) modifies all three terms; Antichrist's miracles, signs, and wonders are **false** not in the sense that they are fakery but that they lead to false conclusions about who he is. They will cause people to believe the lie that he is a divine being and worship him. John saw that Antichrist's deluded followers "worshiped the beast, saying, 'Who is like the beast, and who is able to wage war with him?'" (Rev. 13:4; cf. vv. 12–15). Antichrist will mislead the world **with all the deception . . . wickedness** has at its disposal; he will muster all of evil's undiluted, unrestrained, seductive power to tempt the world to give him unprecedented influence over it.

HIS INFLUENCE

for those who perish, (2:10b)

Antichrist's malevolent, deceptive, deadly influence will extend to all **those who perish.** Only God's elect will not be taken in (Matt. 24:24). The unregenerate, being children of the arch-liar Satan (John 8:44), will inevitably fall for the lies of his emissary (cf. 1 Cor. 2:14; 2 Cor. 4:3–4). Through him, Satan will deceive the whole world (Rev. 12:9); all those who "[receive] the mark of the beast and those who [worship] his image" (Rev. 19:20; cf. 2 Cor. 4:4).

DO NOT BE UNBELIEVING

because they did not receive the love of the truth so as to be saved. For this reason God will send upon them a deluding influence so that they will believe what is false, in order that they all may be judged who did not believe the truth, but took pleasure in wickedness. (2:10c–12)

Specifically, unbelievers will be deceived by Antichrist and perish because **they did not receive the love of the truth so as to be saved.** The phrase **the love of the truth** appears only here in the New Testament, and adds a compelling thought to Paul's argument. The unregenerate are eternally lost, not because they did not hear or understand the truth, but because they did not **love** it. The **truth** includes both "the word of truth, the gospel" (Col. 1:5), and the Lord Jesus Christ, who is truth incarnate (John 14:6; cf. 1:17; Eph. 4:21). Unbelievers do not welcome either Jesus or the gospel He proclaimed. Their antipathy to the truth is not intellectual, but moral, and their self-imposed blindness leaves the unredeemed under a damning level of satanic deception. It is not surprising, then, that Antichrist will deceive the entire lost world.

The Bible clearly teaches that those who go to hell do so because they reject the truth. Speaking of Jerusalem's rejection of the truth, Jesus lamented, "Jerusalem, Jerusalem, who kills the prophets and stones those who are sent to her! How often I wanted to gather your children together, the way a hen gathers her chicks under her wings, and you were unwilling" (Matt. 23:37). John 3:19–20 says, "This is the judgment, that the Light has come into the world, and men loved the darkness rather than the Light, for their deeds were evil. For everyone who does evil hates the Light, and does not come to the Light for fear that his deeds will be exposed." To the unbelieving Jews Jesus declared, "You do not have His word abiding in you, for you do not believe Him whom He sent. You search the Scriptures because you think that in them you have eternal life; it is these that testify about Me; and you are unwilling to come to Me so that you may have life" (John 5:38–40). He reiterated that truth later in John's gospel:

> Therefore I said to you that you will die in your sins; for unless you believe that I am He, you will die in your sins. . . . But because I speak the truth, you do not believe Me. Which one of you convicts Me of sin? If I speak truth, why do you not believe Me? He who is of God hears the words of God; for this reason you do not hear them, because you are not of God. (John 8:24, 45–47)

Because the unredeemed **did not receive the love of the truth** they "do not know God and . . . do not obey the gospel of our Lord Jesus" (1:8). They willfully choose to love their sin, believe Satan's lies, and hate the gospel and the Lord Jesus Christ. They are like those Jewish leaders described in John 12:42–43 who "believed in Him, but because of the Pharisees they were not confessing Him, for fear that they would be put out of the synagogue; for they loved the approval of men rather than the approval of God." In Matthew 10:37 Jesus taught that salvation involves loving Him above all else: "He who loves father or mother more than Me is not worthy of Me; and he who loves son or daughter more than Me is not worthy of Me."

The terrifying reality is that God will seal the fate of those who hate the gospel by sending **upon them a deluding influence so that they will believe what is false.** Though, as noted above, Antichrist will deceive people with satanically empowered false miracles, signs, and wonders, his deception only will succeed because it fits into God's sovereign purpose. He will sentence unbelievers to accept evil as if it were good and lies as if they were the truth. Those who continually choose falsehood will be inextricably caught by it. In the words of Proverbs 5:22, "His own iniquities will capture the wicked, and he will be held with the cords of his sin." They will be abandoned by God to the consequences of their choice to reject the gospel.

The story of Pharaoh is a grim reminder that God will judicially harden the hearts of those who persist in hardening their hearts against the truth. Because Pharaoh hardened his heart (Ex. 8:15, 32; 9:34; 1 Sam. 6:6), God hardened Pharaoh's heart, fixing him in a path from which he could never return (Ex. 4:21; 7:3; 9:12; 10:1, 20, 27; 11:10; 14:4, 8).

In Isaiah 6:9–10, a passage quoted repeatedly in the New Testament (Matt. 13:14–15; Mark 4:12; Luke 8:10; John 12:40; Acts 28:26–27; Rom. 11:8), God said to Isaiah, "Go, and tell this people: 'Keep on listening, but do not perceive; keep on looking, but do not understand.' Render the hearts of this people insensitive, their ears dull, and their eyes dim, otherwise they might see with their eyes, hear with their ears, understand with their hearts, and return and be healed." God told Isaiah that He would sovereignly prevent hard-hearted rejecters of the truth from responding to his preaching. Similarly, Jesus spoke in parables not only to reveal spiritual truth to believers but also to conceal it in judgment on unbelievers (Matt. 13:11–13; Luke 8:10). There comes a day that those who persistently reject the truth will be unable to believe it; God will harden their hearts and fix them in the path they have chosen.

God's use of Satan and Antichrist as instruments of His judgment finds a parallel in the Old Testament. Through the prophet Micaiah, God pronounced judgment on the wicked king Ahab:

Micaiah said, "Therefore, hear the word of the Lord. I saw the Lord sitting on His throne, and all the host of heaven standing by Him on His right and on His left. The Lord said, 'Who will entice Ahab to go up and fall at Ramoth-gilead?' And one said this while another said that. Then a spirit came forward and stood before the Lord and said, 'I will entice him.' The Lord said to him, 'How?' And he said, 'I will go out and be a deceiving spirit in the mouth of all his prophets.' Then He said, 'You are to entice him and also prevail. Go and do so.' Now therefore, behold, the Lord has put a deceiving spirit in the mouth of all these your prophets; and the Lord has proclaimed disaster against you." (1 Kings 22:19–23)

Because of Ahab's rebellion and unfaithfulness, God allowed Satan to deceive him through false prophets. In the future, God will again use Satan as an instrument of His judgment, **in order that they all may be judged who did not believe the truth, but took pleasure in wickedness.** Satan will, through Antichrist and the false prophet, delude the world into believing the lie that Antichrist is God. Unbelievers will be confirmed in that belief because they will choose not to love the truth, but rather to take **pleasure in wickedness.**

As indicated earlier, Romans 1 also illustrates God's judicial abandonment of unrepentant sinners: "Even though they knew God [vv. 19–20], they did not honor Him as God or give thanks, but they became futile in their speculations, and their foolish heart was darkened" (v. 21). Because of that, the passage declares three times that "God gave them over" (vv. 24, 26, 28) to the consequences of their own sinful choices (vv. 24–28; cf. Gen. 6:3; Judg. 10:13; 2 Chron. 15:2; 24:20; Matt. 15:14; Acts 7:38–42; 14:16).

Do Not Be Insecure

But we should always give thanks to God for you, brethren beloved by the Lord, because God has chosen you from the beginning for salvation through sanctification by the Spirit and faith in the truth. It was for this He called you through our gospel, that you may gain the glory of our Lord Jesus Christ. (2:13–14)

Paul's fifth exhortation to eliminate fear of the future is to understand the great doctrine of salvation. With a few words, the apostle sweeps the reader across the vastness of God's redemptive plan to affirm the believer's security in that plan. Again, Paul's intent is not pedagogical but pastoral. Those who reject the truth that believers are eternally secure cannot look forward with confident hope to Christ's coming. To believe that Christians living in unconfessed sin when the Lord returns will go to hell can only engender dread and fear—especially since sinless perfection in this life is unattainable (1 Kings 8:46; Ps. 143:2; Prov. 20:9; Eccl. 7:20; 1 John 1:8,10).

But the Thessalonians did not need to fear they had lost or could lose their salvation, because God's choice of them is irrevocable. Salvation began with God's loving choice in eternity past and will continue until glorification in the future (Rom. 8:29–30). Jesus emphatically declared the utter impossibility that any of God's elect should ever be lost:

> All that the Father gives Me will come to Me, and the one who comes to Me I will certainly not cast out. . . . This is the will of Him who sent Me, that of all that He has given Me I lose nothing, but raise it up on the last day. For this is the will of My Father, that everyone who beholds the Son and believes in Him will have eternal life, and I Myself will raise him up on the last day. . . . No one can come to Me unless the Father who sent Me draws him; and I will raise him up on the last day. (John 6:37, 39–40, 44)

> My sheep hear My voice, and I know them, and they follow Me; and I give eternal life to them, and they will never perish; and no one will snatch them out of My hand. My Father, who has given them to Me, is greater than all; and no one is able to snatch them out of the Father's hand. (John 10:27–29)

That glorious truth caused Paul to **always give thanks to God for** the Thessalonians, knowing that they were **brethren beloved by the Lord.** In contrast to the unredeemed, who refuse to love and obey the truth, are those who willingly do both; in contrast to those whom God judges are those He redeems; in contrast to those who believe Satan's lies are those who believe God's truth; in contrast to those who follow Antichrist are those who follow Christ.

God's work of salvation began with His sovereign, uninfluenced, undeserved love. That love was the basis for His election of believers (Eph. 1:4–5). God's electing love is not conditioned on any merit in its recipients, as Moses reminded Israel: "The Lord did not set His love on you nor choose you because you were more in number than any of the peoples, for you were the fewest of all peoples" (Deut. 7:7).

Flowing out of God's predetermined love is His sovereign choice of believers, whom He **has chosen . . . from the beginning for salvation.** God "chose us in Him before the foundation of the world" (Eph. 1:4); He "has saved us and called us with a holy calling, not according to our works, but according to His own purpose and grace which was granted us in Christ Jesus from all eternity" (2 Tim. 1:9). The redeemed are those whose names were "written from the foundation of the world in the book of life of the Lamb who has been slain" (Rev. 13:8; cf. 17:8). For that reason, the New Testament commonly refers to believers as the "elect" (Matt. 24:22, 24, 31; Mark 13:20, 22, 27; Luke 18:7; Rom. 8:33) or the "chosen" (Matt. 22:14; Rom. 11:7; Col. 3:12; 2 Tim. 2:10; Titus 1:1; 1 Peter 1:1).

The doctrine of God's sovereign, elective love has several practical benefits. It crushes human pride (Titus 3:5), since God gets all the credit for salvation. It exalts God (Ps. 115:1), as He receives praise for His love. It produces joy (1 Peter 1:1–2, 6, 8), as believers rejoice in their salvation. It grants unimaginable privileges (Eph. 1:3). It promotes holiness in the lives of the elect (Col. 3:12–13). Finally, and most relevant to Paul's purpose in this passage, it provides security (Phil. 1:6).

God's sovereign election of believers becomes operative in their lives through **sanctification by the Spirit and faith in the truth. Sanctification** is the work of the **Spirit** that sets believers apart from sin to righteousness (cf. Rom. 15:16; 1 Cor. 6:11; 1 Peter 1:2). This miracle starts at salvation and includes a total transformation, so that the believer is born again (John 3:3–8) and becomes a new creature (2 Cor. 5:17; Gal. 6:15). The **sanctification** that begins at regeneration does not, of course, mean that believers do not sin (see the discussion above). But it does ensure that those set apart from sin to God will lead lives of progressive sanctification, of increasing holiness toward Christlikeness (John 17:17; Rom. 6:1–22; 2 Cor. 3:18; Gal. 5:16–25; Phil. 3:12; Col. 3:9–20; 1 Thess. 4:3–4; 5:23; 1 Peter 1:14–16; 1 John 3:4–10).

The human factor in God's sovereign, loving election and regeneration is **faith in the truth.** Salvation is "by grace . . . through faith" (Eph. 2:8). It is those who "believe in the Lord Jesus [who] will be saved" (Acts 16:31). To the Romans Paul wrote, "If you confess with your mouth Jesus as Lord, and believe in your heart that God raised Him from the dead, you will be saved; for with the heart a person believes, resulting in righteousness, and with the mouth he confesses, resulting in salvation" (Rom. 10:9–10). The truth that salvation is by faith in the true gospel permeates the New Testament (e.g., Mark 1:15; John 1:12; 3:15–16, 36; 5:24; 6:40, 47; Acts 10:43; Rom. 1:16; 1 Tim. 1:16; 2 Tim. 3:15; 1 Peter 1:9; 1 John 5:1). The Spirit regenerates those who hear and believe the truth by granting them repentance (Acts 11:18; 2 Tim. 2:25) and the gift of faith (Eph. 2:8–9).

The next element in God's redemptive plan reaches back chronologically before the third. The apostle's declaration **It was for this He called you through our gospel** refers, as always in the New Testament epistles, to God's effectual call of believers to salvation (e.g., Rom. 1:6, 7; 1 Cor. 1:2, 9, 24, 26; Gal. 1:6; Eph. 4:1, 4). The gracious call of the

Holy Spirit is irresistible (Rom. 8:30); the gospel is not merely words and facts but "the power of God for salvation to everyone who believes" (Rom. 1:16).

All of those gospel realities lead to the ultimate goal of God's redemptive plan—**that** believers **may gain the glory of our Lord Jesus Christ** (cf. 1:10, 12). That firm statement of the security of salvation reveals that God loved, chose, called, and transformed believers for the purpose of eternally reflecting the glory of Christ to them and through them (cf. 1 John 3:1–2; Rom. 8:29; 1 Cor. 15:42–49; Phil. 3:21). Since no purpose of His can be thwarted (Job 42:2), nothing can separate believers from His saving love (Rom. 8:35–39).

Based on this sovereign scheme, there was no need for the Thessalonians to be insecure about their salvation, anxious about the Lord's return, or fearful that they were in the Day of Judgment of the ungodly. They, like all believers, were not destined for judgment but for glory, for "God has not destined us for wrath, but for obtaining salvation through our Lord Jesus Christ" (1 Thess. 5:9).

Do Not Be Weak

So then, brethren, stand firm and hold to the traditions which you were taught, whether by word of mouth or by letter from us. Now may our Lord Jesus Christ Himself and God our Father, who has loved us and given us eternal comfort and good hope by grace, comfort and strengthen your hearts in every good work and word. (2:15–17)

Paul concluded his discussion with a sixth exhortation to the Thessalonians, to **stand firm and hold to the traditions which** they **were taught, whether by word of mouth or by letter from** Paul and his companions (cf. 1 Thess. 3:8). He gave similar exhortations to the Corinthians (1 Cor. 15:58; 16:13), the Ephesians (Eph. 6:11, 13, 14) and the Philippians (Phil. 4:1). He wanted the Thessalonians not to be weak or vacillating but to hold their spiritual ground and keep their grip on the truth. Specifically, the apostle urged them to **hold to the traditions which** they **were taught.** The concept of tradition has been loaded down with a lot of cultural and ecclesiastical baggage over the centuries. But Paul did not have in mind a body of extrabiblical tradition that is equal to God's revelation in Scripture; in fact, the Bible condemns such human tradition (Isa. 29:13; Matt. 15:3, 6; Mark 7:8–9, 13; Col. 2:8). The Greek word translated **traditions** literally means "things handed down" and refers here to divine revelation (cf. 3:6; 1 Cor. 11:2), **whether** given

by word of mouth or by letter. The Thessalonians were to hold fast to what God had handed down, both orally and in writing, through Paul and the other apostles. Believers must hold fast to the "faith which was once for all handed down to the saints" (Jude 3; cf. 1 Tim. 6:20; 2 Tim. 1:14).

As he did in his first epistle (1 Thess. 3:11–13) and would frequently do in his subsequent epistles to other churches (e.g., Rom. 16:25–27; 1 Cor. 16:23), Paul gave a benediction, praying that God would comfort and strengthen the church. Paul understood that they could not obey his exhortation in their own strength but needed instead to depend on God's power. He expressed that balanced view of the Christian life when he wrote to the Colossians, "For this purpose also I labor, striving according to His power, which mightily works within me" (Col. 1:29; cf. 1 Cor. 15:10).

The pronoun translated **Himself** stands in the emphatic position in the Greek text, which could be translated, "Now may Himself our Lord Jesus Christ and God our Father." The pronoun governs both **Lord Jesus Christ** and **God our Father,** viewing both as the source of comfort. That provides powerful evidence of Christ's deity; He is fully equal with the Father in person, power, and respect.

Jesus and the Father **loved** believers from all eternity. Because of that love, which permanently and irrevocably granted believers **eternal comfort and good hope by grace** at salvation, the apostle prayed that both **Jesus Christ** and **God** the **Father** would **comfort and strengthen** the Thessalonians' **hearts in every good work and word** by this unshakable promise of future glory.

As they anticipate the return of Jesus Christ for His own, believers must not be deceived, forgetful, ignorant, unbelieving, insecure, or weak. They will not experience the terrible judgment of the Day of the Lord, because their salvation is secure. God loved them, chose them, redeemed them, and would glorify them. They must therefore be strong and courageous, "looking for the blessed hope and the appearing of the glory of our great God and Savior, Christ Jesus" (Titus 2:13).

What the Pastor Desires from His People

25

(2 Thessalonians 3:1–5)

Finally, brethren, pray for us that the word of the Lord will spread rapidly and be glorified, just as it did also with you; and that we will be rescued from perverse and evil men; for not all have faith. But the Lord is faithful, and He will strengthen and protect you from the evil one. We have confidence in the Lord concerning you, that you are doing and will continue to do what we command. May the Lord direct your hearts into the love of God and into the steadfastness of Christ. (3:1–5)

Being a pastor is the highest calling for a godly man, not only in privilege, but also in obligation. Therefore anyone who preaches and teaches the Word of God and offers himself as a spiritual shepherd for God's flock must meet the highest of divinely established standards. It is the church's duty to measure and hold their pastors to those standards, which Scripture so clearly and precisely defines. In a command that applies to all shepherds, Jesus told Peter, "Tend My sheep" (John 21:17). In the early days of the church, the Twelve resolved, "We will devote ourselves to prayer and to the ministry of the word" (Acts 6:4). Paul, pointing to his own example, exhorted the Ephesian elders concerning the serious and comprehensive responsibilities they had as shepherds of God's church:"For I did not shrink from declaring to you the whole purpose of God. Be on guard for yourselves and for all the flock, among which the Holy Spirit has made you overseers, to shepherd the church of God which He purchased with His own blood" (Acts 20:27-28). Both Paul and Peter set forth God's requirements for shepherding His flock (1 Tim. 3:1-7; 4:6-11; 2 Tim. 3:16-4:5; Titus 1:5-9; 1 Peter 5:1-4; cf. Heb. 13:7, 17).

Scripture is equally clear in stating the duties and responsibilities Christians have to their pastors. In his first letter to them, Paul instructed the Thessalonians about these: "We request of you, brethren, that you appreciate those who diligently labor among you, and have charge over you in the Lord and give you instruction, and that you esteem them very highly in love because of their work" (5:12-13; see the discussion of those verses in chapter 14 of this volume). Believers are to obey that admonition so that their pastors may do their work "with joy and not with grief, for this would be unprofitable for [the flock]" (Heb. 13:17b). When pastor and people each fulfill their clear, scripturally mandated responsibilities to one another, God blesses the church and makes it powerful, effective, and joyful.

This text provides additional insight, directly from Paul's heart, regarding what any dedicated, devoted pastor desires from his people. The apostle set forth four fundamental and obvious desires he had of the Thessalonians: that they would pray for him, that they would trust the Lord, that they would obey his divinely revealed teaching, and that they would grow spiritually.

PASTORS DESIRE THEIR PEOPLE'S PRAYERS

Finally, brethren, pray for us that the word of the Lord will spread rapidly and be glorified, just as it did also with you; and that we will be rescued from perverse and evil men; for not all have faith. (3:1-2)

Paul was without equal as a gifted and effective minister of God. His natural abilities were immense—he had the best rabbinical education; he was a brilliant, logical, and persuasive thinker and communicator; and he was spiritually perceptive and possessed much experience in missions and church planting. But none of those qualities stood alone as the source of his effectiveness. Paul testified to the Colossians, "I labor, striving according to His power, which mightily works within me" (Col. 1:29). He placed no confidence in the flesh but knew that whatever ministry success he enjoyed was due to the power of God at work in his life— a power that energized his natural giftedness for supernatural impact (cf.

Gal. 2:20). Since he depended on the Lord for every aspect of his ministry, he frequently requested his people to pray for him (Rom. 15:30–32; Eph. 6:19–20; Col. 4:3; 1 Thess. 5:25; Philem. 22; cf. 2 Cor. 1:11; Phil. 1:19).

Paul faithfully prayed for the Thessalonians (1 Thess. 1:2; 2:13; 3:9–13; 5:23, 28; 2 Thess. 1:11; 2:16–17; 3:16, 18) and for the other people to whom he ministered (Rom. 1:9–10; 10:1; 2 Cor. 13:7, 9; Eph. 1:16, 18; Phil. 1:4, 9; Col. 1:3, 9; 2 Tim. 1:3; Philem. 4, 6), but he likewise needed their prayers. In his travels he constantly faced difficulty, danger, and loneliness (Acts 9:23–25; 13:50; 14:4–6; 16:16–34; 17:1–9, 14; 19:13–41; 27:26–44; 28:1–10; 1 Cor. 4:8–13; 2 Cor. 4:8–12; 6:4–10; 11:22–33; 2 Tim. 3:11). He either had to support himself (Acts 20:33–35; 2 Cor. 11:9; 2 Thess. 3:7–9) or rely on the support of others (1 Cor. 9:7–11; Gal. 6:6; cf. 1 Tim. 5:17–18). He usually preached to audiences who did not want to hear him and at places to which people did not invite him in the first place (Acts 17:16–34; 26:24–32). He depended on God's power to strengthen and sustain him (1 Cor. 2:1–16; 2 Cor. 4:1–15; 6:3–10; 10:7–18; 12:7–10; Phil. 3:7–14; Col. 1:24–29; 1 Tim. 1:12–17; cf. Acts 16:6–10; 18:9–11; 23:11; 27:22–26), and he knew the prayers of believers before God's throne opened that divine power through him.

Finally (*loipos*) can have the sense of finality, but it literally means "for the rest," or "besides that" (e.g., 1 Cor. 1:16). Paul used the same term in Philippians 3:1 and 1 Thessalonians 4:1, and in neither instance was he ready to conclude his epistle; he was simply making a transition ("besides that . . . this"). In several uses of the word, it marks the transition from the letter's doctrinal content to its practical content, as it does here. By it Paul marked his subject change from eschatology to matters of practical sanctification.

First he invited the Thessalonian **brethren** to **pray for** his co-workers and him (**us**). **Pray** is in the present tense (*proseuchesthe*), meaning that he asked the Thessalonians to "continually pray," or "make prayer a constant pattern" in their lives (cf. 1 Thess. 5:17 and the discussion of that verse in chapter 16 of this volume). His use of the preposition **for** (*peri*) actually denotes "about," "concerning," "with reference to"; thus Paul asked that in their continual prayers and intercessions they would remember his needs. Even with his influence, success, respect, and fame, this request demonstrated Paul's meekness and humility. The man who was inarguably the strongest of spiritual leaders requested prayer from new believers (cf. 1 Cor. 2:1–5; 2 Cor. 10:12–17; 1 Tim. 1:12–17). It also showed his confidence in the inherent power of prayer (Eph. 3:14, 20; Phil. 4:6; 1 Tim. 2:8). Paul's request is a good reminder that even the newest believers have the privilege, in the Spirit, through prayer, of participating in the release of God's power (cf. Eph. 2:18; Heb. 10:19) on behalf of the strongest, most experienced servants of God.

The first specific request Paul made was for the success of his message, which he identified as **the word of the Lord.** The inspired writers of the Old and New Testaments use that phrase again and again to refer to divine revelation (e.g., Gen. 15:1, 4; Num. 3:16; 36:5; Deut. 5:5; Josh. 8:8; 1 Sam. 3:7, 21; 1 Kings 6:11; 12:24; 2 Kings 7:1; 1 Chron. 11:3; Ezra 1:1; Ps. 18:30; Isa. 1:10; Jer. 1:4; Dan. 9:2; Hos. 4:1; Mal. 1:1; Acts 11:16; 1 Peter 1:25). The New Testament writers most frequently associate it with the gospel (cf. Acts 8:14, 25; 13:5, 44, 46, 48, 49; 15:35–36; 16:32; 19:10, 20). **The word of the Lord** comes first as the good news of salvation, which, when savingly believed, brings more understanding of the divine revelation through the Scripture. Paul's passion was that the gospel of salvation would **spread rapidly and be glorified.** That he wrote to the Thessalonians from Corinth, where there was much hostility and overt opposition to Paul's preaching (cf. Acts 18:4–6), revealed his heightened passion for the gospel.

Spread rapidly (*trechō*) literally means "to speed on," or "to make progress" (cf. Ps. 147:15; Acts 19:20). Paul wanted them to pray that the Word would advance like a strong runner, moving ahead unobstructed and unhindered, to attain new ground. That concern was always on his heart because he lived for the successful preaching of the gospel (Acts 20:24; 26:19; Rom. 1:15–17; 10:1; 15:20–21; 1 Cor. 1:17; 2 Cor. 2:17; 5:18–20; Phil. 1:15–18; 2 Tim. 1:8–12; Titus 1:1–3; cf. Gal. 6:14). He would later write to the Ephesians, "Pray on my behalf, that utterance may be given to me in the opening of my mouth, to make known with boldness the mystery of the gospel" (Eph. 6:19; cf. Col. 4:2–4).

Be glorified (*doxazō*), meaning to be praised, honored, and exalted, expresses the apostle's desire that the gospel be received with the proper respect, that people would accept and affirm it as the saving truth of God. Paul's preaching at Antioch in Pisidia (Acts 13:44–49) presents one picture of what he desired concerning the gospel's acceptance:

> The next Sabbath nearly the whole city assembled to hear the word of the Lord. But when the Jews saw the crowds, they were filled with jealousy and began contradicting the things spoken by Paul, and were blaspheming. Paul and Barnabas spoke out boldly and said, "It was necessary that the word of God be spoken to you first; since you repudiate it and judge yourselves unworthy of eternal life, behold, we are turning to the Gentiles. For so the Lord has commanded us, 'I have placed you as a light for the Gentiles, that You may bring salvation to the end of the earth.'"
>
> When the Gentiles heard this, they began rejoicing and glorifying the word of the Lord; and as many as had been appointed to eternal life believed. And the word of the Lord was being spread through the whole region. (cf. 16:11–15, 28–34; 17:11–12; 19:18–20)

Paul knew people such as those Jews at Pisidian Antioch would repudiate and blaspheme the gospel. But he also knew that many others would embrace it by faith, as the Gentiles did, and as they and some Jews did at Thessalonica (Acts 17:1–4). Paul wanted the Thessalonians to pray that the same kind of thing would happen again, and as if to encourage them that such a reception was again possible, he added, **just as it did** [occur] **also with you**. At the initial preaching of the gospel in Thessalonica, both Jews and Gentiles believed. It was only a little later, when more and more Gentiles believed, that some unbelieving Jews violently objected to what was happening (vv. 5–9). But overall, the Thessalonians had had a positive response to the gospel (1 Thess. 1:5–9), and Paul longed for that to occur among other peoples in other places (cf. 1 Tim. 2:3–4).

Second, Paul asked the Thessalonians to pray for the safety of the gospel messengers (cf. Rom. 15:30–31). As already noted from the book of Acts (see also 18:12–17), he constantly faced hostility to his ministry. Therefore he asked them to pray that he would **be rescued from perverse and evil men**. The apostle was not concerned merely about self-preservation or personal comfort and safety (2 Cor. 4:7–12; 11:22–33; Phil. 1:19–30; 3:7–14; Col. 1:24–29); but he did desire that God would protect him as he ministered (cf. 2 Cor. 1:8–10); otherwise people would not hear his message.

Paul identified the source of danger as **perverse and evil men**. **Perverse** (*atopos*) literally means "out of place," and denotes what is unbecoming or inappropriate (cf. Luke 23:41; Acts 25:5; 28:6). Here it refers to men who were improper, wrongfully out of place, unrighteous, or as one writer described them, "morally insane." As if to underscore how dangerous those men were, Paul further described them with the adjective **evil** (*ponēros*), meaning "malignant," or "aggressively wicked." He desired deliverance from the threats and power of such enemies of the gospel whom Satan used to prevent his companions and him from preaching the saving message (cf. 1 Thess. 2:18).

The saints probably assumed that because they had received the gospel so eagerly, such positive response was normal for everyone who heard the message. But their acceptance was far from the pattern for many (Acts 14:4–6; 16:16–24, 37–40; cf. Matt. 19:16–22; Luke 4:28–30; John 6:60–66; 7:1–5, 40–44; 8:48–59; 10:22–39; Acts 4:1–21; 5:17–41; 7:54–8:3; 12:1–4), so Paul cautioned them that **not all have faith**. Some insert the definite article, "not all have *the* faith," to make **faith** refer to the content of the Christian faith. But the phrase more likely means not everyone *believes* the gospel. However, either way Paul's point is the same: **not all** will believe, and those who reject may be hostile to the gospel. This reality moved Paul to call the Thessalonians to pray that as he and his companions preached **the word** of the gospel, it would triumphantly go forth unhindered and be believed.

PASTORS DESIRE THAT THEIR PEOPLE TRUST IN THE LORD

But the Lord is faithful, and He will strengthen and protect you from the evil one. (3:3)

When he wrote this letter, Paul was in Corinth, so he could not ensure firsthand how strong the Thessalonians' trust in God through all their trials and persecutions would remain. But no matter what difficulties faced them, Paul knew **the Lord** would be **faithful** to accomplish His purposes for them. Toward the end of his life, the apostle testified to the truth of God's faithfulness:

> At my first defense no one supported me, but all deserted me; may it not be counted against them. But the Lord stood with me and strengthened me, so that through me the proclamation might be fully accomplished, and that all the Gentiles might hear; and I was rescued out of the lion's mouth. The Lord will rescue me from every evil deed, and will bring me safely to His heavenly kingdom; to Him be the glory forever and ever. Amen. (2 Tim. 4:16–18)

God is so faithful that, as they trust in His spiritual provisions, believers will always be able to handle assaults from the world's evil system: "God is faithful, who will not allow you to be tempted beyond what you are able, but with the temptation will provide the way of escape also, so that you will be able to endure it" (1 Cor. 10:13). Scripture is replete with many other affirmations of the Lord's faithfulness (e.g., Deut. 7:9; Pss. 36:5; 40:10; 89:1–2, 8, 24, 33; 92:2; 119:75, 90; Isa. 49:7; Lam. 3:23; 1 Cor. 1:9; 1 Thess. 5:24; Heb. 10:23; 1 Peter 4:19; 1 John 1:9).

Paul went on to tell the Thessalonians how God would express His faithfulness to them. **Strengthen and protect** are synonymous with "establish and guard." God will firmly establish believers on the inside and guard them on the outside **from the evil one** (most likely a reference to Satan; cf. Matt. 13:19, 38; John 17:15; 1 John 2:13–14; 3:12; 5:18–19). The Lord fills His children with internal spiritual strength (2 Cor. 4:16; Eph. 3:16) while He shields them from external attacks (Eph. 6:16). Jude summarized this concept well when he wrote that God "is able to keep [believers] from stumbling, and to make [them] stand in the presence of His glory blameless with great joy" (Jude 24).

PASTORS DESIRE THEIR PEOPLE'S
OBEDIENCE TO WHAT IS TAUGHT

We have confidence in the Lord concerning you, that you are doing and will continue to do what we command. (3:4)

The third pastoral desire Paul had for the Thessalonians was that they continue their pattern of obedience to God. Based on what they were already **doing** (1 Thess. 1:3, 6–8; 3:12–13; 4:1), Paul had **confidence in the Lord** that they would **continue to do what** he taught them. As their pastor, he had spent much time explaining the Word of God, and in so doing he had the authority to **command** that they obey it (cf. 1 Tim. 4:11).

Scripture is replete with such commands for obedience. In fact, David described the entirety of God's Word as a command: "The commandment of the Lord is pure, enlightening the eyes" (Ps. 19:8). In the Great Commission, Jesus defined as commands the many things He taught, and He expected believers to obey them: "Teaching them to observe all that I commanded you" (Matt. 28:20). Even the gospel contains the twofold command to repent and believe (Mark 1:15; cf. 6:12; Matt. 3:2; 4:17; Acts 2:38; 3:19; 17:30; 26:20). Thus it is the duty of all believers, as it was for the church at Thessalonica, to obediently follow the divine commands (Scripture) their pastor gives them—whether he is present or absent (cf. 2 Cor. 10:1, 11; 13:2, 10; Phil. 2:12).

PASTORS DESIRE THEIR PEOPLE TO GROW SPIRITUALLY

May the Lord direct your hearts into the love of God and into the steadfastness of Christ. (3:5)

Because of his confidence in God's faithfulness to His elect, and based on their delight in obeying God's commands (1 Thess. 1:3, 6–8; 2 Thess. 1:3–4), Paul anticipated the best from the Thessalonians. But he desired that they continue in their spiritual growth, so he asked that **the Lord direct** their **hearts** toward that objective. **Direct,** "make straight," is the same word (*kateuthunō*) used in 1 Thessalonians 3:11 to indicate the removing of all obstacles and hindrances as someone opened a pathway or road. Paul did not want their spiritual progress to come to a halt, but rather that **the Lord** would clear the way so their **hearts** or inner persons would move **into the love of God.**

The phrase **of God** in the Greek can be either an objective or subjective genitive: **into** God's **love** for the believer, or the believer's **love** for God. The Greek grammar provided Paul with a certain ambiguity of expression so that he could convey a complete, well-rounded sense of truth to the Thessalonians. In this context, therefore, the phrase is probably both objective and subjective. J. B. Lightfoot noted, "The Apostles availed themselves . . . of the vagueness or rather comprehensiveness of language, to express a great spiritual truth" (cited in Leon Morris, *The First and Second Epistles to the Thessalonians, The New International Commentary on the New Testament* [Grand Rapids: Eerdmans, 1989], 249). Paul desired that his audience go down the pathway deeper and deeper into God's love for them, which in turn would cause them to love Him more and more.

Second, the apostle desired that God would **direct** the Thessalonians' **hearts** to grow stronger in **the steadfastness of Christ.** That phrase also contains a certain degree of ambiguity in meaning. Paul could have referred either to Christ's **steadfastness** (*hupomonē,* also rendered "patience," as in "patient enduring") with believers, or believers' patience in His strength, through their endurance. Paul wanted the Thessalonians to increasingly understand how patient Christ was with their sins, problems, and struggles and to understand better His own endurance in trials (cf. Matt. 4:1–11; 26:59–68; Luke 22:39–53; John 18:33–38; 19:1–11), so that they would have greater spiritual endurance (cf. Heb. 2:17–18; 4:15–16). He desired that they learn from their Savior's example and move forward in love and patience under persecution (cf. Matt. 5:10–12; Rom. 12:12; Gal. 6:9; Eph. 6:18; Col. 1:23; 2 Tim. 3:12; Heb. 3:6, 14; 6:10–11, 19; 12:2–3; 1 Peter 4:13).

So in this passage, the apostle Paul provides an excellent example of genuine pastoral concern that his people prosper spiritually and thereby contribute to the edification and glorification of Christ's church. No shepherd of a local congregation could ask more from his flock than that they pray for him, trust in the Lord, obey what is taught from the Word, and grow spiritually.

Work: A Noble Christian Duty (2 Thessalonians 3:6–15) 26

Now we command you, brethren, in the name of our Lord Jesus Christ, that you keep away from every brother who leads an unruly life and not according to the tradition which you received from us. For you yourselves know how you ought to follow our example, because we did not act in an undisciplined manner among you, nor did we eat anyone's bread without paying for it, but with labor and hardship we kept working night and day so that we would not be a burden to any of you; not because we do not have the right to this, but in order to offer ourselves as a model for you, so that you would follow our example. For even when we were with you, we used to give you this order: if anyone is not willing to work, then he is not to eat, either. For we hear that some among you are leading an undisciplined life, doing no work at all, but acting like busybodies. Now such persons we command and exhort in the Lord Jesus Christ to work in quiet fashion and eat their own bread. But as for you, brethren, do not grow weary of doing good. If anyone does not obey our instruction in this letter, take special note of that person and do not associate with him, so that he will be put to shame. Yet do not regard him as an enemy, but admonish him as a brother. (3:6–15)

As he so often does in his epistles Paul returns from the lofty heights of theological instruction (chaps. 1 and 2) to the basics of practical Christian living. For Paul, theology was not merely abstract reasoning, but practical truth to affect daily life. In this passage, he discusses the universally practical issue of work.

People from Paul's day to the present have had a wrong view of work. In fact, our society proudly displays its skewed view of work on the back of its cars. "I owe, I owe, so off to work I go," reads one bumper sticker, reflecting the view that work is a necessary evil; nothing more than a way to pay off debts and fund one's lifestyle. Another, extolling the virtue of laziness, proclaims, "Work fascinates me—I can sit and watch it for hours." License plate frames announce that people would rather be fishing, flying, RVing, golfing, skiing, sailing, hiking, camping, four wheeling—anything but working. In our materialistic, self-indulgent society, many people play at their work and work at their play. Others work only to achieve prosperity, success, fame, and early retirement.

Such perspectives rob work of any intrinsic value. In essentially valueless work, people display that disdain for the effort itself in doing only enough to avoid being fired, getting away with whatever cheating they can, considering long hours and hard work to be counterproductive, remaining loyal to their opportunity and employer only until they get what they perceive as a better, more lucrative opportunity, and in general showing utter indifference to the quality of their work.

Throughout history, cultures have denigrated the value of work. Even in Jewish thinking, doing menial labor was inferior to studying God's law. One rabbi expressed that view in the following prayer:

> I thank thee, O Lord, my God, that thou hast given me my lot with those who sit in the house of learning, and not with those who sit at the street corners; for I am early to work and they are early to work; I am early to work on the words of the Torah, and they are early to work on things of no moment. I weary myself, and they weary themselves; I weary myself and profit thereby, and they weary themselves to no profit. I run, and they run; I run towards the life of the age to come, and they run towards the pit of destruction. (Cited in Leland Ryken, *Work and Leisure in Christian Perspective* [Portland, Ore.: Multnomah, 1987], 65–66)

Many cultured Greeks and Romans also viewed manual labor as beneath their dignity, fit only for slaves or the lower classes. Aristotle declared working as a craftsman or a trader to be "devoid of nobility and hostile to perfection of character" (cited in Ryken, 64). In a similar vein the Roman author Cicero wrote, "The toil of a hired worker, who is paid only for his toil and not for artistic skill, is unworthy of a free man and is sordid in character.... Trade on a small retail scale is also sordid" (cited in Ryken, 65).

A low view of work also found its way into the church. The church father Eusebius wrote,

> Two ways of life were thus given by the law of Christ to His Church. The one is above nature, and beyond common human living; . . . wholly and permanently separate from the common customary life of mankind, it devotes itself to the service of God alone. . . . Such then is the perfect form of the Christian life. (*The Proof of the Gospel*, I, 8)

For Eusebius, first-class Christians serve God alone; second-class Christians engage in secular employment. That dichotomy between secular and sacred occupations reached its full flower in the monasticism of the Middle Ages. It was not until the Reformation that Luther, Calvin, and the other Reformers restored work to its God-given place of dignity.

Like any other aspect of life, work viewed apart from God appears to have little value. In Ecclesiastes Solomon asked:

> What advantage does man have in all his work which he does under the sun? (1:3)

> For what does a man get in all his labor and in his striving with which he labors under the sun? (2:22)

> What profit is there to the worker from that in which he toils? (3:9)

> This also is a grievous evil—exactly as a man is born, thus will he die. So what is the advantage to him who toils for the wind? (5:16)

Seeing it from a purely human perspective, Solomon argued that work is futile:

> Thus I considered all my activities which my hands had done and the labor which I had exerted, and behold all was vanity and striving after wind and there was no profit under the sun. . . . Thus I hated all the fruit of my labor for which I had labored under the sun, for I must leave it to the man who will come after me. (2:11, 18)

> I have seen that every labor and every skill which is done is the result of rivalry between a man and his neighbor. This too is vanity and striving after wind. . . . There was a certain man without a dependent, having neither a son nor a brother, yet there was no end to all his labor. Indeed, his eyes were not satisfied with riches and he never asked, "And for whom am I laboring and depriving myself of pleasure?" This too is vanity and it is a grievous task. (4:4, 8)

> As he had come naked from his mother's womb, so will he return as he came. He will take nothing from the fruit of his labor that he can carry in his hand. This also is a grievous evil—exactly as a man is born, thus will he die. So what is the advantage to him who toils for the wind? (5:15–16)

> All a man's labor is for his mouth and yet the appetite is not satisfied. (6:7)

It is only when work is viewed from God's perspective that its value may be seen:

> There is nothing better for a man than to eat and drink and tell himself that his labor is good. This also I have seen that it is from the hand of God. (2:24)

> Every man who eats and drinks sees good in all his labor—it is the gift of God. (3:13)

> Furthermore, as for every man to whom God has given riches and wealth, He has also empowered him to eat from them and to receive his reward and rejoice in his labor; this is the gift of God. For he will not often consider the years of his life, because God keeps him occupied with the gladness of his heart. (5:19–20)

The Christian faith, however, does not accept any utilitarian work ethic. There is no such thing as a secular job for a Christian; all work is a spiritual duty to be done as an opportunity to give glory to God (1 Cor. 10:31). The Christian view of work affirms several truths.

First, God exalted work by commanding it. It is often ignored that the familiar fourth commandment not only prescribes the keeping of the Sabbath on the seventh day, but work on the other six (Ex. 20:9). That is God's command as much as the day of rest. Its importance is clear from its inclusion in the Decalogue.

Second, God Himself sets the example of work for all to follow. God works in Creation (Gen. 1:1), preservation (Heb. 1:3), providence (1 Chron. 29:11), judgment (Acts 17:31), and redemption (Gal. 4:4–5). The Lord Jesus Christ is also working: by redeeming people (Gal. 3:13), building His church (Matt. 16:18), interceding for His people (Rom. 8:34), and preparing a place in heaven for them (John 14:1–3). Likewise, the Holy Spirit works by convicting sinners (John 16:8), regenerating them (Titus 3:5), and indwelling them (2 Tim. 1:14).

Third, work is a feature of the creation mandate and is therefore a normal part of man's existence. The psalmist expressed that truth in Psalm 104:14: "He causes the grass to grow for the cattle, and vegetation for the labor of man, so that he may bring forth food from the earth." That man should work to produce food is a part of the natural course of events: "Man goes forth to his work and to his labor until evening" (v. 23). Work is not a result of the curse, since God commanded Adam to work in the Garden before the Fall (Gen. 2:15). The Fall did not initiate work, but cursed it (Gen. 3:17–19), making it laborious and painful.

Fourth, work is a gift from God. Man's occupation with it provides development of skill and productivity, significant contribution, value, meaning, and fulfillment in life. It also prevents idleness which, as clearly seen in the indolent of every society, is debilitating and destructive. It is well said that "idle hands are the devil's workshop." God also gave work to man as a means of demonstrating the image of God in him, who by work is providing for the needs of all in his care. God's gift of work grants the satisfaction of serving the needs of other people.

Finally, the biblical work ethic affirms that all work can be elevated above the mundane by being done for the Lord Himself. In Ephesians 6:5–7 Paul commanded:

> Slaves [employees], be obedient to those who are your masters according to the flesh [employers], with fear and trembling, in the sincerity of your heart, as to Christ; not by way of eyeservice, as menpleasers, but as slaves of Christ, doing the will of God from the heart. With good will render service, as to the Lord, and not to men.

Some of the Thessalonian believers were not living consistently with this biblical view of work. They were causing strife in the church by refusing to work and leeching off the rest of the congregation. Paul does not reveal what their motives were. They may have been influenced by the prevailing Greek and Jewish views of work, noted above, and felt it was beneath their dignity. Perhaps they believed that since Christ could return at any moment, work was pointless. Or they may just have been lazy (the Bible condemns laziness in such passages as Prov. 10:26; 12:27; 15:19; 24:30–34). Paul did not mention their motives for failing to work because none of them are valid; there is no excuse for someone who has the ability and opportunity to work not to do so.

Since this was the third time that Paul had had to deal with this issue (3:10; 1 Thess. 4:11–12), he bluntly and directly confronts those who stubbornly refused to work. This passage contains six incentives to motivate those sinning to repent and get to work: disfellowship, example, survival, harmony, shame, and love.

DISFELLOWSHIP

Now we command you, brethren, in the name of our Lord Jesus Christ, that you keep away from every brother who leads an unruly life and not according to the tradition which you received from us. (3:6)

Since those refusing to work had obstinately disregarded his instruction while he was there (3:10) and his exhortation in his first letter (4:11–12; 5:14), Paul here issued a stern **command** regarding them. The Greek verb translated **we command** is in the emphatic position in the sentence; Paul was not offering a suggestion, but issuing an order. This **command** was not based on his, Silas's, and Timothy's authority; it was issued **in the name of our Lord Jesus Christ** and carried the full weight of His authority. Therefore it was to be obeyed instantly and unquestioningly.

When Paul ordered the Thessalonians to **keep away from every brother** who refused to work he was commanding them to shun them. And there were to be no exceptions. As previously noted, there is no valid excuse for anyone who is able to work and has the opportunity to do so to be idle. The verb translated **keep away** is a form of the verb *stellō* which, when used in the middle voice, means, "to avoid," "shun," or "pull back from." Paul commanded the rest of the congregation to separate from and ostracize **every** idle **brother.**

In the context of Matthew 18, this is the third step in the process of church discipline. Step one is to confront the sinning believer privately; step two is to confront him again with two or three witnesses present; step three is to tell the offense to the congregation and cut the offender off from the normal life of the church. For those who persist in sinning after the first three steps, step four is to remove them from the fellowship altogether (treat them as unbelievers; Matt. 18:17). Since a disciplined sinner was still to be regarded as a **brother** (cf. 3:15), this disfellowshiping stopped short of the complete and final (barring repentance) excommunication of step four.

Those who refused to work were placed in the category of those guilty of leading **an unruly life.** In a military sense, *ataktōs* (**unruly**) refers to "being out of rank," "out of line," or "out of order." It was also used in extrabiblical Greek writings to refer to apprentices being truant from work (William Barclay, *The Letters to the Philippians, Colossians, and Thessalonians*, rev. ed. [Louisville, Ky.: Westminster, 1975], 217–18). Paul described the **unruly** in verse 11 (the only other time the word appears in the New Testament) as "doing no work at all, but acting like busybodies."

Such idle, lazy, out-of-line behavior was definitely **not according**

to the tradition which the Thessalonians had **received.** As noted in the discussion of 2:15 in chapter 24 of this volume, **tradition** (lit.,"something handed down") refers to divine revelation given through the apostles. The concept of an extrabiblical body of tradition equal in authority to Scripture is foreign to the New Testament (cf. 2 Tim. 3:16–17). The inspired **tradition** they had **received** from Paul, both orally (3:10) and in writing (1 Thess. 4:11–12), forbade idleness. Therefore, those who refused to work were guilty of rejecting God's Word.

That the indolent believers faced church discipline shows the seriousness with which God views failing to work. Since true believers cherish the fellowship of other believers, being cut off from it should be painful enough to effect a change in their behavior. The drastic step of church discipline was also necessary to protect the church's reputation with outsiders. The world must also know that God does not tolerate indolence and laziness.

EXAMPLE

For you yourselves know how you ought to follow our example, because we did not act in an undisciplined manner among you, nor did we eat anyone's bread without paying for it, but with labor and hardship we kept working night and day so that we would not be a burden to any of you; not because we do not have the right to this, but in order to offer ourselves as a model for you, so that you would follow our example. (3:7–9,)

The apostle Paul would have agreed wholeheartedly with the statement of the Puritan Thomas Brooks, "Example is the most powerful rhetoric" (cited in I. D. E. Thomas, *A Puritan Golden Treasury* [Carlisle, Penn.: Banner of Truth, 1977], 96). Therefore, he bracketed this section with the phrase **you . . . follow our example.** The Greek verb used in both instances is a form of the verb *mimeomai;* the related noun is the source of the English word *mimic.* Paul was an example for the Thessalonians to imitate because he himself imitated the Lord Jesus Christ (1 Cor. 11:1). He was a model of gospel preaching (1 Thess. 1:6), enduring suffering (2:2), honesty and integrity (2:3–5), humility (2:6), gentleness (2:7), affection (2:8), self-sacrifice (2:8), holiness (2:10), and prayer (3:10). Just as they followed his example in those areas (1:6), they needed to follow his example of hard work (2:9).

The phrase **you yourselves know** appeals to the Thessalonians' firsthand knowledge of the missionaries' exemplary behavior (cf. 1 Thess. 2:1; 3:3; 5:2; Acts 20:18,34); they **did not act in an undisciplined manner.**

The Greek verb translated **act in an undisciplined manner** is related to the word translated "unruly" in verse 6 and "undisciplined" in verse 11. The missionaries' industriousness was in sharp contrast to the lazy indolence of the idle members of the congregation. Reinforcing that contrast, Paul declared, **Nor did we eat anyone's bread without paying for it.** The phrase to **eat . . . bread** refers metaphorically to food and sustenance (cf. Gen. 3:19; 43:32; Amos 7:12; Matt. 15:2; Luke 14:15). Though they apparently stayed at Jason's house (Acts 17:7), the missionaries did not eat at his expense. They insisted on paying for their own food and perhaps their lodging; **with** strenuous **labor and hardship** they **kept working night and day so that** they **would not be a burden to any of** the Thessalonians—a truth the apostle had also reminded them of in his first epistle (1 Thess. 2:9; cf. Acts 20:34; 1 Cor. 4:12).

Paul made it clear that his reason for doing manual labor was **not because** he, Silas, and Timothy did **not have the right to** receive support for their intense work of preaching and teaching. He did not always forgo accepting support from the churches to which he ministered. In fact, the Philippians twice sent him a gift during his stay in Thessalonica (cf. Phil. 4:16), and he also received support from other churches while ministering in Corinth (2 Cor. 11:8–9). He particularly chose to work in Thessalonica so that those who refused to work could not point to his not working as justification for their idleness. Instead, the missionaries dignified work by offering themselves **as a model for** the believers to **follow.**

Paul plainly taught that as an apostle and preacher he was entitled to full support. In Galatians 6:6 he wrote, "The one who is taught the word is to share all good things with the one who teaches him." He instructed Timothy that "the elders who rule well are to be considered worthy of double honor, especially those who work hard at preaching and teaching" (1 Tim. 5:17). But his most detailed exposition of that principle is in 1 Corinthians 9:3–14:

> My defense to those who examine me is this: Do we not have a right to eat and drink? Do we not have a right to take along a believing wife, even as the rest of the apostles and the brothers of the Lord and Cephas? Or do only Barnabas and I not have a right to refrain from working? Who at any time serves as a soldier at his own expense? Who plants a vineyard and does not eat the fruit of it? Or who tends a flock and does not use the milk of the flock? I am not speaking these things according to human judgment, am I? Or does not the Law also say these things? For it is written in the Law of Moses, "You shall not muzzle the ox while he is threshing." God is not concerned about oxen, is He? Or is He speaking altogether for our sake? Yes, for our sake it was written, because the plowman ought to plow in hope, and the thresher

to thresh in hope of sharing the crops. If we sowed spiritual things in you, is it too much if we reap material things from you? If others share the right over you, do we not more? Nevertheless, we did not use this right, but we endure all things so that we will cause no hindrance to the gospel of Christ. Do you not know that those who perform sacred services eat the food of the temple, and those who attend regularly to the altar have their share from the altar? So also the Lord directed those who proclaim the gospel to get their living from the gospel.

Paul began by asking a series of rhetorical questions, each demanding an affirmative answer. Just as he had a right to eat and drink (v. 4) and be married (v. 5), he also had a right to refrain from physical labor and give himself totally to the hard work of ministry (v. 6). The apostle then presented a series of analogies to further demonstrate his point (v. 7). Soldiers have a right to have their expenses paid; those who plant vineyards have a right to the fruit they produce; those who tend flocks have a right to what they produce. Using the proverbial illustration of an ox threshing grain, the Law teaches that those who minister are to be cared for (vv. 8–10). Those who pour their lives into ministering to, teaching, and nurturing others have the right to expect their support (vv. 11–14).

Since Paul humbly labored to meet his needs in addition to his ministry, how could anyone else justify not doing so? But despite all of Paul's hard work to be a godly model for them, some still refused to work. For them, stern measures were in order.

SURVIVAL

For even when we were with you, we used to give you this order: if anyone is not willing to work, then he is not to eat, either. (3:10)

To the missionaries' example, Paul added a pointed command. The divinely revealed, authoritative, axiomatic truth that those who are **not willing to work** are **not to eat** was not new to the saints. Ignorance was not their problem, **for even when** the missionaries **were with** them, they **used to give** them that **order.** Paul had also discussed this issue in his first epistle (4:11; 5:14). His point is simple: if people get hungry enough, they will work to get food. As Solomon put it, "A worker's appetite works for him, for his hunger urges him on" (Prov. 16:26). Believers who have the opportunity and the ability to work for their own food are to do so. Those who do not are worse than unbelievers (1 Tim. 5:8).

It is important to note that Paul addresses here the issue of those **not willing to work,** not those unable to work. Both individual believers and the church as a whole have a responsibility to care for the poor

(Matt. 6:2, 3; Gal. 2:10; 1 Tim. 5:4; Heb. 13:16; James 2:15–16; 1 John 3:17). But neither the world nor the church owes a living to those too lazy to work. We are used to "entitlements" in our society. This is the idea that those who will not work hard are entitled to be paid money taken from those who do. The results of the welfare culture are visible for all to see—family breakups, immorality, crime, hopelessness, meaninglessness, and bitterness.

HARMONY

For we hear that some among you are leading an undisciplined life, doing no work at all, but acting like busybodies. Now such persons we command and exhort in the Lord Jesus Christ to work in quiet fashion and eat their own bread. But as for you, brethren, do not grow weary of doing good. (3:11–13)

Word had come to Paul that despite his exhortations, both in person (3:10) and in writing (1 Thess. 4:11–12), some in the congregation were still unwilling to work. How he was able to **hear** about those **leading an undisciplined life** is not known, but somehow news of the continuing problem reached Corinth from Thessalonica. *Ataktōs* (**undisciplined**) is the same word translated "unruly" in verse 6. The **undisciplined** were **doing no work at all, but acting like busybodies.** There is a play on words in the Greek; Paul says they were not *ergazomenous,* but *periergazomenous;* "not busy, but busybodies." Not content with refusing to work productively, they used their unoccupied time to wander around interfering in the lives of others in the church (cf. 1 Tim. 5:13). The nonworkers were an irritant, creating disunity and discord by being a burden on those who did work. That was beginning to affect the loving harmony and effective witness of the assembly of faith.

Now such persons, writes Paul, **we** strongly **command and** gently **exhort in the Lord Jesus Christ to work in quiet fashion and eat their own bread.** A corollary to the familiar Pauline concept of being **in the Lord Jesus Christ** (cf. Rom. 8:1; 16:3, 7; 1 Cor. 1:30; 2 Cor. 5:17) is the unity of those united with Him (Rom. 12:5; 1 Thess. 2:14). To preserve that precious unity, the indolent members of the flock were commanded **to work in quiet fashion and eat their own bread.** They were to settle down, stop meddling in other people's affairs, and begin leading an ordered life of quiet, consistent work. By so doing they would cease being a burden and become a blessing, thereby promoting harmony in the church.

Paul encouraged the rest of the **brethren** who were faithfully working **not** to **grow weary of doing good** (cf. Gal. 6:9). The danger was that they would **grow weary** of the deadbeats and become indifferent to real needs. As noted above, God's people must not ignore their responsibility to care for those in need. David wrote, "The righteous is gracious and gives. . . . All day long he is gracious and lends" (Ps. 37:21, 26). In Psalm 41:1 he added, "How blessed is he who considers the helpless" (cf. Ps. 112:9). Solomon was also aware of the need to care for the poor: "He who gives to the poor will never want, but he who shuts his eyes will have many curses" (Prov. 28:27). In Isaiah 58:7, God commends those who "divide [their] bread with the hungry and bring the homeless poor into the house." In Luke 14:12–14 Jesus said,

> And He also went on to say to the one who had invited Him, "When you give a luncheon or a dinner, do not invite your friends or your brothers or your relatives or rich neighbors, otherwise they may also invite you in return and that will be your repayment. But when you give a reception, invite the poor, the crippled, the lame, the blind, and you will be blessed, since they do not have the means to repay you; for you will be repaid at the resurrection of the righteous."

Paul reminded the Ephesian elders, "In everything I showed you that by working hard in this manner you must help the weak and remember the words of the Lord Jesus, that He Himself said, 'It is more blessed to give than to receive'" (Acts 20:35). The prescription for church unity was for the nonworkers to go to work, and for the entire congregation to care for those in genuine need. Obviously, this was directed at the men who had the responsibility to provide for their families, while the women kept the home (cf. Titus 2:3–5). Even young widows were to marry husbands who would rescue them from being busybodies (cf. 1 Tim. 5:11–14).

SHAME

If anyone does not obey our instruction in this letter, take special note of that person and do not associate with him, so that he will be put to shame. (3:14)

Since this was the third time Paul had dealt with this issue, **anyone** who still refused to **obey** his **instruction in this letter** was being sinfully obstinate. Therefore, he commanded the rest of the assembly to take **special note of** such a **person.** He was to be marked out for serious attention—the rest of the congregation was **not** to **associate with him.** The strong double compound verb _sunanamignumi_ (**associate with**) literally means, "to mix up together with." The church individually and collectively was to withdraw fellowship from such persons and avoid them. They were probably to be denied the privilege of taking communion. Surely they were not to be allowed to participate in the love feast, since feeding them a meal would condone and perpetuate their indolent behavior. The pressure of isolation was to be brought to bear on them to produce repentance.

The purpose of this third step in the church discipline process (cf. the discussion of v. 6 above) is that those who refuse to work **will be put to shame.** The verb translated **be put to shame** is a form of the verb *entrepō,* which literally means, "to turn in on oneself." The idea is that isolation from the fellowship would cause the sinning believers to reflect on their condition, see themselves for the wicked, recalcitrant sinners that they were, be ashamed, and change their behavior. The repentance and restoration of the sinning member is always the goal of church discipline.

LOVE

Yet do not regard him as an enemy, but admonish him as a brother. (3:15)

Since this is not yet the fourth and final stage of the discipline process, the faithful members of the assembly must **not regard** the one being disciplined **as an enemy** (cf. Matt. 18:17). Since he had not yet been put out of the fellowship (1 Cor. 5:2) and delivered to Satan (1 Cor. 5:5; 1 Tim. 1:20), the congregation was not yet to treat him "as a Gentile and a tax collector" (Matt. 18:17), but to **admonish him as a brother.**

This point provides a much-needed balance to the discipline process, noting that the motive for disciplining sinning believers is love. Galatians 6:1 gives the proper attitude for those engaged in the discipline process: "Brethren, even if anyone is caught in any trespass, you who are spiritual, restore such a one in a spirit of gentleness; each one looking to yourself, so that you too will not be tempted."

Our culture's work ethic has eroded, but the biblical work ethic remains constant. When Christians diligently pursue the vocation to which God has called them, God is honored. Therefore, "All who are under the yoke as slaves are to regard their own masters as worthy of all honor so that the name of God and our doctrine will not be spoken against" (1 Tim. 6:1).

A Prayer for Divine Enablement (2 Thessalonians 3:16–18) **27**

Now may the Lord of peace Himself continually grant you peace in every circumstance. The Lord be with you all! I, Paul, write this greeting with my own hand, and this is a distinguishing mark in every letter; this is the way I write. The grace of our Lord Jesus Christ be with you all. (3:16–18)

This brief letter has been filled with high drama. Its three short chapters have described God's retribution on the wicked rejecters of the Lord Jesus Christ, and their eternal destruction in hell (1:6–10). It has discussed God's judgment of the sinful world in the Day of the Lord (2:1–2). It has also predicted the coming of the final Antichrist, the blasphemous abomination of desolation he will commit, and his ultimate destruction at the return of Jesus Christ (2:3–12). It has warned of deceiving wolves in sheep's clothing (2:2–3) and rebuked lazy Christians (3:6–15). In short, it has up to this point been a tempestuous letter. But this concluding passage is like the calm sea after a violent storm.

The Thessalonian church, so strong in many ways, had been tormented by persecution, false doctrine, fear, and sin. In the main body of this letter, Paul gave them detailed instructions for dealing with those issues. But he knew that no matter how well they understood the information he had given them, they could not implement it in their own strength. Therefore, he periodically punctuated this letter's instruction with pleas that God would enable believers to conform to it. After instructing them about the coming of Christ in judgment, bringing eternal destruction on the wicked (1:5–10), Paul wrote:

> To this end also we pray for you always, that our God will count you worthy of your calling, and fulfill every desire for goodness and the work of faith with power, so that the name of our Lord Jesus will be glorified in you, and you in Him, according to the grace of our God and the Lord Jesus Christ. (1:11–12)

After his discussion of the Day of the Lord and the rise and fall of the final Antichrist (2:1–15), Paul once again closed a section of exhortation with a prayer: "Now may our Lord Jesus Christ Himself and God our Father, who has loved us and given us eternal comfort and good hope by grace, comfort and strengthen your hearts in every good work and word" (2:16–17).

In chapter 3, Paul asked the Thessalonians to pray for his effective ministry and for protection from his enemies (vv. 1–2). He then instructed them about God's faithfulness and urged them to continue to obey what he had taught them (vv. 3–4). That section closed with the prayer, "May the Lord direct your hearts into the love of God and into the steadfastness of Christ" (v. 5).

Verses 6–15 discussed the problem of those who refused to work and detailed the church's responsibility to discipline them. Then, for the fourth time in this epistle, the apostle expressed the desire of his heart in a prayerful benediction to God for them (vv. 16–18) that He would energize their spiritual maturity.

De (**Now**) marks a transition, as Paul moves from command and exhortation (vv. 6–15) to benediction and prayer (vv. 16–18). This passage does not record an actual prayer, but rather expresses the desire of his heart that constantly rises as a cry for God's blessing. He calls upon God to grant four blessings that are essential for spiritual maturity: peace, strength, truth, and grace.

PEACE

Now may the Lord of peace Himself continually grant you peace in every circumstance. (3:16*a*)

Paul's first request here, as in his other letters (cf. 2 Cor. 13:11; Eph. 6:23), is for that highly prized, yet elusive reality, **peace.** The world defines **peace** as the sense of calm, tranquility, quietness, contentment, and well-being that comes when everything is going well. But that definition, frankly, is shallow. A calm, tranquil feeling can be produced by lies, self-deception, unexpected good fortune, the absence of conflict and trouble, biofeedback, drugs, alcohol, even a good night's sleep. Such peace is fleeting and easily destroyed. It can be shattered by the arrival of conflict and trouble, as well as by failure, doubt, fear, bitterness, anger, pride, difficulty, guilt, regret, sorrow, anxiety over circumstances beyond one's control, being disappointed or mistreated by others, making bad decisions—in short, by any perceived threat to one's security.

But true spiritual **peace** is completely different from the superficial, ephemeral, fragile human peace. It is the deep, settled confidence that all is well between the soul and God because of His loving, sovereign control of one's life both in time and eternity. That calm assurance is based on the knowledge that sins are forgiven, blessing is present, good is abundant even in trouble, and heaven is ahead. The peace that God gives His beloved children as their possession and privilege has nothing to do with the circumstances of life.

That peace has several characteristics. First, it is divine, deriving from **the Lord of peace Himself.** The pronoun *autos* (**Himself**) stands in the emphatic first position in the Greek text. The God who is peace grants peace to believers. It is the very essence of His nature, one of His attributes. God is at all times at perfect peace, without any discord within Himself. He is never under stress, worried, anxious, fearful, unsure, or threatened. He is always perfectly calm, tranquil, and content. There are no surprises for His omniscience, no changes for His immutability, no threats to His sovereignty, no doubts to cloud His wisdom, no sin to stain His holiness. Even His wrath is clear, controlled, calm, and confident.

Scripture makes it clear that peace characterizes and flows from every member of the Trinity. "God of peace" is a common title for the Father (e.g., Judg. 6:24; Rom. 15:33; 16:20; 1 Cor. 14:33; 2 Cor. 13:11; Phil. 4:9; 1 Thess. 5:23; Heb. 13:20). First Thessalonians 5:23 calls the Father "the God of Peace"; Jesus Christ is here called **the Lord of peace.** Taken together, the two passages reveal Christ's deity and equality with the Father, since both are the source of peace. Isaiah 9:6 gives Him the title "Prince of Peace"; speaking of Christ, Ephesians 2:14 says, "He Himself is our peace." The Holy Spirit is also the source of **peace. Peace** is part of the fruit of the Spirit (Gal. 5:22), while Paul wrote in Romans 14:17, "The kingdom of God is not eating and drinking, but righteousness and peace and joy in the Holy Spirit."

In the perfectly harmonious working of the Trinity, the Father decreed peace, the Son purchased it (cf. Acts 10:36; Rom. 5:1; Col. 1:20), and the Holy Spirit brings it.

Second, divine peace is a gift from God. It is His good pleasure to graciously **grant** it to those who belong to Him. The priestly blessing of Israel reads in part, "The Lord lift up His countenance on you, and give you peace" (Num. 6:26). In Psalm 29:11 David declared, "The Lord will bless His people with peace," while Psalm 85:8 adds that "God the Lord ... will speak peace to His people, to His godly ones." In Isaiah 57:19 God Himself promises "Peace, peace to him who is far and to him who is near" (cf. Isa. 26:3, 12). Paul prayed, "Now may the God of hope fill you with all joy and peace in believing" (Rom. 15:13). Peace also comes from the Lord Jesus Christ, who promised, "Peace I leave with you; My peace I give to you" (John 14:27; cf. 16:33; 20:19, 21, 26). Peace is such an integral part of the New Testament that it appears in the greetings of all of Paul's epistles, as well as in 1 Peter, 2 Peter, 2 John, 3 John, Jude, and Revelation.

God does not give true spiritual peace to unbelievers, for it is a feature of salvation (Rom. 15:13). Isaiah 48:22 bluntly states, "There is no peace for the wicked,' says the Lord" (cf. 57:21; Jer. 6:14; 8:11; Ezek. 13:10, 16). The peace the wicked experience is the false peace of delusion. The Puritan pastor Thomas Watson wrote:

> Peace flows from sanctification, but they being unregenerate, have nothing to do with peace. . . . They may have a truce, but no peace. God may forbear the wicked a while, and stop the roaring of his cannon; but though there be a truce, yet there is no peace. The wicked may have something which looks like peace, but it is not. They may be fearless and stupid; but there is a great difference between a stupefied conscience, and a pacified conscience. . . . This is the devil's peace; he rocks men in the cradle of security; he cries peace, peace, when men are on the precipice of hell. The seeming peace a sinner has, is not from the knowledge of his happiness, but the ignorance of his danger. (*Body of Divinity* [reprint; Grand Rapids: Baker, 1979], 182)

The false peace of the unregenerate also has several components. It is the peace of presumption. It is based on pride, not truth, stemming from thinking oneself to be worthy before God. Those who have it are under the mistaken notion that God will accept them because they are good people. It lulls those headed for hell into a false sense that all will be well.

In addition, the false peace of those who are enemies of God separates peace and holiness—two realities that God has joined. Psalm 85:10 affirms that true peace is inseparably linked with holiness when it declares, "Righteousness and peace have kissed each other." Isaiah 32:17 adds, "The work of righteousness will be peace." Only a foolish, deceived man could boast,"I have peace though I walk in the stubbornness of my heart" (Deut. 29:19). Watson notes, "You may as well suck health out of poison, as peace out of sin" (*Body of Divinity,* 183).

Furthermore, unlike true peace, which grows stronger through trials, false peace cannot survive the tests of life. Trouble severely shakes it and leaves it in despair. The false peace enjoyed by unbelievers will be of no comfort when the Day of the Lord comes: "While they are saying, 'Peace and safety!' then destruction will come upon them suddenly like labor pains upon a woman with child, and they will not escape" (1 Thess. 5:3).

A third element of the divine peace that God gives to believers is that it is **continually** available. Why then does Paul pray for believers to experience it? Because though true peace is always available it can be interrupted. Weak or disobedient Christians may find their peace disturbed by the same sins, doubts, fears, and anxieties that destroy the false peace of the unredeemed.

How may a believer's interrupted peace be restored? First, by trusting God. In Psalm 42:11 the psalmist asked himself, "Why are you in despair, O my soul? And why have you become disturbed within me? Hope in God, for I shall yet praise Him, the help of my countenance and my God" (cf. v. 5; 43:5).

Second, peace that is forfeited by sin can be restored by repentant obedience. God promised Israel, "If you walk in My statutes and keep My commandments so as to carry them out . . . I shall also grant peace in the land" (Lev. 26:3, 6). To the Romans Paul wrote that there will be "glory and honor and peace to everyone who does good" (Rom. 2:10). "If you would have peace," counseled Thomas Watson, "make war with sin" (*Body of Divinity,* 185).

Third, peace may be restored by accepting God's chastening:

> Behold, how happy is the man whom God reproves, so do not despise the discipline of the Almighty. For He inflicts pain, and gives relief; He wounds, and His hands also heal. From six troubles He will deliver you, even in seven evil will not touch you. In famine He will redeem you from death, and in war from the power of the sword. You will be hidden from the scourge of the tongue, and you will not be afraid of violence when it comes. You will laugh at violence and famine, and you will not be afraid of wild beasts. For you will be in league with the stones of the field, and the beasts of the field will be at peace with you. You will know that your tent is secure, for you will visit your abode and fear no loss. (Job 5:17–24)

Fourth, peace may be restored by walking in the Spirit, since peace is an element of the fruit of the Spirit (Gal. 5:22).

Fifth, peace may be restored by loving God from the heart and avoiding legalism. In Galatians 6:16 Paul wrote,"And those who will walk by this rule [by faith in the power of the Spirit], peace and mercy be upon them."

Sixth, those whose peace has been interrupted need to pray that the God of peace and the Prince of Peace will restore it.

A fourth element of the divine peace that God continually gives the redeemed is that it exists **in every circumstance.** It is unaffected by anything in the worldly realm because it is based on the promise of eternal salvation (Heb. 5:9) made by the God who cannot lie (Titus 1:2). It is anchored in the reality that "He who began a good work in [believers] will perfect it until the day of Christ Jesus" (Phil. 1:6). This unbreakable, unassailable, transcendent peace, so utterly unlike worldly peace (John 14:27), stabilizes the Christian in every situation (cf. Phil. 4:7).

Paul longed for God to grant the Thessalonians peace so that no matter what their circumstances were, they would experience settled confidence and unshakable joy amid the storms of life.

STRENGTH

The Lord be with you all! (3:16b)

At first glance, this seems like a puzzling statement; since God is omnipresent (cf. Ps. 139:7–12), how could He not **be with** them **all?** But Paul did not have some benign sense of God's presence in mind, but rather His presence to empower believers to live for His glory. The psalmist rejoiced over that strengthening presence in Psalm 46:1:"God is our refuge and strength, a very present help in trouble." It was His enabling presence that the Lord Jesus Christ spoke of in Matthew 28:20 when He said, "I am with you always, even to the end of the age." He promised the Twelve, shocked and saddened by the revelation that He would soon be leaving them,

> I will ask the Father, and He will give you another Helper, that He may be with you forever; that is the Spirit of truth, whom the world cannot receive, because it does not see Him or know Him, but you know Him because He abides with you and will be in you. I will not leave you as orphans; I will come to you. (John 14:16–18; cf. Acts 1:8)

Believers need God's strengthening presence for several reasons. First, it enables them to resist temptation. First Corinthians 10:13 promises,"No temptation has overtaken you but such as is common to man; and God is faithful, who will not allow you to be tempted beyond what you are able, but with the temptation will provide the way of escape also, so that you will be able to endure it." Christ's strength will open up the path for believers to flee temptation.

Second, believers need God's strength to face Satan and his demon hordes. In Ephesians 6:10–13 Paul instructed Christians how to prepare for spiritual warfare:

> Finally, be strong in the Lord and in the strength of His might. Put on the full armor of God, so that you will be able to stand firm against the schemes of the devil. For our struggle is not against flesh and blood, but against the rulers, against the powers, against the world forces of this darkness, against the spiritual forces of wickedness in the heavenly places. Therefore, take up the full armor of God, so that you will be able to resist in the evil day, and having done everything, to stand firm.

Third, believers need God's strength to effectively serve Him. "I was made a minister," wrote Paul, "according to the gift of God's grace which was given to me according to the working of His power" (Eph. 3:7). To the Colossians he added, "For this purpose also I labor, striving according to His power, which mightily works within me" (Col. 1:29). He praised "Christ Jesus our Lord, who has strengthened me, because He considered me faithful, putting me into service" (1 Tim. 1:12). The writer of Hebrews expressed his wish for his readers that "the God of peace, . . . equip you in every good thing to do His will, working in us that which is pleasing in His sight" (Heb. 13:20–21).

Fourth, believers need God's strength to persevere. Paul wrote confidently to Timothy, "The Lord will rescue me from every evil deed, and will bring me safely to His heavenly kingdom; to Him be the glory forever and ever. Amen" (2 Tim. 4:18). Jude reminded his readers that God "is able to keep you from stumbling, and to make you stand in the presence of His glory blameless with great joy" (Jude 24).

Fifth, believers need God's strength to endure trials. Paul wrote in 2 Corinthians 12:9–10:

> And He has said to me, "My grace is sufficient for you, for power is perfected in weakness." Most gladly, therefore, I will rather boast about my weaknesses, so that the power of Christ may dwell in me. Therefore I am well content with weaknesses, with insults, with distresses, with persecutions, with difficulties, for Christ's sake; for when I am weak, then I am strong.

Sixth, believers need God's strength to effectively evangelize the lost world. Jesus said in Acts 1:8, "You will receive power when the Holy

Spirit has come upon you; and you shall be My witnesses both in Jerusalem, and in all Judea and Samaria, and even to the remotest part of the earth" (cf. Matt. 28:18–20). After his conversion Paul "kept increasing in strength and confounding the Jews who lived at Damascus by proving that this Jesus is the Christ" (Acts 9:22; cf. 18:9–10; 2 Tim. 4:17).

Paul's prayer in Ephesians 3:16–19 summarizes believers' need for God's power in every aspect of life. He prayed that God

> would grant you, according to the riches of His glory, to be strengthened with power through His Spirit in the inner man, so that Christ may dwell in your hearts through faith; and that you, being rooted and grounded in love, may be able to comprehend with all the saints what is the breadth and length and height and depth, and to know the love of Christ which surpasses knowledge, that you may be filled up to all the fullness of God.

Philippians 4:13 succinctly states, "I can do all things through Him who strengthens me." God provides all the strength necessary to serve and glorify Him to those who trust Him, obey Him, accept His chastening, walk in the Spirit, love Him from the heart, live by the Word, and faithfully pray.

TRUTH

I, Paul, write this greeting with my own hand, and this is a distinguishing mark in every letter; this is the way I write. (3:17)

Paul interrupts his benediction for the church, which resumes in verse 18, to deal with another vital issue. He was deeply concerned that they have God's truth. Since he was the agent of that truth, he did not want them confused about which were his authentic writings; therefore, he decided to **write this** closing **greeting with** his **own hand.**

As noted in the discussion of 2:2 in chapter 23 of this volume, false teachers had come to Thessalonica claiming that the Day of the Lord had arrived. They produced a forged letter supposedly from Paul to support their lies. They may also have denied the authenticity of his first epistle, since it contradicted their false teaching. Paul normally dictated his letters to an amanuensis (cf. Rom. 16:22), much like a modern business executive dictating a letter to his secretary. But to prevent forgery and affirm their authenticity, he apparently personally signed each of them (cf. 1 Cor. 16:21; Gal. 6:11; Col. 4:18; Philem. 19); his distinctive signature became the **distinguishing mark in every letter** he wrote.

As was the apostle John (2 John 4; 3 John 4), Paul was deeply concerned about truth. In 2 Corinthians 4:2 he wrote, "We have renounced the things hidden because of shame, not walking in craftiness or adulterating the word of God, but by the manifestation of truth commending ourselves to every man's conscience in the sight of God" (cf. 7:14; 12:6; 13:8). Because his many enemies often branded him a liar, Paul repeatedly affirmed that he spoke the truth: "I am telling the truth in Christ, I am not lying, my conscience testifies with me in the Holy Spirit" (Rom. 9:1); "As the truth of Christ is in me, this boasting of mine will not be stopped in the regions of Achaia" (2 Cor. 11:10); "For this I was appointed a preacher and an apostle (I am telling the truth, I am not lying) as a teacher of the Gentiles in faith and truth" (1 Tim. 2:7).

Just as God is the God of peace and strength, so also is He the God of truth (Ps. 31:5; Isa. 65:16; cf. 2 Chron. 15:3; Jer. 10:10; John 7:28; 17:3; 1 Thess. 1:9; 1 John 5:20; Rev. 6:10). His words are truth (2 Sam. 7:28), He is abundant in truth (Ps. 86:15), He is true even if all men are liars (Rom. 3:4), and He cannot lie (Num. 23:19; 1 Sam. 15:29; Titus 1:2; Heb. 6:18).

The Lord Jesus Christ, being God, is also the truth. John 1:14 describes Him as "full of grace and truth"; verse 17 says, "grace and truth were realized through Jesus Christ"; in John 7:18 He referred to Himself as "He who is ... true"; in the familiar words of John 14:6, He is "the way, and the truth, and the life"; Ephesians 4:21 declares that "truth is in Jesus"; Revelation 3:7 describes Him as "He who is holy, who is true"; verse 14 as "the Amen, the faithful and true Witness"; and Revelation 19:11 says that He "is called Faithful and True."

The Holy Spirit, the third member of the Trinity, is also truth. John three times calls Him "the Spirit of truth" (14:17; 15:26; 16:13), while 1 John 5:6 affirms that "the Spirit is the truth."

Paul wanted the church to be the "pillar and support of the truth" (1 Tim. 3:15). But to do so, it must be able to distinguish between "the spirit of truth and the spirit of error" (1 John 4:6). The only benchmark for doing so is the "word of truth" (Col. 1:5; 2 Tim. 2:15; James 1:18), which is why Paul was so deeply concerned to guard, protect, and assure the authenticity of the revelation God gave him.

GRACE

The grace of our Lord Jesus Christ be with you all. (3:18)

Paul concludes his prayer wish and the epistle by expressing his desire that **all** those who have put their faith in the Lord Jesus Christ continue to experience **grace. Grace** is God's undeserved goodness and benevolence granted to those who in no way deserve it. Saving grace was decreed by God (Ps. 84:11) and given through **our Lord Jesus Christ** (cf. John 1:17; Rom. 5:15; 1 Cor. 1:4; Titus 2:11). **Grace** is essential, not only for salvation (Acts 15:11; 18:27; 20:24; Rom. 3:24; Gal. 1:6, 15; Eph. 1:7; 2:5, 8; 2 Tim. 1:9; Titus 3:7), but also for endurance (2 Cor. 12:9; cf. Prov. 3:34), service (Rom. 12:6; Eph. 4:7; 1 Tim. 1:12–14; 1 Peter 4:10), growth (Acts 20:32; Heb. 13:9; 2 Peter 3:18), and giving (2 Cor. 8:1). Believers experience God's enabling, sanctifying grace by trusting Him, obeying His Word, enduring chastening, doing good, walking in the Spirit, and praying.

There is a wonderful mystery to living the Christian life to the glory of God. To do so requires all the understanding, obedience, commitment, dedication, and effort that the redeemed can give. But all of that would be futile were it not for the peace, strength, truth, and grace that only God can supply. Paul had the balance when he wrote, "For this purpose also I labor, striving according to His power, which mightily works within me" (Col. 1:29).

Bibliography

Arndt, W. F. and F. W. Gingrich. *A Greek-English Lexicon of the New Testament and Other Early Christian Literature.* Chicago: Univ. of Chicago, 1957.

Best, Ernest. *The First and Second Epistles to the Thessalonians.* Black's New Testament Commentary. Peabody, Mass.: Hendrickson, 1988.

Bruce, F. F. *1 & 2 Thessalonians.* Word Biblical Commentary; vol. 45. Waco, Tex.: Word, 1982.

Carson, D. A., Douglas J. Moo, and Leon Morris. *An Introduction to the New Testament.* Grand Rapids: Zondervan, 1992.

Findlay, G. G. *The Epistles of Paul the Apostle to the Thessalonians.* Reprint; Grand Rapids: Baker, 1982.

Gromacki, Robert G. *New Testament Survey.* Grand Rapids: Baker, 1974.

Guthrie, Donald. *New Testament Introduction.* Rev. ed. Downers Grove, Ill.: InterVarsity, 1990.

Harrison, Everett F. *Introduction to the New Testament.* Grand Rapids: Eerdmans, 1968.

Hendriksen, William. *New Testament Commentary: Exposition of Thessalonians, Timothy, and Titus.* Grand Rapids: Baker, 1981.

Hiebert, D. Edmond. *An Introduction to the New Testament Volume Two: The Pauline Epistles.* Chicago: Moody, 1977.

————. *The Thessalonian Epistles: A Call to Readiness.* Chicago: Moody, 1977.

Marshall, I. Howard. *1 and 2 Thessalonians.* The New Century Bible Commentary. Grand Rapids: Eerdmans, 1983.

Morris, Leon. *The First and Second Epistles to the Thessalonians.* The New International Commentary on the New Testament. Grand Rapids: Eerdmans, 1989.

Pfeiffer, Charles F. and Howard F. Vos. *The Wycliffe Historical Geography of Bible Lands.* Chicago: Moody, 1967.

Ramsay, Sir William M. *St. Paul the Traveler and Roman Citizen.* Reprint; Grand Rapids: Baker, 1975.

Smith, T. W. *What the Bible Teaches: 2 Thessalonians.* Kilmarnock, Scotland: John Ritchie, 1983.

Thomas, Robert L. "1, 2 Thessalonians." In *The Expositor's Bible Commentary,* vol. 11. Edited by Frank E. Gaebelein. Grand Rapids: Zondervan, 1979.

Wanamaker, Charles A. *The Epistles to the Thessalonians.* The New International Greek Testament Commentary. Grand Rapids: Eerdmans, 1990.

Wilson, Geoffrey B. *1 & 2 Thessalonians.* Edinburgh: Banner of Truth, 1975.

Wilson, T. E. *What the Bible Teaches: 1 and 2 Thessalonians.* Kilmarnock, Scotland: John Ritchie, 1983.

Indexes

Index of Greek Words

Index of Scripture

9:3	235	14:17	199	**Ezra**		
10:19	90	15:10	134	Ezra 1:1	294	
12:18	184	20:1	134			
17:19–20	89	23:6	158	**Nehemiah**		
18:16	235			2:19	209	
28:1	66	**First Kings**		8:10	184, 185	
28:15	66	1:34	134	9:28–29	210	
29:14–15	62	1:39	134	13:18	66	
29:19	315	1:41	134			
29:29	204	3:9	199	**Esther**		
31:7–8	50	6:11	294	3	264	
31:23	50	8:10	137	4–9	264	
32:35	111, 180,	8:46	286			
	236, 241	12:24	294	**Job**		
33:2	234	19:10	62	1:5	202	
		21:10	158	1:6–21:12	7	
Joshua		22:19–23	285	2:3	121	
1:5–9	50	22:22	71	2:6	72	
1:8	198			2:8	71	
1:8–9	58	**Second Kings**		5:17–24	315	
8:8	294	6:22	181	8:5	87	
22:22	272	7:1	294	17:9	20	
		17:13	64	18:21	242	
Judges		20:1–6	255	23:12	198	
2:10	108, 242	20:12–17	256	32:21–22	41	
6:24	313	22:17	66	37:23	241	
6:34	134			42:1–6	226	
10:13	285	**First Chronicles**		42:2	89, 141, 254,	
19:22	158	11:3	294		278, 288	
		28:9	91			
First Samuel		29:11	302	**Psalms**		
2:12	158, 242			1:1–2	198	
2:30	260	**Second Chronicles**		1:1–6	210	
3:7	294	6:30	91	1:2	108	
3:21	294	7:16	202	1:2–3	58	
4:21	62	15:1–2	64	2:8–9	246	
6:6	284	15:2	285	2:11	184	
12:19–23	255	15:3	319	4:1	187	
13:3	134	21, 22	264	4:3	103	
15:29	319	24:18	66	5:2	87	
16:5	202	24:19	64	5:9	41	
16:7	91, 230	24:20	285	5:11	81, 184	
16:12–13	202	24:20–21	62	8:4–6	209	
		24:20–22	64	9:10	194	
Second Samuel		29:19	272	9:17	242	
6:15	134	36:16	64, 66	12:3	41	
7:28	319			16:8–9	184	
10:12–13	50			16:8–11	185	

12:1–4	60, 295	16:1–5	167	17:15	6, 77
12:6	125	16:6–10	4, 118, 293	17:16–34	293
12:11–16	187	16:11–15	294	17:23	108
13:1–3	167, 173, 202	16:12–40	118	17:30	244, 297
13:1–4	89	16:13	3	17:30–31	65
13:2–4	166	16:14	193	17:31	28, 234, 302
13:5	294	16:16–24	34, 295	18:1	7
13:8	71	16:16–34	82, 293	18:3	169
13:9–11	168	16:19	118	18:4–6	294
13:33–35	28	16:19–34	223	18:4–7	5
13:36	125	16:22–25	25	18:5	6, 7, 8, 77, 223
13:40–50	61	16:23	213	18:5–7	78
13:43	207	16:25	118	18:9–10	318
13:44	57, 294	16:26	269	18:9–11	293
13:44–49	294	16:28–34	294	18:12	8
13:46	245, 294	16:29	118	18:12–17	8, 61, 295
13:46–48	20	16:31	287	18:23	79
13:47	164	16:32	294	18:25	143
13:48	193, 245, 294	16:34	184	18:27	320
13:49	294	16:37	222	19:8–10	61
13:50	213, 293	16:37–40	295	19:10	294
14:1–7	61	17:1	3	19:13–41	82, 293
14:1–20	82	17:1–4	24, 56,	19:18–20	294
14:4–6	293, 295		60, 295	19:19	172
14:16	285	17:1–9	223, 293	19:20	294
14:19–20	61	17:1–10	68, 82	19:22	78, 223
14:21–22	79	17:1–15	78	19:29	4
14:22	89, 166, 207,	17:2	5	20:4	4
	229, 248	17:2–3	56	20:4–5	78
14:23	167	17:2–4	97	20:17	167
15:2ff.	167	17:4	13, 57,	20:18	305
15:3	185		222, 223	20:18–20	169
15:8	118	17:5–6	35	20:19	184
15:11	320	17:5–8	60	20:21	20, 27
15:20	104, 105	17:5–9	3, 295	20:24	294, 320
15:22	222	17:5–10	24, 222	20:27	111, 141
15:22–29	167	17:6	4	20:27–28	292
15:23–29	196	17:7	5, 35, 306	20:28	59, 165,
15:27	222	17:8	5		166, 167
15:29	104	17:9	72	20:28–31	32
15:32	79, 222	17:10	60, 64, 223	20:29–30	80, 136
15:35–36	294	17:10–11	197	20:29–32	76
15:40	13, 223	17:10–14	118	20:31	170, 177, 178
15:41	79	17:11	108, 195, 199	20:32	58, 89, 103,
16–18	7	17:11–12	294		104, 108, 170,
16:1	223	17:13	269		202, 320
16:1–3	13, 78,	17:14	77, 118,	20:33–34	41
	222, 223		223, 293	20:33–35	293

Index of Subjects

The MacArthur New Testament
Commentary series includes:

Matthew 1–7
Matthew 8–15
Matthew 16–23
Matthew 24–28
Mark 1–8
Mark 9–16
Luke 1–5
Luke 6–10
Luke 11–17
Luke 18–24
John 1–11
John 12–21
Acts 1–12
Acts 13–28
Romans 1–8
Romans 9–16
First Corinthians
Second Corinthians
Galatians
Ephesians
Philippians
Colossians & Philemon
First & Second Thessalonians
First Timothy
Second Timothy
Titus
Hebrews
James
First Peter
Second Peter & Jude
First–Third John
Revelation 1–11
Revelation 12–22

www.MoodyPublishers.com | 1-800-678-6928